POST-REALISM

POST-REALISM

THE RHETORICAL TURN IN INTERNATIONAL RELATIONS

EDITED BY
FRANCIS A. BEER AND ROBERT HARIMAN

Michigan State University Press

East Lansing

All Michigan State University Press books are produced on paper which meets the requirements of American National Standard of Information Science—Permanence of paper for printed materials ANSI Z39.48-1984.

Michigan State University Press
East Lansing, Michigan 48823-5202

03 02 01 00 99 98 97 96 1 2 3 4 5 6 7 8 9

Library of Congress Cataloging-in-Publication Data

Post-Realism : the rhetorical turn in international relations /
    [edited by] Francis A. Beer and Robert Hariman.
            p. cm. — (Rhetoric and public affairs series)
    Includes bibliographical references and index.
    ISBN 0-87013-422-1. — ISBN (invalid) 0-87013-461-1 (ppk.)
    1.International relations and culture. 2.Persuasion (Rhetoric) 3. Realism.
  4.World politics—1989—-Decision making. 5. Cold War. I. Beer, Francis A.
  II. Hariman, Robert. III. Series.
JX1255.P67   1996
327.73'009'045—dc2096   6848
                                                                CIP

CONTENTS

ACKNOWLEDGMENTS

This volume began as an outline on a single sheet of paper soon after the authors met at the Scholars Workshop in the Rhetoric of Political Argumentation, which was sponsored by the Project on the Rhetoric of Inquiry at the University of Iowa and by the National Endowment for the Humanities. We are indebted to John Nelson for cajoling us into participating in the workshop and for his early encouragement of the project, and to the workshop participants for their critical readings of our individual chapters as well as their vital embodiment of the values, and value, of interdisciplinary conversation. Our work also benefited in similar manner from the Faculty Rhetoric Seminar at the University of Iowa. Early versions of some of the chapters were presented at annual conventions of the International Studies Association, American Political Science Association, Speech Communication Association, Western Political Science Association, Western States Communication Association, and the Alta Conference on Argumentation. We are grateful for the interest and criticisms provided by the many scholars who took the time to attend to these early drafts.

As with any edited volume, we cannot list all the readers on whom the individual authors relied for each of the essays, but you know who you are. We also are grateful for the reviews provided by the anonymous readers for the Michigan State University Press and for the careful and thorough work of the series editor, Marty Medhurst. Above all, we thank the authors themselves—for their good work, their suggestions and encouragement regarding the volume as a whole, and their patience.

We also appreciate the help with the index provided by both Kate Neckerman and the Drake Center for the Humanities, and we are especially grateful to Rachel Buckles, whose secretarial skill and personal unflappability saved the day so many times when coordinating the work of eighteen people in four countries through a maze of computer systems, faxes, phones, express mailings, and more. Her contribution, like all the others, reminds us how much scholarship is the work of a community.

Finally, we each have been sustained and inspired by our families. The unique individuals in them—Diana, Omar, Marie, and Jeremy; Jane, David, and Katherine—have taught us much about the joys of a common life. Their intelligence and passion, wit and constancy remind us that scholarship, like politics, should be inspired by a love of the real world.

I
REFIGURING REALISM

RESTRUCTURING REALISM

FRANCIS A. BEER AND ROBERT HARIMAN

REALISM AND RHETORIC IN
INTERNATIONAL RELATIONS

The conduct of international relations has always involved skillful
use of persuasive discourse. Relations between states might
depend on factors such as military capability and natural
resources, but the decisions made about the conduct of peace and war
are also a result of the successes, failures, habits, and nuances of persuasive appeal among elites and publics alike. For the most part, however, academic research in international relations has not focused on
the forms and effects of conversations, speeches, debates, narratives,
or discourses in political practice. This systematic inattention to the
role of words in foreign affairs is the result of a specific intellectual
history that emphasized the material bases of international politics as
it "really" was. Political realism, historically known as reason of state
or *Realpolitik*, was contrasted with both the utopian tendencies of
philosophical idealism and the liberal overvaluing of verbal agreements that was epitomized at Munich. As it was linked to the modern
valorization of scientific method, the doctrine of political realism
became the dominant theory within the contemporary discipline of
international relations. By 1960, political realism had "swept the field
in the United States"; one more recent study suggested that 90 percent
of the hypotheses in behavioral studies in the discipline were realist
in conception.[1]

There has been a corresponding lack of attention to foreign affairs
in rhetorical studies, which have been directed largely to domestic
politics and national literatures. Recently, however, we have seen a
convergence of interests, a bridging of the realist's unexamined divisions between foreign and domestic politics and between the languages of politics and of inquiry. On the one hand, scholars in
rhetoric have produced a number of critical studies of foreign policy
discourse.[2] These studies reveal that foreign policy decision making is

1

influenced powerfully by modes of persuasive appeal that realist explanation overlooks or presumes irrational or even replicates dangerously. On the other hand, "dissident" scholars in the discipline of international relations have taken a linguistic turn.[3] By drawing on a number of linguistic methodologies ranging from Chaim Perelman's anatomy of rhetoric to various post-structuralisms, these initiatives not only explicate phenomena that were excluded from realist explanatory schemes but also suggest how realist discourse operates as a rhetoric influencing the world it purports to describe.

Periodic criticisms of the realist paradigm have not substantially altered either the conventional wisdom of international studies or its considerable influence over foreign affairs. For most political scientists and the many practitioners they school, the analysis, explanation, and evaluation of international relations begins and usually ends with the realist paradigm. Consequently, any reconsideration of international studies has to come to terms with realism: considering how it produces and limits knowledge of foreign affairs, how it describes and structures political practice, how it contains untapped resources and misleading directions, and how it needs to be adapted to changes in world politics and in the conduct of inquiry. Rhetorical scholars have additional interests as well. The realist paradigm is a superb example of persuasive success in twentieth-century modernist culture, and, so long as realist assumptions structure international study, such inquiry will not be hospitable to the rhetorical tradition. By identifying how realism works as a persuasive discourse, one can challenge its hegemony within international studies and demonstrate how a rhetorical sensibility can contribute to more sophisticated and strategic understanding of foreign affairs.

STORY TIME: REALISM'S NARRATIVE STRUCTURE

The first step in accounting for the rhetoric of realism is to recognize how realist explanation relies on stories about both the world and itself. Recent work in the rhetoric of inquiry has identified how various modes of explanation depend on more or less explicit designs otherwise thought of as "literary," "rhetorical," "imaginative," or "artificial."[4] In particular, compelling accounts of the world often are organized by narrative structures. These narratives can include pervasive myths or powerful formal designs that are dominant in many literatures, or nuanced adaptations of canonical texts in a specific discipline. In any case, the narrative is a source of coherence, meaning, and appeal.[5] Realism is no exception; indeed, its several versions all are grounded firmly in two intertwined stories about the world and about realism's place in it.

Realism's Story of the World

Realism's persuasive power comes partly from its presentation of a taut narrative of world politics. This narrative appears most of the time not in strict story form, but rather in the manner of the *narratio* in a classical oration: that portion of the speech providing a statement of the circumstances of the case.[6] The *narratio* was designed to set the scene for the exposition of arguments, which it preceded. (The predominant usage was in legal argumentation, just as in today's standard format for the legal brief.) The classical handbooks note that narrations can be legendary (involving obviously imaginary characters such as Chiron the centaur), historical (involving actual past characters such as the Peloponnesian War), or "realistic" (involving things that could have happened such as Rousseau's stag hunt). Whatever the type of account, persuasive success usually requires that it be brief, clear, and plausible. The realist's narrative of world politics exemplifies these qualities of persuasive exposition. It sets the scene, and in so doing both structures subsequent argument and defines the natural attitude of the discourse—its most reliable, core knowledge of the world.

Some of the important elements of this narrative are included in the following sketch. In the discourse of realism, nation-states are the primary actors in world politics. Since these states necessarily inhabit a condition of anarchy, they learn to conduct their foreign policies on the basis of national interest defined in terms of power. Consequently, they calculate and compare benefits and costs of alternative policies and rank each other according to their power, which is measured primarily in terms of material and especially military capabilities. Thus, national foreign policy decision makers use whatever means are most appropriate, including direct violence, to achieve the ends of national interest defined in terms of power.

This narrative usually is augmented with several additional claims as well, which establish it as an account of a permanent, ubiquitous, essential condition. These facts of international competition, we are told, are grounded in human nature and confirmed by political history. The key to success in this real world of nation-states competing for survival is to see things as they are rather than as we would want them to be. Alternative accounts are either delusions temporarily afforded by circumstances of relative peace or prosperity, or special pleading by those who lack the capability to defend themselves otherwise. The story of realism continues indefinitely, for it is a story of the fatal limitations of human nature.

The persuasive power of this narrative should not be underestimated. In a few sentences, it produces a coherent account of the international environment that coordinates all the key elements for representing human motivation: an actor (the nation-state) in a scene (the condition of anarchy, a state of nature) uses an agency (calculation) to act (the application of force) for a purpose (national interest).[7] In addition, by articulating this simple but powerful calculus as a universal, even tragic condition, the narrative suggests that it, and it alone, can equip one to survive and explain the natural conditions of state competition.[8] Its full significance, however, becomes more evident in conjunction with realism's other story.

Realism's Story of Itself

Realism complements this story of a world of raw power and rational calculation with a story about itself. In this tale, realism is the primary actor in the world of theory, with power greater than other theories. This story of self-justification develops in three parts. First, realism appears as the natural outgrowth of the dominant development in world politics: the formation of the nation-state. Realism's roots are entwined with the history of the classical and medieval city-states and its branches cover the essential elements of modern foreign policy: state sovereignty and the corresponding monopoly on violence. As it has been developed by those who were key figures in the ascendancy of the state, and by those who were present at crucial periods of global conflict between the great powers of the modern era, realism alone is capable of accounting for decisions for peace and war in a world of states. Realism becomes the only indigenous theory of international relations and foreign policy in the modern world, the only effective way to reason in the domain of world politics. Within this story, realism alone can encompass the Eurocentric world system, the American century, the Pax Americana, and the New World Order. Like the states that it valorizes, realism becomes the privileged form

for international order, the hegemonic discourse in modern international relations.

Realism is, secondly, embedded in a history of ideas. The geneal-
ogy of realism is a theoretical chronology and a collective biography.
It goes from antiquity to modernity, coterminous with our historical
records. Realism's ancestors include Mencius, Lao Tzu, and
Thucydides. Modern realists include Machiavelli, Bodin, Hobbes,
Richelieu, Ranke, Meinecke, Friedrich von Ghent, Clausewitz, Aron,
Carr, Wight, and Bull. Contemporary American realism ranges from
the writings of Mahan, Spykman, Mackinder, Lippmann, Kennan, and
Morgenthau to the modern neorealist theory of Keohane, Waltz, and
their collaborators. This story has a theme as well: It is a story of men
with the intellectual courage to admit that humanity is red in tooth
and claw, and with the strength to push through the pressures of common opinion and official doctrine to advance rational analysis of the
world as it is, not as either the few or the many would like it to be.
Realism, while reducing world history to a story of dominant states
(and dominant leaders), also reduces the history of ideas to a story of
dominant thinkers writing the discourse that will prevail because of
its monopoly on reason.

Finally, realism presents itself as one version of the most powerful
narrative of our time: the story of the development of modern science.
What was grounded in world history and identified by a long line of
great theorists now has been validated by scientific investigation. In
this story, only realism has identified the basic conditions and fundamental laws of international relations. One of the most important
tenets of realist theory is the assertion that realism expresses without
distortion the permanent essence of politics between nations, the core
structures and processes of contemporary world politics. It accounts
for phenomena today as well as millennia ago, just as it will be able to
account for any future condition. Most important, it escapes the influences of its own historical moment. Thus, realism exemplifies the theoretical norms of scientific positivism. Realist theory is general,
simple, and logical. It is parsimonious, buying a great deal with very
little. Realism is empirically correct and comprehensible. The
hypotheses of realism, Morgenthau tells us, are consistent with "the
facts."[9]

Obviously, this summary of realism does not include every nuance
or implication. Nor would we claim that it is likely to be untrue
because it is so internally coherent. On the other hand, it should be

apparent that realism depends on standard means of rhetorical justification: It provides elegant "grand narratives" that make sense of the world while advancing the speaker. Stated otherwise, realism simultaneously operates as an epistemology, an ontology, and a rhetoric. First, the realist claims to be seeing the world clearly and so presumes that objective knowledge is available to anyone who knows how to acquire it. Second, the realist claims that politics is a competition among states pursuing power that can be achieved through rational calculation, and so presumes that attention to other practices or values is a distraction inevitably leading to failure to survive or to understand the consequences of political acts. Finally, the realist acts as a realist in order to obtain persuasive power; the declaration of one's objective understanding of the elements of power invariably operates as an appeal to be granted priority over others who are comparatively benighted. As Hans Blumenberg has observed, "in the modern age anti-rhetoric has become one of the most important expedients of rhetorical art, by means of which to lay claim to the rigor of realism, which alone promises to be a match for the seriousness of man's position (in this case, his position in his 'state of nature')."[10] As these three claims are articulated together in realist discourse, and particularly as they are counterpoised against other discourses labeled utopian, idealistic, moralistic, legalistic, ideological, partisan, emotional, or rhetorical, the persuasive effect is comprehensive. Realism becomes not just an account of world politics, but the predominant context for explanation, evaluation, and action.

CRITICISM AND CHANGE: POST-REALISM

Several converging circumstances are inducing a reconsideration of realist discourse. Recent events in Eastern and Central Europe have made it plausible that realists can be unrealistic, unable to even recognize the self-destruction of a major state. The war in the Persian Gulf has demonstrated the continuing violence and self-validating character of realist policies, while also illustrating new dimensions of international complexity ranging from instantaneous worldwide communication to an awareness of long-term environmental damage.

These political changes are matched by intellectual changes. Although realism has been challenged for contradictions and deficiencies on its own terms for the last half century, now other perspectives are raising new epistemological issues and suggesting different approaches to the study of international relations.[11] Moreover, the tenor of the debate has changed. The point now is not to repudiate realism but to understand it as a discursive practice and draw on it selectively while articulating alternative languages for understanding international relations. Instead of proving its interpretive inadequacy, one has to account for its readings (e.g., Thucydides), follow similar patterns of argument (e.g., about a canon for international studies), and reformulate its fundamental concerns (such as the necessity of strategic thinking). In some cases, the critique aims at restoration of an earlier, more complex version of realism; in other cases, the intent is to go well beyond the constraints of realist explanation. In any event, these linguistically oriented critiques have begun the movement from anti-realism to post-realism.

Of course, post-realists do contest many of realism's central claims about itself and about the world. Realists believe that realism is the only story of world politics. Post-realists assert that realism is only one story among many; although it is an important story, it provides neither the only plausible explanation nor the only possible world. Instead of accepting a world of states as a natural world, post-realists note how realist discourse replicates the dynamics of state legitimation. Just as the state defines itself as the sole vehicle for the political process, so does the realist define power politics as an autonomous realm, separated from the obligations of law, religion, custom, and the like. Just as the state defines rational conduct as that which can be measured and maximized by state administration, so does the realist project a persona of autonomous expertise and instrumental rationality. In short, the discourse of realism and the practices of the modern state are mutually reinforcing. Each operates according to a similar skein of relationships that can be interpreted as either linguistic or social practices. Such reciprocal theoretical and political relations between the state and realism are subtle and complex. Post-realist inquiry contends that they need to be explored further before we accept the hegemonic claims of either.

Post-realists challenge realist history, holding that important theorists in the realist canon were not realists as the realists describe them. Thucydides is an important example, as the realist figure to whom the most attention has been paid. Realist political scientists construct Thucydides as the founding father of realism; yet they tend to read him selectively and very simply, featuring a few passages with little attention to the lexical designs in any given passage or to the relationship of the parts of the text to the whole or to the contexts of composition and reception. The realist's Thucydides becomes a simple text with a clear lesson; its use does not require interpretation.

Other readers see Thucydides quite differently: He becomes a master of dialectical argumentation, a dramatist, or an ironist.[12] In these readings, realism is one discourse among many and an object of considerable ambivalence. Thucydides does indeed present realism as a mode of inquiry but also as a cause of the Athenian defeat. He is attempting to trace the dynamics of the war but also is recounting the collapse of cultural understanding brought about by the war. The post-realist does not deny the relevance of Thucydides, or of a Thucydidean realism, but recognizes how the realist appropriation has been used to invent a tradition to legitimate contemporary forms of authority.[13]

Similarly, post-realists note how realism draws from a limited historical base. Most theorists in the realist canon are American or European. Nor are there representatives of different publics, or classes, or religious movements, or cultures of resistance, or technologies, or markets. Moreover, as feminist theorists have taught us, the problem is not merely one of identifying and rectifying specific exclusions, but of recognizing the profound limitations and distortions that occur within a perspective that has been constructed through the negation of crucial areas of human experience.[14] Realist reliance on its canon, and the narrow range of that canon, produces far too selective an account of the actual determinants of political history and of the potential capacity for action within the varied forms of human collectivity. For example, realism provides too simple a story of the rise of the modern state. Post-realism need not deny the state's monopoly of force or its competition with other states, but it should recognize the state's dependencies on legal, economic, and communicative processes and on patterns of cooperation among states and among nations or peoples independently of state policies. Realism sees too few origins, and too many epiphenomena.

Post-realists also offer a range of criticisms of realism's scientific status. We note the following claims: (a) Realism has not produced an irrefutable body of scientific knowledge because it has not been tested adequately or produced sufficiently consistent empirical findings. (b) Realism is not likely to do so, because it is a form of local knowledge, limited by its historical circumstances, and unaware of and disposed to remain unaware of these limitations. (c) Realism could not do so, for it relies on modes of inquiry that are self-validating, or it lacks sufficient conceptual resources, or is limited by too many self-imposed constraints to provide an adequate explanation of international politics. (d) Even if scientifically productive, realism should meet other criteria as well, since it is a mode of action in the world it explains. Consequently, realism must also be evaluated, or developed, as a mode of self-reflection and practical wisdom. In doing so, the realist has to account for all that has been hidden behind the facade of scientism, including involvement with nationalism and imperialism, imposition of an artificial poverty of concepts and information on international studies, and foreclosing debate in the public sphere about foreign policy.

Contemporary realist responses to these criticisms cede a good deal of ground. Realists assert that realism is true, but perhaps not always in standard empirical ways. Realist theory is discontinuously or contingently true. It expresses the essence of world politics, but specific pieces of material evidence at particular times may not directly confirm particular hypotheses. Realist history is not a veridical, word-for-word stenographic record, but a virtual history, presented as if it were real, as it would have happened in accord with the laws of international politics. Realist policy makers act as if they were rational power maximizers, even though they may not be consciously aware that they are doing so. Decision makers "will act as if they solved certain . . . problems, whether or not they actually solve them."[15] The hidden hand writes history through the actors without necessarily requiring their conscious knowledge or cooperation. Realist doctrine is normatively true because decision makers do err. Realism is the doctrine that policy makers should follow if they were rational, even though they may not actually be so.[16]

To summarize these arguments, the post-realist holds the realist accountable for all the criticisms that have accumulated around that body of theory, while adding more as well. These additional criticisms generally are of a particular bent: They begin with the investigation of realism as a language and end with judgments in terms of any of the ideological, ethical, or other considerations that the realist would rule out. Yet post-realism has to recognize that its own story of the collapse of realism should not be a tale of intellectual dishonesty or bad faith. It will have to invent a tradition as well, and its own formulations can neither invalidate realist claims in every case nor escape entanglement in discursive practices and historical processes beyond its complete apprehension or control. Furthermore, the post-realist accepts the burden of not only criticizing realism but of replacing or refiguring it. To do that, the post-realist needs to suggest how a linguistic turn can be compatible with the conventional aspirations of a social science.

REALISM, RHETORIC, AND SCIENCE

This book accepts the challenge to reconsider the dominant language of international relations in respect to both new international conditions and the intellectual resources available within the context of postmodern theory. The project begins with a shift in perspective: We analyze political realism as a persuasive discourse rather than as a positive theory. We need not deny that realist claims can be veridical representations of an external world, but we also recognize that realist discourse can be believed and have effects independent of its truth value. Realism communicates not only propositions but also attitudes (which are incipient actions); it both represents the world and structures relationships among the speakers, subjects, and audiences of world politics; it describes some events yet also deflects awareness of others. Realism is not only a set of ideas but also a mode of symbolic action.[17]

This approach allows us to recover an intellectual richness in the tradition of realism, a richness lost within the late-modern emphasis on empirical observation and structural explanation.[18] We also open a post-realist space, structured not by a rigid opposition between realism and idealism (or even between authority and dissent) but by a radical inclusiveness. We confront realists with what they have excluded from their calculations, although we do not wholly abandon the calculus of power realists know so well. This critique begins as a revisionary project and then becomes more extroverted. These two movements are reflected in the structure of the volume, which first provides rereadings of major realist texts and then offers reformulations of important concepts and models of decision making in international relations.

The return to major realist writers exemplifies a broad rhetorical perspective. We introduce rhetorical studies, the tradition of linguistic analysis most attuned to the political realm, into the linguistic turn already taking place in the study of international relations. Rhetoric, arguably the first political science, offers an analytical program that works well with the common sense and enduring concerns of foreign affairs. The rhetorical tradition includes appreciation of the dynamics of power, valorization of both argument and style, a focus on negotiation, involvement in the dialectic of elites and their publics, a strategic sensibility, and an ambivalent mixture of technical skill and ethical themes.[19]

Within the rhetorical perspective, one takes words seriously but not for their own sake alone. The emphasis is on discourse—with a corresponding wariness of the conventional distinctions between speech and action, language and reality—yet the interest is in the effect the discourse has on conduct. Rhetorical analysis probes the relationship between the content, forms, and functions of discourse and it demonstrates the capacity of speech to affect judgment and action, particularly in respect to political decision making. Thus, realist ideas do not occur transcendentally but rather through the conventions of realist discourse, which also determine how and how well realism functions to produce knowledge, craft policy, secure agreement, or motivate other forms of action.

The rhetorical tradition carries two other assumptions that can contribute directly to international studies: First, it assumes that the appeal and rationality of both political practice and scientific inquiry go beyond their reliance on empirical observation and logical calculation. Instead, rhetorical analysis asks a question of crucial importance for both the political practitioner and the social scientist: What are the appropriate criteria and standards for determining the rationality of any particular discourse?[20] (This question should be familiar to those who have criticized neorealism for its undue reliance on strictly scientific norms of theory construction.) Second, the rhetorical tradition offers itself as a common language for integrating different (disciplinary) accounts of complex phenomena. By serving as a metalanguage for identifying, comparing, and assessing different norms of argument and habits of disciplined conversation, the vocabulary of rhetoric might not fulfill the premodern ideal that "eloquence is one" but it can provide pragmatic service in an academy composed of many, highly specialized vocabularies.[21] In other words, rhetoric as a tradition of erudition has a broader range than the conventional modern conceptions of rhetoric as either the practice of propaganda or the criticism of the formal elements of literary texts.

These limiting conceptions prevailed during the formation of the American academic disciplines in the twentieth century.[22] This process applied a "politics of separation" that divided scientific inquiry from public discourse and gave realism a privileged space in international studies.[23] Such divisions were the means of disciplinary consolidation and the basis for claims to academic status. Consequently, arguments that alter the relationship between scientific inquiry and rhetorical practice are not likely to persuade established realists. In Lakatosian terms, it seems that a shift to a more interpretative inquiry involves only semantic resolution of pertinent problems.[24]

A post-realist perspective, however, has to step outside of this standoff between a narrow conception of science and a derogatory conception of rhetoric. The point is not to abandon the social scientific ideal—though we certainly encourage "enhanced reflexivity" regarding both ideal and actuality—but to recognize that the continued development of the social sciences requires and recommends broadening the definition of scientific inquiry.[25] Indeed, the need for a more expansive conception of the scientific enterprise, independent of one's commitment to a positivist core, has been evident for some time. In international studies, such an expansion is already underway. On the one hand, research programs in artificial intelligence, cognitive science, and political psychology have each required significant adjustment of the narrow conception of positivist inquiry, just as they have offered examples of how a more integrative science might work. On the other hand, obviously self-reflexive and rhetorically sensitive work can make its way between established norms and radical innovations without abandoning or reifying scientific standards. Thus, the many linguistic turns available today might induce vertigo but they need not impel an abandonment of scholarly argument or scientific analysis. Science and language are at odds only within a simplistic conception of each. Positive and interpretive analyses can indeed be compatible if one allows a more complex understanding of both the object and method of the human sciences and admits to the corresponding partiality of any mode of explanation. These are indeed exciting times for international studies, and also demanding times, for now rigor alone is not enough.

Perhaps this shift from a narrow to a broader conception of the social sciences reflects their maturation. Just as the natural sciences have long since moved beyond the simple empiricism that marked their early development, so are the social sciences moving beyond simple oppositions between positive and interpretive theories, data analysis and textual criticism. Social scientific analysis may still rely on proven techniques for controlled observation and inference of objective events. Yet it can also have a richer sense of context that comes from recognizing that scientific explanation must begin and end in conversation with other forms of scholarly investigation, including historical, philosophical, and critical inquiries. The maturing social science presumes a complex field of analytical frameworks and includes a good-faith effort to address questions raised by reflection on one's own conditions of belief. A linguistic turn may be evaluated not as the end but as a means for disciplinary growth.

TEXTS AND CONTEXTS

The essays in this volume offer various examples of how post-realist inquiry may begin. Taken as a whole, they represent a rhetorical engagement with the canon and conventions of international studies, critical reflection on the persuasive appeals and effects characterizing realism, and new interpretations of the conduct of foreign affairs. We hope these initiatives are evident in the following outline of the subsequent chapters:

The first six essays provide new readings of prominent Anglo-American realists whose works were formed in the crucible of the Second World War and the Cold War and who helped to establish realism as the dominant discourse of the era. Although not all the important figures could be included, those represented herein were major influences on both sides of the Atlantic, in academic, governmental, and public forums, for several generations.

We begin in the present. Henry Kissinger continues to be a highly publicized exemplar of, and apologist for, the discourse of realism. Robert Hariman's analysis draws on classical rhetorical theory to identify how Kissinger's public address develops the three modes of appeal constituting any persuasive act. Realist discourse persuades in part because it articulates sharply defined and highly consistent depictions of its speaker, subject, and audience. Kissinger's late-modern realism confers executive authority on the speaker, constructs an idealized model of world order, and limits considerably the role of the public in the determination of foreign policy.

George Kennan dominated the previous generation of foreign policy analysts. By examining the imagery of several of Kennan's most influential texts, Robert Ivie demonstrates how Kennan's work included the irrational emotionalism that he otherwise condemned. Kennan's suppression of explicitly emotional argument in the conduct of foreign affairs was matched by a subterranean current of fear, while his depiction of international order was matched by distorted images of democratic polity. Ivie suggests that Kennan's realism was self-defeating, for it activated chronic insecurities that could not be allayed and relied on beliefs about policy formation that cut it off from important resources for strategic action.

Reinhold Niebuhr was a pivotal figure in the formation of the mentality of the Cold War, for he promulgated realism to an important public audience that was a potential source of opposition. James Aune examines several representative samples of Niebuhr's public address to identify, first, how Niebuhr's work both exploited and neutralized the tension between power and conscience, and, second, how he functioned as a "vanishing mediator," allowing an essentially secular perspective on international relations to displace an earlier, theological world view. Aune's account does double duty, for it tells part of the story of how realism came to dominate American political thought, and it also suggests why realists might want to reread Niebuhr when contending with the awakening of religious movements throughout the third world and former Soviet Union.

British historian E. H. Carr was the author of the first major statement of modern realism, a leading figure in British political debate during and after the Second World War, and an important influence on American academic work as well. Charles Jones examines the persuasive designs in Carr's texts to illustrate Carr's ambivalence toward realism and his attempt to work out an explicitly normative approach to policy formation. From his diction through his arguments to the choice of genres and formation of his *œuvre*, Carr was simultaneously articulating and qualifying realism while attempting to influence public opinion and policy-making elites on the Right and the Left. Rhetorical sophistication did not guarantee success, however, and Carr became party to easy misrepresentation of his work, although today he merits rereading by those hoping to reconcile realist analysis with a liberal democratic agenda.

Martin Wight was a second pillar of British realism. Roger Epp reminds us that Wight should be remembered for more than his codification of power politics. Wight was influenced by Niebuhr, saw himself as someone struggling with the dialectic between order and justice, and labored to develop a theory of international politics that could both incorporate and criticize realist preoccupations. Epp's revisionary reading highlights three themes that qualify Wight's realism: historical indeterminacy, moral tension, and the linguistic and dialogical character of political theory. Wight might be said to prefigure post-realism, for he holds to some of the core beliefs of realist doctrine but strives to overcome its limitations by moving to more interpretative modes of inquiry.

Like all the other individuals featured in this section, Hans Morgenthau was actively involved in both academia and public debate, and often he is singled out as the most important figure in the establishment of modern realism. Thomas Goodnight examines *In Defense of the National Interest* in order to assess Morgenthau's ingenious response to the rhetorical context of his time. Goodnight argues that Morgenthau redefined foreign policy discourse according to the norms of civic humanism in order to negotiate the excesses of the nuclear age. Morgenthau's work stands as a model for foreign policy deliberation, one that includes sound rules for practical reasoning, countermeasures against competing and more dangerous rhetorics, and a commitment to prudence that includes continued cultivation of the public sphere. Obviously, Goodnight's valorization of this classical realism, understood now in terms of its better rhetorical strategies, provides a basis for criticism of later versions of realist discourse.

These rereadings of prominent figures in the recent history of realism are not the only means for refiguring international relations. We look backward so that we can look forward; we read in order to write. The third and fourth sections of this volume identify strategies for rewriting basic concepts and important practices of international relations in order to understand and address the problems of the twenty-first century. They demonstrate the practical import of understanding how action and inquiry are essentially experiences with language. They also illustrate the manner in which post-realists are beginning to offer accounts of the world that move well beyond discussions of the theoretical adequacy of realism.

The third section recasts foundational concepts within a discursive context and offers additional concepts to support new directions in inquiry. We begin with sovereignty, for that is where realism begins. Sovereignty is the first qualification and encompassing narrative of realist calculation; it accounts for the definitive exercise of power while codifying continued political disorder. Jean Elshtain reviews a wide range of texts to illustrate how sovereignty is a boundary-setting discourse that structures fundamental political relationships both between and within states. Elshtain's description of sovereignty is one model of a post-realist analysis, for she emphasizes how sovereignty has been constituted discursively within the complex tradition of political theory, while also recognizing that it is a deeply embedded condition of modern life. Elshtain objects to both uncritical use and utopian dismissal of the concept, and she suggests how richer versions of political identity are becoming available for understanding and development.

Once established, the desire for sovereignty becomes transmuted into concerns about security. Paul Chilton examines this concept which is at once highly metaphorical and representative of the most basic requirements of human survival. Chilton's anatomy of the metaphoric structure of American usage in the post-war period illustrates once again how thoroughly the discourse of realism can create and manage what it sets out to describe. In particular, the realist's uncritical reliance on the container metaphor (as in, "the need to contain Soviet aggression") and related metaphoric schemas produced an internal logic impervious to contrary evidence and capable of reproducing itself in any political situation. Chilton's analysis suggests how these metaphoric linkages can be loosened and redefined. The point is not to do without the concept of security, but to modify and expand the concept so that it can be the means for more realistic and more humane approaches to international politics.

Despite all their talk about sovereignty and security, realists in major states rarely have to face the loss of either. Prestige and reputation are always at risk, however, and are at least as important as any other motive in international relations. Jennifer Milliken reminds us that powerful states and influential realists alike have been obsessed with these tokens of social approval. Milliken demonstrates that realists put great stock in the concepts, yet fundamentally and characteristically misunderstand them as force effects rather than as social attributions. Their unreflective dependency on the metaphoric designs structuring the concepts allows them to avoid empirical confirmation of the claims made about what is at stake and what has been gained or lost. Milliken's revision leads to reconsideration of the nature of political power, while reminding us that prestige and reputation often can be secured more reliably through persuasive skill rather than the invasion of third world countries.

Realists often speak of the "nation-state," but the emphasis clearly is on the latter term, and in the high modernist formulations of neorealism any systematic recognition of nationalism drops out altogether.

Yosef Lapid focuses on this progressive effacement of nationalism in the discourses of realism. Lapid argues that a somewhat awkward though valuable engagement with nationalism in classical realism did not survive translation into the logic of neorealist analysis. Through critical examination of the neorealist definitional strategies, Lapid identifies how "scientific" explanation was purchased at great cost in descriptive capability. By looking for concepts that are not already complicitous with the state's monopoly on its own meaning, Lapid re-opens the relationships between nation and state and nationalism and sovereignty. It becomes clear that post-realism has to contend with the resurgence of nationalism across the globe while also considering workable political outcomes other than a proliferation of states.

When rewriting realist concepts, one also has to consider larger structures of meaning that influence the whole system of terms and produce specific political effects. V. Spike Peterson has discussed the pervasive influence of gender bias in political and philosophical thought, and in this volume she examines its particular embedded-ness in the discourse of realism. Realism draws on the masculinist gender bias of Western philosophy, as do many other discourses, but it also reifies the hierarchical dichotomy of masculine-feminine that is essentialized in processes of Western state making. Peterson argues that realism perpetuates the subordination of "the feminine" (women, the Other, and rhetoric) that is basic to Western philosophy, political theory, and state forms. These historical interdependencies mean that a refiguring of realism requires a rethinking of masculinity. Her argu-ment calls for more fundamental changes than the incorporation of women's rights into diplomatic agendas and demonstrates the contin-ued importance of feminist critique for post-realist inquiry.

Finally, one has to rewrite the whole story. And the story of politi-cal realism is part of the story of the modern era. James Der Derian contributes to the ambitious project of rewriting realism by linking it to the many related discourses in the modern episteme of recording reality. Der Derian gives us a genealogy of realism that runs through philosophical, literary, artistic, and disciplinary debates. He decon-structs realism in order to save it, however; the challenge is to find a new language capable of engaging the realities of a world being made over by the comprehensive exchange of capital and information and the displacement of politics by technologies of acceleration. In such a world, political realism will require many voices and continual rene-gotiation of the terms of understanding.

The final set of essays in this volume examine actual practices of foreign policy decision making in order to identify overlooked opportunities for policy formation. By identifying where and how foreign policy is crafted, one can begin to rewrite the terms of negotiation. The section begins with a case study of executive decision making about Vietnam. David Sylvan and Stephen Majeski focus on the rhetorical norms of the distinctive culture at the top of the foreign policy hierarchy. Members of that culture probably would agree with, or even be flattered by, the authors' assumption that they are oriented toward rhetorical skill and problem solving. But they might not recognize their dependence on the rhetorical figure of place specifications. Sylvan and Majeski demonstrate how the definition of place is a key determinant of subsequent state action yet escapes argumentative scrutiny within the culture of policy makers. This analysis not only suggests that the realists' account of policy formation is quite unrealistic, but also that their lack of precision makes it impossible for them to use their theories to criticize or improve on the details of actual policies.

Contrary to the preference of some realists, the executive culture is not the only forum for decision making about foreign affairs. Roxanne Doty examines the heated public debate over U.S. colonization of the Philippines to demonstrate how foreign policy coalesces within and is influenced by the public sphere. She demonstrates how the actual language of policy formation differed considerably from realist calculations yet resulted in outcomes consistent with realist valorizations of state power, geopolitical control, and a balance of forces. Because the public debate turned more on questions of racial and gender identity (and their implicit motives of domination) than on calculations of national interest and global power, the realist is not disposed to understand the real grounds for decision. Doty's analysis also reminds us that post-realism's attention to other languages of policy formation carries no guarantee of better decisions.

The next essay identifies international relations with the public sphere in its widest and most fragile form. By focusing on the advocacy of indigenous peoples for recognition and protection in global politics, Franke Wilmer identifies a political movement that should not have any significance according to the precepts of realism, yet both records and challenges some of the most profound and yet unrecognized consequences of the modern state system. Wilmer argues that the indigenous peoples' assertion of rights is creating a new context for the conduct of international relations. This context defines modernization and globalization as the dominant processes altering all international relationships among states and peoples; it recognizes marginal sites as new loci in international relations that are indicative of new modes of political action; it changes the ideal of global community from an orderly system of states to a political community of diverse cultures; and it sees normative discourses and persuasive enterprises as inevitable and important means for conducting foreign affairs. Wilmer's advocacy for peoples lacking states, military forces, and material resources can trigger habitual dismissal, but it holds out the possibility of more realistic appraisals of both local conflicts and global processes.

The last case study in this volume emphasizes this distinction between being a realist and being realistic. By examining the discourse of committee deliberations in the U.S. Senate regarding Cambodia, Francis Beer and Robert Boynton validate an alternative model of policy formation. In this model, institutions, groups, and individuals all are important participants in a complex political process held together by persuasive discourse and practical reasoning. As a realist would recommend, state actions are based on calculations of power and interest in respect to objective assessment of situational constraints, but on much more as well. Foreign policy cognition is "thick" with cultural memory, emotion, and morality, and state action requires skillful negotiations that build agreement among diverse constituencies. This model qualifies the ideal of explanatory simplicity in order to understand the complexities of international politics.

The volume concludes with a discussion of the relationship between ethics and strategy in post-realist inquiry. These two topics represent both the continuing engagement and permanent standoff between realism and other, more normative, approaches to politics and inquiry. They also raise the one sure challenge to post-realism: "Isn't it the case," the realist can say confidently, "that post-realism, like every other attempt to improve the human condition, can only be sustained during a period of relative peace, security, or affluence? Isn't it inevitable that hostilities will resume, pressures be brought to bear on the state, and then will we not all become realists again or perish?" The form of argument here is presumptive—it is similar to claiming that there are no atheists in foxholes—but the point is a sharp one nonetheless. The final chapter of this volume accepts this challenge by suggesting how post-realism can articulate a richer, more powerful conception of the strategic intelligence inevitable in international relations. A corresponding revaluation of ethical thinking also is required, for effective strategies in a postmodern world will have to recognize contingencies of moral assertion. We argue that the narrow identification of strategic analysis with realism is itself not strategic, and we offer a broader, more discursively oriented, conception of strategic thinking for negotiation of increasingly complex realities.

INTERESTS AND AGENDAS

These essays share several theoretical interests and point toward an agenda for subsequent research that should challenge scholars in several disciplines. The common denominator of the volume is its linguistic turn: All the essays presume that human behavior is determined by specific, complex relationships between language, world view, and action. The behavior of states is no exception—in fact, "the behavior of states" is a good example of how what we say influences how we see the world, which in turn influences how we act in the world, and how, by acting, we remake the world in the image of our discourse.

This general orientation leads to a second theme, which is that there is no radical demarcation between the practice of inquiry and other social or political practices. This is particularly true of realism, which is both a theoretical account of a realm of political practice and a discourse having specific origins and effects within that realm. The disavowal of moral innocence for the terms of scholarly understanding follows from this volume's emphasis on language: The relationship between language and the practice of inquiry parallels the relationship between language and political practice. There are differences between practices, of course—for example, the conduct of international affairs might be explicitly political and only implicitly investigative, while academic work in international relations is the reverse. In each case, what one thinks and does is determined in part by what one says, and every practice—inquiry included—is somewhat blind at any moment to what else could be said about what it does. Obviously, this perspective blurs the distinction between knower and known, subject and object of inquiry, and it is likely to diminish expert authority while emphasizing responsibility for the effects of expert discourses. It need not compromise inquiry on behalf of other values, however. Indeed, by attending to the intricate relationships between discourse and action in more explicitly political venues, one can acquire the means for more reflexive development of the language of inquiry. For example, by identifying how political actors actually argue among themselves, one can fill in the idea of prudence, a seemingly important but largely empty category in classical realism.[26]

The comparison between political practice and the political dimension of scholarship goes deeper yet. A dominant discourse not only describes a wide range of phenomena, it also reinscribes a set of social relations within the description. Post-realism challenges the suspension of disbelief and develops the previous themes as a "hermeneutics of suspicion." It looks behind claims to reason, morality, or legitimacy for mixed motives, alliances of mutual self-interest, and the like. In its most radical form, it presumes strong linkages among forms of domination or authority. Although many of the essays in this volume do not pursue this connection, the critique of realism highlights the relationship between the dominant academic codification of international relations and the chronic problems of modern global politics. Although academic work is not necessarily the cause of war, insecurity, or injustice, it is not entirely innocent either and it can identify corrective measures. This capacity for influence is particularly available in the discipline of international relations since it is directly wired into the bureaucracies of international politics. Yet, the essays in this volume suggest that one result of the work of the past five decades has been a trained incapacity in assessing processes of modernization, political economy, nationalism, and other determinants of foreign affairs.

Part of the problem is that such incapacity is very difficult to avoid. Precisely because of the emphasis on linguistic horizons and historical constraints, the post-realist has little basis for faulting individuals retrospectively. Furthermore, the essays in this volume take on an additional interest which amplifies the concerns raised thus far. The post-realist perspective is committed to the analysis of change. More specifically, it assumes that the current historical moment is one of accelerated change, even transformation, of some of the basic conditions of global politics. The complaint about realism is in part that, however well it might have described the events of mid-century or prepared decision makers to make tough decisions correctly at that time, its formulations now obscure key elements of change and perpetuate strategies of decision making that are becoming increasingly dysfunctional. The failure of prominent realists to predict and even to admit to the collapse of the Soviet Union (as many other analysts were accurately anticipating and reacting to events) is an object lesson in being blinded by one's discourse. The perpetuation of the national security state after that event and amidst other widespread economic, cultural, and political changes could become the story of an equally comprehensive error.

In the hope of overcoming such mistakes, the post-realist emphasizes analysis of the available means for representing events and motivating action. This emphasis identifies both discursive constraints and powers of invention. Many of the essays have identified how realism limits observation, interpretation, and action. These analyses directly challenge claims regarding its universal and exhaustive scope, while showing how it also can misfire in specific situations. Yet the interest in the discourses of international relations goes beyond such critique to consider how any of them, including realism, are productive and generative. A productive discourse builds something, in this case, a self-sufficient political order. A generative discourse creates resources for innovative problem solving and for articulating new experiences and modes of action. Whether looking at how realism works, or identifying alternative discourses in world politics, many of the essays in this volume have attempted to identify specific examples of how discourse may be used to these ends. This is but an extension of the basic interest of classical rhetoric, which was the discovery of how specific rhetorical maneuvers could be appropriated for continued reapplication to the ever-changing problems of negotiating advantage and securing agreement.

In the spirit of that tradition, the essays here are ultimately pragmatic in orientation. There is no interest in discursive or moral or political purity. The essays are to be judged by their contribution to identifying actual means of persuasion as they rework texts for additional use, modify concepts for better application, and recommend particular models of decision making. Likewise, the pluralism that is invoked from time to time is to be one that works in practice, which, of course, inevitably will be a pluralism subject to criticism on its own terms.

These interests can be developed in many directions, and the selection of essays here was never intended to be definitive. That said, they do suggest an agenda for scholarly research. This agenda draws together work in both international relations and communication studies. It includes terms unfamiliar on each side while doing more than look for common ground. Some of its basic elements are outlined in the following pages:

The first project is the analysis of specific political cultures. Modern realism has promulgated the idea that the scene of international politics is a universal state of nature. Of course, this natural condition is but an artistic design—the flat, abstract surface of late modernism. Post-realism brings back a more familiar representationalism, one that registers the many colors characterizing the cultural dimensions of political life. The full statement of the analytical move here is that every political act is meaningful only within the context of some culture that can be identified in part by communicative norms, and that politics typically involves negotiating between different cultures. The cultures of international politics include the national and regional cultures already built into many standard formulations such as the "nation-state" and the "West," as well as the ethnic and religious cultures that provide perennial disruptions of realist conceptions of global order. They also include the culture or cultures of diplomacy, the culture of high-level decision making, the culture of the public sphere, and the institutional or intellectual cultures of political theory and commentary. These cultural foci in turn lead to further possibilities for critical analysis in terms of several dialectics: for example, between local and global processes, between governmental and commercial enterprises, or between elites and publics. The point is not merely to build into political calculation an anthropological account of how relevant actors experience politics, although that would be of considerable value. The focus on culture brings in the recognition that international politics is a negotiation of meanings, that cultural interpretation is the key to identifying both empirical error and resources for collaboration, and that international studies will be no better than their means for identifying the cultural determinants of state action.

This emphasis on cultural interpretation requires texts. Thus, the second item on the agenda is the recovery and revisionary reading of influential texts. This volume began by reconsidering canonical works and that project is likely to be continually rewarding. But these rereadings also were acts of recovery, not only of lost meanings, for they often involved bringing in other (and often more "public") works. Other essays pointed to the related task that also lies ahead, which is to identify and analyze the full array of discourses that shape both routine and crucial decisions in the international arena. This task is not likely to be glamorous, for it leads directly into bureaucracies, "non-political" venues, procedures of recording and accounting, and the like. It also holds out the best possibilities for integrating more ambitious theoretical projects in social theory with conventional concerns of international studies. In addition, identifying the texts of international politics leads from the archives to positions of advocacy. The emphasis here has been on politically marginal voices, particularly those of stateless peoples and of women everywhere, but the possibility exists that many other interests can be brought to light as well. Ultimately, the emphasis on interpretive analysis suggests a correspondingly comprehensive development of a public sphere.

These initiatives need to be consolidated into a theory of power. The task of supplementing realist theory is daunting. We might have to qualify some of our theoretical ideals, such as parsimony, or reexamine the relationship between individual case and theoretical generalization. A post-realist theory has to acknowledge the factors of "power politics" while also accounting for discursive power. It has to recognize both natural constraints and constitutive practices. It has to account for state actions while tracking the many social, cultural, technological, and economic practices that typically are overlooked in state-oriented explanations. It has to balance intentionalist, structuralist, and poststructuralist definitions of how discourse works. It has to be oriented toward both prudence—the crafting of normative and expedient political decisions—and imagination—the presentation of alternative futures.

Finally, this agenda includes consideration of the various means, forums, effects, and models of persuasion. Scholars in rhetoric will recognize that we have just begun to identify the persuasive techniques likely to be employed in the discourses of international relations. Let us stress as well that such analysis should not be limited to the influence of realism. Scholars in international relations will have noticed that we have expanded somewhat the venues for political influence. Traditionally, rhetorical awareness in international studies has been relegated to diplomatic conversations or to the business of propaganda. The essays in this volume feature executive, legislative, academic, and perhaps surprisingly, public arenas. Likewise, the consideration of persuasive effect has expanded beyond charming an ambassador or manipulating the masses to suggest how discourse can constitute identity, structure deliberation, and constrain action. Some of the essays also set out models for high quality persuasive exchange. Some of these are defined negatively, as they criticize particular habits of usage, while others feature positive examples. These include models of practical reasoning and of theoretical argument, and they involve various combinations of critique and reappropriation of the realist tradition.

So it is that post-realism does not so much negate realism as situate it as one form of life among the many others it would deny or control. Where realism was a grand narrative, it has become one story among others. Where it was a theory validated by political history, it has become a mode of action often culminating in tragedy. Where it was a persona characterized by the mental toughness demanded for survival in a state of nature, it has become a linear mindset resistant to innovation in conditions of contingency, choice, and abundance. Yet post-realism can never wholly do without realism, for one has to presume that there will always be both those grasping for power and an ideology to rationalize their conduct once successful.

Postmodern culture does not wholly break with the modern. It reappropriates the elements of modernity as they lose coherence and become by turns alienated or oddly coincident or recombinant. Just so, post-realism coexists with realism as it has become a radically local, provisional, or paradoxical doctrine. Postmodern theory deconstructs and reconstructs modern thought by recourse to those intellectual traditions and symbolic materials that it had repressed. Likewise, post-realism reconceptualizes international relations by reactivating those modes of cognition and action that were largely excluded from the realist's calculations of power. This richer articulation begins by reintroducing the rhetorical tradition into both the theory and practice of international relations. By defining realism as a persuasive discourse and the conduct of foreign policy as a complex of persuasive practices, the door opens for a comprehensive process of revision and innovation. This perspective provides critical readings of realist texts, new interpretations of realist concepts, detailed accounts of practical decision making, realignment of the elements of strategy, reactivation of an ethics indigenous to the international community, recasting scientific analysis in a more explicitly interpretive mode, and replacing the norms and cognitive habits of power-driven monocultures with the intellectual and political skills needed to thrive in a period of multicultural global change.

We do not presume to have fully articulated this agenda. We have attempted to suggest the usefulness of a rhetorical perspective in the study and practice of international relations. Whether reconsidering how the present came to be, understanding what is happening and what choices are available today, or preparing for the challenges of the twenty-first century, we need to realize that we live in a world of meaning and that many of our opportunities and limitations are of our own making. While ever aware of tough choices, our fate could turn out to be a story of missed opportunities. If we are to cheat this fate, it might well be by pursuing not only power but other interests as well, including emancipatory interests. If we are to control our destiny, it might be by valuing not only order but diversity. Ultimately, success or failure will be determined not only by the realities of human nature but also by our capacity for learning, imagination, and innovation. Perhaps this volume can be one contribution toward discovering new possibilities for global politics.

NOTES

1. Robert Keohane, ed., *Neo-Realism and its Critics* (New York: Columbia University Press, 1986), 9; John A. Vasquez, *The Power of Power Politics: An Empirical Evaluation of the Scientific Study of International Relations* (New Brunswick, N.J.: Rutgers University Press, 1983), 162-70.

2. For example, see the bibliography in Martin J. Medhurst, Robert L. Ivie, Philip Wander, and Robert L. Scott, *Cold War Rhetoric: Strategy, Metaphor and Ideology* (New York: Greenwood Press, 1990). More recent examples include: Denise M. Bostdorff, *The Presidency and the Rhetoric of Foreign Crisis* (Columbia: University of South Carolina Press, 1994); Martin J. Medhurst, ed., *Eisenhower's War of Words* (East Lansing: Michigan State University Press, 1994); Cori E. Dauber, *Cold War Analytical Structures and the Post Post-War World* (New York: Praeger, 1993); Lynn B. Hinds and Theodore O. Windt, Jr., *The Cold War as Rhetoric: The Beginnings* (New York: Praeger, 1991).

3. See Richard K. Ashley and R. B. J. Walker, "Speaking the Language of Exile: Dissident Thought in International Studies," *International Studies Quarterly* 34 (1990): 259-68. See also Frederick M. Dolan and Thomas L. Dumm, eds., *Rhetorical Republic: Governing Representations in American Politics* (Amherst: University of Massachusetts Press, 1993); James N. Rosenau, *Global Voices: Dialogues in International Relations* (Boulder, Colo.: Westview Press, 1993); David Campbell, *Writing Security: United States Foreign Policy and the Politics of Identity* (Minneapolis: University of Minnesota Press, 1992); James Der Derian, *Antidiplomacy: Spies, Terror, Speed, and War* (Cambridge: Blackwell, 1992); James Der Derian and Michael J. Shapiro, eds., *International/Intertextual Relations* (Lexington, Mass.: Lexington Books, 1989).

4. Herbert W. Simons, ed., *The Rhetorical Turn: Invention and Persuasion in the Conduct of Inquiry* (Chicago: University of Chicago Press, 1990), and Simons, ed., *Rhetoric in the Human Sciences* (London: Sage, 1989); Richard Harvey Brown, *Social Science as Civic Discourse: On the Invention, Legitimations, and Uses of Social Theory* (Chicago: University of Chicago Press, 1989); John S. Nelson, Allan Megill, and Donald N. McCloskey, *The Rhetoric of the Human Sciences: Language and Argument in Scholarship and Public Affairs* (Madison: University of Wisconsin Press, 1987); Donald N. McCloskey, *The Rhetoric of Economics* (Madison: University of Wisconsin Press, 1985); Hayden White, *Metahistory: The Historical Imagination in Nineteenth-Century Europe* (Baltimore: Johns Hopkins University Press, 1973).

5. Richard Harvey Brown, "Narrative in Scientific Knowledge and Civic Discourse," in *Current Perspectives in Social Theory*, ed. John Wilson (Greenwich, Conn.: JAI Press, 1991); Anthony P. Kerby, *Narrative and the Self* (Bloomington: Indiana University Press, 1991); Roger C. Schank, *Tell Me a Story: A New Look at Real and Artificial Memory* (New York: Charles Scribner's Sons, 1990); Paul Ricoeur, *Time and Narrative*, trans. Kathleen Balmey, 3 vols. (Chicago: University of Chicago Press, 1988); W. J. T. Mitchell, *On Narrative* (Chicago: University of Chicago Press, 1981).

6. [Cicero], *Ad Herennium* 1.8.12-1.9.16, trans. Harry Caplan, Loeb Classical Library (Cambridge: Harvard University Press, 1954).

7. Kenneth Burke, *A Grammar of Motives* (Berkeley: University of California Press, 1969).

8. Joel H. Rosenthal, *Righteous Realists: Political Realism, Responsible Power and American Power in the Nuclear Age* (Baton Rouge: Louisiana State University Press, 1991).

9. Hans Morgenthau, *Politics Among Nations: The Struggle for Power and Peace*, 4th ed. (New York: Knopf, 1967), 3.

10. Hans Blumenberg, "An Anthropological Approach to the Contemporary Significance of Rhetoric," in *After Philosophy: End or Transformation?*, eds. Kenneth Baynes, James Bohman, and Thomas McCarthy (Cambridge: MIT Press, 1987), 454.

11. There is a growing contemporary literature that builds on the already extensive library of thought that is critical of realism. Examples of recent work include: Jaap W. Nobel, "Morgenthau's Struggle with Power: The Theory of Power Politics and the Cold War," *Review of International Studies* 21 (1995): 61-86; Steven Forde, "International Realism and the Science of Politics: Thucydides, Machiavelli, and Neorealism," *International Studies Quarterly* 39 (1995): 141-60; Richard Little, "Neorealism and the English School: A Methodological, Ontological and Theoretical Reassessment," *European Journal of International Relations* 1 (1995): 9-34; Brian C. Schmidt, "The Historiography of Academic International Relations," *Review of International Studies* 20 (1994): 349-68; Charles W. Kegley, Jr., "The Neo-

Idealism Movement in International Studies? Realist Myths and the New International Realities," *International Studies Quarterly* 37 (1993): 131-46; Friedrich Kratochwil, "The Embarrassment of Changes: Neo-Realism as the Science of Realpolitik without Politics," *Review of International Studies* 19 (1993): 63-80; Michael C. Williams, "Neo-realism and the Future of Strategy," *Review of International Studies* 19 (1993): 103-22; Inis H. Claude, Jr., "The Tension between Principle and Pragmatism in International Relations," *Review of International Studies* 19 (1993): 215-26; Ronen P. Palan and Brook M. Blair, "On the Idealist Origins of the Realist Theory of International Relations," *Review of International Studies* 19 (1993): 385-99; K. J. Holsti, "International Relations at the End of the Millennium," *Review of International Studies* 19 (1993): 401-8; Francis A. Beer and B. J. Balleck, "Realist/Idealist Texts: Psychometry and Semantics," *Peace Psychology Review* 1 (1993): 38-44. For representative examples of work that moves beyond the old stalemates, see note 3.

12. Michael W. Doyle, "Thucydidean Realism," *Review of International Studies* 16 (1990): 223-38; Daniel Garst, "Thucydides and Neo-Realism," *International Studies Quarterly* 33 (1989): 3-28; Hayward Alker, Jr., "The Dialectical Logic of Thucydides' Melian Dialogue," *American Political Science Review* 82 (1988): 805-20; J. Peter Euben, *Greek Tragedy and Political Theory* (Berkeley: University of California Press, 1986); James Boyd White, *When Words Lose their Meaning: Constitutions and Reconstitutions of Language, Character and Community* (Chicago: University of Chicago Press, 1984); Robert R. Connor, *Thucydides* (Princeton N.J.: Princeton University Press, 1984); Hunter R. Rawlings III, *The Structure of Thucydides' History* (Princeton N.J.: Princeton University Press, 1981); Marc Cogan, *The Human Thing: The Speeches and Principles of Thucydides' History* (Chicago: University of Chicago Press, 1981); Peter R. Pouncey, *The Necessities of War: A Study of Thucydides' Pessimism* (New York: Columbia University Press, 1980).

13. Eric Hobsbawm and Terence Ranger, eds., *The Invention of Tradition* (Cambridge: Cambridge University Press, 1983).

14. Christine Sylvester, *Feminist Theory and International Relations in a Postmodern Era* (Cambridge: Cambridge University Press, 1993); V. Spike Peterson and Anne Sisson Runyan, *Global Gender Issues* (Boulder, Colo.: Westview Press, 1993); Cynthia Enloe, *The Morning After: Sexual Politics at the End of the Cold War* (Berkeley: University of California Press, 1993); Betty A. Reardon, *Women and Peace: Feminist Visions of Global Security* (Albany: State University of New York Press, 1993); Ruth H. Howes and Michael R. Stevenson, eds., *Women and the Use of Military Force* (Boulder, Colo.: Lynne Rienner, 1993); J. Ann Tickner, *Gender in International Relations: Feminist Perspectives on Achieving Global Security* (New York: Columbia University Press, 1992); V. Spike Peterson, ed., *Gendered States: Feminist (Re)Visions of International Relations Theory* (Boulder, Colo.:

Lynne Rienner, 1992); Rebecca Grant and Kathleen Newland, eds., *Gender and International Relations* (Bloomington: Indiana University Press, 1991); Jean Bethke Elshtain and Sheila Tobias, eds., *Woman, Militarism, and War: Essays in History, Politics, and Social Theory* (Savage, Md.: Rowman and Littlefield, 1990); *Millennium: Journal of International Studies* 18, no. 2 (1988): Special Issue on Women and International Relations; Jean Bethke Elshtain, *Women and War* (New York: Basic Books, 1987).

15. Christopher Achen and Duncan Snidal, "Rational Deterrence Theory and Comparative Case Studies," *World Politics* 61 (1989): 143-69.

16. Dean R. Gerstein, R. Duncan Luce, Neil J. Smelser, and Sonja Sperlich, eds., *The Behavioral and Social Sciences: Achievements and Opportunities* (Washington, D.C.: National Academy Press, 1988).

17. Kenneth Burke, *A Rhetoric of Motives* (1950; reprint Berkeley: University of California Press, 1969); *A Grammar of Motives.*

18. Richard K. Ashley, "The Poverty of Neorealism," in Keohane, *Neorealism and Its Critics.*

19. Thomas M. Conley, *Rhetoric in the European Tradition* (Chicago: University of Chicago Press, 1993); Stanley Fish, "Rhetoric," in *Critical Terms for Literary Study*, eds. Frank Lentricchia and Thomas McLaughlin (Chicago: University of Chicago Press, 1990); Brian Vickers, *In Defense of Rhetoric* (Oxford: Clarendon Press, 1988); Terry Eagleton, "A Small History of Rhetoric," *Walter Benjamin, or Towards a Revolutionary Criticism* (London: Verso, 1981); Samuel Ijsseling, *Rhetoric and Philosophy in Conflict: An Historical Survey* (The Hague: Martinus Nijhoff, 1976). Cross-disciplinary initiatives include: R. H. Roberts and J. M. M. Good, *The Recovery of Rhetoric: Persuasive Discourse and Disciplinarity in the Human Sciences* (Charlottesville: University Press of Virginia, 1993); John Bender and David E. Wellerby, eds., *The Ends of Rhetoric: History, Theory, Practice* (Stanford: Stanford University Press, 1990); David Zarefsky, "How Rhetoric and Sociology Rediscovered Each Other," in *The Rhetoric of Social Research: Understood and Believed*, ed., Albert Hunter (New Brunswick: Rutgers University Press, 1990); Gerald B. Wetlaufer, "Rhetoric and Its Denial in Legal Discourse," *Virginia Law Review* 76 (1990): 1545-97.

20. Francis A. Beer, "Words of Reason," *Political Communication* 11 (1994): 185-201; Aristotle, *On Rhetoric*, trans. George A. Kennedy (New York: Oxford University Press, 1991); Aristotle, *Nicomachean Ethics*, trans. Terrence Irwin (Indianapolis: Hackett, 1985); Blumenberg, "An Anthropological Approach"; Martin Hollis and Stephen Lukes, *Rationality and Relativism* (Cambridge: MIT Press, 1983); Richard J. Bernstein, *Beyond Objectivism and Relativism: Science, Hermeneutics, and Praxis* (Philadelphia: University of Pennsylvania Press, 1983); Chaim Perelman and L. Olbrechts-Tyteca, *The New Rhetoric*, trans. John Wilkinson and Purcell Weaver (Notre Dame: University of Notre Dame Press, 1969).

21. Cicero, *De Oratore* 3.5.23, trans. E. W. Sutton and H. Rackham, Loeb

Classical Library (Cambridge: Harvard University Press, 1976); Nelson, et al., *Rhetoric of the Human Sciences*; Richard McKeon, "The Uses of Rhetoric in a Technological Age: Architectonic Productive Arts," in *Rhetoric: Essays in Invention and Discovery*, ed. Mark Backman (Woodbridge, Conn.: Ox Bow Press, 1987).

22. Dorothy Ross, *The Origins of American Social Science* (Cambridge: Cambridge University Press, 1991); Peter Novick, *That Noble Dream: The "Objectivity Question" and the American Historical Profession* (Cambridge: Cambridge University Press, 1988); Gerald Graff, *Professing Literature: An Institutional History* (Chicago: University of Chicago Press, 1987); Bruce A. Kimball, *Orators and Philosophers: A History of the Idea of Liberal Education* (New York: Teachers College Press, 1986); David M. Ricci, *The Tragedy of Political Science: Politics, Scholarship and Democracy* (New Haven: Yale University Press, 1984); Alexandra Oleson and John Voss, eds., *The Organization of Knowledge in Modern America, 1860-1920* (Baltimore: Johns Hopkins University Press, 1979); Thomas Haskell, *The Emergence of Professional Social Science: The American Social Science Association and the Nineteenth-Century Crisis of Authority* (Urbana: University of Illinois Press, 1977); Burton J. Bledstein, *The Culture of Professionalism: The Middle Class and the Development of Higher Education in America* (New York: W. W. Norton, 1976); Laurence R. Veysey, *The Emergence of the American University* (Chicago: University of Chicago Press, 1965).

23. Timothy Engstrom, "Philosophy's Anxiety of Rhetoric: Contemporary Revisions of a Politics of Separation," *Rhetorica* 7 (1989): 209-38; Stanley Hoffmann, "An American Social Science: International Relations," *Daedalus* 106 (1977): 41-60, and *Contemporary International Relations: The Long Road to Theory* (Englewood Cliffs, N.J.: Prentice Hall, 1960).

24. Imre Lakatos, "Falsification and the Methodology of Scientific Research Programmes," in *Criticism and the Growth of Knowledge*, eds., Lakatos and Alan Musgrave (Cambridge: Cambridge University Press, 1970): 118-19.

25. Yosef Lapid, "The Third Debate: On the Prospects of International Theory in a Post-Positivist Era," *International Studies Quarterly* 33 (1989): 215-54.

26. Joseph Dunne, *Back to the Rough Ground: 'Phronesis' and 'Techne' in Modern Philosophy and in Aristotle* (Notre Dame: University of Notre Dame Press 1993); Eugene Garver, *Machiavelli and the History of Prudence* (Madison: University of Wisconsin Press, 1987); Robert Hariman and Michael Leff, eds. *The Discourses of Prudence* (forthcoming).

II
REREADING REALIST
WRITERS

Critics of realism often point to its impersonality. Realist doctrine presumes an objective world that operates according to natural laws; its first lesson is to look for those constraints on action that will thwart one's intentions; it culminates in rational analysis. Yet this impersonal model can not be quite right, for it is difficult to think of realism without thinking of realists. Realism is not only a set of precepts but also the personae of Kissinger, Kennan, Niebuhr, Morgenthau, and others. It is both a tradition of political thought and a genealogy of thinkers, each of whom has affected its direction, authority, and influence. Curiously, individual realists loom larger than representatives of idealist doctrines. Past idealists like Grotius, Kant, and even Woodrow Wilson visit us today only in ghostly form.

These are small ironies, but they point to some features of self-definition. Perhaps realism is not only a program for rationality but also a narrative of self-determination. As we suggested in Chapter One, the realist narratio includes an intellectual history of heroic individuals speaking the truth. Prominent advocates of realism might go a step further by presenting themselves as exemplars of the autonomy and capacity for effective action that their counsel would provide the state. Stated rhetorically, realism's capacity for influence seems to depend on development of an ethos characteristic of its major precepts. Study of this "ethical" dimension of realist discourse offers special opportunities for uncovering both self-deception and complexity, *the distinctive genius of realism and the mistakes likely to result from its commonplace imitation.*

The story of the tradition's resurgence after Munich and its hegemony in the post-war period usually is told as a story of great minds and classic works. Carr's The Twenty Years' Crisis, *Wight's* Power Politics, *and Morgenthau's* Politics Among Nations *restructured academic study in England and the U.S. Kennan's Long Telegram and "X" article caused a similar reorientation in the NATO foreign policy establishment. Despite differences on specific issues, Kennan and Niebuhr were powerful influences on a generation of opinion leaders throughout the U.S., shaping public discussion of politics, foreign and domestic, around the precepts and themes of realism. Soon thereafter, Kissinger was schooling the global elite at Harvard and subsequently would become a major public figure reiterating realist maxims for several decades. Other individuals could be named and other stories could be told as well, but it seems that any reconsideration of the authority of realism needs to begin by rereading its major authors.*

The essays in this section are arranged so that one order will represent several patterns of interpretation. First, they move from the present back into the past. Kissinger is still publishing major statements of his perspective on foreign affairs to great media fanfare. Kennan also continues to receive some attention in his previous circles of influence, although more in respect to questions of historical interest than on current questions of policy. Niebuhr's disciples, a generation of preachers, academics, and journalists, have not yet retired, but his name and works are largely out of circulation despite the fact that no other cleric has achieved anything like his stature in public debate. Wight, Carr, and Morgenthau are now figures from the past. They have been canonized, but their work has acquired iconic status. They are names to be invoked more than writers who are read carefully for new insights.

As the essays in this section work back through this genealogy, they follow other changes that have occurred across the several generations of realist advocacy. Thus, the second principle of arrangement is from a relatively simplified contemporary realism to the more complex formulations of the founders. One might argue for the relative merits of simplicity or complexity, and whether political theory ought to contain dynamic tensions or be free of contradictions, but it seems hard to deny the relevance of such questions. This sense that the earlier statements were richer is reflected in a third pattern for the essays here, which range from those that offer a straightforward critique of the discourse of realism to those presenting revisionary adjustments. This alignment might confirm the defense of classical realism, as it suggests that the founders adequately anticipated their critics. Even so, defenders of realism also should acknowledge that richer, more flexible interpretations have not been readily available to several generations of disciplinary readers. In fact, another irony emerges: It seems that if there is to be a stronger, more complex and more flexible realism, it will only emerge from a rhetorical turn.

Although these essays reflect varied academic perspectives, they all examine the texts of major realists in order to determine their persuasive techniques, intentions, constraints, or effects. They illustrate how any realism is located not in a state of nature or in the unchangeable record of history, but in a text that was crafted for influence yet remains open to alternative interpretations. Although focused on prominent individuals, their interest is finally in the discourse of realism as it can be used by a wide range of actors and audiences. Some analyze the implications of rhetorical forms while others provide functionalist explanations of changes in rhetorical stance, but all are identifying how realism works as a language for political thought and action. Whether objecting to realism or revising it, they demonstrate that any realism depends not only on observation and analysis but also on advocacy and assent. Thus, by grounding realist argument in the speakers, texts, and audiences of its recent history, post-realism begins.

ROBERT HARIMAN

HENRY KISSINGER
REALISM'S RATIONAL ACTOR

One consequence of realism being deeply embedded in Western culture is that it can operate effectively in fragments. The entire code can be activated any time we are reminded, e.g., that people are by nature self-interested, that law is useless without enforcement, or that testaments of common ideals are mere rhetoric. As we accept these and similar nostrums, we enter a world of states competing for power, experts capable of calculating advantages, and idealists and other amateurs counseling folly. As these beliefs cohere, they shape our attitudes, our sensitivities (or lack of them), and our political identity.

Some speakers are particularly adept at activating the entire discursive code through succinct statements, as when Henry Kissinger counsels that "We must not equate tough rhetoric with strong action, nor can we wish away tough realities with nostalgic hopes."[1] Through the juxtaposition of "reality" with objectivity and force, and against rhetoric and idealism, such maxims activate a fundamental set of relationships between speaker, subject, and audience. When Kissinger informs his audience that "there must be realistic negotiations," the audience understands his statement not because they are familiar with other advisors who are promoting the value of unrealistic negotiations, but because his words offer reassurance while delimiting the world of foreign affairs and enhancing his authority.[2] Such phrases can carry additional meanings—in this case, an appeal for compromise—but these have to operate within the larger discursive context. Kissinger's public record demonstrates more than a knack for such statements, and his prominence over several decades of public life demonstrates how considerable persuasive power can result from concentration of the discourse of realism into a single persona.

Kissinger provides an ideal case for consideration of how realism operates as a persuasive public discourse: His academic career in international studies established him as a model realist.[3] He presided over our foreign affairs under two presidents during a period of exceptional intensity in American foreign policy.[4] He also achieved extraordinary prominence in the public sphere; though an unelected official, he became a celebrity by producing a prolific run of essays, reports, speeches, interviews, and memoirs that were accompanied by continuous publicity and promotion in the mass media. Not incidentally, throughout this period of "superstar" status and subsequently as one of the highest paid public speakers in America, Kissinger's performance has never varied. Like other late-modern actors, he plays the same, minimalist character whatever the script.

In short, Kissinger is an influential speaker and writer who epitomizes realist discourse. His prominence comes from a genius for the conventional, and his example highlights how the persuasive appeals characterizing realist rhetoric function in public address. Through analysis of the persuasive designs in his texts, we can identify how the discourse of realism structures public deliberation.[5] This analysis features the coordination of the three dimensions of the speech act known as *logos*, *pathos*, and *ethos*. This triad comes from Aristotle's *Rhetoric*, where it is the first of several sets of analytical terms that together identify the persuasive text as a mode of action, having an institutional orientation, involving practical reasoning, managing emotions, requiring stylistic competency, and otherwise organizing symbolic action for strategic effect.[6] The terms *logos*, *pathos*, and *ethos* mark three modes of appeal that are potentially available during any moment of persuasive communication. As one is persuaded, it can be because the persuasive discourse has presented a plausible representation of the subject of the speech (*logos*), a pertinent identification of the audience (*pathos*), or a reassuring portrait of the speaker (*ethos*). These elements of the persuasive process often have been included under different names in contemporary discussions of representation, hegemony, and the like. Such discussions certainly go beyond the scope of the Aristotelian vocabulary, yet not always in a manner useful for the analysis of public discourse. The Aristotelian triad still offers a precise and highly economical set of terms for analyzing the basic grammar of appeal in a text that operates as a mode of action.

By adhering to this simple structure, one can identify when realism is the dominant discourse within a speech text or series of texts, even though its appeals are not numerically superior to other forms of address. That is, the discourse of realism becomes a dominant mode of understanding and action in a public statement when its various, often fragmentary, appeals cohere into mutually reinforcing conceptions of subject, audience, and speaker. As long as these basic modes of address are articulated in the idiom of realism, the speaker may also appeal for strategic purposes to democratic values, standards of justice, and other ideals without having to risk deferring to them. This formula for rhetorical power applies to both the individual speech text and sustained performance through a number of texts. When it is augmented by coordinated use of rhetorical figures—that is, stock verbal techniques of definition, transformation, inclusion, and exclusion—the discourse can articulate a wide field of political relationships. In particular, it reveals how the discourse of realism generally constricts public speech and contributes to the monopolization of power.

Logos

As Henry Kissinger speaks, every word comes out slowly, carefully, freighted with the gravity of his subject. His premeditated, measured, somber tone gives perfect inflection to his discourse, which tells us that he is going to confront reality while others will be swayed by "prophecy," "propaganda," or "rhetoric." This technique of contrasting a real world with a world of words can function as both a local appeal, often used early in an address to dismiss alternative conceptions of the subject and announce the authority of the speaker, and the master trope structuring our most basic sense of what it is he is talking about.[7] Kissinger's subject, he tells us, is nothing less than the fundamental reality of international politics—a hard reality known by contrast with the illusions fostered by language. Note how the design operates in Kissinger's praise of Bismarck: "I think he is the first modern statesman in this sense: that he attempted to conduct foreign policy on the basis of an assessment of the balance of forces, unrestrained by the clichés of a previous period."[8] Likewise, Kissinger's subject will not consist of opinions or values or laws, nor will it involve modulating interpretations. All of these elements in political understanding become but counters in a situation that can be apprehended clearly if we have but the will to do without the distractions and desires imbued in words.

For example, the lead essay in *American Foreign Policy*, which has served as the major statement of Kissinger's political philosophy, reduces the possibilities for international order to a choice between two philosophical perspectives, that of the "statesman" and the "prophet."[9] The description of the first figure introduces each of the basic elements in the realist paradigm: "The statesman manipulates reality; his first goal is survival; . . . his view of human nature is wary"; he also is suspicious of eloquence, committed to structures rather than personalities, and believes that gradualism is the key to stability.[10] Here Kissinger neatly summarizes the realism of his generation of scholarship: the combination of pessimism, reason, and will found in classical realism has been augmented by increased emphasis on structural norms. Furthermore, this world system consists of states competing for survival, where the only rational orientation is toward achieving power. Finally, Kissinger legitimizes this world by contrasting it to prophecy. Kissinger's use of the term does not imply divine guidance, but rather the human tendency to be swept away by a spellbinding discourse of totalizing purpose and unrealistic goals. This design then can perform additional duty in this particular text as an allegorical account of the domestic crisis over the war in Vietnam.

This strategy of definition is supported further by the realist epistemology, which Kissinger's text supplies in short order. The reason the gap between reality and prophecy is so great is that these positions reflect "two lines of thought which since the Renaissance have distinguished the West from the part of the world now called underdeveloped (with Russia occupying an intermediary position). The West is deeply committed to the notion that the real world is external to the observer, that knowledge consists of recording and classifying data— the more accurately the better. Cultures which escaped the early impact of Newtonian thinking have retained the essentially pre-Newtonian view that the real world is almost completely *internal* to the observer." The text even goes further: "Empirical reality has a much different significance for many of the new countries than for the West because in a certain sense they never went through the process of discovering it."[11] The full implication of this claim is staggering: the world is rightfully ours, for only we have endured the hard work of discovering it. Here the imperialistic capability of realism is revealed in vulgar detail. The claim to know the world is a claim of ownership, and the claim that one is equipped to see the world as it really is confers authority over those who would think about it differently.

This construction of the subject of international relations structures thinking about a wide range of policies. The topic of human rights illustrates how Kissinger relies on the realist conception of reality to keep foreign policy within the narrow orbit of realist calculation. Liberal befuddlement with "'justice'" or other such ideals is highlighted by presenting these ideas as terms and by reminding his audience of others' weakness for utopian visions. For example, the attempt of the Congress to tie economic relations to human rights issues reflected an infatuation with "easy slogans" and raised the question "whether we will use our moral convictions to escape reality."[12] Not surprisingly, Kissinger's approach is presented in terms of "the scope and limits of a realistic policy"[13] and defines the situation as a choice between two forms of linkage: "when policymakers relate two separate objectives in negotiation" and "by virtue of reality."[14] Contrary to the liberal administration's emphasis upon "moral values and concern for human rights," we were reminded reprovingly that "Reality is more complex" and told that undue emphasis upon human rights produces "geopolitical disintegration."[15]

This conception of the world of international relations can lead to certain discursive anomalies, however. The claim to have a special purchase on reality rings a bit hollow when it comes in a speech that is dominated by abstraction. Frequently when reading Kissinger's speeches one can get the disconcerting feeling that the address could be about any number of alternative worlds, for Kissinger practices his structuralism with a vengeance, constantly displacing particular situations with highly abstract formulations that seem valid either everywhere or nowhere. This melding together of a realist tone and a structuralist diction is augmented by his use of history. The invocation of history's lessons occurs periodically, often as part of the assertion of a will to know reality, yet there is a marked paucity of actual historical analyses or arguments. For example, "history is marked by brief moments when an old order is giving way to a pattern new and unforeseen . . . We face such a moment today. Together let us face its realities."[16] What those other moments might have been like, we have to surmise for ourselves. This monolithic figure of "history," like "reality," often fulfills tactical functions in the realist's speech as well: displacing alternative accounts, reinforcing the appeal to "stability," and so forth. In every case, the structure of argument is enthymematic and the missing premise can be supplied unreflectively by the audience because the discourse of realism already is embedded deeply within the political culture. Realism is a discourse authorizing its speaker to intervene in the world, to manipulate reality, but it does not require that one specify more than that one knows the difference between what is real and what is not real.

Kissinger's public address brings out other features of realism as well. The subject of realism is always a world of states. We can read this phrase as both a world of *states* and a *world* of states. The more common sense is the former: realists always see states, rather than peoples, markets, regional cultures, disease gradients, or ecosystems. Although Kissinger should be credited for attempting during the last decade to see beyond the state system (in part perhaps because he began to work for private corporations), the perception of states as the only or dominant agencies in the world of international affairs remains a constant throughout his work. More important to Kissinger's realism, however, is his emphasis upon the systemic character of international relations, which is designated by his frequent use of such terms as "balance of power" or "balance of forces," "equilibrium," and "stability." The unique task of the political leader is to be the manager of this system. We are told frankly that maintaining the system is more important than peace or justice. (These latter terms usually are put in quotes. The implication is that peace and justice are enculturated terms, subject to disputed definition, whereas equilibrium and stability are terms applying to the whole system and hence incontestably rational.) Furthermore, every state has a weight in the system determined universally by its concentration of force. Consequently, all action is determined first, by the two great superpowers of the U.S. and Russia, and second, by the other "industrial democracies" of Europe and Japan, and by no one else. Witness, for example, the condescension in these remarks: "As for the Third World nations now meeting in Cuba, when I was in office I never read their resolutions, I regret to tell you, which is just as well because I might have said something rather nasty."[17] Ultimately, this discourse results not just in nastiness but in the reduction of diplomacy to the maneuvers of "geopolitics"—i.e., to a political topography.[18] This topographical sensibility is a hallmark of realism: The realist's world becomes a denuded world subject to powers of observation and control, a world of spaces, forces, and targets. Likewise, power is imagined as an autonomous, material force whose dynamics will always lie below our knowledge of peoples, cultures, and languages. Ultimately, this construction of the subject of international relations produces the central dilemma of realism: successful performance of this form of rationality increases the propensity to violence.

The spatial diction of a system of states is reinforced by related figures of temporality. Kissinger's conception of international order is legitimated in part by his nostalgia for the international system of the nineteenth century. As his title *A World Restored* implies, the Congress of Vienna achieved nothing less than the recovery of a prior, foundational order after a period of revolutionary chaos. As we are again in a period of revolution, the implication is clear that we have much to learn from "the guardians of the equilibrium of the nineteenth century," or at least from someone who has studied them.[19] The interesting aspect of this appeal to history is that it is so thoroughly a restatement of modernism, as is revealed when he meditates upon the secret of the "'guardians'" success. Contrary to the ideological conflicts of today (and apparently without regard to 1848), in those days "diplomats spoke the same language, not only in the sense that French was the lingua franca, but more importantly because they tended to understand intangibles in the same manner."[20] Thus a unified Europe was the issue of a univocal Europe, in fact, one where the most important matters could be left unsaid. To complete the structure of this appeal, in successful periods of international relations, univocality displaces heteroglossia, an elite corps of diplomats displaces democratic pluralism, and commitment to management of the system of states displaces redressing local injustices. Also, the sense of historical succession that one might expect from historical study is displaced by the conception of a rational system that can be abandoned but discovered and maintained anew without loss. Diplomacy includes the task of removing the obstacles in the contemporary period to re-establishing this system. As we shall see, the solution requires persuasive skill, for Kissinger's audience is part of the problem.

PATHOS

As the realist text promotes rational political calculations constructing an orderly system of states to restrain treacherous human nature, it has to do so in a manner that includes an identity for the audience who would live in this world. This identity will have to include a plausible account of how one is to act and to be acted upon. A moral anomaly arises at this point, for realism implies that we should act in a manner we would not want to suffer; at the least, we have to manipulate others and perhaps abandon those in need of human charity to maintain the stability of the system. This anomaly is eased within the confidently imperial state, for the audience can assume that they will not face reciprocity with those they are conquering; recall that an appeal to the reversals of history did not faze the Athenians at Melos. The anomaly becomes more worrisome, however, for those in a *liberal* imperial state. As Kissinger understands the problem, "Americans are, in some sense, in a state of permanent rebellion against the contemporary realities of world affairs."[21]

Kissinger's realism succeeds, I believe, because it assuages the anxieties of liberal imperialism. Circumstantially, his rise to power coincided with the national trauma of Vietnam, the revolutionary success of the Organization of Petroleum Exporting Countries (OPEC), and the humiliation of Watergate. Generally, this was a period in which the American public had to admit to the evils and the costs of its empire while also recognizing that its imperial status was both valuable and precarious. Kissinger's realism seems admirably adapted to this condition. As he expounds such basic symbols as "stability," and "rationality," he often sets this advice amid a review of ambivalence in foreign affairs. American policy (pre-Kissinger) always is described as an unstable, inconsistent flux: The indecision, ambivalence, and reversals in domestic politics, combined with a pervasive penchant for the illusions of idealism and ideology, produce oscillations between "isolationism and interventionism," "suspicion and euphoria," "idealism and pragmatism," among others.[22] In every case, the greater error than either alternative is the oscillation (and presumed indecision); against such error, the realist offers a carefully calculated program for gradual gains over the long term, a policy of low though constant risk and little change legitimated by an overarching rationality.

Specific moral qualms or criticisms are addressed further through the emphasis upon the legitimacy of major states, frequent recurrence to bi-polarism (especially when the morality or cost of a policy is challenged), and attribution of a defective political psychology to his critics. Although these designs are at work throughout his *œuvre*, Kissinger's memoirs offer particularly rich examples. The sacrifice of small states to grand designs (think of Melos) is rationalized through the example of Cambodia: "Strategically, Cambodia could not be considered a country separate from Vietnam."[23] (According to the same logic, Belgium cannot be considered a separate country from France.) Lest one begin to relax and think of more democratic policies, the reductive logic and constant danger of bi-polarism survives even amidst détente: "The Kremlin no doubt hoped that détente would sap the will to resistance of the democracies. . . . Brezhnev . . . was not abandoning hope for advancing the prospects of a global Communist victory." Kissinger's intentions have been thwarted only by our "national hysteria" about Vietnam and the accompanying lack of "confidence" in the Congress and the public. The psychological cast of this claim is revealed further when the requirements for effective foreign affairs are contrasted with Kissinger's enemies: the media, who are shameless provocateurs of public opinion, the academics, who are given over to "hyperbole" and "overweening righteousness," and the students, whose idealism resulted from being brought up by "skeptics, relativists, and psychiatrists," and who were "stimulated by a sense of guilt encouraged by modern psychiatry and the radical chic rhetoric of upper middle-class suburbia."[24]

These claims do more than rationalize the speaker's policies. Kissinger's critics are defined in terms of their anxieties and psychological weaknesses, which are inseparable, it seems, from the identity of a democratic public. Left to their own devices, public decision makers would be incapable of controlling themselves, much less a hostile power, precisely because they live within the psychological turmoil that results from multivocality. To compensate for this indecision and susceptibility to inappropriate moral scruples, the realist orients the audience toward an external, objective, and seemingly value-neutral conception of political order. By simultaneously activating and assuaging anxieties about disorder, the persuasive text produces the effect of quiescence.[25] By articulating the audience as a source of weakness in the conduct of foreign policy, the text strengthens the realist's claims about the external political environment and the proper locus of control.

This management of the audience culminates in what might be the major symbol of Kissinger's speech, the evocation of world order. The overriding orientation of American foreign policy is summarized as "laying foundations of international order" such that we can control our future.[26] This symbolic orientation is evident as early as *A World Restored*, which begins with a tribute to stability that positions it between those wishes and prayers constituting the goal of peace and the aggression sure to result from succumbing to such ideals. In *American Foreign Policy*, its logic is laid out with textbook clarity: "International politics recognizes no sovereign or even quasi-sovereign power beyond the nation-state. Thus in international affairs the age-old struggle between order and anarchy has a political as well as a legal dimension. . . . The unrestrained quest for predominance brooks no legal restraints. . . . In the international arena stability requires a certain equilibrium of power. Our basic foreign policy objective inevitably must be to shape a stable and cooperative global order out of diverse and contending interests."[27] This teleology has an impressive symbolic economy, deriving order from anarchy and unity from axioms of radical individuation. All criticisms have to defer to this goal, and the realist ought to respond confidently since ultimately the obstacles to its achievement are subjective conditions of the audience. "A world of turmoil and danger cries out for structure and leadership. . . . This requires confidence—the leaders' confidence in their values, the public's confidence in its government, and the nation's collective confidence in the worth of its objectives."[28] There are both psychological and moral implications for those influenced by this appeal. Psychologically, the discourse of world order makes instability into a major anxiety, change automatically a threat to control, and executive leadership the only credible mode of action. Morally, of course, the discourse rationalizes the status quo. What might need to be recognized is that the psychological condition could be the more dangerous, the greater cause of ruinous acts and the condition less capable of being identified or countered by other speakers.

Thus, the vision of world order functions ideologically. It masks American hegemony, for clearly the world order to come looks very much like the status quo, and every American increase in power is defined as contributing to world order while every Russian or other major power advance is suspected of disrupting that order.[29] More important, the symbol of world order provides the necessary indirection for managing the ambivalence of liberal empire. World order is different from national power precisely because it allows us to imagine hegemony without oppression of others, control without resentment by others, centrality without responsibility for others, and the practice of power without corruption. It is at this most imperial moment that the realist discourse once again proves to be a premier discourse of modernity, for the symbol of world order gives us a new world that is a rational world and known objectively to be so. Thus, the discourse leads to a "paradox of purity": as it becomes a global design, realism becomes transformed into the idealism that it would displace.[30] For those oriented toward this totalizing vision, the only question that remains is, what are the characteristics of the one who will lead us there?

ETHOS

There is some irony but no accident that realists such as Machiavelli or Kissinger come to be known as powerful personalities. The realist discourse might construct a world of blurred outlines in a fog of abstractions, and it can interpolate an audience that is mired in its anxieties, but these seeming weaknesses are more than compensated by its assertion of the realist himself. Realism is a discourse that portrays the speaker as someone who has power over nature because of superior intelligence and power within society because of the autonomy that comes from lacking social restraint while possessing self-control. This stylizing of the speaker is a crucial element in realism's rhetorical success; it authorizes who can speak authoritatively and how they should speak, while masking the speaker's actual political dependencies and motivating allegiance or deference.

Kissinger's rhetoric provides definitive examples of the realist's ethos. Perhaps the first sense one gets of his persona is that of an Olympian detachment from the details and anxieties of the many events brought together under the broad sweep of his gaze. As he reminds us that "history is replete with examples" of various maxims, and as his policies are rationalized by the abstract diction of his structuralist analyses, and as he contrasts his perspective with "sentimental" (i.e., liberal) and "ideological" (i.e., conservative) reactions, the consistent implication is that he deserves our confidence (a reaction matching his confidence in himself) because he has obtained a secure perspective above the fray. This higher position is reinforced by two related appeals which establish the speaker's rationality by contrast with two forms of corruption, the ordinary human dependencies on our emotions and our institutions.

The opposition between reason and emotion gives Kissinger's realism its high modernist tenor. Throughout his career, he has told us that if emotion lies on one side, then reason must be on the other, and that statecraft only succeeds through controlling one's emotional responses. Whether we take Metternich or Bismarck as our model, the lesson is the same. Metternich, we are reminded approvingly, was "'not a man of strong passions and of bold measures; . . . [he was] a

great talent; cool, calm, imperturbable and calculator *par excellence*,'"
and he succeeded because he was "a 'scientist' of politics, coolly and
unemotionally arranging his combinations. . . . Because he considered
policy a science, he permitted no sentimental attachments to interfere
with his measures."[31] Bismarck in turn "urged that foreign policy had
to be based not on sentiment but on an assessment of strength. . . .
Policy depended on calculation, not emotion."[32] These models are
reinforced by Kissinger's assessment of his contemporaries, who generally are susceptible to "charismatic" leadership, "ideological rigid-
ity," and the emotional swings of American foreign policy. This
emotionalism seems particularly prevalent in his opponents, who in
turn are aligned with the mass media. Even when Kissinger claims "a
special feeling" for the students protesting his extension of the war,
he quickly sets the record straight: "They were, in my view, as wrong
as they were passionate. . . . Emotion was not a policy."[33]

Kissinger himself emerges as a premier performer of rationality. He
defines diplomacy as the practice of restraining force and his perspective on any problem generally is a cautionary tale about the need to
control our emotional reactions. His memoirs, which of all his texts
are the most devoted to the analysis of personalities, offer a series of
vignettes on Richard Nixon that provide melodramatic contrast
between the president and his secretary. Nixon is characterized as an
edgy combination of personal turmoil and social awkwardness, and
Kissinger comes off as an unflappable man of reason providing cool,
confident management of any problem. As Nixon's awkwardness signifies socio-emotional life and its dangers, so Kissinger becomes the
personification of rationality, itself defined as the absence of excessive emotion: "I was at peace with myself, neither elated nor sad."[34]

This opposition between reason and emotional response (and the
social determination of emotional life) is strengthened by Kissinger's
supposed aversion to institutions. Whenever the rationality of his policies is misunderstood or subverted, it is because someone is already
hidebound by institutionally induced error. Stated otherwise,
Kissinger defines himself against several other stock characters, all of
whom have institutional obligations. The most direct opposition is
between the "statesman" and the "bureaucrat," who is the dominant
character in those areas of government for which Kissinger had some
responsibility.[35] The technical expert also is denigrated, however, as is
the domestic politician: the first for being insensitive to politics and
the second for being too sensitive. As these and other characterizations

are played out, a rather depressing picture develops: Politicians are too quick to sacrifice policy for political gain, bureaucrats honor only their own interminable and arbitrary practices, and experts lack the perspective to manage their expertise. Academicians are at once too aloof and too righteous, citizens are either ignorant or too caught up in their ideals as the mass media inflame their passions. Against all this, the leader of nations stands alone. As we survey the contest, we can sense that realism develops reason as an *heroic* act.[36]

The sovereignty of the rational actor has even more subtle origins, however. Not only does Kissinger stand alone, his authority remains undefined. For example, in an essay reviewing the three available kinds of leadership in foreign affairs, all are faulted, and the direct implication is that the writer represents an additional approach, by implication one superior to the others if only because it has achieved a superior perspective. This strategy typifies the Kissinger persona, which is an assertion of sheer autonomy. The perspective of statecraft emerges from seeing the limitations of all other perspectives, and this unique standpoint is the most authoritative because it is the only one not defined in terms of an institutional practice. Kissinger need not honor the obligations of representation (as does a politician) or of service (as does the bureaucrat) or of method (as does the expert). It is, of course, an assertion of executive power, but not one defined in terms of the traditions and limitations of the executive branch of the government. It is pre-eminent because it is the one undefined space at the center of the government. This autonomy is further articulated through two lesser devices: First, Kissinger's well-publicized appreciation of secrecy functions neatly in his discourse as a sign of empowerment, with power defined as exemption from public accountability. Second, Kissinger foregrounds the steady, controlled, realist persona through his frequent emphasis upon the contingent and changing nature of political reality. The implication is that one cannot rely upon the customary reactions determined by the social roles of bureaucrat, technician, etc. when contending with a reality that does not stay fixed. Only the sovereign analyst has the character capable of maintaining control amidst change.

In sum, Kissinger's persona is a superb enactment of the modern conception of rationality. Against conventional divisions of modern society, he stands as an autonomous individual; against the illusions and desires of personal life, he offers us his commitment to reason, which is not just mere calculation but a program for self control. Here we have professionalism without a profession: someone so capable he need answer only to his few peers and who would not succumb to the pursuit of self-interest, yet who has none of the corresponding limitations on his perspective that would come from specialized training or institutional affiliation. This is the figure of the bourgeois autocrat: one who merits authority because he has no social location to compromise his application of the powers of reason. It is a persona drawing upon potent strategies for composing the modern self and it offers itself as the figure naturally suited to managing states.

REALISM AND THE PUBLIC SPHERE

Perhaps it seems unfair to reduce Kissinger's career to the characteristic performance in his public address. Surely it seems presumptuous to judge realism on the basis of its expression by one speaker during a particular moment in history. Yet Kissinger's public address does provide an adequate basis for partial, provisional assessments of realism's political character and consequences. In particular, we should consider how realism affects other discourses also potentially available for decision making. Recall that the realist acquires power as a speaker by defining others as more disposed to error because they are too discursive, too caught up in words (like "human rights") to see the world. My analysis suggests that realism exemplifies the aggressiveness it finds elsewhere in the world: it attacks and drives out other discourses, and reconfigures the public sphere in a manner advantageous to maintaining its power. Not only is it the case that "diplomatic power could not exist without the structure of a text," it matters which text is supplying the structure, and when the realist text is structuring international relations specific dangers arise.[37]

Kissinger gives us one model of how the realist would control public debate. One form of control stems from the monotony of realism. Kissinger's performance of his rational persona is achieved in large part through his diction, which is largely devoid of ornament, illustration, word play, or wit. He rarely hazards a metaphor, other figures are used even less frequently, and when a striking illustration is chosen it sometimes is used redundantly in several texts. Obviously, he cannot speak without recourse to figuration at some deep level of meaning, but his discourse has a uniformly flattened surface that neither appeals to the imagination nor sparks argumentative engagement. (Kissinger's speeches often follow a similarly monotonous organizational pattern:

after a serious beginning there is one joke, then a preview of the three points to be covered, followed by his pronouncements on each, leading to a brief summation and a peroration to some ideal endorsed by the audience but otherwise unnecessary for the argument.) The important point here is that this elimination of tropes and troping is an elimination of speakers and perspectives. It is one thing to be dull, but here we have uniformity as a means for maintaining executive power. Stated otherwise, whereas realism posits its plain speech as the means for mapping reality, that plainness also construes the speaker as someone already in possession of reality, already empowered and not open to objection or alternative interpretation. Once this plainness becomes conventional, a more figurative discourse then signifies either foolishness or demagoguery, that is, something requiring either condescension or rational restraint. The cumulative effect is to disengage rather than to engage the audience, to drain emotion rather than to harness it, to induce complacency rather than an active consensus.

This constriction of public debate into a narrowly defined circumference of rational speech is matched by more explicit divisions of authority as well. Realism divides the public sphere into several sectors of decision making, with the whole configuration advantageous to the realist. First, politics is separated from all other dimensions of social life: states become sheerly political entities, power the only objective of political activity, and politics an autonomous realm of action and judgment. As a consequence, all manner of speakers and discourses can be discredited for being insufficiently experienced in political affairs (or too contaminated by "artistic," "economic," or other concerns). Second, foreign affairs are separated from domestic policy; the consequence is that public debate becomes something that assumes the single capability of supporting or subverting foreign policy (as it does or does not provide the consensus necessary for a state to throw its weight around internationally). Third, the executive office is defined as the only legitimate locale for negotiation and decision, for how else can a state have the necessary secrecy, rapid response time, and willingness to risk violence that are essential to survival in a condition of anarchy? This last division is particularly interesting because it not only restricts the context of public debate and public accountability, but also restricts the sphere of technical or professional discourses, including not incidentally the professional foreign service officer.[38] Although realism benefits from its alignment with the discursive conventions of scientific culture, it also interferes with the application of disciplinary and institutional expertise in political decision making. In Kissinger's words, "The solutions will not be worthy of the opportunity if left to technicians. They must be addressed at the highest level."[39]

This division of labor is complemented by realism's appeals for a quiescent public. Kissinger's public address constructs an explicit but very limited role for the public audience. The public is the reservoir of those essential resources of national will, national unity, and the like—i.e., psychological bases of power necessary for any state to mobilize its resources. Diplomacy, we are told, has become more complicated since the advent of democratic states: qualities once required only of the ruler now have to be found more generally and the diplomat has to assume the additional burden of educating the democratic masses.[40] This conception of public debate seems to require an additional, totalizing grandiosity to sustain its plausibility: "Let us not paralyze ourselves by a rhetoric of weakness. . . . Nowhere has the West been defeated for lack of strength. Our setbacks have been self-inflicted, either because leaders chose objectives that were beyond our psychological capabilities or because our legislatures refused to support what the executive branch believed was essential."[41] As legislators can only support or refuse to support policy, it appears that publics never define the national interest, which must be something independent of public ideals or actions. Any alternative conception of public affairs is further obstructed as Kissinger draws upon other characteristic appeals: "The public atmosphere was hardly hospitable to nuance. For the war had set in motion forces transcending the issues and emotions that went beyond the substance of the debate," and subsequent protests were "conspicuously and generally approvingly covered by the media."[42] The public is something acted upon, rather than acting, affective rather than rational, and something to be evaluated in respect to the executive's plans, rather than the reverse.

Thus, as realism operates as one discourse within the public sphere it also attempts to reconfigure public address as a simulacrum of the world the realist would manage. When the realist dominates, all public debate can become normed to the conventions of rational speech and executive authority, based on calculations of interest and risk, capable of persuading elites to compromise and of persuading masses to maintain the national consensus needed to enforce systemic stability. Furthermore, as it achieves hegemony, the realist discourse depersonalizes politics. By bringing us to see states rather than peoples and power rather than personalities or texts, the practices of realism sup-press all those terms of identification with others that activate our conscience and put a brake on violence.

This reduction of sensibility leads to additional faults as well. However much it counsels restraint among states, realism becomes a standing excuse for aggression by states within their own borders. Although discounting the traditional trappings of authority, it natural-izes autocracy, and while checking the worst tendencies in ideologi-cal speech, it imbues the alienation and indifference habitual to an imperial world. Although I also want to avoid alternative dystopias of mass hysteria, capricious leadership, and violent upheavals, the choice is not likely to be between order and chaos. As the system con-tinues its absorption of the lifeworld, we are more likely to stand between one form of order or another, between a realist rhetoric of state management and other discourses attempting to place that sys-tem into another context. The shift from a world of states to a world of discourses need not simplify our choices, however. For they are not separate worlds. Notice, for example, how this theory of discourses competing for public influence reproduces some of the elements of realism. The issue is not one of discursive purity—or of the purity of our ideals—but rather discerning how to avoid reduction to the mod-ernist structures likely to be both empowering any discursive act in the modern world and inhibiting our capability to escape the modern forms of violence. This is the problematic of post-realism, and one that can benefit from the analysis of public address. By identifying the discourses competing within the public sphere to define the conduct of international relations, we realize the opportunity for a more cre-ative politics.

NOTES

1. Henry A. Kissinger, *American Foreign Policy*, 3d ed. (New York: W. W. Norton, 1977), 302.

2. Kissinger, *American Foreign Policy*, 137.

3. Walter Isaacson, *Kissinger: A Biography* (New York: Simon & Schuster, 1992); Kenneth W. Thompson, *Morality and Foreign Policy* (Baton Rouge: Louisiana State University Press, 1980); Michael Joseph Smith, *Realist Thought from Weber to Kissinger* (Baton Rouge: Louisiana State University Press, 1986); Stanley Hoffmann, "An American Social Science: International Relations," *Daedalus* 106 (1977): 41-60. Kissinger's latest work—which I received as this essay was close to publication—provides ample illustration

of how much he continues to depend on the language of realism. See especially the first chapter of *Diplomacy* (New York: Simon & Schuster, 1994).

4. Isaacson, *Kissinger*; Robert D. Schulzinger, *Henry Kissinger: Doctor of Diplomacy* (New York: Columbia University Press, 1989); Richard C. Thornton, *The Nixon-Kissinger Years: The Reshaping of American Foreign Policy* (New York: Paragon House, 1980).

5. Perhaps I should emphasize that I am not conducting a biographical study of Kissinger, of which there are plenty available. Likewise, the means of persuasion evident in public address need not derive their meaning or significance primarily from their relationship to the author's background and beliefs. For the latter emphasis in respect to Kissinger, see Harvey Starr, *Henry Kissinger: Perceptions of International Politics* (Lexington: The University Press of Kentucky, 1984); Stephen Walker, "The Interface Between Beliefs and Behavior: Henry Kissinger's Operational Code and the Vietnam War," *Journal of Conflict Resolution* 21 (1977): 129-68. Of course, full consideration of any one of Kissinger's texts would have to account for at least the specific situation and task he was facing, his pertinent beliefs and attendant circumstances, and his use of the conventions of the particular communicative genre.

6. *Aristotle on Rhetoric: A Theory of Civic Discourse*, trans. George A. Kennedy (New York: Oxford University Press, 1991).

7. For discussion of realism's dependency upon this trope, see the concluding chapter of this volume, and "No Superficial Attractions and Ornaments: The Invention of Modernity in Machiavelli's Realist Style," in Robert Hariman, *Political Style: The Artistry of Power* (Chicago: University of Chicago Press, 1995).

8. Henry A. Kissinger, *For the Record: Selected Statements, 1977-1980* (Boston: Little, Brown, 1981), 161; see also 119-20 for the précis of realism that accompanies this assessment.

9. This distinction is reactivated in the second chapter of *Diplomacy*, where Kissinger contrasts his American hero, Theodore Roosevelt, a "warrior-statesman," and his foil, Woodrow Wilson, "the prophet-priest."

10. Kissinger, *American Foreign Policy*, 46-47.

11. Ibid., 48, 49.

12. Ibid., 211.

13. Ibid., 308.

14. Henry A. Kissinger, *For the Record*, 88.

15. Ibid., 286-87.

16. Kissinger, *American Foreign Policy*, 182.

17. Kissinger, *For the Record*, 247.

18. Theodore Draper, "Kissinger's Apologia," *Dissent* 27 (1980): 246 ff.; Hariman, "No Superficial Attractions and Ornaments."

19. Kissinger, *American Foreign Policy*, 56.

20. Ibid., 55; *A World Restored: Metternich, Castlereagh and the Problems of*

Peace 1812-22 (Boston: Houghton Mifflin, 1957), 320.

21. Henry A. Kissinger, *Observations: Selected Speeches and Essays 1982-84* (Boston: Little, Brown, 1985), 63.

22. Ibid., 7-8, 60-65; *White House Years* (Boston: Little, Brown, 1979), 1476; *American Foreign Policy*, 95, 147, 200, 302; *Diplomacy*, chaps. 1 and 31.

23. Kissinger, *White House Years*, 486.

24. Ibid., 297, 509-17, 1252, 1254, 1257.

25. Murray Edelman, *Politics as Symbolic Action: Mass Arousal and Quiescence* (New York: Academic Press, 1971).

26. Kissinger, *White House Years*, 1251.

27. Kissinger, *American Foreign Policy*, 218. Note how this passage relies on the realist *narratio* and the trope of contrasting real power with a more discursive, e.g., "legal," alternative.

28. Ibid., 212.

29. Noam Chomsky, *Towards a New Cold War: Essays on the Current Crisis and How We Got There* (New York: Pantheon, 1982), 167; Philip Green, *Deadly Logic: The Theory of Nuclear Deterrence* (Columbus: Ohio State University Press, 1966), 245.

30. Kenneth Burke, *A Grammar of Motives* (1945; reprint Berkeley: University of California Press, 1969), 35-38.

31. Kissinger, *A World Restored*, 11-12, 319.

32. Henry A. Kissinger, "The White Revolutionary: Reflections on Bismarck," *Daedalus* 97 (1968): 906-7.

33. Kissinger, *White House Years*, 510; *Diplomacy*, 834.

34. Kissinger, *White House Years*, 1476.

35. Kissinger, *American Foreign Policy*, 17-26, 29 ff.; Dan Caldwell, *Henry Kissinger: His Personality and his Politics* (Durham, N.C.: Duke University Press, 1983), 15-18; Marvin Kalb and Bernard Kalb, *Kissinger* (Boston: Little, Brown, 1974), 78-99; I. M. Destler, "Can One Man Do?" *Foreign Policy* 5 (1971-72): 28-40.

36. Donna Gregory, "Foreword" to *International/Intertextual Relations: Postmodern Readings of World Politics,* eds. James Der Derian and Michael J. Shapiro (Lexington, Mass.: Lexington Books, 1989), xvii.

37. Jacques Derrida, "No Apocalypse, Not Now (Full Speed Ahead, Seven Missives, Seven Missiles)," *Diacritics* 14 (1984): 26.

38. Gordon A. Craig and Alexander L. George, *Force and Statecraft: Diplomatic Problems of Our Time* (New York: Oxford University Press, 1983), 60-72.

39. Kissinger, *American Foreign Policy*, 103.

40. Ibid., 11-16, 54-55, 91-97, and ff.

41. Ibid., 394.

42. Kissinger, *White House Years*, 288, 289.

ROBERT L. IVIE

REALISM MASKING FEAR
GEORGE F. KENNAN'S POLITICAL RHETORIC

Fear is a feature of human nature that political realists typically factor into their pessimistic view of international affairs. The world as it actually "is," they assume, consists of nation-states inherently conflicted over competing interests and limited resources, arbitrating their differences and seeking security through the elusive agency of power. Humankind is motivated less by morality and law than by fear and greed, motives which must be managed through the intelligent application of power—not just military power, but economic and ideological might as well. Providing for national security and fulfilling national interests are constant aspirations and tenuous achievements in an essentially anarchic international environment.[1] George F. Kennan is no exception among realists holding this view of "man's fallen nature."[2] In Kennan's words, we "run around . . . encumbered" by our "demonic side . . . wholly unamenable to reason . . . restrained only by some form of force. Violence is the tribute we pay to original sin."[3] Fear and insecurity, no less than jealousy and ambition, are "prime movers of events."[4]

Kennan's response to the savagery of the human condition has been to advance the ideal of civility in the orderly and rational pursuit of national self-interest.[5] He is, as Greg Russell observes, an elitist who "yearns for a civilized meritocracy of skill and intellect," a man who, in his own words, prefers "hierarchy and authority over compromise and manipulation," who harbors a "distaste amounting almost to horror for the chaotic disorder of the American political process."[6] The manner and method of pursuing one's objectives is more real to him than the goals—"normally vainglorious, unreal, extravagant, even pathetic"—that people and nations strive to achieve.[7] His elitist cynicism about democratic process and the management of foreign affairs makes him yearn for the order and stability of a balance of power among great nations, and causes him to fear for the survival of civilization itself in an irrational age of nuclear weaponry and advanced technology.[8] The unifying theme in Kennan's extensive writing, according to Barton Gellman, is that "the quality of a civilization is the only true measure of its purposes, its methods, and its prospects in world affairs. A society's internal health is logically precedent to its relationship with the external world."[9]

The cultivation of civility compensates for Kennan's "realistic" assumptions about human nature by exacting, perhaps inadvertently, a heavy price. That is to say, the ideal of an orderly and rational management of power compounds the problem of national *in*security, exaggerating the external threat by turning it inward—basing it inextricably on a pessimistic prognosis of society's internal health. Even Kennan's later attempt to correct an overly frightful image of the Soviet threat, an image which he was largely responsible for creating in the earliest phase of the Cold War, relies on a conceptual framework that underscores the nation's inherent susceptibility to barbarism. Ironically, Kennan's political realism masks the fear to which his political rhetoric panders, even as it purports to warn against "a monster of our own creation."[10] Because his rhetoric assumes that a purely rational agent should preside on matters of public policy, instead of acknowledging the inevitability of pathos in civic discourse, Kennan advances a self-defeating realism by constituting a threat that cannot be allayed. His appeal to civility ultimately serves to control emotions by suppressing them; it attempts to manage unacknowledged affect instead of understanding its influence on deliberative processes, thus amplifying and distorting feelings of insecurity that are capable of becoming perverse influences on "rational" thinking.

Kennan's model of the rhetoric-reality relationship is typical of political realists who equate rhetoric with the devices of propaganda which are employed of necessity by the elite to protect the masses from themselves, and who presume that the governing elite have access to an objective, rational discourse with which to calculate real national interests and devise appropriate strategies for protecting those interests. At most, such a model allows for the possibility of realists becoming bewitched by their own propaganda, thus acknowledging a wider scope and greater influence of rhetorical discourse, but not without retaining the idea that a better, rational alternative is available for freeing them from their own rhetoric. Only by understanding realism itself as a rhetorical construction and by assuming no recourse to an objective logic of politics are we able to perceive how realism is an expression of fear grounded in images of irrationality and instability. Such a discourse is comprehensible and influential only within its own rhetorically constructed context of fear. Thus, my purpose is to examine Kennan's rhetorical construction and reassessment of the Soviet threat in order to identify the conceptual imagery through which his political realism contributes to an exaggerated sense of national insecurity and thereby perpetuates a fear of civilization's inevitable demise. The analysis reveals a far different mentality than that which Kennan-the-realist purports to be necessary for the proper conduct of foreign affairs. Instead of the cool, calculating diplomat, we discover suppressed fear, lurid imagery, and demonizing rhetoric, which places him out of touch with "the existing structure of American democracy."[11]

As an exercise in criticism, the goal of examining Kennan's fear-inducing discourse of realism is to identify and evaluate its rhetorical architecture, i.e., to critique its strategic design as a motivating construct of political reality which comprises our prevailing sense of civic substance and propriety. Metaphorical concepts, as I have argued elsewhere, constitute the foundation of any such reality-defining discourse.[12] The strategic constructions that organize our lives originate as fertile metaphors that become literalized beyond recognition as they are elaborated into conventional definitions of situations. Thus, literalized metaphors are key components of political thought that shape the culture of political elites as well as the public. Kennan's metaphorical thinking, in particular, is the source of his construction of the Soviet threat. I review his otherwise familiar writings on the subject of containment in order initially to highlight and contextualize key metaphorical influences on his thinking and subsequently to suggest a reformulation of political realism itself that is neither self-validating nor self-defeating to the extent that it incorporates a more rhetorically sophisticated account of democratic polity.

KENNAN'S CONSTRUCTION OF THE SOVIET THREAT

As the acknowledged father of the containment doctrine, Kennan played a major role in articulating the rationale for the Truman administration's post-war "get tough" policy toward America's recent ally, the Soviet Union. This was the period of his Foreign Service career when, as the government's leading expert on Russia, he was

explicitly hostile to the Soviets and rhetorically alarmist in his characterization of the threat posed to the United States. In Kennan's
view, Stalin, "endowed with [a] rather feverish political imagination,"
had abandoned Western civilization in the pursuit of "conspiratorial
thinking, secretiveness, cruelty, unscrupulousness, and oppor-
tunism."[13] Two documents that received considerable attention during this period were the 8,000-word "long telegram" sent to the
Department of State on 22 February 1946 from Kennan's diplomatic
post in Moscow and the "X" article on "The Sources of Soviet
Conduct" published "anonymously" in the July 1947 issue of *Foreign
Affairs*. Both reveal the conceptual imagery with which the architect
of containment built his rhetorical edifice of national peril in the service of political realism.

The Long Telegram

A haunting image of death pervades and dominates Kennan's
analysis in the long telegram from Moscow, an image that draws upon
a set of metaphorical concepts portraying Soviet strength as a function
of America's weakness and its susceptibility to unhealthy influences.
Kennan's dominant metaphor is one of sickness and disease bolstered
by figures of fire, subversion, and darkness, all of which puts Western
civilization in a symbolic framework of grave risk. Kennan's interpretation of the danger, in other words, transforms his perception of
American inadequacies into a vision of apocalyptic doom.

The metaphor of sickness is introduced into the long telegram by
observing the "Kremlin's neurotic view of world affairs," i.e., the "traditional and instinctive Russian sense of insecurity" that historically
"afflicts" all Russian rulers and causes them to seek their own security at the expense of others, by spreading a dogma that views the outside world as "bearing within itself germs of creeping disease and
destined to be wracked with growing internal convulsions until it is
given [the] final *coup de grace* by [the] rising power of socialism."
Marxism, which "smoldered" for fifty years in Western Europe and
finally "caught hold and blazed" in a backward Russia, is a "fig leaf"
of Soviet respectability used to tempt the "ignorant" and "desperate"
of a "war-torn outside world" with "honeyed promises" that are
"more dangerous and insidious than ever before." The "subtle
intrigue" of which the Russians are past masters operates in a "subterranean plane" of "oriental secretiveness" designed to keep opponents

in the "dark" and to "penetrate," through this "underground" and "conspiratorial" cover, a number of especially vulnerable groups such as "labor unions, youth leagues, women's organizations, [and] racial societies." The goal of this "paralyzing" strategy is to "undermine [the] general political and strategic potential of major western powers" by disrupting "national self-confidence" and stimulating "all forms of disunity." The "poor will be set against rich, black against white, young against old, newcomers against established residents, etc." Where suspicions exist among Western powers, "they will be fanned; where not, ignited" by such "underground methods."

Kennan's solution is to prescribe the "same courage, detachment, objectivity, and same determination not to be emotionally provoked or unseated by [Soviet neurosis], with which [a] doctor studies [an] unruly and unreasonable individual." Avoiding "hysterical anti-Sovietism" and defeating the communist threat depends on the "health and vigor of our own society," for world communism is like a "malignant parasite which feeds only on diseased tissue." Thus, the United States government must take "courageous and incisive" measures to solve the "internal problems" and "deficiencies of our own society," including improved discipline, in order to "cling to our own methods and conceptions of human society." The alternative is to succumb to the disease of Soviet-dominated communism and thus "to become like those with whom we are coping."[14]

Clearly, Kennan based his prognosis on what for him were pessimistic premises. The disease of international communism threatened Western civilization by infecting the most vulnerable groups among the emotional and uninformed democratic masses, including especially women and ethnic minorities.[15] Kennan's fundamental doubts about democracy's internal health and its ability to respond intelligently and deliberately to a grave communist threat predisposed him incongruously to expect the worst even while criticizing the public for seeing the Soviets as the incarnation of evil. Correcting the deficiencies of American society would require more than a mere reform and thus amounted to a feeble gesture of hope in Kennan's otherwise bleak assessment. Indeed, he later observed that his telegram read "exactly like one of those primers put out by alarmed congressional committees or by the Daughters of the American Revolution, designed to arouse the citizenry to the dangers of the Communist conspiracy." The "sensational" effect of "this elaborate pedagogical effort" resulted from a momentary state of receptivity in

Washington—a "subjective state of readiness"—regardless "of the fact that the realities which it described were ones that had existed, substantially unchanged, for about a decade." In Kennan's view, this raised the question of "whether a government so constituted should deceive itself into believing that it is capable of conducting a mature, consistent, and discriminating foreign policy," a question that continued to plague him increasingly over the years and that he consistently answered in the negative.[16]

The Sources of Soviet Conduct

Kennan's image of an unhealthy democratic polity exposed to the deadly ideological germs of communism establishes the essentially pessimistic context of his advocacy of containment as the best possible response to the sources of Soviet conduct. Within this framework, containment—as a test of political will, fortitude, and wit—pits democracy's essential weakness against totalitarianism's principal strength. The implicit attitude of the "X" article, despite Kennan's lame suggestion to the contrary, is one of democracy containing the seeds of its own destruction.[17]

"The political personality of Soviet power," Kennan observes, is the product of an ingrained communist ideology reinforced by the circumstances of established totalitarian power. Stalin and his followers share a sense of "insecurity" and a brand of "fanaticism," "unmodified by any of the Anglo-Saxon traditions of compromise," that within its "Russian-Asiatic world" is "too fierce and too jealous to envisage any permanent sharing of power" inside or outside the Soviet sphere. Ideology taught that the outside world is hostile and that it is "their duty eventually to overthrow the political forces beyond their borders." Thus, in an ironic extension of his own fears of democratic irrationality and incivility to a threatening construction of Soviet neuroses and insecurities, Kennan concludes that the "machinery" of Soviet security rests on the "the iron discipline of the Party" and its patient "quest for absolute power" as it foresees the "inevitability of the eventual fall of capitalism." Kennan vividly characterizes the machinery of Soviet power:

> The accumulative effect of these factors is to give to the whole subordinate apparatus of Soviet power an unshakable stubbornness and steadfastness in its orientation. This orientation can be changed at will by the

Kremlin but by no other power. Once a given party line has been laid down on a given issue of current policy, the whole Soviet governmental machine, including the mechanism of diplomacy, moves inexorably along the prescribed path, like a persistent toy automobile wound up and headed in a given direction, stopping only when it meets with some unanswerable force.

Since "the Kremlin is under no ideological compulsion to accomplish its purposes in a hurry," it "has no compunction about retreating in the face of superior force" and thus presents the West with an "unceasing constant pressure"—a "fluid stream which moves constantly, wherever it is permitted to move," until it fills "every nook and cranny available to it in the basin of world power." This means, as Kennan observes, that the Soviet threat cannot be effectively countered "by sporadic acts which represent the momentary whims of democratic opinion." Instead, it requires "a long-term, patient but firm and vigilant containment of Russian expansive tendencies."

If the United States can sustain such a policy over a period of ten to fifteen years, Kennan speculates, it might be able to weaken and eventually defeat its totalitarian adversary. Such a victory depends upon "the degree to which the United States can create among the peoples of the world generally the impression of a country which knows what it wants, which is coping successfully with the problems of its internal life and with the responsibilities of a World Power." Because "the palsied decrepitude of the capitalist world is the keystone of Communist philosophy," any "exhibitions of indecision, disunity and internal disintegration within [the United States] have an exhilarating effect on the whole Communist movement." The Kremlin must encounter "frustration indefinitely" in order for its power to disintegrate eventually and its aspirations to mellow gradually.

The Soviet challenge, Kennan concludes, stands as a "test of the over-all worth of the United States." Providence could not devise a "fairer test of national quality." The entire security of the American people as a nation depends upon "their pulling themselves together."[18] Nowhere, though, does Kennan offer the opinion that Americans will indeed prove their worth by pulling themselves together in order to pass the test of containment and thus preserve their security. Instead, he provides what Lynn Hinds and Theodore Windt call a "chilling portrait" of Soviet expansionism that stresses "fanaticism [and] dictatorial powers unrelieved by any Western civilities."[19] The machinery of disciplined Soviet power is aligned ominously against the sporadic and whimsical responses of democratic opinion.

KENNAN'S REASSESSMENT OF THE SOVIET THREAT

Contrary to the relatively common view that Kennan reversed course by revising downward his assessment of the Soviet threat after the early years of the Cold War, he instead maintained rhetorical continuity in his characterization of a nation and world at risk. As Michael Polley notes, any change in Kennan's brand of realism by the 1970s was more a matter of tone than substance; in fact, his "viewpoint grew more pessimistic and more urgent in tone" as a consequence of his "doubts about the quality of American society" and his fundamental belief that "a nation's diplomacy could only be as effective as [its] social system."[20]

In 1951, with the publication of *American Diplomacy, 1900-1950*, Kennan had written that there exists "a very significant gap between challenge and response in our conduct of foreign policy" which puts us in "grave peril" and thus requires us to "face up unsparingly to our weaknesses." The machinery of government accounted in his mind for much of the trouble, for the executive was held hostage to "the erratic and subjective nature of public reaction to foreign-policy questions." Public opinion was a poor guide on matters of foreign policy since it could be so easily "led astray into areas of emotionalism and subjectivity." Because a stronger reliance on the principle of professionalism would run counter to "strong prejudices and preconceptions" in the public mind, the United States was condemned to continuing the practice of "diplomacy by dilettantism" and by implication would remain incapable of avoiding moralistic excesses in its response to international problems.[21]

In 1977, Kennan began *The Cloud of Danger* with a similar warning that the nation's "internal constitution and habits" hamper its ability to act effectively on the international scene. These internal conditions include "the congenital deficiencies" of American government which "rule out the privacy, the flexibility, and the promptness and incisiveness of decision and action" that are necessary to the conduct of foreign policy by a great state. Moreover, they include an inability to cope effectively with the domestic problems of violent crime, inflation, unemployment, transportation, declining educational standards, corrupt mass communications, pornography, and environmental deterioration. The United States, he concludes, "cannot be a source of hope and inspiration to others against a background of resigned failure and deterioration of life here at home." In particular, America's congenital inability to act effectively on the international scene entails the grave danger of "carry[ing] us all to destruction" by letting the Soviet-American nuclear arms race become wholly uncontrollable.[22]

Kennan marks the year 1973 as the beginning of a new phase of increased hostility in Soviet-American relations, when "the Soviet Union appeared in a far more menacing posture than had been the case for the past decade." This ominous new tendency continued to grow until it reached its apotheosis during the Reagan era as a "full-fledged war scare accompanied by a high degree of general anti-Soviet hysteria." The origin of this hysteria was subjective rather than objective, i.e., it reflected "a subconscious need on the part of a great many people for an external enemy—an enemy against whom frustrations could be vented, an enemy who could serve as a convenient target for the externalization of evil, an enemy in whose allegedly inhuman wickedness one could see the reflection of one's own exceptional virtue." National frustration and the failures of American society, he reasons, stimulated this subconscious need for an external enemy. Such subconscious states of mind proved too great a temptation for politicians "anxious to avoid involvement with the bitter internal issues of the day and eager to reap, instead, the easy acclamations usually produced in our society by a vigorous ringing of the chauvinist bell." Such emotionalism, oversimplification, and dramatization of reality had undermined the chances of Western civilization surviving the tremendous dangers of the nuclear age.[23]

Survival, in Kennan's view, demands fundamental changes in American government and society that, while not impossible to make, may require more time than is available in order to avoid a final catastrophe. Statesmen will have to overcome "that subjectivity that caused Americans to be strongly pro-Soviet at the height of the Stalin era and equally anti-Soviet in the days of Khrushchev, and to acquire a greater steadiness and realism of vision before the phenomenon of Soviet power." Politicians will have to learn not to exploit "the image of a formidable external rival in world affairs." Such an "unreal image" of an "utterly inhuman adversary" causes us to lose rational control of our "fearful capacity for suicidal destruction."[24]

The problem of the Soviet threat, as Kennan sees it, has always been one of how to pursue a rational middle course between hysteria and euphoria. Prior to the Korean War and the death of Stalin, he argues, the problem was caused by the political left—people with "a naive, overtrusting, overidealistic view of what was then Stalinist power." It is this sort of "left-wing deviation" against which his "X" article and the policy of containment are aimed. After Stalin's death, the opponents of a realistic policy toward the Soviets came from the political right—people "unable to see the curious mix of the negative and the positive, of the discouraging and the hopeful, in the Soviet political personality."[25] It is this group that motivates Kennan's reassessment of the Soviet threat. In both cases, Kennan sees the common thread of a flawed society unable to contend with the irrational impulses of human nature. His opinion of humankind, always low, is that they shall forever remain "part animal, governed by their emotions and subconscious drives rather than by reason."[26] Their irrational impulses create the sickness within that constitutes the threat from without, whether that threat takes the form of an ideological virus infecting unsuspecting victims or an exaggerated image of the enemy prompting nuclear suicide. The Soviets are a threat in either case only because an unhealthy American polity is incapable of responding rationally to external realities.

KENNAN'S REALISM AND RHETORIC OF FEAR

Kennan's quest for civility in the conduct of international relations compounds the problem of fear inherent to political realism. Civility is the rational mask of realism worn to cover the fear engendered by his rhetoric, a rhetoric that diagnoses democracy as a terminal disease and prescribes an elitist remedy which removes issues of foreign policy from the realm of public deliberation. Kennan's prescription for a better world simply does not apply to a democratically constituted polity.[27] It exacerbates the problem by insinuating a turn toward authoritarianism. Realists such as Kennan assume that fear and greed (i.e., emotion and interest) are not just basic human motives but are also base characteristics of the human condition, characteristics for which nation-states must compensate by the expert management of power. Of course, if Kennan were correct about the inherent flaws of democracy, the United States would have collapsed at the end of the Cold War instead of its Soviet adversary and the problems of capricious, irrational foreign policy would not have been evident throughout history in elite, authoritarian governments.

Kennan, however, believes that the real enemy is within; as he noted in 1987, the concept of containment should be revised "to recognize that a large proportion of the sources of our troubles and dangers lies outside the Soviet challenge." There is much in American life, he suggests, that needs to be restricted. Quite simply, "the first thing we Americans need to learn to contain is . . . ourselves." Left uncontained, our worst inclinations put Western civilization itself at grave risk. The "compulsions, the suspicions, the anxieties" engendered by the nuclear weapons race, for instance, might easily lead to catastrophic consequences. Another source of instability that needs to be contained is our neglect of the worldwide environmental crisis. Lack of stewardship of nonrenewable energy resources and pollution of our water and atmosphere threatens to undermine the environment "as a support system for civilized living." Such environmental destructiveness reflects the character flaws of an undisciplined people living beyond their means, spending themselves into a disastrous budgetary deficit, and becoming inundated by uncontrolled immigration "of great masses of people of wholly different cultural and political traditions."[28] This distrust of democracy, however, ignores the destructive influences of capitalism and industrialization on the environment, fails to recognize environmentalism as a democratic movement, and overlooks the terrible environmental degradation occurring within disciplined, authoritarian societies.

Nevertheless, Kennan maintains that the need for democratic self-containment is nowhere greater than in the application of morality to foreign policy. Too often our "sensibilities" have dictated foreign policy to the detriment of our national interests, leading us to various ill-considered interventions under the banner of democracy, human rights, and other such moralistic slogans and principles. Democracy, a "loose term," contrives to cover such a variety of abuses in other countries that it works against American interests, when those interests would be better served by "a wise and benevolent authoritarianism" rather than dictatorships that claim "the legitimacy of mass support." Thus, Kennan warns against succumbing to "the histrionics of moralism at the expense of its substance. By that is meant the projection of attitudes, poses and rhetoric that cause us to appear noble and altruistic in the mirror of our own vanity but lack substance when related to the realities of international life." Failure to contain such irrational impulses decreases our chances of averting "the two apocalyptic catastrophes that now hover over the horizons of mankind"—

suicide by nuclear holocaust and reckless disregard of the environment, both entailing the final destruction of civilization.[29]

Kennan's conceptual image of containing ourselves—of controlling our destructive emotional impulses—entails a Platonic constraint on human freedom in order to insure the welfare and happiness of the republic. Specifically, it cycles back to a treatise he wrote in 1938, but never published, extolling the benefits of authoritarian rule by experts. Democracy, he wrote, can only succeed in small European countries with homogeneous populations, not in America's cauldron of democratic chaos where "boss-ridden democracy" has been corrupted by the "bewildered ignorant masses," including especially aliens and naturalized citizens, nonprofessional women, and blacks, all of whom should be disenfranchised. The United States should be ruled by an elite minority trained to keep the larger national interest as its guiding principle.[30] As Stephanson observes, this distrust of the *demos* and desire to form an elite group of guardians was "a thinly disguised attempt to adapt Plato's *Republic* to American conditions."[31]

Kennan's longstanding fetish for order and control and his desire to suppress human emotions in the conduct of civic affairs makes his critique of the American experience irrelevant at best and, at worst, conducive to exaggerating the external threat and to condoning authoritarianism. Yet, even Kennan does not consider seriously the possibility of fundamentally altering the American constitution to empower a governing elite, leaving him pessimistic about the future and devoid of suggestions for enhancing the odds of avoiding nuclear or environmental catastrophe. Ironically, his initial analysis of the Soviet threat and his subsequent reassessment, both of which point to uncontained irrational impulses as the source of the danger, undermine still further the nation's capacity for constructive international relations. He achieves the reverse of what he sets out to accomplish by constructing a symbolic orientation that, if taken seriously, underscores freedom's fragility. Conceptualizing democracy—the symbol of civilization—as unhealthy (on the one hand subject in its weakened state to the untoward influence of ideological infection and on the other hand suicidal in its neurotic response to the Soviet threat) exaggerates its vulnerability to the forces of savagery.

Regardless of his best efforts to reassure Americans that their communist adversaries are not as barbaric as they once seemed under Stalin's fierce rule, Kennan's balanced characterization of Soviet aspirations and his realistic assessment of the limitations on their freedom of action still convey the threatening image of a totalitarian challenge to freedom's tenuous survival. The very existence of a totalitarian alternative is problematic symbolically to the extent that freedom and democracy are characterized rhetorically as succumbing to unhealthy influences. That which is inherently frail and feeble, as a function of unbridled emotionalism, irrational impulses, and moralistic sensibilities, needs a totally antiseptic environment free of foreign ideological germs to insure against its demise. Thus, Kennan's symbolic orientation, stripped of its impracticable provision for empowering a reliably rational diplomatic elite, transforms any accommodation of Soviet great-power interests into the appearance of a dangerous flirtation with frail democracy's doom.

The basic limitation of Kennan's political realism in a democratically constituted polity, then, can be traced to the key assumption that emotion is a sickness of the masses that must be contained by the rational management of power in the pursuit of objective national interests. Simply put, he lacks any positive regard for the deliberative role of political rhetoric in the conduct of civic affairs, for that would acknowledge the existence of impassioned rationality in the affairs of state—a notion that is reduced to oxymoronic nonsense when one is as accustomed as Kennan to opposing objective reality to subjective feelings. Thus, Kennan cannot appreciate the essential strength of democracy—that interests are composed in deliberation and that competing interests necessarily vie for adherence through the agency of fallible arguments grounded in human sentiment. Instead, he chooses to mask the operation of emotion in a facade of objective realism, reducing an essential influence to a base and dangerous flaw of human nature.

Kennan's elitist determination to contain the affective dimension of human nature within the fragile vessel of rational civility undermines the realism of his politics—at least insofar as realism places a premium on a balanced apprehension of and relationship to the actual conditions of political conduct and attempts to avoid the extremities of dogmatism on the left and the right. Failure to recognize the whole of political reality, as R. N. Berki argues, leads to an idealism either of imagination or nostalgia. Political realism, he observes, ought to stand at the midpoint between possibilities imagined and limitations experienced. It strives to transcend partial and one-sided accounts that idealize the future or the past. It "combines purpose with observation and analysis," recognizing that "values are an integral part of political reality."[32] To do otherwise results in a simplistic dichotomy between naive utopianism and cynical determinism—which, in Kennan's case, petrifies reality by failing to appreciate its heterogeneity and dynamism along with its laws and continuities, and which attempts to arrest human nature through an enlightened exercise of power aimed at preserving law and order and preventing civilization from descending into chaos.

Kennan's unrealistic desire to contain, and thus repress, the nation's democratic impulse alienates him from the essential character and inherent strength of the polity, thereby promoting cynicism and fear where otherwise one might find more cause for confidence in the deliberative process. Hence, invoking democracy instead of wishing to suppress it would make Kennan more of a realist, both by acknowledging the normative component that is inherent to political realism and by realizing more of the existing culture's potential for discerning, even constituting, its interests. As Berki observes, regarding the normative component of political realism, even the grim positivism of *Realpolitik* is "moralistic in that its advocates usually find ultimate justification for the 'realistic' . . . maintenance of power and government in eternal moral laws which govern an eternally corrupt human nature." Not only do they adopt the assumption of determinism, which is itself subject to critical examination, but additionally they entertain "visions of new worlds" and hold "strong underlying moral convictions."[33]

Acknowledging the moral authority of democracy would require political realists such as Kennan to confront the dissociation of reason and rhetoric, to question the tenuous opposition between the civility of elite rationality and the barbarism of public deliberation, and thus to explore ways of accommodating "the actual forces of political life."[34] Practicing democracy realistically, instead of fearing it intuitively, would entail a different normative theory than Kennan's elitism, one that recognizes the role of power in politics without assuming the objectivity of interests and reason. "Democratizing rationality," as John S. Dryzek has argued, involves a discursive or communicative conception of practical reason guiding instrumental action that does not resort to authoritarianism or reduce to objectivism.[35]

Dryzek's notion of communicative rationality provides an initial approximation of how political realists might transcend the fear-inducing dichotomization between elite rationality and public deliberation revealed so clearly in Kennan's cynicism. From Dryzek's perspective, the health of the nation can be enhanced by maximizing the practice of communicative rationality instead of minimizing it; democratizing rationality is a cure (rather than a disease) which promotes uncoerced interaction by resurrecting authentic public discourse and acknowledging the authority of a good argument. Instrumental and communicative rationality coexist in a world of imperfect knowledge, he observes, where instrumental rationality can flourish only under the condition of free criticism. Thus Dryzek, following Jürgen Habermas, advances the counterfactual ideal of an open society as the speech situation by which to hold actual practice accountable. The normative imperative of practical reason serves as his procedural standard, replacing the normative authority of technical expertise.[36]

Realism, understood as a persuasive discourse, need not be grounded permanently on an image of domestic disease and instability nor dependent on the emotion of fear for its existence and effect, as it is in Kennan's case and as it has been historically materialized and socially sedimented in decades of conventional wisdom. Kennan's fear of domestic emotionalism motivates his appeal to elite rationality as a means of suppressing fear, which in turn predisposes him to an irrational impulse disguised by his own discourse. In Kennan's case, at least, the realist's explicit acknowledgement of pessimism is based on the latent emotionality of his discourse, i.e., on a dialectic of suppressing and activating fear which presumes (unrealistically) to quarantine domestic instability in order to conduct international affairs objectively and rationally. Contrary to realism's conventional insistence on the irrelevance of the domestic sphere, then, Kennan's conception of international affairs entails a debilitating image of the domestic polity. Thus, political realism's claim to validity would seem to hinge, at least in the present instance, on the legitimacy of its model of domestic politics. Recognizing that the business of the community is conducted rhetorically and that national interests are rhetorically derived would help not only to unmask the self-perpetuating dialectic of fear in Kennan's particular construction of political realism but also to foster a broader reassessment of one of realism's basic assumptions.

As it stands, Kennan's rhetorical naivete renders his model unworkable. Instead of achieving objectivity in the conduct of international affairs, it promotes nostalgia for a mythic past ill-suited to present conditions; his elitism would suppress diversity and foster sexism and racism in a misguided desire to restore the health of the body politic. Disease, as the metaphor that frames his pessimistic picture of an unwieldy American democracy, effects an enfeebling apprehension of freedom's fragility, misjudges the rhetorical vitality of American political culture, and exaggerates the nation's vulnerability. Thus, the republic is goaded into fearing itself.

Kennan's diagnosis of the nation's political illness represents the reality of his own bodily experience more accurately than the condition of the society it purports to depict, for it is a metaphor grounded in his physical ailments. As a freshman at Princeton University, he contracted scarlet fever and never completely regained his health, suffering intermittently from a chronic case of ulcers and related afflictions throughout his adult life. The inspiration for his Platonic vision of an authoritarian utopia ruled by experts came in 1935 from his study of a model medical insurance law imposed on Austria by its reactionary central government in the absence of the "demagoguery" and "public wrangling" for which "democratic politicians" were infamous—a study he undertook while recovering from a severe attack of ulcers induced by his stressful assignment in Moscow.[37] Again, Kennan was bedridden when he composed the long telegram in which, as Daniel Yergin has observed, he "assumed the guise of a doctor."[38] By his own account, Kennan was "taken with cold, fever, sinus, tooth trouble, and finally the aftereffects of the sulpha drugs administered for the relief of these other miseries" as he "suffered the daily take of telegrams and other office business" brought to the bedroom where he diagnosed the disease of Soviet communism and prescribed its remedy.[39] Moreover, when his views were publicly criticized by Walter Lippmann and later Dean Acheson, Kennan fell ill enough to require hospitalization.[40] Clearly, the democratic exercise of public debate was a sickening experience for him.

The bodily foundation of Kennan's guiding conceptual image projects the disease within the authorial body onto the external world of politics, a disease that can only be contained by measures antithetical to a democratic society. His key metaphorical concept, the organizing principle of his political realism, yields a fear of diversity and a rhetoric of suppression that blinds him to the possibility of communicative rationality and the security of legitimizing national interests in public deliberation. Conceiving political realism as itself a rhetorical discourse subject to the criticism and refinement of its leading metaphorical concepts thus serves to deliteralize and neutralize troublesome terms that might otherwise remain reified. Understood as an overextended analogy, then, the "disease" of domestic democracy in Kennan's realism need not tyrannize realistic accounts of international affairs. Kennan's version of realism, like others, professes to represent external conditions only, but his rhetoric smuggles in unrealistic representations of internal, "domestic," conditions to which it is never held accountable, which are self-validating, which are dangerously hostile to democratic politics, and which contribute to an exaggerated sense of national insecurity. This kind of realism depends upon a lurid distortion of democratic life that identifies Kennan, in Michael Smith's words, with "an idealized picture of the prerevolutionary, preideological international system of the early eighteenth century."[41] He yearns for a simple, orderly world—a mythic world of univocal rationality that never existed and most certainly does not exist today—and thus he fails to speak to "the requirements of mass democracy,"[42] to the inevitability of pathos playing a key role as one of the complexities of communicative rationality that constitute contemporary public life and define the present conditions of political realism. Lifting the mask of aristocratic civility is the first step toward dispelling mythic fears of the demos and to reversing a tradition of self-loathing that distorts the construction of national interests and exaggerates the danger from external enemies.

NOTES

1. Anantha Sudhaker Babbili, "Understanding International Discourse: Political Realism and the Non-Aligned Nations," *Culture and Society* 12 (1990): 313-15; Robert G. Gilpin, "The Richness of the Tradition of Political Realism," *International Organization* 38 (1984): 289-304; Hans Morganthau, *Politics Among Nations* (New York: Alfred A. Knopf, 1973), 3-4.

2. Greg Russell, "Searching for Realism's Grand Design: George F. Kennan and the Ethics of American Power in World Affairs," *The Political Science Reviewer* 19 (1990): 201.

3. George F. Kennan, *Realities of American Foreign Policy* (Princeton, N.J.: Princeton University Press, 1954), 48. For a recent elaboration on "the demonic side of human nature" and the "cracked vessel" that is man, see George F. Kennan, *Around the Cragged Hill: A Personal and Political Philosophy* (New York: W. W. Norton and Co., 1993), 17-36, but especially 28-32.

4. George F. Kennan, "History and Diplomacy as Viewed by a Diplomatist," *The Review of Politics* 18 (1956): 171.

5. Michael Polley, *A Biography of George F. Kennan: The Education of a Realist* (Lewiston, N.Y.: The Edwin Mellen Press, 1990). In particular, Polley argues that Kennan's "desire for order in international relations was a major factor in [his] attitude toward the Soviet Union" (14). See also, Anders Stephanson, *Kennan and the Art of Foreign Policy* (Cambridge: Harvard University Press, 1989), 245.

6. Russell, 203; George F. Kennan, *Memoirs, 1950-1963* (Boston: Little, Brown and Co., 1972), 322.

7. George F. Kennan, *Memoirs, 1925-1950* (Boston: Little, Brown and Co., 1967), 199; Stephanson, 200.

8. Walter L. Hixson, *George F. Kennan: Cold War Iconoclast* (New York: Columbia University Press, 1989), 8-10, 16.

9. Barton Gellman, *Contending with Kennan: Toward a Philosophy of American Power* (New York: Praeger, 1984), 140.

10. Quoted in Russell, 239.

11. Michael Joseph Smith, *Realist Thought from Weber to Kissinger* (Baton Rouge: Louisiana State University Press, 1986), 189.

12. Robert L. Ivie, "Metaphor and the Rhetorical Invention of Cold War 'Idealists,'" *Communication Monographs* 54 (1987): 165-82; Robert L. Ivie, "Cold War Motives and the Rhetorical Metaphor: A Framework of Criticism," in Martin J. Medhurst, et al., *Cold War Rhetoric: Strategy, Metaphor, and Ideology* (New York: Greenwood Press, 1990), 71-79; Robert L. Ivie, "The Metaphor of Force in Prowar Discourse: The Case of 1812," *The Quarterly Journal of Speech* 68 (1982): 240-54; Robert L. Ivie, "Images of Savagery in American Justifications for War," *Communication Monographs* 47 (1980): 279-94.

13. Kennan, *Memoirs, 1925-1950*, 57; Thomas G. Paterson, *Meeting the Communist Threat: Truman to Reagan* (New York: Oxford University Press, 1988), 121.

14. The original text of the long telegram is reprinted in John H. Etzold and John Lewis Gaddis, eds., *Containment: Documents on American Policy and Strategy, 1945-1950* (New York: Columbia University Press, 1978), 50-63.

15. Hixson, 8; David Mayers, *George Kennan and the Dilemmas of U.S. Foreign Policy* (New York: Oxford University Press, 1988), 56-58.

16. Kennan, *Memoirs, 1925-1950*, 294-295.

17. It is worth noting that Kennan's rhetorical vision of the threat, common among cold warriors, illustrates a classic case of projecting onto the Soviets his own beliefs and anxieties, including his view of American society as prone to emotionalism and irrationality, his perception of the outside world as hostile, and his admiration of authority and discipline.

18. All quotations are from George F. Kennan [X], "The Sources of Soviet Conduct," *Foreign Affairs* 25 (1947): 566-82.

19. Lynn Boyd Hinds and Theodore Otto Windt, Jr., *The Cold War as Rhetoric: The Beginnings, 1945-1950* (New York: Praeger, 1991), 201.

20. Polley, 128.

21. George F. Kennan, *American Diplomacy, 1900-1950* (Chicago: University of Chicago Press, 1951), 81-89.

22. George F. Kennan, *The Cloud of Danger: Current Realities of American Foreign Policy* (Boston: Little, Brown and Co., 1977), 3-26, 202.

23. George F. Kennan, *The Nuclear Delusion: Soviet-American Relations in the Atomic Age* (New York: Pantheon Books, 1982), xix-xxiii, xxx. Kennan renews his analysis along these same lines in *Around the Cragged Hill*, where he discusses "the pathological form" of Americans' attitudes toward their nation as "a terrible disease of the human spirit," an "emotional compulsion," and a "form of contagious hysteria" (78-84); moreover, he bemoans the nation's material and mental "addictions" that make it a "sick" society (113, 157-58).

24. Kennan, *The Nuclear Delusion*, 46-47, 56-57.

25. Ibid., 67.

26. Ibid., 72.

27. Polley, 160.

28. George F. Kennan, "Containment Then and Now," *Foreign Affairs* 65 (1987): 889-90.

29. George F. Kennan, "Morality and Foreign Policy," *Foreign Affairs* 64 (1985-1986): 208-9, 212-13, 216, 218.

30. Quoted in Stephanson, 217-19.

31. Stephanson, 219.

32. R. N. Berki, *On Political Realism* (London: J. M. Dent and Sons Ltd., 1981), 31, see also 27-30.

33. Ibid., 16, 18.

34. Ibid., 33.

35. John S. Dryzek, *Discursive Democracy: Politics, Policy, and Political Science* (New York: Cambridge University Press, 1990), 9.

36. As Dryzek noted, an argument parallel to his is advanced by Richard K. Ashley, *The Political Economy of War and Peace* (London: Frances Pinter, 1980), 205-30. Although Dryzek's position is grounded in Aristotelian notions of politics and practical reason, recognizing persuasion as the primary means in collective life for deliberating values and exercising prudential judgment on matters of public policy, his conception of communicative rationality remains unrealistically non-rhetorical in its Habermasian distrust of strategic discourse. Proofs in public deliberation, as Aristotle understood, are inherently affective in their reasoned adaptation to audiences. Pathos necessarily commingles with logos when opposing rhetors deliberate on issues of public policy, each advancing his or her best case in a realm of uncertain knowledge and conflicted values. Such is the nature of persuasive discourse as it legitimates action and constitutes political reality. Thus, Dryzek's model of communicative rationality needs to encompass the rhetorical and strategic aspects, as well as the public dimension, of political dis-

course in order to dispel the fear of democracy that confounds Kennan's realism.

37. Hixson, 7-8; Mayers, 49-50.
38. Daniel Yergin, *Shattered Peace: The Origins of the Cold War and the National Security State* (Boston: Houghton Mifflin Co., 1977), 168.
39. Kennan, *Memoirs, 1925-1950*, 294.
40. Hixson, 73, 181.
41. Smith, 190.
42. Ibid., 191.

JAMES ARNT AUNE

REINHOLD NIEBUHR AND THE RHETORIC OF CHRISTIAN REALISM

It is very difficult for an academic audience at the end of the twentieth century to imagine a time when the college preaching circuit
was a way for theologians to influence large numbers of students
and make a good income, or a time when listening to preaching was at
least an occasional experience even for secular intellectuals. Religion
remains an important legitimating device for the Republican Party
and for what remains of the civil rights movement among African
Americans, but religious symbols and themes—the sin of national
pride, the tension between the *civitas dei* and *civitas terrena*—have
been effectively expelled from academic discourse about politics and
international relations.

Critics of the expulsion of religious language and argument from
the academic study of politics often forget the positive intentions that
lay behind it.[1] Such an expulsion was partially motivated by a recognition of the destructive effects of religious extremism in political life,
especially foreign policy. It is a common criticism of American foreign policy during the Cold War that it was animated by the rhetoric
of "prophetic dualism," in which conflict between the United States
and the Soviet Union was depicted in essentially religious terms.
According to Philip Wander, such rhetoric was useful in appealing to
certain constituencies (Bible-Belt Protestants and working-class
Catholics) whose support was essential for foreign policy success.[2] It
also had the advantage of stifling debate, since public discourse conducted in essentially moralistic/religious terms presumes that it is
impossible to argue with God's will.[3]

Contemporary theorists of liberal democracy, perhaps in part reacting to the abuses of religious argument during the Cold War, "either
omit religion from their theories or assign it a subsidiary role."[4] In a
larger sense, it appears that the liberal tradition and religion may be

ultimately incompatible, because religion "is a form of social life that mobilizes the deepest passions of believers in the course of creating institutions that stand between individuals and the state."[5]

The seemingly stark contrast between the liberal tradition and religion may obscure the role of religion in forming the realist tradition in international politics. The American Protestant theologian Reinhold Niebuhr has been called "the most important figure in American realism"[6] and the dean of the "righteous realists."[7] Niebuhr deeply influenced the secular realist theorists E. H. Carr, Hans Morgenthau, and George Kennan (to whom is often attributed the phrase "Niebuhr is the father of us all").[8]

It is customary to read Niebuhr in tandem with Morgenthau, Kennan, and Lippmann as accomplishing a threefold persuasive task for the political and intellectual elite in the United States after World War II. First, they provided a moral grounding for the "exorcism" of isolationism in American politics.[9] Second, they provided a prudential grounding for the rejection of crusading tendencies by both the right and the left. Third, they justified strenuous efforts to "contain" the Soviet Union.

Yet is is not immediately clear what religious rhetoric has to do with such a political program. Robert W. Cox simply locates Niebuhr with Morgenthau as "European-formed thinkers" who "introduced a power-oriented view of mankind into an American milieu conditioned by eighteenth-century optimism and nineteenth-century belief in progress."[10] When international relations theory developed an increased sense of disciplinary identity in the late 1950s, it seemed increasingly to "[excise] theology and theologians from the subject as such."[11]

The place of religious discourse in academic inquiry into politics and international relations has received new impetus from the rise of the Christian Right in the United States (as well as other fundamentalisms worldwide) and from a pervasive sense, after the end of the Cold War, that "tragedy and despair" should not have the "final word" in discussions of political practice.[12] An examination of Niebuhr's work may prove useful both for the reconstruction of realism after the Cold War and for an understanding of the rhetorical role played by religion in both popular and elite politics.

I proceed in this essay by focusing on an essential tension in Niebuhr's work: the contradiction between the claims of power and the claims of conscience. First, I attempt to demonstrate the significance of this contradiction for Niebuhr's primary audience, the American religious and intellectual elite, during the Cold War period. Second, I provide a surface reading of the texture of Niebuhr's rhetoric, identifying recurring points of strain or ambiguity which generate objections to Christian realism. Finally, I argue, based on a structural reading of the fundamental opposition of power and conscience, that Niebuhr's rhetoric served as a kind of "vanishing mediator" similar to the role played by Protestantism itself in the transition to a capitalist worldview. That is, it provided the means for an essentially secular view of international relations to win out over an earlier theological one by neutralizing the power of "idealism."

Even if Niebuhr's work played a role in hastening the disappearance of religious warrants from inquiry into international relations, his Christian/Augustinian emphasis on sin and redemption may provide a useful counterweight to the pessimism of both Weberian and scientific "neorealism," as well as to the abstract rationalism of much contemporary political and moral thought.[13] The focus of my paper, however, is less on the reconstruction of realist doctrine than on the investigation of the instability of Niebuhr's realism as it was forged through decades of rhetorical engagement with audiences and opponents.

The uneasy coupling of religion and realism may stem from a rhetorical problem possessed by realistic arguments. The rhetorical problem is that realism has a limited usefulness as a device for motivating mass audiences. Realism may serve as a prudential guide for action, but it cannot (at least in its neorealist form) provide much grounding for the values of the nation-state. There thus may be a cycle of alternating "realisms" and "idealisms" in the discourse and practice of politics and international relations, mediated at least in part by the shifting role of transcendent or religious appeals in public argument.

Reinhold Niebuhr addressed several audiences throughout his career. He first addressed Christians who believed that Christianity is about otherworldly concerns. These he sought to involve in democratic politics. A second audience consisted of Christians who blindly assumed that the United States was uniquely blessed by God. These he sought to convict of the sin of pride. A third audience consisted of liberal Christians who abhorred violence and who possessed a naive faith in the ability of Christian liberal rhetoric to establish the Kingdom of God on earth. Niebuhr's first major work, *Moral Man and Immoral Society* (1932), was an attack on the pacifism of the liberal Christians and Socialists with whom he had worked in the 1920s.

Niebuhr presented a qualified defense of the use of force and violence by responsible Christians. He also criticized the "social inertia" of optimistic liberal reformers, and defended a rhetorical role for intellectuals as providing the "illusions" and "oversimplifications" needed to motivate the working class.[14]

Niebuhr's insistence that only justice, not love, was capable of attainment in politics was an important influence on a fourth audience, Christian and secular elites involved in the process of making decisions about public policy. These elites were subject to the twin temptations of utopianism and the abandonment of moral principle. Niebuhr's influence stemmed from his remarkable ability to maintain a tension between the claims of power and the claims of conscience.

Moral Man and Immoral Society was a particular influence on realists such as E. H. Carr as early as the 1930s.[15] The realism of that volume, however, was concerned with the qualified defense of violence and class struggle. Niebuhr's realism was to change profoundly with the rise of the Cold War. The situation of the American intellectual elite during the Cold War was a deeply contradictory one. The New Deal and the G. I. Bill provided an expanded public role for intellectuals. This expansion of opportunity included a conscious commitment to a meritocracy that transcended ethnicity and class (if not yet gender). Their greater public role, however, opened intellectuals to attack by the radical right.

Intellectuals also experienced a sense of responsibility for their role in the horrors perpetrated by Nazism and Stalinism, as well as a sense that scientific rationality itself lay behind both totalitarianism and the nuclear threat. It is not surprising that much of the serious writing, both fiction and nonfiction, of the period exhibited a "structure of feeling"[16] in which characters are alienated outsiders, suspended between contending groups, classes, and nations, discovering that solutions to their problems will occur (if at all) not through politics but through some form of transcendence. This was the period in which public theologians such as Niebuhr and Paul Tillich preached to packed auditoriums on college campuses, and novelists such as William Golding and John Updike explored the social implications of the Christian doctrine of original sin in their bestselling novels.

Gene Wise describes the period as dominated by a "Counter-Progressive Paradigm," a reaction against the optimistic assumptions of an earlier, Progressive generation of literary critics, historians, and theologians. The Counter-Progressives shared a common style of thinking and arguing:

> These thinkers weren't as certain as Progressives that one could see straight into realities, so they spent much time studying myths and symbols and images of reality. They were also intrigued by nuances and enjoyed tracking down incongruities in the American experience. Words like "paradox," "ambiguity," and "irony" sounded often through their writings.[17]

Wise identifies Niebuhr as a central figure in the Counter-Progressive paradigm (along with Lionel Trilling and Richard Hofstadter). If traditional religious practice was no longer possible for most intellectuals after World War II, the Counter-Progressive paradigm arguably made it possible to treat religious myths and symbols with greater respect than they had enjoyed in the academy for many years.

It is difficult for later audiences to understand the influence Niebuhr possessed. It is a common criticism of Niebuhr that his preference for the sermon as a mode of communication limited his long-term influence. He was not a rigorous thinker in the Germanic mode of Karl Barth or Paul Tillich, his chief rivals for the mantle of the most important Protestant theologian of the century. Further, his concern for oral communication and adaptation to occasion conveys a sense of being uninterested, as William Lee Miller writes, in "formal, classificatory thought," with the result being that some years later Niebuhr seems just to sit "there repeating his paradoxes, ironies, perils, and dialectics cold upon the printed page."[18] It is probably no accident that the most readable of the Niebuhr anthologies, Larry Rasmussen's *Reinhold Niebuhr: Theologian of Public Life*, consists of paragraphs from Niebuhr cut from longer treatises and arranged thematically.[19]

Yet such criticisms of Niebuhr may simply miss the manner in which his discursive practice matched the way most people and cultures actually do moral work: in the conversation, the speech, and the brief journalistic essay. If that is the case, then strictly rhetorical analysis may be a "realistic" corrective to other forms of inquiry.

A rhetorical analysis is concerned above all with "the appropriate, the occasional, the ad hoc in past performances," as opposed to the transhistorical judgments characteristic of philosophical and scientific inquiry.[20] The two examples which follow illustrate typical

Niebuhrian rhetorical strategies and ethical arguments. The first is a sermon, "We See Through a Glass Darkly," delivered first at St. George's Episcopal Church, New York City, 17 January 1960, and later reprinted in *Justice and Mercy*.[21] The second is a column from *Christianity and Society* (later *Christianity and Crisis*) in spring 1950.[22]

I select these two examples because they are short enough to be analyzed in their entirety in a brief essay and because they are representative of the two rhetorical stances Niebuhr tried to keep in tension throughout his career. The first is the stance of the preacher seeking to allay his audience's anxiety. The second is the stance of the intellectual seeking to justify a realistic view of secular politics. These two stances create the public persona of Niebuhr as theologian of Christian realism, mediating the tensions between religion and politics, conscience and power, and the private and public spheres through his skillful rhetoric. Both essays illustrate typical Niebuhrian strategies: provoke and partially allay anxiety, heighten a sense of irony and paradox, and identify Christian virtue as a mean between two extremes.

In "We See Through a Glass Darkly," Niebuhr is preaching on a text from St. Paul, the so-called "Hymn to Love" of I Corinthians 13, a passage often read at Christian weddings. Niebuhr uses the traditionally private, familial associations of the Pauline text to expound a message about public responsibility.

He begins by noting that it is shortly after the New Year, and thus the theme of permanence and change is an appropriate one. St. Paul draws our attention to the fact that our knowledge is partial—"we see through a glass darkly"—as we move through time. What does not change? Three things: faith, hope, and love. How darkly do we see? We seem to be able to know the "strange drama of the past" reasonably well, and there are certain regularities in human life—birth, growth, death—that we can observe in ourselves, our families, and in whole civilizations. But as we imagine our family before us, we know that the destiny of our children is uncertain, and we have to leave them in the hands of God.[23]

A conventional Protestant sermon of the time might leave the audience there, but Niebuhr characteristically heightens tension by shifting abruptly from the private to the public. What about the collective destiny of the nation? There is a faith we share with our founding fathers—our "liberal democratic faith." But they could not have foreseen "a civilization where we maintain a tolerable justice by fantastically complex equilibria of power." They also were less powerful than we are. We have been "vaulted to the position of seeming omnipotence." Yet we are now less free because of our omnipotence. Further, our attempt to divide the world "according to the dogmas of the Cold War" has been proven to be temporary. Our faith in progress has been dashed by the "nuclear dilemma."[24]

The particularly tense quality of Niebuhr's Christian realism appears in the transition between these two sections of the sermon. He has provided a qualified defense of nuclear power-politics, but he goes on to reject Western pride: We must accept that "the drama of history" is not "to be played for the sake of *our* security, or for the security of *our* nation or the security of *our* civilization."[25] Just as we cannot expect our own family to be miraculously protected from harm, we cannot expect either that "Western civilization will survive untouched and that Communism will perish." Mature hope is an ability to "rejoice in the whole drama of human history, including the terrible anxieties of the nuclear age."[26]

Like hope, love has a childish and mature aspect as well. Mature love is about responsibility. Although Christian love is sacrificial love, like that of Jesus on the Cross, we must be very careful about how we treat sacrificial love as an ideal: "All the justice we have is a justice which has transmuted the sense of responsibility in various balances of power in order to prevent the strong from taking advantage of the weak, by making the weak a little stronger but not too strong. Always we are dealing with sinful man."[27]

As he concludes, Niebuhr returns to the private sphere with a familial example: "probably no happy family has ever existed purely by a sense of justice." Love as "mutual forbearance" makes family life possible.

Niebuhr summarizes by saying that faith, hope, and love each have an immature moment as well as a mature, abiding moment. In his concluding prayer he praises God's wisdom and power as beyond human understanding, and asks for "grace to apprehend by faith the power and wisdom which lie beyond our understanding."[28]

As with most of Niebuhr's writings, this sermon is about human pride, a sense of the limitations of human nature and knowledge, a "realistic" view of the possibilities of justice as contrasted with a naive liberal view, and an affirmation of God's majesty and inscrutability. Its rhetorical function is less an exhortation to action—although not to act is a sin—but an exhortation to examine one's conscience for signs of pride. The fundamental movement of ideas and images is from the personal and familial out to the public and then back to the personal and familial again. It appears as if the primary realm of sacrificial love and forgiveness is the family rather than the public realm, where different rules are in effect. Yet the very centrality of public issues in the sermon undercuts the essentially private sort of Christianity with which the audience might be more comfortable.

The abrupt transitions, the fondness for the ironic phrase ("tolerable justice"), the heightening and limited release of psychological tension—all are hallmarks of the Niebuhrian style. The fundamental shape of the argument is this: Here are two extremes, with the preferred stance somewhere in-between, but locating that in-between spot requires constant shifting, running, like Alice in Looking-Glass land, as fast as you can in order to stay in the same place. As Richard Fox writes, Niebuhr used a recurring strategy (Fox calls it "the debater's ancient ploy") of presenting the opposition in extreme or simplistic terms, and then rejecting the opposition as simplistic.[29]

From a rhetorical standpoint, public moral argument is crafted out of such moments as this sermon. Like the sermon, the function of the editorial or opinion column is to provide an orientation toward events, even if its form dooms it to rapid obsolescence. My second example from Niebuhr's public address illustrates the same strategies we have seen in the sermon: provoke and partially allay anxiety, heighten a sense of irony and paradox, and identify virtue as a constantly shifting mean between extremes. There is also an additional strategy—the search for a mean between the discursive and the material—that complements his other strategies.

In the spring of 1950, shortly before the start of the Korean War, there was debate over the development of the hydrogen bomb by the United States. In a column in *Christianity and Society*, Niebuhr argued about the ethics of the H-Bomb. He begins with a familiar set of tensions. The age brings "new perils and possibilities," "the possibility of mutual mass annihilation," although such a peril occurs against the backdrop of an unchanging human nature: "Yet we are no different from our fathers. Our present situation is a heightened and more vivid explication of the human situation." The fundamental human situation is a lack of power over the course of history, despite our illusion that each new conquest over nature will give us such mastery. It is when we try to curb the destructive consequences of such power that "the whole ambiguity of the human situation is more fully revealed."

Niebuhr then provides a narrative of the factors in the development of the hydrogen bomb. First, the order to develop it was done without public debate. The development probably would have been ratified by public debate, anyway, but the lack of that debate "represents a real threat to the democratic substance of our life." Second, we are in a "tragic" situation: we appear to need to develop the hydrogen bomb, because of risks that the enemy may develop it as well, and yet it, "if used by us against our enemies, would mean our moral annihilation." Niebuhr asks, "What shall we do?"[30]

The first answer (as always) is the naive liberal one: "The pacifists have a simple answer." There are two problems with the pacifist argument to renounce use of such a weapon. First, we do not have the moral authority to "risk annihilation or subjugation for the sake of saying no to this new development of destruction." Pacifists simply do not understand how history works: "This answer assumes that it is possible to summon the human will to defy historical development with a resounding no."

A hallmark of the realist creed is that simple answers are by definition bad answers. Simple answers also tend to misinterpret the relationship between rhetoric and reality. Note how Niebuhr here is arguing for a proper understanding of the place of discourse in a democracy. The temptation of the powerful is to dispense with democratic discourse, while the temptation of pacifists is to rely on discourse alone to resist evil.

Second, the pacifist argument that unilateral renunciation of the hydrogen bomb by the United States would "soften the Russian heart" ignores the extent to which the Russians are themselves caught up in their own discursive net: "Granted the Russian hope and belief that it has the possibility of bringing its peculiar redemption to the whole world, it is not likely to be impressed by a 'moral' gesture from what it believes to be a decadent world."

Another pacifist answer is to return to the negotiating table with the Russians, but "the Russians are almost certain to demand general disarmament as the price for any agreement in the field of atomic energy." To do so, however, would mean accepting Russian domination of Eastern Europe.[31]

The position Niebuhr defends—"the most feasible possibility"—is that of the eleven scientists "who have suggested that we produce the

H-Bomb but make a solemn covenant never to use it first." There are three good reasons for this position. First, it would reassure an anxious world. Second, it would deter forces in the United States "who are placing undue reliance on the bomb and who may, if we are not careful, so develop our defenses that we could not win a war without using the bomb." Third, it would "counteract all those tendencies in our national life which make for the subordination of moral and political strategy to military strategy."

The scientists' proposal thus restores the proper balance between the discursive and the material in American political deliberation. It neither ignores the communicative function of foreign policy, nor the material realities of warfare in the nuclear age.

Finally, however, the proposal sends a much deeper moral message: "We would be saying by such a policy that even a nation can reach the point where it can purchase its life too dearly. If we had to use this kind of destruction in order to save our own lives, would we find life worth living?" If we ask this question we are not like those cynics who fail to recognize the possibility of "moral transcendence over historical destiny."[32]

These two short pieces by Niebuhr illustrate the ad hoc and occasional quality of his reflections on social ethics and foreign policy as well as his characteristic rhetorical strategies: the heightening of anxiety in the minds of his audience, the use of both the Christian message and the trope of irony to allay that anxiety partially, and the depicting of opposing positions in extreme or simplistic terms. Niebuhr asks his Christian audience not to flee from "history," and asks his secular audience not to ignore "eternity"—two opposing forces momentarily reconciled in Niebuhr's rhetoric.

Yet the subsequent disappearance in academic international relations of Niebuhr's religious spin on realist rhetoric, as well as the fragmentation of the Niebuhrian theological tradition into liberationist and neoconservative wings, require explanation. A larger explanatory framework for understanding the development of Christian realism requires attention to the underlying semiotic structure of Niebuhr's rhetoric. I will argue that Niebuhr's style represents an attempt to reconcile the same irreconcilable social conflicts or contradictions that were present in Max Weber's work.

A strictly surface reading of the style of Niebuhr's rhetoric reveals a split between two types of audiences: those motivated chiefly by the claims of power and those by the claims of conscience. This split mirrors the oppositions between public/private and history/eternity that organized both the sermon and the editorial. We saw that "history" becomes a place in which God's judgment is experienced, but not God's grace, which is inevitably given only in the private sphere.

Max Weber's classic essay, "Politics as a Vocation" centers on the tension between "ethics" and "politics." He creates a dichotomy between an "ethic of ultimate ends" and an "ethic of responsibility." This dichotomy should be familiar to readers of Niebuhr, since it parallels his distinction between an ethic of love and an ethic of justice. Niebuhr was one of the first to introduce Weber's work to an American audience.[33] Roger Epp, attempting to recover a place for Christian realism after the Cold War, claims that Niebuhr is different from Weber in his rejection of pessimism.[34] I will argue, however, that Niebuhr seems equally as pessimistic as Weber, but is more skillful at providing a set of rhetorical motivations to combat the "social inertia" of an ethic of responsibility.

Weber's project was to reject, as Fredric Jameson puts it, "all philosophies which—the Hegelian world spirit and the Marxist dialectic just as much as Christian providence—seek to convince us that some teleological movement is immanent in the otherwise chaotic and random agitation of empirical life."[35] Weber's ethic of responsibility was intended to replace these illusions of human self-fulfillment. Weber also wished his audience to realize that it was not ideas but material and ideal interests that govern human action.

In his discussion of the oppositions between the roles of the priest and the prophet in religious life, Weber argues that it is the prophet who releases "the world from magic and in doing so" creates the basis for our modern science and technology, and for capitalism.[36] This role of religion as a mediator of social change appears in the more well-known argument about the relationship between Protestantism and rise of capitalism. Weber argued that the Lutheran and Calvinist notion of a *Beruf* or "calling" helped to mediate the transition from feudal peasant labor to modern industrial labor.[37]

A "suspicious" reading of Niebuhr would examine the way in which his Weberian roots can be turned against him. One way of reading Niebuhr's rhetorical career is in much the same way as Weber reads the role of the prophet in the transition from magic to science and the role of Protestantism in the transition from feudalism to capitalism. Niebuhr may have been a kind of "vanishing mediator," accomplishing the translation of European views of power and interest into an American idiom for the purposes of mediating the contradiction between the need to preserve American economic interests and the belief in America's unique moral position in world politics.

It was essential in the early days of the Cold War that American elites be educated away from both the optimistic internationalism of Henry Wallace and the paranoid nativism of Joseph McCarthy if the long term interests of the United States were to be served. The popularity of Niebuhr's position among elites stemmed from his skillful rhetorical union of two discourses normally kept separate: the language of power and the language of conscience.[38]

As Niebuhr wrote, a "realistic analysis" of politics reveals "a constant and seemingly irreconcilable conflict between the needs of society and the imperatives of a sensitive conscience. This conflict, which could be most briefly defined as the conflict between ethics and politics, is made inevitable by the double focus of the moral life. One focus is on the inner life of the individual, and the other in the necessities of man's social life."[39]

Niebuhr's argument, directed against Christian critics of the radical labor movement in the 1930s, is structured in precisely the same way as Niebuhr's defense of the hydrogen bomb in 1950. There are essentially two positions to be rejected: those of elites who reject conscience in the name of power, and those of Christian liberals or pacifists who reject power in the name of conscience. If we represent these positions semiotically, following Jameson's discussion of Weber, we end with the following ideological positions and mediations.[40]

Christian
Realists

Power   **Conscience**

Elites   *Liberals,*
(U.S./Soviets)   *Pacifists*

       Without   **Without**
       Conscience   **Power**

The Masses, Women

If we leave the analysis at this point, it would account for many of the arguments raised by leftist critics of Niebuhr: his androcentic notion of sin, his inability to understand third world liberation movements, and his seeming endorsement of religious symbolism merely as a necessary illusion. First, as Plaskow writes, Niebuhr's sense of sin is only appropriate for male powerholders. If pride is the greatest public sin for Niebuhr (insistence on the security of "our nation or our civilization") what of the sins more characteristic of those (women and minorities) who have less frequently participated in the public sphere?[41] Fox, who is otherwise sympathetic to Niebuhr, writes that Niebuhr was unable to understand "the concrete cultures of American working people."[42] Can Niebuhr account for the sins of sloth or sensuality to which those "others" of universalizing liberal discourse are prone?[43]

Second, does Niebuhr's rejection of Christian liberalism's naive view of justice make it possible for Christians to be more politically effective or does it legitimize some of the more unappealing aspects of American power politics? Niebuhr seems never to have taken the claims of national liberation movements (other than Zionism) seriously nor considered the possibility of internal dissent within the Soviet Union.[44]

Third, as Stanley Hauerwas has argued, Niebuhr appears to neutralize the political impact of the Christian message by providing a theological rationale "for why Christians should not seek to make their theological commitments relevant for social policy and strategy."[45] Niebuhr is no more a believer in a literal Last Judgment than Max Weber. The sermonic rhetorical form, intended to combat social inertia, displaces ultimate meaning into the personal realm. History functions only as the place of judgment for Niebuhr, never redemption. Niebuhr may have simply been a Machiavellian in disguise, rejecting any narrative form—nationalist *or* Christian—of redemptive politics.[46]

If we return to a more properly rhetorical level of analysis, we can see how each ideological position described in the previous chart also requires an additional mediation between itself and a mass audience. The elites criticized by Niebuhr never presented their cynical arguments in "realist" terms, at least not in public. The mediation of the claims of power and conscience by the rhetoric of Christian realism presents practical problems when viewed as a rhetoric for a mass audience. If the masses must be exhorted to fight in Korea or Vietnam, expend billions of dollars of public money on armaments, and risk nuclear annihilation it is unlikely that they will do so by understanding the irony of American history. Niebuhr, otherwise critical of liberal naivete for its social inertia, seems to have shared the liberal assumption that education and reasoned discourse—embodied in that great saint of Cold War liberalism, Adlai Stevenson—could gradually subdue the American tendency toward self-righteousness.

Perhaps what Niebuhr's career illustrates is the way in which "realism" can become the primary marker of a gulf between elite and popular audiences which has intensified since the Vietnam War. It may not be so much the dark brooding Manichaeanism of prophetic dualism that is most characteristic of American popular reflections on politics and foreign policy, so much as a fundamental optimism grounded in a vague sense of being blessed by divine favor.[47]

If "Christian realism" was an unstable compound when brought into the rhetorical realm, it was also ideologically unstable for Niebuhr's self-professed followers. Despite their theological agreement, followers of Niebuhr frequently split on political grounds. Martin Luther King, Jr., was deeply influenced by Niebuhr. So were the neoconservatives Richard John Neuhaus and Michael Novak. Niebuhr himself split with other followers of Christian realism, notably Paul Ramsey and Hubert Humphrey, over the the Vietnam War.[48]

What these left and right Niebuhrians shared was a rejection of both the optimism and privatism of the mainstream American audience. It was only natural that when the clergy who had seized on the leftward pole of Christian realism began preaching in the accents of liberation theology in the 1980s that this would appear to many American laity as a call to neglect one's family, neighborhood, and friends.

Some of the contradiction between right and left interpretations of Niebuhr stems from the instability of his critique of elite behavior during the Cold War. Look, for instance, at the status of the United States in the semiotic rectangle established by the opposition of power and conscience. Christian realism, in order to maintain a consistently prophetic stance, could not allow the United States itself to occupy the space mediating between power and conscience. That would run the risk of national pride. On the other hand, to refuse pride of place to the United States was to risk constructing what later would be called a "myth of equivalence" between the United States and the Soviet Union.

The fact that the Soviets and the Americans can be read as occupying the same semiotic space (prideful power) accounts for the almost claustrophobic quality of some of Niebuhr's prose during the Cold War. The passages at the end of Niebuhr's central reflection on American politics, *The Irony of American History*, illustrate the sort of strain an advocate and audience must undergo to sustain a consistent Christian realist position. In a commentary on Lincoln's second inaugural address, Niebuhr draws on Lincoln's authority to clarify a middle course between Communism and uncritical Americanism. Niebuhr first criticizes those who do not recognize Communism to be as evil as the slavery against which Lincoln fought. He identifies a "sentimental softness" in liberal culture, with "its inability to comprehend the depth of evil to which individuals and communities may sink, particularly when they try to play the role of God in history."[49]

On the other hand, we must not "establish the righteousness of our cause by a monotonous reiteration of the virtues of freedom compared with the evils of tyranny." To do this "offers us no insight into the corruptions of freedom on our side and it gives us no understanding of the strange attractive power of communism in a chaotic and impoverished world."[50] Just as Lincoln reminded his listeners that "the Almighty has his own purposes," so too we "must be reminded that the true God can be known only where there is some awareness of a contradiction between divine and human purposes, even on the highest level of human aspirations."[51]

The awkwardness of sustaining a thoroughgoing demonization of Communism while resisting deifying Americanism is perhaps reflected in the tortured periods of the penultimate paragraph:

> There is, in short, even in a conflict with a foe with whom we have little in common the possibility and necessity of living in a dimension of meaning in which the urgencies of struggle are subordinated to a sense of awe before the vastness of the historical drama in which we are jointly involved; to a sense of modesty about the virtue, wisdom, and power available to us for the resolution of its perplexities; to a sense of contrition about the common human frailties and foibles which lie at the foundation of both the enemy's demonry and our vanities; and to a sense of gratitude for the divine mercies which are promised to those who humble themselves.[52]

What Niebuhr seems not to have recognized, however, is that humility is a property affordable only by those who have won a decisive victory—a lesson Lincoln perhaps understood. Niebuhr's appeals

could only work for an audience naturally at home in irony.
Niebuhr's irony was grounded in the Christian virtue of humility, and
yet irony as a consistent perspective on the world tends "to dissolve
all belief in the possibility of positive political actions," as Hayden
White has observed.[53] Ironic rhetoric is a poor motivator for mass
audiences, although it may serve as a check on the political ambitions
of intellectuals.

There is a sense, then, in which the discourse of Christian realism
can be turned against itself. If people, classes, and nations are motivated by sinful pride as well as by justice, then it is unrealistic to
assume that a rhetoric dominated by irony, anxiety, ambiguity, and an
endless search for the mean will be of much use in the public arena.
Caught between its elitism and the sin of pride, the discourse of
Christian realism became too much a language of alienation, even as it
habituated public audiences to accept America's involvement in the
world of power politics.

The net result of a Christian realism, however useful it may be in
checking the ambitions of elites and conquering political withdrawal
by Christian audiences, is to make Christian faith and Church authority utterly irrelevant as a source of good reasons for particular policy
decisions. Did Niebuhr, then, like Protestantism itself in Weber's narrative, simply serve as the rhetorical pretext or mediator for the final
secularization of American political and foreign policy argument, at
least among elites? Niebuhr himself was a liberal in the religious
sense, even as he warred against the political consequences of liberal
idealism. Christianity for him was quite literally reduced to a
rhetoric—a set of symbols, appeals, and principles of prudence that
could be used to allay anxiety and avoid grievous political error.[54]

The critique of utopianism, the commitment to the rule of law, the
defense of democratic decision making, and a skeptical stance toward
politics as a means of salvation—all these are positive legacies of
Niebuhr's work. A new realism appropriate to the post-Cold War
world will need to take some lessons from Niebuhr in how to defuse
the explosive power of religion in national and ethnic conflicts. Even
so, advocates of Christian realism will need to consider how long a
religion inherently centered on God's saving actions in history can
survive when those actions are displaced from history into the individual soul. This displacement, whether the product of some
Weberian iron law of secularization or of the homogenizing tendencies of American class society, is what makes the rhetoric of Christian

realism both significant as a historical mediator and so potentially meaningless as part of a living religious tradition.[55]

NOTES

1. See Stephen Carter, *The Culture of Disbelief* (New York: Basic Books, 1993).
2. Philip Wander, "The Rhetoric of American Foreign Policy," *Quarterly Journal of Speech* 70 (1984): 339-61.
3. See Adolph L. Reed, Jr., *The Jesse Jackson Phenomenon* (New Haven: Yale University Press, 1986), 41-60.
4. Carter, *The Culture of Disbelief*, 42.
5. Mark Tushnet, *Red, White, and Blue: A Critical Analysis of Constitutional Law* (Cambridge: Harvard University Press, 1988), 248; cited in Carter, 42.
6. Michael Joseph Smith, *Realist Thought from Weber to Kissinger* (Baton Rouge: Louisiana State University Press, 1986), 17.
7. Joel Rosenthal, *Righteous Realists: Political Realism, Responsible Power, and American Culture in the Nuclear Age* (Baton Rouge: Louisiana State University Press, 1991).
8. See Roger Epp, "The 'Augustinian Moment' in International Politics: Niebuhr, Butterfield, Wight, and the Reclaiming of a Tradition," *International Politics Research Paper*, No. 10 (Aberystwyth, Wales: University College of Wales, 1991), 1-2, 22n. 4.
9. Stanley Hoffmann, "An American Social Science: International Relations," *Daedalus* 106, no. 3 (1977): 47-48.
10. Robert W. Cox, "Social Forces, States and World Orders: Beyond International Relations Theory," in *Neorealism and Its Critics*, ed. Robert O. Keohane (New York: Columbia University Press, 1986), 240-41.
11. Epp, "The 'Augustinian Moment' in International Politics," 20.
12. Ibid.
13. Ibid.
14. Reinhold Niebuhr, *Moral Man and Immoral Society* (New York: Charles Scribner's Sons, 1932), 221-22, 277. See also Richard Fox's discussion of the book in *Reinhold Niebuhr: A Biography* (New York: Pantheon, 1985), 136-41.
15. Epp, 1.
16. Raymond Williams, *The Long Revolution* (New York: Columbia University Press, 1961), 48, 65-71.
17. Gene Wise, *American Historical Explanations*, 2d ed. (Minneapolis: University of Minnesota Press, 1980), 84.
18. William Lee Miller, "Some Customer," *Christianity and Crisis*, 3 February 1986, 21-22.
19. Larry Rasmussen, *Reinhold Niebuhr: Theologian of Public Life* (Minneapolis: Fortress Press, 1991).

20. Nancy Struever, *Theory as Practice: Ethical Inquiry in the Renaissance* (Chicago: University of Chicago Press, 1992), xi.

21. Reinhold Niebuhr, "We See Through a Glass Darkly," in *Justice and Mercy*, ed. Ursula Niebuhr (Louisville: Westminster/John Knox Press, 1974), 29-37.

22. Reinhold Niebuhr, "The Hydrogen Bomb," *Christianity and Society* 15 (1950): 235-37.

23. Niebuhr, "We See Through a Glass Darkly," 30.

24. Ibid., 31.

25. Ibid., 32-33.

26. Ibid., 34-35.

27. Ibid., 36.

28. Ibid., 37.

29. Fox, *Reinhold Niebuhr*, 169-70.

30. Niebuhr, "The Hydrogen Bomb," 235.

31. Ibid., 236.

32. Ibid., 237.

33. Fox, *Reinhold Niebuhr*, 102.

34. Epp, "The 'Augustinian Moment,'" 19.

35. Fredric Jameson, "The Vanishing Mediator; or, Max Weber as Storyteller," *The Ideologies of Theory, Vol. 2: The Syntax of History* (Minneapolis: University of Minnesota Press, 1988), 10.

36. Ibid., 17.

37. Max Weber, *The Protestant Ethic and the Spirit of Capitalism*, trans. Talcott Parsons (New York: Charles Scribner's Sons, 1958).

38. Niebuhr, *Moral Man and Immoral Society*, 4: "Politics will, to the end of history, be an area where conscience and power meet, where the ethical and coercive factors of human life will interpenetrate and work out their tentative and uneasy compromises."

39. Ibid., 257.

40. Any "story," whether literary or philosophical, can be described as a narrative system of characters or agents which is then transformed into "an exchange mechanism by which some final illusion of harmony, some final 'imaginary' solution of the contradiction it articulates, can be generated," Fredric Jameson, *Wyndham Lewis, The Modernist as Fascist* (Berkeley: University of California Press, 1979), 99. Jameson's semiotic rectangle, modified from A. J. Greimas' work, is "the representation of a binary opposition (two contraries), along with the simple negations (or contradictories) of both terms (the so-called sub-contraries), plus the various possible combinations of these terms, most notably the 'complex term' (ideal synthesis of two contraries) and the 'neutral' term (ideal synthesis of two sub-contraries) (Jameson, *Wyndham Lewis*, 99n. 9.).

41. Judith Plaskow, *Sex, Sin, and Grace: Women's Experience and the Theologies of Reinhold Niebuhr and Paul Tillich* (Washington, D.C.: University Press of America, 1980), 92-94.

42. Fox, *Reinhold Niebuhr*, 139.
43. See Plaskow, and Beverly Wildung Harrison, "Niebuhr: Locating the Limits," *Christianity and Crisis*, 17 February 1986, 36-39.
44. See Charles Kammer, *Ethics and Liberation: An Introduction* (Maryknoll, N.Y.: Orbis, 1988), 168-77.
45. Stanley Hauerwas, *Against the Nations: War and Survival in a Liberal Society* (Notre Dame: University of Notre Dame Press, 1992), 32.
46. On Machiavellian politics as the rejection of redemptive politics, see Nancy Struever, *Theory as Practice*, 151.
47. See Don Browning, *A Fundamental Practical Theology: Descriptive and Strategic Proposals* (Minneapolis: Fortress Press, 1991), 172.
48. Fox, *Reinhold Niebuhr*, 284-85.
49. Reinhold Niebuhr, *The Irony of American History* (New York: Charles Scribner's Sons, 1952), 172-73.
50. Ibid., 173.
51. Ibid.
52. Ibid., 174.
53. Hayden White, *Metahistory: The Historical Imagination in Nineteenth Century Europe* (Baltimore: Johns Hopkins University Press, 1973), 38.
54. Some may find the "liberal" label inaccurate, since Niebuhr is often considered to be "neo-orthodox" theologically, but his rejection of the physical resurrection of Jesus as well as of individual immortality places him closer to liberalism than to the neo-orthodoxy of Karl Barth. See Fox, *Reinhold Niebuhr*, 215, and Hauerwas, *Against the Nations*, 31.
55. For an argument that Niebuhr capitulated to the homogenizing force of American Protestant taste as part of his own upward social mobility, see John Murray Cuddihy, *No Offense: Civil Religion and Protestant Taste* (New York: Seabury Press, 1978), 31-47.

CHARLES JONES

E. H. CARR

AMBIVALENT REALIST

The *Twenty Years' Crisis* is the of the work of E. H. Carr most familiar to students of international relations. In this book Carr took great pains to situate himself precisely half way between utopianism and realism.[1] Yet the strategy has generally been regarded as little more than a flourish. Carr has consistently been taken for a political realist. A lecture not long ago by William Fox, subtle and knowledgeable in its treatment of Carr, unhesitatingly referred to "Carr's realist vision" and his "version of realist doctrine," and Carr certainly exhibited many of the characteristic marks of the realist school.[2] Earlier critics like Hugh Trevor-Roper were never in any doubt that Carr was a realist.[3] In works on foreign policy, nationalism, and international relations, written during the ten years that followed his departure from the British Foreign Office in 1936, Carr laid characteristic emphasis on power, conflict, and constraint. Above all, he repeatedly derided the League of Nations and, more generally, all those approaches to the problem of world order that he termed naively voluntaristic.

Carr was, in addition, a consistent friend of the state, especially the large multinational state, at times quite cavalier in consigning national self-determination to the past. Norman Stone found him quoting Rosa Luxemburg with approval to the effect that Ukrainian nationalism was "the ridiculous farce of a few university professors and students."[4] The post-war settlement of 1919, he believed, had created far too many small states in the name of national self-determination, many of which were simply not economically viable in modern conditions.[5] Finally, he repeatedly expressed a belief in historical continuity—even progressive continuity—though always stopping short of crude determinism.

One last characteristic serves to tie Carr still closer to the realist school. Like many North American realists he believed firmly that the role of the intellectual in political life was to persuade statesmen, and those close enough to influence them, to adopt prudent policies; but he had to act within a political culture rather more resistant to movement between academic and official posts, and with a class background falling tantalizingly short of what was required for automatic social access to the topmost echelon of policymakers in Britain. For all this, from the moment he left the Foreign office to the end of his service at *The Times* (London) in 1946, Carr never desisted from his attempts to influence public policy.

Yet Carr was no straightforward realist. There were already hints of a liberal modification of his attitude toward the state as early as 1939. These can equally well be read as anticipations of a Cold War world of more or less permanently allied blocs, or of what would now be called complex interdependence, or of regional integration short of federalism in, for example, a "Europe of Nations."[6] Over the next five years these were to be developed more fully. Again, realism became associated after 1945 with the political Right and with a hawkish willingness to fight against Communist aggression in the last resort. But Carr was very clearly a man of the Left. Like many other Britons of his generation he was less a Marxist socialist than a collectivist liberal; but his sympathy with the Soviet experiment was evident. Nor was Carr a warmonger. Quite the contrary; up to the very eve of war in 1939 he continued to advocate appeasement.

The argument of this essay is that the same ambivalence between realism and idealism that pervaded so much of Carr's political thinking also marked the rhetorical method of his texts. Choice of rhetorical method, it is suggested, provides one more way of distinguishing between the political realist and his idealist opponent. In all aspects of literary expression, Carr remained undecided, more or less consciously exploiting the tensions between thoroughgoing realism and a more pragmatic, liberal stance. Carr's rhetoric, like his politics, was almost realist, but not quite.

This claim will be made good first of all by clarifying in a little more detail the ways in which Carr's political and ideological stance differed from that of a stock, Anglo-American *realpolitik* position before going on to outline his views on rhetoric and propaganda. These views cut him off still further from the common-sense empiricism of the British political Right but also distinguish him from the most ruthless rhetoricians of the classical realist tradition. A second section examines in some detail Carr's rhetorical intentions and the methods he employed to achieve them, moving from small details of language, through the marshaling or structuring of arguments, to choice of genres and the gradual formation of an *œuvre*. The third section considers the reception of Carr's work, arguing that the devices which he employed in pursuit of his rhetorical intention often proved self-defeating. As the Cold War took shape, Carr implicitly admitted defeat, retiring into the rhetorical wilderness of a multi-volume history of the Soviet experiment. One of the strongest and most decisive voices of the British Left in the 1940s, he was finally rendered powerless by the compromises he had made in the vain attempt to influence policy without sacrificing intellectual integrity.

CARR'S DISTINCTIVE REALISM

State, War, and Ideology

Neither in his political program nor in his ideological preferences was Carr a textbook realist. His views on the centrality of the state in international relations were significantly qualified by the germ of a concept of complex interdependence. He also appears heterodox in the company of later realists for his passionate advocacy of appeasement, his left-wing political stance, and his treatment of power.

It is true that Carr frequently acknowledged the supposed necessity of large multinational states as the only political form capable of securing individual rights in an industrialized and capitalist world. Yet he already recognised, before the Second World War, "that there may be a size [of state] which cannot be exceeded without provoking a recrudescence of disintegrating tendencies."[7] Accurately foreseeing that sovereignty would, in the future, become "more blurred and indistinct than it is at present," Carr imagined a world in which formal imperialism was far less important than the clustering of nominally independent states, sustained or created by nationalist cultural reactions to modernity, around a few leading powers.[8]

By 1944 Carr had gone rather further, reaching the conclusion that the massive concentration of military power implied by clusters of this sort would require a system of checks and balances more substantial than the mere blurring of sovereignty. This was to be provided partly by functional international organizations working within the overarching economic and military frameworks provided by large multinational states. Carr, the longstanding opponent of grandiose projects for world government, saw no prospect of any revival of the political organs of the League of Nations; but he did see a future for "the so-called 'technical' organs of the League of Nations, including the International Labour Organization."[9] In addition, Carr looked for a revival in international law and hoped to see "systems of joint planning and organization between countries or groups of countries agreeing to pursue full employment policies in common, or to share in the economic development of backward areas; . . . such regional policies [corresponding] in part, *though not necessarily or exclusively*, with the multinational groupings of power."[10] In short, Carr's position on the state system was more functionalist than realist.

Further difficulties in characterizing Carr as a realist stem from his attitude to war. War appeared to Carr to be above all an institution for accommodating changes in relative power and redressing the injustices that resulted from such changes. Narrow legal discussions about which power was the aggressor were effectively swamped by historic shifts in the underlying power balance. The climax of *The Twenty Years' Crisis*—the chapter immediately preceding the book's conclusion—consists in a treatment of "Peaceful Change." In it, Carr argues in favour of virtual acquiescence by states in changing balances of military and economic capabilities, to be achieved through negotiation backed by the ultimate threat of force. His chief point, here as elsewhere, was that even though no supranational authority could be devised, on the lines of the League of Nations, that would take this task from states, they could realistically hope to shoulder it themselves.

In support of this contention, Carr cited the example of industrial relations. In those states where government had stood clear of the contest between labour and employers, he argued, hard bargaining, punctuated by strikes and lockouts, had produced a gradual improvement in the position of organized labor, reflecting the rising power of this new force. At the same time, the rules of engagement had gradually transformed themselves without any intervention from a superior authority. Long years of war and diplomacy in labor relations had, by Carr's day, "produced on both sides a willingness to submit to various forms of conciliation and arbitration, and ended by creating something like a regular system of 'peaceful change.'"[11] Hedged though it is with realist caveats, this argument runs on to the conclusion that was to earn Carr more obloquy than any other single sentence he wrote. "If the power relations of Europe in 1938 made it inevitable that Czecho-Slovakia should lose part of her territory, and eventually her independence"—Carr declared—"it was preferable (quite apart from any question of justice or injustice) that this should come about as a result of discussions round a table in Munich rather than as the result . . . of a war."[12] North American realists after 1945, by contrast, would see in the policies of appeasement pursued by the major democracies in the 1930s a chief cause of the Second World War. Determined to avoid another general war, Henry Kissinger placed great emphasis on the willingness of major powers to engage in limited wars in order to avoid all-out war.[13] This hawkish stance was very far from Carr's position.

Because the Cold War was perceived to be not simply a contest between great powers, but an ideologically charged struggle between Left and Right, realism came to be regarded as a doctrine of the Right. Here, too, Carr was out of line. Some of the most influential British appeasers of the 1930s were also Conservatives, and their arguments often masked pro-German sympathies or, more interestingly, strong Catholic or Anglo-Catholic anti-Bolshevik convictions.[14] Yet even when he had the opportunity to mix with this circle, Carr kept clear. *The Times* had become closely associated with the appeasement lobby through the editorials of Geoffrey Dawson and Robert Barrington-Ward. There was indeed a social as well as an intellectual link to the notoriously pro-appeasement Cliveden set, named after Nancy Astor's English country house, through John Astor, one of the proprietors of *The Times*, though he seldom visited the house. Carr neither courted nor was adopted by the Cliveden set, preferring to be identified as a man of the Left. His sympathy with the Russian revolutionary tradition had already found clear expression in works on Herzen and Bakunin.

Finally, Carr shared the realist view that power was indivisible and rooted in the state.[15] This doctrine applied just as much to power over opinion as it did to military or economic power. Accordingly, Carr believed that control over the mass media, concentrated in few hands by their very nature, must be assumed by the state if community were to be preserved from the depredations of vested interests.[16] Yet, while characteristically dismissive of any possibility of supranational, as distinct from national opinion, Carr concluded his treatment of power with the idealistic observation that competing national propaganda machines, however loud or subtle, could never quite suppress truth, and that truth would in the end be sought out because of the "inherent utopianism of human nature."[17] For him to have said otherwise would, of course, have been to declare the futility of his own attempts to foster rational public debate and change official policy.

Carr's Realist Rhetoric

It might reasonably be objected that a desire to influence policy was and remains something common to all political commentators, realist and idealist alike, the difference lying solely in the nature of the policies advocated. But against this it may be argued that realists have their own attitude toward the whole business of influencing the policy process: that they are more self-consciously manipulative in their use of language, more concerned than idealists to engage policy makers directly rather than to convert a wider public. What is perhaps chiefly distinctive about the attitude of the realist tradition to propaganda is the degree to which its adherents characteristically place success higher than either truth or transparency, persuasion before candor, and the privacy of the council chamber ahead of wider public debate. This contrasts strongly with, for example, the faith Kant placed in the public use of reason as a means to Enlightenment, where "public use" consists in the exercise of reason not as a rule-bound member of some order or hierarchy—be it priest, officer, or bureaucrat—but as a citizen of the world.[18]

The antecedents of a twentieth-century realist attitude to rhetoric are well known. Here it may be enough to observe that both Machiavelli and Hobbes are claimed by Carr as precursors of modern realism, and that both go out of their way to win the trust of their readers—a trust they proceed to abuse—by pointing to the plain and unadorned character of their prose, purged of the old rhetorical devices of appeal to authority, excessive classical allusion, elaborate metaphor, and the like.[19] Hobbes went further, arguing that the reason men are unable to live in the ordered, self-regulating anarchy of bees and other creatures is precisely their ability, through language, to deceive one another. For this reason he urged counselors, when assisting the deliberations of princes, to avoid all "metaphorical" speeches, tending to stir up the passions.[20] Yet styles claiming to be cleansed of rhetoric simply acquire a distinctive rhetorical force; and Hobbes and Machiavelli gained, through their privileging of a "literal" style which they had themselves created, a substantial and generally unperceived degree of control over their readers.

For Carr, the issue of persuading policymakers was not purely tactical, as it had perhaps been for Machiavelli, or part of a broader materialism, as it was for Hobbes, but part and parcel of a social scientific methodology greatly influenced by his reading of Karl Mannheim.[21] Not only did Carr take from Mannheim the central antithesis in his argument between realism and utopianism,[22] he also adopted a position very close to Mannheim's on the sociology of knowledge. This second borrowing was much more fundamental than the first since, by forcing the problems of relativism and reflexivity upon his attention, it led Carr to a fresh understanding of the position of the intellectual in society and of his voice and texts in the policy process.

The leading argument against the sociology of knowledge went like this. One could hardly argue that other people thought as they did because of their social circumstances without conceding the same to be true of oneself. But full acceptance of this reflexive argument might easily lead to a failure of confidence in the thinker's own views, that loss of "a right of moral judgment and a ground for action" which Carr acknowledged to be among the implications of consistent realism.[23] Consistency seems to demand that one's own views be regarded as themselves open to sociological explanation and so no more than conditionally true. This realization in turn may easily lead to enervating moral relativism: the unwillingness to take one's own views as the basis for action in preference to the beliefs of other cultures, other nations, and other faiths. This line of reasoning led the work of Mannheim, and similar Marxist arguments about social conditioning and false consciousness, to be viewed as a serious threat to concepts of objectivity, truth, rationality, and even personality, considered quite fundamental to liberal individualism. The sociology of knowledge presented a challenge to the universal validity and application of Western political and cultural values.

Carr himself certainly suffered from no kind of moral funk. He knew what he thought and could, when he felt it appropriate, come right out with it. The explanation of his relative immunity from moral relativism is to be found in the second chapter of *The Twenty Years' Crisis*. Carr understood Mannheim's own solution to the problem but went beyond it. Mannheim felt that the intelligentsia acquired a measure of objectivity through relative disengagement from the processes of production and exchange, and consequent immunity from social conditioning. But Carr, while admitting this, pointed out that the corollary of this immunity was "detachment from the masses whose attitude is the determining factor in political life."[24]

How might this detachment be overcome? The intellectual, it seemed, could only be sure of exerting power by commanding the mass of national opinion formers as well as the much smaller policy-making elite. Speaking solely to the policy makers was not enough, as the rejection of the League of Nations by the American people had shown.[25] This belief in the importance of public opinion might be seen as a departure from orthodox realist contempt for popular participation in the foreign policy process. But Carr's response to the admitted power of public opinion was realist, though not at first completely so. Consideration of middle-class as well as strictly elite opinion guided his choice of genre and determined the adoption of a deceptively clear style in much of his work; it led him into the Ministry of Information and to *The Times*. But the light did not dawn soon or fully enough to make *The Twenty Years' Crisis* a wholly cynical or wholly effective realist text.

One reason for this delay is almost certainly that Carr was still struggling during the later 1930s with the very particular implications of the sociology of knowledge for rhetoric and publicity. By stressing the importance of social conditions in determining views about society, Mannheim's approach necessarily downgraded the role of authors in both generating and interpreting the texts that came from their pens. Thus distanced from their texts, authors were bound to become more conscious of the social character and persuasive function of language and correspondingly less willing to accept it as a transparent medium for the faithful expression of some increasingly implausible inner self. This insight, following directly from Carr's doubts about the relative autonomy of the intelligentsia, could hardly do other at the time than lead him in the direction of a more instrumental and manipulative use of language. But this distinctive rhetorical strategy misled and irritated some readers, was perceived by others as part of an attack on rationality itself, and provided countless polemical opportunities to a varied host of opponents.

Carr's Rhetorical Intention

How are the nuances of Carr's liberal or utopian realism expressed in the details and construction of his texts and in his particular and cumulative choices of what kinds of texts to produce? It seems appropriate first to pay attention to *The Twenty Years' Crisis*, as the least realist of his works, and, in particular, to identify some of the most common metaphors and structural devices employed there.

Dichotomy and Dialectic: Gender and Anthropomorphism

The most frequently employed argumentative figures in *The Twenty Years' Crisis* are dichotomy and dialectic. The first two parts of the book work through a series of pairings which echo the basic division between utopia and reality. The first is associated with free will, theory, law, naivety, and radicalism; the second, conversely, with determinism, practice, power, sterility, and conservatism.

Alongside dichotomy, especially in the early chapters of the book, Carr deploys a set of anthropocentric metaphors which are trichotomous, resting on the terms "infancy," "maturity," and "senility." The pairing "infancy / old age" is, to a point, just one more dichotomy; but poised between the two lies maturity, which, by implication, is a leading intellectual characteristic of the third part of the book, where Carr is to put forward his own views following his presentation and subsequent dismissal of both utopianism and realism. The problem is that the order in which the book unfolds is not the natural, but the dialectical order:

not —	infancy	maturity	senility
but —	infancy	senility	maturity
	(thesis)	(antithesis)	(synthesis)

Both utopianism and realism, as Carr portrays them in the early chapters, are stalking horses. They display discreditable extremes in order to win support from those readers who think of themselves as moderate for the compromise that Carr will unveil in the later chapters of his book. One must assume the prime target readership to be the British policy-making elites of the day: almost entirely male, largely middle-aged or elderly, and for the most part conservative in politics. To flatter these readers into concurrence Carr very early on introduces the notion of utopianism as youth or immaturity. "The science of international politics is in its infancy," he announces in the opening sentence of the book.[26] Realism, however, is the philosophy of sterile old age.[27] In place of the two extremes, Carr offers a seductive compromise of romantic pragmatism—"mature thought" as he calls it—standing perfectly poised between youth and age, just as Titian pictured the cardinal virtue of prudence. *"Ex praeterito praesens prudentur agit ni futura actione deturpet"*—"From past experience the present acts prudently lest future action be vitiated."[28]

A second problem with Carr's deployment of this set of terms arises from his implicit gendering of "youth" and "maturity." The dialectic runs thus:

youth	senility	maturity
female	male	offspring

Realism is associated with analysis which is "hard" and "ruthless," and so with an inability, in isolation, to alter, act, or create. When the political scientist reaches the limits of what may be achieved by utopianism—the stage of adolescence—the moment will come "when purpose by itself is seen to be barren [rather than sterile or impotent], and when analysis of reality has forced itself upon him. . . ."[29] Whether this rape is homosexual or heterosexual is scarcely the point; its patriarchal character is clearly implied by contradictions in the final column of the following schema.

Temporal	Past	Present	Future
Natural	Infancy	Maturity	Senility
Dialectical	Infancy: thesis	Senility: antithesis	Maturity: synthesis
Organic/ gendered	Infancy: female	Senility: male	Maturity: offspring
Reference	Utopianism (idealism)	Carr's third view or Realism?	Realism or Carr's third view?

What do ambiguities in Carr's use of anthropocentric images, presented here in tabular form, amount to? There is space in them for the elderly to read the offer of resumed maturity and potency, and for the realist (as male) to assume authority over and anticipate acquiescence from the utopian (female). There is certainly room for readers to develop quite divergent readings of Carr's realism.

Authority

The possibly unconscious identification, through this use of anthropocentric terms, of the author as mature male is reinforced by the stance that Carr developed toward his readers. Instead of adopting the Machiavellian ploy of an apparently simple and literal language in which author and reader are fully complicit, one with another, Carr chose to present himself as the professor addressing his pupils (maturity speaking to adolescence). *The Twenty Years' Crisis* is announced as "An Introduction" to international relations.[30] On the same title page Carr describes himself, truthfully of course, as "Professor." The immediate implications are of authority as well as authorship, but, secondarily, of a more utopian address and accessibility to a wide and untutored audience. Carr moves quickly to provide a further boost for his own authority as initiate, or revealer of mysteries. In the preface the reader is promised analysis of "the underlying and significant, rather than the immediate and personal, causes of the disaster [the outbreak of war]."[31] The theme of induction, even initiation, into a public science of social relations formerly conducted in secret, persists through the titles of part 1 and chapter 1: "The Science of International Politics" and "The Beginnings of a Science."[31] Authority is further reinforced by a barrage of references to the classics of European political philosophy far in excess of that needed for the achievement of the book's polemical aim.

There is no deceptively innocent Machiavellian style here. Instead, one group of readers is held in thrall while nods and winks are offered to the careful reader, by which Carr subverts the authority he has assumed. He is scathing toward the "metaphysicians of Geneva [who] found it difficult to believe that an accumulation of ingenious texts prohibiting war was not a barrier against war itself"; yet he *writes* to offer a method of averting war through the appeasement of rising powers.[32] He quotes with approval Churchill's claim in 1932 that at no previous time had "the gap between the kinds of words which statesmen used and what was actually happening in many countries was so great as it is now."[33] Is this to be taken as a general invitation to mistrust propaganda and, more generally, to reject the claim of political texts to represent the world? But Carr's intention is not destructive; rather it is to succeed in the attempt to persuade readers of the possibility of translating his policy proposals into reality. Discussing propaganda, or "power over opinion," in a text intended precisely to exert power over opinion, Carr argues at length for the inseparability of military and economic power from each other and from control of the media. He concludes that state control over the media is inevitable, and that ideas of independent world opinion as a political force are illusory, since "propaganda is ineffective as a political force until it acquires a national home and becomes linked with military and economic power."[34] Yet he puts forth this view as a private person, and a forceful independent critic of his own government on the brink of war.

In such ways as this Carr attempted an extraordinary balancing act in which, as realist, he strove to maintain control and superiority over his readers while, as idealist or liberal, he sought in Kantian fashion to extend the public use of reason to the conduct of foreign policy.[35] The invitation to a wider public was there, but it was as often an invitation to submission as to empowerment.

Pleasing both Left and Right

Carr employed dichotomy and dialectic for substantive reasons, to set limits, as it were, to the position he intended to take in the later, longer (and least often read?) parts of his book. He employed them, also, for their rhetorical value in affirming his authorial power and hooking the right-wing readership that he later intended to play into the midstream. But in seeming contradiction to this second objective, Carr used dichotomy to keep the Left on board. For the dialectical method is also the German, and so the Marxist, method. *The Twenty Years' Crisis* moves in stately Hegelian progress from thesis (utopianism) to antithesis (realism) and on to synthesis (Carr's own position). This first, theoretical, synthesis is then played out through a further, practical, dialectical progression. Small linguistic clues of Carr's familiarity with the German philosophical tradition and with Marxism abound, as, for example, his use of the term "reproduction" in the context of dialectical reasoning.[37]

Very early in the book, a more specific mason's handshake is offered to the observant Marxist. Carr distinguishes between the physical and the social sciences. In the latter, the purpose of the investigator must always be numbered among the facts to be examined; there can be no complete objectivity. "Purpose and analysis become part and parcel of a single process."[38] Immediately, Carr goes on to cite Marx in support. Straightway, then, he disclosed an understanding of a central Marxist attitude toward scientific methodology and a familiarity with the canonical works. But at the same time he playfully negated his own standing as scientist and authority by the clear implication that he too, like any political scientist, must be regarded as purposive: a negation, however, that might easily float past the untutored reader.

Elsewhere, his account of the origins of the First World War is the purest Leninism in both its stress on 1900 as the turning point in international relations and the linking of territorial and economic aspects of imperialist competition.[39] Indeed, the specific debt to Lenin, among authors in the Marxist canon, becomes more and more obvious as the book proceeds; direct references to Lenin's works (11) exceed those to Marx and Engels singly (2, 3) and jointly (4).

Nor are these the only whiffs of Marxism in the book. Germany and Italy, regimes of the totalitarian Right, are highlighted as the have-not or revisionist states to which Britain and the other status quo powers are urged to make concessions proportionate to the current, rather than to some bygone distribution of power, so that general war may be avoided. Yet the argument applies with equal force to the Soviet Union. Carr may have reckoned he had much more chance of persuading British Conservatives to allow the Soviet Union to resume its place among the Great Powers by first putting forward the parallel and equally necessary—if to him less palatable—case for Germany.

Also intriguing is the sheer space offered to the Marxist reader within Carr's dichotomous schemes. Utopianism is aligned with the Left. Realism, however, is a little confusingly derived by Carr through German idealism and Marxism.[40] Earlier, the strategy of opposition to individualist liberalism pursued through the early chapters and, most of all, the assault upon liberal political economy, panders just as much to the critical appetites of Marxists as of British Conservatives and Unionists. Again, the seemingly Rightist characterization of the Left as more theoretical and the Right, by contrast, as wise and pragmatic, is implicitly nuanced in favour of the "realist" Soviet regime by the observation that "when Left parties . . . are brought into contact with reality through the assumption of political office, they tend to abandon their 'doctrinaire' utopianism and move towards the Right."[41]

Yet for all this barely concealed appeal to the socialist Left, Carr was able to hold a large section of the Tory readership of *The Times* in thrall, at least during the middle passage of the war. Soon after Carr's arrival, Barrington-Ward expressed admiration for his willingness to work in partnership, molding his "advanced views in such a way that they will seem to our constituency the most normal and inevitable truths." This enthusiasm only began to dwindle in mid-1943, as Barrington-Ward, having more and more to "tone down" the leaders of his deputy, ruefully noted that "the political effects of what he writes are not always plain to him."[42]

The Architecture of The Twenty Years' Crisis: *Deploying Two Realisms*

Carr did not restrict himself to addressing simultaneously two ideologically opposed readerships in *The Twenty Years' Crisis*; he also attempted to deploy two versions of realism in order to exploit the space between them.

To this end, dichotomy, so powerful a technique in the first and second parts of the book, is re-deployed in Part 3. Where utopianism-radicalism-theory and realism-conservatism-practice had formed neat columns in the first half of the book to provide the two extremes, now *theoretical* positions of whichever political orientation—radical or conservative—are pitted against their *practical* or pragmatic counterparts. In privileging practical over theoretical reason at this point, Carr perhaps reveals Kantian, rather than Anglo-Saxon, liberal antecedents.[43] Doctrinaire conservatism, just as much as doctrinaire liberalism, is to be subordinated in concrete political situations to the needs of the moment. "Every political situation contains mutually incompatible elements of utopia and reality, of morality and power."[44]

The reason for this switch in the use of dichotomy is to retain the powerful rhetorical tool of a supposed spirit of pragmatism, compromise, and moderation in order to seduce the Right into pragmatic adoption of what might at first seem doctrinally unacceptable policy proposals including economic planning, Western European integration under British leadership, and acquiescence in Soviet denial of national self-determination in Eastern Europe: the very package that Carr was to hammer home in innumerable *Times* editorials of the 1940s.

Genres and Œuvre: To Whom Was Carr Speaking?

Carr's range of writings and publications was considerable. Leaving the Foreign Office in his mid-forties, he found in the Wilson chair of international politics at Aberystwyth, to which he was appointed in 1936, the academic base from which to take part in the quickening national debate on foreign policy. For two years, from 1937 to 1939, he chaired a research group on nationalism for the Royal Institute of International Affairs at Chatham House, hard by Westminster and the royal palaces. Later, on the outbreak of war, he went to the Ministry of Information to develop British propaganda for use abroad before joining the staff of *The Times* in January 1941. Already responsible for some editorials while still at the ministry, he now became a regular contributor and served for more than five years as assistant editor. After the war, more narrowly academic than ever before, he devoted himself primarily to a massive history of the Soviet revolution and its consequences. Throughout it all, he was a regular reviewer for *The Times Literary Supplement.* His *œuvre* consisted of everything from daily journalism to multi-volume history.

Rhetoric consists in the persuasive use of language. Persuasion rests just as much in the choice of genre and the manner of publication as in the construction of arguments and the employment of tropes. Carr was well aware of this. One section of *The Twenty Years' Crisis*, the part of chapter eight dealing with "power over opinion," was separately published prior to the book in pamphlet form.[45] The same treatment was given to the section of *Conditions of Peace* that dealt with nationalism.[46] "The Two Scourges," his most celebrated *Times* editorial, sold more than 10,000 copies in pamphlet form.[47] And if *The Twenty Years' Crisis* was so allusive and forbidding to the novice as to belie its claim to be simply an introduction to a new academic discipline of international relations, the same cannot be said for his work of the same year on British foreign policy, genuinely plain and popular in its literary style.[48]

By publishing parts of longer works in pamphlet form, by writing and editing popular treatments of foreign policy, and by his work at the British propaganda ministry, but above all by his command of the *Times* leader, Carr displayed considerable rhetorical awareness and judgment. In attempting to define more precisely the audiences Carr intended to reach through this varied *œuvre*, it may be best to employ his own technique of dialectic to examine his progress from the utopianism of *The Twenty Years' Crisis*, through the realism of Carr's time at the Ministry of Information, to the compromise between public and private power achieved at *The Times*.

The political variety of the intended audience for *The Twenty Years' Crisis* has already been indicated. The extent of the audience and its social complexion have been touched upon in the discussion of Carr's casting of the book as an "Introduction" (implying access) and his contradictory adoption of a highly allusive manner, bristling with erudition (implying elitist exclusion). Was the audience intended to be numbered in hundreds or in tens of thousands? The sheer difficulty and rhetorical treachery of the book implies the former. This, in turn, might be taken to imply that *Crisis* was a realist book, because aimed at the policy-making elite rather than at a wider public. Not so: *Crisis* is an idealist book, because it is public, in two important senses.

First there is the implicit, but scarcely hidden display of ambiguity through those contradictory uses of dialectic which were examined earlier. The text teases its readers with an exposure of Carr's own doubts. While there is manipulation, it is imperfectly concealed, almost wanting to be found.

Secondly, though Carr had been a civil servant, and was very shortly to join the civil service once again to help direct the British wartime propaganda effort overseas, he wrote *The Twenty Years' Crisis* as a citizen of the world, not a member of any organization. Accordingly the book was public in the sense of not being bound by any code of restrictive rules. (Only a private citizen can write a fully public text). In this respect *Crisis* contrasts strongly with the other major work in which Carr was actively engaged during the later 1930s, the report on nationalism produced collectively and anonymously by the Chatham House study group which he chaired.[49] This difference between unrestricted and official authorship is significant given Carr's belief that the tendency in his time was for the state more and more to dominate the media. Because it was least restricted by loyalties to others, *Crisis* was the most personal, and therefore—paradoxically—the most public—of Carr's works of this period.

A thorough account of the next, and most realist, phase in Carr's career, is difficult to provide. The Ministry of Information war aims files in the Public Record Office preach the importance of backing law with force, the military obsolescence of the smaller European states, the consequent need for post-war federation, a certain disdain for the alleged diplomatic inexperience and archaic liberalism of United States leaders, and the need to create a welfare state in Britain in order to appear fully democratic and post-imperial in the eyes of potential allies. But it is anybody's guess whether this or that phrase came from Carr's pen, reflected his influence, or simply expressed a more broadly derived collegiate view with which he concurred.

Work at *The Times* fell precisely between *Crisis* and Carr's work at the Ministry of Information. More than the first, it was designed to appeal beyond the London elite of policy makers to a more numerous national class of opinion formers. Like the second, it was strictly speaking a team effort aimed at two audiences. Publicly directed at winning acceptance from a wide and influential swathe of British elite opinion for a "peaceful revolution," *The Times* leading articles had also a more private and, hence, a more realist aspect.[50] As a member of the editorial team at *The Times* under Barrington-Ward, Carr was speaking directly to the governments of the United States, the Soviet Union, and Britain through a daily newspaper still, at that time, regarded as the mouthpiece for a British government that, ironically, could no longer control it as it had done in the 1930s.[51] Furthermore, his editorials were composed in the clear and forthright style of authentic realism.

To whom were *The Times* editorials addressed? An example will make this clear. Published on 5 December 1940, "The Two Scourges" caused a considerable stir. In it Carr sought to place unemployment on all fours with war. Both evils had to be dealt with if there was ever to be real security. Domestic economic and social reconstruction must therefore be thought through by the British government and publicly debated long before victory was in sight.

Was Carr expressing a sincerely held welfarist view? Certainly; but he was attempting more than this. Editorials were calibrated for their impact both on the middle-class readership at large and on a much narrower audience of policy makers, at home and abroad. The origin of "The Two Scourges" provides an insight into the rhetorical consciousness of the editorial team at *The Times*. The idea for the piece stemmed from a conversation between Lord Lothian, British ambassador to Washington, and Geoffrey Dawson, then still editor, in which the former claimed that the United States would never trust Britain fully as a democratic ally unless there were signs of a full employment policy for the post-war period. The United States' official mind was already well on the way to the theory, later to be used to justify the creation of the Bretton Woods system, which attributed the war chiefly to economy insecurity, mediated through unemployment, mass support for political extremism, consequent changes in regimes, and the imperative need of new populist administrations of the Right to use rearmament to counter the unemployment that had brought them to office. Carr came into Dawson's room during the conversation and Dawson suggested he try an editorial on this theme.

The aim was not, then, solely to address and persuade the readership of *The Times*. It was written with an eye to the arras: to those undeclared statesmen abroad who regarded *The Times* as the quasi-official British newspaper. Nor was this incident exceptional. Dawson and his successor Barrington-Ward were constantly aware of the propaganda impact of their newspaper. As early as July 1940, Barrington-Ward and Carr had come to a clear shared understanding of this task, and of its delicacy. Their views, by and large, were shared by the co-chief proprietor, John Astor.[52] *The Times*, Barrington-Ward confided to his diary, "almost alone in the press and certainly first, is trying to get the right 'answer to Hitler' in a statement on our plans for war and peace to show that we are fighting for a new Europe not the old—a new Britain and not the old." He continued: "I wholly agree with Carr;—planned consumption, abolition of unemployment and poverty, drastic educational reform, family allowances, economic organization of the Continent, etc., but all this needs the right presentation."[53]

If the British middle classes had to be made to feel comfortable with a welfare state, North American elite opinion had equally to be persuaded that Britain was more democratic than imperialist at heart. In much the same way, at a later stage in the war, Carr was to urge the British government, through the columns of *The Times*, to withdraw its support for the Greek Right in order to persuade Soviet leaders that Britain was not the "reactionary, imperialist power" pictured by their ideologues.[54] Since both of the superpowers-to-be were, in their different ways, anti-imperialist, Britain had to forge a new identity if it were to continue to exercise legitimate power in the post-war world. And sustained national power was every bit as important an objective for the ill-assorted duo—Carr the advanced liberal and the deeply religious radical Tory, Barrington-Ward—as the explicit objective of social justice.

If they had power to influence foreign perceptions of Britain, the dynamic duo also exerted a degree of influence over the British government. Barrington-Ward had access to Churchill himself, and was able to press him to consider post-war planning from an early point in the war. Resistant on ideological grounds, and because he expected to give way to younger men after the war, Churchill preferred to concentrate on the conduct of the war. But even he succumbed to pressure in April 1942, accepting a memorandum in which Carr summarized the line advocated by *The Times*. Partly in response to continued pressure from *The Times*, Churchill at last devoted an unprecedented broadcast to domestic policy issues on 21 March 1943, sketching a four-year reconstruction plan chiefly designed to keep Tory options open.[55] This gave powerful sanction to the emerging welfarist consensus embedded in British war aims and so actively publicized in *The Times*.

On foreign policy questions, too, Carr had the power, through *The Times*, to irritate if not to persuade the Soviet Premier. The paper was distinguished above all by its line on the Soviet Union. Carr and Barrington-Ward agreed as early as the middle of 1942 that at the end of the war Britain would be too weak to prevent the Russians from dominating, if not occupying the whole of Eastern Europe, at least as far west as Berlin. Anticipating early United States withdrawal from Europe and fearful of reviving the Russo-German alliance by ill-judged and ineffectual opposition to Soviet plans, Carr urged that Britain should accept this extension of Soviet influence.[56]

A number of corollaries followed. Most immediately, the need for good relations with the Soviet Union in the post-war world required that Stalin's demands for a second front to relieve pressure on his forces be promptly met. Later, Britain would have to acquiesce in rough Soviet treatment of Eastern Europe. And in the longer run, Carr argued, the British government would have to tone down its relationship with the United States and take the lead in Western European political and economic cooperation. "It would be the height of unwisdom to assume"—he thundered in May 1945—"that an alliance of the English-speaking world, even if it were to find favour with American opinion, could form by itself the all-sufficient pillar of world security and render superfluous any other foundation for British policy in Europe."[57]

Many would have agreed, then as now; but it was to take almost thirty years for Carr's aspirations to take practical form in British membership of the European Community. In the meantime, his game was nearly up. For a decade, he had aimed multiple messages at multiple audiences, often simultaneously. He had cast himself as counselor to statesmen and free intellectual, whisperer of private words and public thunderer. But when nemesis came in the form of the close alignment of a bankrupt British state with the United States in a Cold War against the Soviet Union, Carr's practical hopes of a welfarist Anglo-Soviet condominium in Europe foundered. And at that point, the multiple rhetorical strategies of the previous ten years proved to be just so many hostages in the hands of his enemies.

CARR'S RECEPTION

In the search for an explanation of the strength of feeling against Carr at the height of the Cold War one must distinguish an impatience with his elaborate and elitist manner, his frequent, seemingly opportunistic inconsistencies and ambiguities, his leanings towards determinism, and his alien social-constructivist methodology from more straightforward dislike of his specific policy proposals. The two certainly fed on one another but remain analytically and perhaps even socially distinct.

The first kind of criticism was most evident in intellectual responses to his longer works; the second in the growing resistance of readership and politicians to his *Times* editorials. By the late 1940s thousands of English men and women with little time for political theory, and who probably did not even know Carr's name, seem nevertheless to have come to loathe a stream of editorials they regarded as the work of a crypto-Communist and a traitor to his country. While Carr may have done a good deal to win elite acquiescence in, or even support for Barrington-Ward's "peaceful revolution" as carried through by the British Labour government after 1945, his influence on foreign policy was less enduring. As concern about post-war Soviet power developed in the mid-1940s, his line on Russia was rapidly identified as a mere transfer from Germany to the Soviet Union of the pre-war policy of appeasement. Carr was denounced in June 1942 by Lord Elibank, speaking in the House of Lords, as "an active danger to this country."[58] Worse was to follow when he and Barrington-Ward opposed the despatch of British troops to Greece late in 1944 to support the incumbent right-wing government. Carr's editorial of 1 January 1945 finally goaded Churchill into a public denunciation of *The Times* in the House of Commons, which was met with "the loudest, largest, and most vicious—even savage!—cheer that I have heard in the House," Barrington-Ward noted ruefully, "a vent for the pent-up passions of three years, a protest against all that has, rightly or wrongly, enraged the Tories in the paper during that time."[59]

As the year wore on the government became less and less patient. By stating the realities of the British position so baldly, in what the Russians regarded as an official newspaper, Carr effectively undermined the negotiating position of British diplomats. The Foreign Office protested, and four months before Carr's departure the political bankruptcy of his partnership with Barrington-Ward was made unambiguously clear when the latter was summoned to the Foreign Office and subjected to a tirade from the Labour Foreign Secretary, Ernest Bevin. Barrington-Ward later noted down the essential points of Bevin's repetitive and emotional attack: "*The Times* did great harm. It was taken abroad for a national newspaper. He was going to tell the House of Commons that it was not, and that it was pro-Russian and not pro-British. I had a lot of pink intelligentsia down there and he didn't believe I was in control."[60] As Britain slipped steadily into the cold embrace of the United States, this mud stuck. Rebecca West, a representative member of the British pre-war Left intelligentsia, "stunned fellow guests at a dinner party [in New York early in 1947] by asserting that *The Times* of London was now a Communist party organ." Taken by her biographer as evidence of near pathological obsession with Communist infiltration, this had in fact become a widely held view of the "thruppeny *Daily Worker*" by the end of the Barrington-Ward era.[61]

Hostile reactions from the intelligentsia were directed at Carr personally rather than *The Times*. His use of stalking horses lent itself to misinterpretation, whether it was the political utopianism which he was to reintroduce in a more robust form in the second half of *The Twenty Years' Crisis* or the seemingly pro-Axis position intended to win support for concessions to all revisionist powers. The prompt reaction of Susan Stebbing, a philosophically sophisticated reviewer of *Crisis*, is instructive. She proceeded to beat Carr about the head with views not so very different from those he had himself reached by the end of the book, seeming to assume he actually held the realist view advanced in chapter five, but effectively demolished in chapter six.[62] Another early critic, Czeslaw Poznanski attacked *Conditions of Peace* for setting economic rationality above nationality as the criterion for political self-determination and *The Twenty Years' Crisis* for its advocacy of appeasement. He accused Carr of a wholly unprincipled view of foreign policy, quite ignoring the fact that the later chapters of *The Twenty Years' Crisis* are wholly devoted—whether successfully or not—to establishing a moral basis for foreign policy.[63] Such attacks were only plausible because of the too life-like features of the straw men set up at the start of the book.

After 1945, judgments of Carr from intellectuals, when they rose above the commonplace and simplistic attacks on appeasement, crypto-Communism, and the like, almost invariably attacked the relativism and determinism that were held to lie at the heart of Carr's method. Hans Morgenthau was among the first. In a faithful and fair review article of 1948, he argued that the root of Carr's problem lay in moral relativism. "Mr. Carr has no transcendent point of view from which to survey the political scene" and for this reason has become "a utopian of power," mistaking preëminent will for right, both in his judgments of politicians and in the exercise of his own literary skills, one presumes. Rightly recognizing Carr as the political romantic he was, Morgenthau concluded that while "it is a dangerous thing to be a Machiavelli . . . it is a disastrous thing to be a Machiavelli without *virtú*."[64] All this, of course, could be of little comfort to those, including Carr, who perceived themselves to be living "after virtue," after the collapse of faith in the moral integrity of the last modernist hope, the Soviet state.

Hugh Trevor-Roper, writing much later, would seize gleefully on what he took to be Carr's about-face, from pro-Nazi appeaser in 1939 to Leninist historian in the 1950s. In a vituperative review of *What Is History* in *Encounter*, he noted Carr's realism and recalled his past support for appeasement before referring sarcastically to the supposed change of mind about the realities of power that had made Carr "the Red Professor of Printing House Square" during the Second World War. Moving on to Carr's work on Soviet Russia, Trevor-Roper accused Carr of writing determinist history, a victor's history in which he allowed "no voice . . . to Lenin's opponents." Just as "the Nazi success-story" which Trevor-Roper suggests Carr might easily have written in the 1930s "has ended in discredit and failure," so, it is implied, the final failure of the Soviet state would demonstrate the intolerance of the history Carr really did write. "No historian since the crudest ages of clerical bigotry," Trevor-Roper concluded, "has treated evidence with such dogmatic ruthlessness as this."[65] The change of mind, in short, was proof of the folly of Carr's advocacy of swimming with the tide of history.

The hostility directed against him has been a measure of Carr's continuing influence. *The Twenty-Years' Crisis* is still in print, and is still read by most undergraduates studying international relations in Britain. *What Is History*, despite Hugh Trevor Roper, was issued in a substantially revised edition as recently as 1987. Attacking Carr was a minor theatre of the ideological Cold War. The point, here, has been neither to substantiate nor to dismiss the criticisms, but to make clear the ways in which his employment of complex rhetorical strategies laid Carr open to specific kinds of attack. Recognizing that the functions of language were both expressive and persuasive, Carr had been close enough to his own parody of realism to opt for persuasion as the more urgent task, but too much the liberal entirely to conceal the means of persuasion from his readers. This tender-heartedness certainly divides Carr from those out-and-out realists, of whatever political hue, who may be termed "opaque" realists: those who believe it not merely permissible but necessary to conceal the rhetorical techniques by which they pursue their ends. It places him instead, along with Richard Rorty, in the company of those "transparent" or "utopian" realists of a democratic and ironic cast of mind—patient, piecemeal, and accepting of contingency—who figure that the trip will not have been worth taking if half the passengers end up not knowing how they got there.

NOTES

1. Early in 1992, I wrote a paper treating Carr's position on nationalism and the multi-national state from 1936 to 1944 and the later reception of his ideas on this subject. The present paper was first drafted not long after. Like two balls in play upon a pool table, the two papers kissed from time to time before (I hope) dropping neatly into their respective holes. The earlier paper is published as "E. H. Carr through Cold War Lenses: Nationalism, Large States and the Shaping of Opinion," in *Chatham House and British Foreign Policy, 1919-1945: The Royal Institute of International Affairs during the Inter-War Period*, eds. Andrea Bosco and Cornelia Navari (London: Lothian Foundation Press, 1994). My particular thanks for their comments upon drafts, and for their help in sorting out what belonged in which paper go to Barry Buzan, David Carlton, Linda Jones, and Robert Hariman.
2. William T. R. Fox, "E. H. Carr and Political Realism: Vision and Revision," *Review of International Studies* 11 (1985): 1, 7.
3. Ved Mehta, *Fly and the Fly-Bottle: Encounters with British Intellectuals* (London: Weidenfeld & Nicolson, 1963), 111.
4. Norman Stone, "Grim Eminence," *London Review of Books* 5, no. 1 (20 January - 2 February 1983).

5. E. H. Carr, *Conditions of Peace* (London: Macmillan, 1942), 60-1.

6. E. H. Carr, *The Twenty Years' Crisis, 1919-1939: An Introduction to the Study of International Relations* (London: Macmillan, 1939), 295-97. Unless otherwise stated, references in this paper are to the first edition, which differs substantially in pagination from later editions.

7. Ibid., 295.

8. Ibid., 296.

9. E. H. Carr, *Nationalism and After* (London: Macmillan, 1945), 47.

10. Ibid., 69 (my emphasis).

11. Carr, *Twenty Years' Crisis*, 271-72.

12. Ibid., 287.

13. James E. Dougherty and Robert L. Pfaltzgraff, Jr., *Contending Theories of International Relations: A Comprehensive Survey*, 3d ed. (New York: Harper & Row, 1990), 108.

14. Michael Astor, *Tribal Feeling* (London: Readers Union, 1964), 136-47.

15. Carr, *Twenty Years' Crisis*, 131-85.

16. Ibid., 170-71.

17. Ibid., 184.

18. Onora O'Neill, "The Public Use of Reason," *Political Theory* 14, no. 4 (1986): 523-51.

19. Niccolo Machiavelli, *The Prince* (Harmondsworth: Penguin Books, 1981).

20. Thomas Hobbes, *Leviathan* (Oxford: Clarendon Press, 1909), 199.

21. Carr, *Twenty Years' Crisis*, x.

22. Karl Mannheim, *Ideology and Utopia: An Introduction to the Sociology of Knowledge* (London: Kegan Paul, 1936).

23. Carr, *Twenty Years' Crisis*, 113.

24. Ibid., 21.

25. Ibid., 21-22.

26. Ibid., 3.

27. Ibid., 15.

28. James Hall, *Dictionary of Subjects and Symbols in Art* (London: Murray, 1974), 255.

29. Carr, *Twenty Years' Crisis*, 13-14.

30. Ibid., iii.

31. Ibid., ix.

32. Ibid., xiii.

33. Ibid., 41.

34. Ibid.

35. Carr, *Twenty Years' Crisis*, 2d ed. (London: Macmillan, 1946), 135, 139.

36. O'Neill, "Use of Reason."

37. Ibid., 26.

38. Carr, *Twenty Years' Crisis*, 6.

39. Ibid., 78.

40. Ibid., 83ff.

41. Ibid., 28.

42. Barrington-Ward's diary, quoted in Stephen Koss, *The Rise and Fall of the Political Press in Britain, "The Twentieth Century,"* vol. 2 (Chapel Hill and London: University of North Carolina Press, 1984), 608, 616.

43. O'Neill, "Use of Reason," 531.

44. Carr, *Twenty Years' Crisis*, 119.

45. E. H. Carr, *Propaganda in International Politics* in Oxford Pamphlets on World Affairs No. 16 (Oxford: Clarendon Press, 1939).

46. E. H. Carr, *The Future of Nations: Independence or Interdependence* (London: Kegan Paul, 1941).

47. Iverach McDonald, *The History of The Times,* "Struggles in War and Peace," vol. 5 (London: Times Books, 1984), 467-68.

48. E. H. Carr, *Britain: A Study of Foreign Policy from the Versailles Treaty to the Outbreak of War* (London: Longman, Green & Co., 1939).

49. Royal Institute of International Affairs, *Nationalism. A Report by a Study Group of Members of the Royal Institute of International Affairs* (London: Oxford University Press, 1940).

50. The quoted phrase is that of Robert Barrington-Ward, editor of *The Times;* McDonald, *Times,* 98.

51. Richard Crockett, *Twilight of Truth: Chamberlain, Appeasement and the Manipulation of the Press* (London: Weidenfeld & Nicolson, 1989).

52. McDonald, *Times,* 82.

53. Ibid., 39.

54. Ibid., 118.

55. Ibid., 100-1, 111.

56. Ibid., 104-7.

57. Ibid., 135-36.

58. Ibid., 105.

59. Ibid., 122.

60. Ibid., 139-40.

61. Victoria Glendinning, *Rebecca West: A Life* (London: Weidenfeld and Nicolson, 1987), 188

62. Susan Stebbing, *Ideals and Illusions* (London: Watts & Co., 1941).

63. Czeslaw Poznanski, *The Rights of Nations* (London: Routledge, 1942), v-vi.

64. Hans J. Morgenthau, *The Restoration of American Politics* (Chicago: University of Chicago Press, 1962), 43.

65. Hugh Trevor-Roper, "E. H. Carr's Success Story," *Encounter* (1962), quoted by Ved Mehta, *Fly and the Fly-Bottle,* 112.

ROGER EPP

MARTIN WIGHT

INTERNATIONAL RELATIONS AS REALM OF PERSUASION

Realism can be a very fine thing: it all depends whether it means the abandonment of high ideals or of foolish expectations.[1]

Everyone is a Realist nowadays.[2]

Martin Wight's reputation as a realist rests primarily on two texts. The first is his 1946 tract, *Power Politics*, which framed what became the conventional analysis of the League of Nations in the language associated now with realism: in the end, the League was a facade made possible, then shattered by a shifting balance of power; it had not supplanted the international anarchy. *Power Politics* was greeted by one emigre scholar as a "brilliant summary of ideas which we share"—ideas which in the "appeasement period" had been a "minor heresy."[3] The second text is the well-known essay whose title—"Why is there no International Theory?"—was to exercise a generation of positivists committed to the scientific pursuit of precisely that. The essay drew a sharp distinction between domestic and international realms. It identified the former as the site of possible progress; therefore, "political theory" could be concerned with the "good life." The latter, however, was the "realm of repetition and recurrence," which admitted no higher objective than order and, ultimately, survival.[4] Consequently, Wight is commonly denoted as not simply a realist but also a pessimist, even by sympathetic interpreters. One critic in retrospect has accused him of no less than having made "pessimism respectable in British international relations."[5]

Wight's place in the company of first-rank postwar realists, for all that, is far from incontestable. Certainly, he was an influential lecturer in the 1950s at the London School of Economics (LSE), one whose imprint on the study of international politics in Britain remains as pervasive—or, for some, as stifling—as it is absent in North America.

But Wight never identified himself in print as a realist. He treated E. H. Carr with disdain, and Hans Morgenthau with a critical coolness. A conscientious objector during the Second World War, he refrained later from much of the polemics raised against "utopians" and "idealists." He seldom resorted to the trademark rhetorical strategy—the intellectual conceit—of claiming to know the world as it was, not as it should be. He retained a certain sympathy, in fact, for the idea of Anglo-American federation that gained a brief prominence before the Cold War deepened, and he once proposed that what was remarkable about the League's collective security system was that it had come close to succeeding. Significantly, his *Power Politics* concluded by addressing the absence of optimism that so distinguished the public mood of 1946 from that of 1919.

Wight's inclusion in this volume is defensible, nonetheless, on the strength of his abiding interest in statecraft and relations among powers. This is what attracts Richard Ashley, who holds up his exemplary "classical" realism against subsequent, scientific varieties.[6] But a rereading of Wight in relation to others who comprise the heterogeneous camp of postwar realism can also contribute to the shaping of a post-realist rhetorical turn. The Wight that emerges from the following analysis offers a keen sense of historical contingency and moral tension. More than that, by situating international theory in a "conversation" among distinct but interwoven traditions that are historically embodied and shaped in particular circumstances by political writers and practitioners, he calls close attention to the politics of language and argument. In effect, he recasts international relations as a realm of persuasion. Wight once admitted in this respect that on examining his "own psyche," he found traces of each of the patterns of thought by which he categorized international theory: realist, rationalist, and revolutionist.[7] His realism, in turn, might be understood to represent one voice—sometimes amplified, sometimes muted—in an internal dialogue of conscience that was projected onto the diverse terrains of public, academic, and even ecclesiastical argument.

In rereading Wight, it is essential to avoid the temptation to treat only those better-known texts that are most obviously about international relations: the revised *Power Politics* and *Systems of States*, published after his death; and the essays in *Diplomatic Investigations*, which he edited with Herbert Butterfield. Wight's thought was worked out in the larger, intersecting debates about human history, war and peace, that engaged historians, philosophers, theologians, and others before international relations became the domain of specialists in fragmented universities. To focus on a narrower list of texts would reinforce the impression that Wight, owing to a pessimistic outlook, chose scholarly detachment over engagement. In truth, he was a regular reviewer, essayist, and lecturer throughout the 1940s and 1950s. A wider survey of his varied public utterances—extending to the book page of *The Observer*, to theological journals, even to the reproachful footnotes he wrote for Arnold Toynbee's *A Study of History*—can help to illuminate his treatment of international relations and, in particular, its transformative potential.

HISTORY AND HUMAN FREEDOM

Among the key elements of Wight's thought is an insistence that a reading of history is embedded in any account of international politics.[8] To some extent all expressions of postwar realism shared, if only implicitly, in this insistence, or rather inherited it, given that their immediate target was what remained of the complacent liberal teleology of peace. The realist strategy, typically, was to deny certain futures or at least their foreseeable prospect. Wight's turn to history, however, was more deliberate and nuanced, owing to his academic training, his intimidating erudition, and also to an eschatological Christianity to which this essay will return. In the first instance, historical argument was a means of assailing those "false expectations" generated by political and theological progressivisms. Yet, even in the late 1940s, and increasingly so as the study of international relations became dominated by realism, then ossified into social-scientific discourse, he challenged static or cyclical assumptions about history that issued in either testable hypotheses or existential despair. The historicity of the modern state-system was proof for him of its open-endedness.

The claim that Wight's reading of history emphasized freedom and contingency must begin at its weakest point: his own description of international relations as the "realm of repetition and recurrence." As commentators have shown, the dichotomies that surround the phrase—domestic/international, good life/survival—do not bear up to critical scrutiny,[9] however much they reinforce a powerful "inside-outside" discourse.[10] Moreover, as Morgenthau once observed, Wight had refuted his own historian's scepticism about generalization; for, surely, recurrent patterns were the stuff of hypotheses, laws, and predictions.[11]

Wight, however, used the phrase "repetition and recurrence" on only one occasion in print. The essay in which it appeared was a deliberately provocative inaugural paper read in 1959 for the British Committee on the Theory of International Politics. It asked why there was no speculative tradition of international theory akin to the body of political theory stretching from ancient Greece to the modern era, only scattered reflections on war and the likelihood of its abolition. Wight proposed two reasons for the paucity and the "intellectual and moral poverty" of past theoretical efforts. One was the "intellectual prejudice imposed by the sovereign state," a point on which interpreters seldom dwell. The other was the belief in progress, a predisposition more readily frustrated by international than by domestic politics; Sir Thomas More and Henry IV returned to England and France would encounter, in relations between them, "much the same melodrama."[12]

This was not, however, Wight's final or only word on the subject. That same year, for example, he wrote of international relations that the "regularities [are] so tenuous, . . . the consequences of any course of action so speculative, each crisis is so marked by historical uniqueness, that it is extraordinarily difficult to organize diplomatic experience into a system, let alone a theory."[13] Such claims cannot be conflated with the more recent, so-called structural realism, notably of Kenneth Waltz, that has rendered history a null set and that projects a future inevitably like the present.[14]

Wight, contrarily, had stressed already in the introduction to *Power Politics* that the modern state-system was "by no means the rule in history" despite "the illusion that it is normal." Power politics, in strictest terms, emerged only with sovereign states out of the gradual dissolution of European Christendom, a "revolution in loyalties" accompanied by a transformation in the language of political rule from medieval *right* to modern *power*.[15] A significant marker in this transformation was the appearance in 1579 of the phrase, "balance of power," in a book dedicated to Elizabeth I.[16] Language in this view is bound intimately to practice. Accordingly, the modern state-system came into existence when Europeans began to describe their world in terms of a *systema civitatum* or its vernacular equivalents.[17] Wight's meticulous inquiry in *Systems of States* into the chronological and geographical limits of the modern state-system stands in continuity with the distinction among epochs, this sense of historical breaks corresponding with changes in the language of political appeal. He discerned another shift within the modern era near the end of the

eighteenth century, in the transition to the age of ideas, so that an ideological motive could be ascribed to every European war since 1792.[18]
From that point, too, the spread of the "revolutionary creed of
progress" within Europe and the subsequent expansion of the state-
system to include non-Western powers, combined to weaken whatever restraining force still attached to remnants of the medieval
natural-law tradition.[19]

Wight's international history is at times top-heavy with a kind of
philosophic idealism, although he could be as likely to consider, for
example, that the increasing economic and technological unification
of the world since about 1789 had blurred the distinction between
"international" and "civil" conflict.[20] It may be instructive here to
remember his assertion that the subject could not be understood "simply in terms of mechanics. . . . For men [sic] possess not only territories, raw materials and weapons, but also beliefs and opinions."[21] In
any case, the point is that his history does admit of fundamental
changes against mere repetition and recurrence. Wight could inquire
into ancient "state-systems"—Greek, Chinese, Indian—on the assumption of recurrence or of parallels between the present and particular
periods of the past; but the closer he looked the weaker those parallels
became. What gave them force at all was the tendency of participants
themselves to *think* that history was somehow repeating itself, to
interpret their own times through a more ancient prism. Thus, with a
modern state-system "coming to self-awareness at a time when the
models of antiquity were venerated," publicists for Hapsburg, English,
Dutch, and French causes alike could appropriate the slogan of the
Punic War—*Carthago delenda est*—in their favor; or, similarly in the
nineteenth century, the Victorian peace could be compared to the *pax
Romana.*[22]

Beyond the recognition of change, however, Wight hinted at a more
fundamental theological response to the problem of history. His second major essay in *Diplomatic Investigations* concluded with an
appeal to a moral sense that assumed that political life could be
secured "without accepting the doctrine that to preserve it any measures are permissible." The assumption, he added, lay again "within
the province of philosophy of history," and specifically, "belief in
Providence."[23] Wight did not elaborate. His circumspection on this
matter in later life may have been due to the rough reception which
talk of providence, or of divine judgment in history, received from fellow historians like Carr when Butterfield attempted it in the early

1950s. Nonetheless, the idea of providence—ultimately inscrutable, demanding trust rather than anxiety about the morrow, and not merely a liberal synonym for progress—was a consistent, undergirding element of his thought. It appeared in his early defense of pacifism,[24] and informed the eschatological turn in his writing (and preaching) in the decade after the war. In an address to an ecumenical church conference in Switzerland in 1948, and in a BBC radio talk the same year, for example, he reached back to the Augustinian distinctions between the eternal and the temporal, between the divine and earthly cities commingled on earth but separated at the final judgment—all this to challenge optimistic, but also despairing, attitudes toward the worsening East-West crisis. War may be inevitable, "humanly speaking," as the balance of power would prove an insufficient basis of peace. Still, he said, the "incalculable factor" of divine intervention could not be dismissed. While "secular history"—"our air-bubble in eternity," having no intrinsic meaning or inevitable direction—was shaped by human moral freedom, it was not autonomous of the ultimate purposes of an author located outside time. History was made "transparent against the light of eternity, the sum of all depths of destiny." And, in the immediate context, Wight proposed, "hope is a theological not a political virtue"—but by that he did not mean that there was nothing for which to hope.[25]

This dimension of Wight is not well-known or explored, and leaves some interpreters either uncomfortable or mystified. It is not the case as claimed that Wight's idea of providence should have led naturally to a passivity, on the grounds that "choices are not very important and politics is a charade."[26] Wight's commitments may well need sorting-out, but they amount to more than otherworldly disdain, and his theology was more than an eccentricity or one-half of a split personality. It is difficult, indeed, to make sense of Wight without understanding his absorption into the prevailing theological currents of a time when Christianity had regained briefly a respectability in British intellectual circles.

The character of that revival, spanning roughly the 1930s through 1950s, was one of sharp reaction against the accommodationist tendency of liberal Protestantism, with its banal expectation that the "kingdom of God" was being built on earth. The reaction comprised two main strands. One was the neo-orthodoxy emanating from the Continent, which borrowed from Kierkegaard's "either/or" existentialism and language of paradox.

The more important and peculiarly British strand emerged from the Anglo-Catholic movement within Anglicanism. By the 1930s, influenced by French neo-Thomism, it tended to be associated with a rather nostalgic medievalist critique of capitalism, and, in some cases, with a yearning for Christendom or what T. S. Eliot called the "idea of a Christian society" against liberal or "neo-pagan" corruptions. Intimations of this sort can be found in some of Wight's writings. But Anglo-Catholicism embodied a second, pluralist tendency, which stressed the provisional attachment of Christians to all temporal communities. These strands, buttressed in Britain by the influence of theologian Reinhold Niebuhr, made common cause in the 1930s in study groups, ecumenical conferences, and newsletters preoccupied with the problem of disengaging Christianity from an uncritical cultural Protestantism.

Wight was immersed in various ways in these theological debates. In a lengthy analysis on *The Observer's* editorial page before the World Council of Churches' 1948 founding assembly in Amsterdam, he anticipated a cleavage between delegates from the U.S. tending still to a "liberal optimistic" theology and those from the Continent, "who have outgrown all that in the past generation." The crucial point, he added, would be marking where the churches would abandon the conviction that a synthesis was possible with a "post-Christian" civilization.[27] In his Swiss speech several months earlier, reprinted in the first edition of the WCC-sponsored *Ecumenical Review*, he had already indicated something of his own answer as to where the line should be drawn:

> It is in the international sphere that the demonic concentrations of power of the modern neo-pagan world have their clearest expression. Russia and America are the last two Great Powers within the Westernized system of sovereign states. And the characteristic of that system, after centuries in which the Church has had no influence upon its development, is the emancipation of power from moral restraints.[28]

Wight described both remaining powers as apostasies, partitioning the globe in an "inverted and terrifying fulfillment" of the evangelical command. The "problems" that faced a "dissolving Christendom" were, in fact, judgments in the form of four "demonic perversions": war, which was no longer a "purposive and preservative activity"; the state; nationalism, a form of idolatry; and revolution. The ferocity of

Wight's critique of these related evils had scarcely an equal in the disillusioned corpus of inter-war idealism as the League of Nations unravelled in the late 1930s.[29]

This tendency to religious interpretation, full of eschatological intemperance, admittedly is difficult to relate to Wight's more conventional writing on international politics. The differences in language may reflect the different audiences for which Wight wrote. The eschatological language in any case receded from its peak about 1948, as did Wight's fear of war. It is worth remembering, nonetheless, that in his Swiss address as in *Power Politics* one of his stated purposes was to counter a pervasive despair. Here trust in providence conjoined with the study of history. Butterfield's *Christianity and History* (1949) had asserted that there was no "irretrievable disaster" set for this century, and that those who lived, for example, in fear of communist victory showed a distrust of providence and an ignorance of the record of human resilience.[30] There is a strong echo of this assurance near the start of Wight's LSE lectures:

> One of the main purposes of university education is to escape from the Zeitgeist, from the mean, narrow, provincial spirit which is constantly assuring us that we are the summit of human achievement, that we stand on the edge of unprecedented prosperity or *unparalleled catastrophe* . . . . It is a liberation of the spirit to acquire perspective, to recognize that every generation is confronted by problems of the utmost subjective urgency . . . .[31]

History, then, provided both a sense of perspective—not least of the temporality of all regimes—and a measure of detachment, or, perhaps, provisional attachment. Wight drew precisely on such a sense in the very public controversy that raged in 1954 over whether Toynbee's Reith Lectures, *The World and the West*, amounted to a betrayal of "Christian civilization." Wight vigorously defended his former mentor from conservative attacks. The biblical promise that the "gates of hell" shall not prevail against the church, he wrote, did not mean that "the Western world will win all its battles." To regard history from a non-European vantage point, as Toynbee had attempted, was to see the West less as privileged agent of providence and more as aggressor and exploiter.[32]

Wight's equation of history with freedom bears closer consideration as well. Whatever image of *deus ex machina* is invoked by the theological vocabulary of providence and judgment, time and eternity, those who used it most influentially for Wight—Niebuhr and Butterfield among them—did not therefore treat persons as automatons in a predetermined universe. Far from it. The position that Niebuhr developed in the 1940s affirmed that social relations belonged to the realm of human historical construction, which was marked by "endless possibilities" and a "limitless future," and that the capacity of memory "prevents the present reality from appearing as an event of pure natural necessity."[33] Wight essentially endorsed this position. To it he added that history was the "true science" of humanity, because it showed over and over how a free will could modify the course of events. Such voluntarism is striking, and not simply when set opposite the neorealist preference for structural explanations. Wight, who spent a term at the University of Chicago, was fully aware of the pitched battles being fought in American universities at the time over the so-called behavioral revolution. He even suggested that the attraction of the social sciences with their "inexorable laws" was further evidence of the reversion of a post-Christian civilization to cyclical and pre-Christian conceptions of human affairs.[34]

Wight's historical turn meant more than what he called "ransacking the past" for examples to buttress laws, maxims, and contemporary analyses. To do so was to "forget that the past, in its richness and indeterminacy, contains in equal measure clues to the conflicts that have not arisen and the *rapprochements* that will yet succeed."[35] What history did represent was a vast canvas on which irony, the play of chance, human wills, and particular circumstances were interwoven. What it offered was not off-the-shelf maxims but a sense of the essential unpredictability and the limits of instrumental political activity. Precisely for this reason, Wight suggested that diplomatic history was more faithful to the "record of international experience" and the working of the state-system, in all its contingency, than was the self-consciously theoretical literature inspired by social scientific method.[36] His framework did not, in his own terms, limit human autonomy so much as the modern alternatives.

ORDER AND JUSTICE

In June 1946, the *New Statesman and Nation* published a letter from Wight, describing Britain's acquiescence in the Indonesian annexation of the region of Sarawak as the "most repugnant form of imperialism." Wight's letter proposed that the last chance to prevent the annexation lay in the mobilization of *public opinion*—hardly the stuff of postwar realism. But he wondered whether it was already too late.[37]

Wight's intercession on behalf of Sarawak is perhaps insignificant in itself. Though consistent with the criticisms of Western colonialism expressed in his lectures at a time when the future of the empire was a British preoccupation, the letter was not part of any prolonged public campaign. It does serve, however, to raise further doubts about the commonplace associations of Wight with eschatological escapism, an incapacity for moral outrage, or a simple inside-outside dichotomy that left consideration of the "good life" strictly for "domestic politics."

There is instead considerable merit in Hedley Bull's description of Wight as "odd man out" in both history and international politics, concerned ultimately and unfashionably with ethical and theological questions.[38] The significance of this concern should not be understated. Working at a time when there was "no one in the intellectual mood to write about justice"[39]—silenced by a combination of epistemological inhibition and recent experience—Wight promoted an alternative view: that the traditional issues of political theory were played out increasingly at the international level. His assignation of matters of the "good life" to the "domestic" realm, in the essay cited above, may be puzzling in this regard. But, again, there is reason not to accept it as his final word on the subject. It is inconsistent, for example, with his long-held conviction about the erosion over the past two centuries of the distinction between "international" and "civil," or his common criticism of the claim he ascribed to American realists that morality was a creation of, thus largely internal to, particular nations. Wight's work overall could be said to constitute an extended inquiry into the nature of, and the relationship between, legitimacy, power and obligation, and, more elementally, between order and justice.

Not surprisingly that inquiry shaped the focus of the British Committee on the Theory of International Politics, which Butterfield acknowledged later was created and composed to satisfy Wight's interests, and of the volume *Diplomatic Investigations*, a distillation of papers read to it. Wight was an occasional observer at sessions of the short-lived U.S. committee, also funded by the Rockefeller Foundation, which in keeping with the times had segmented "normative" from more rigorous sorts of theory. The introduction to

Diplomatic Investigations noted modestly that the "connoisseur of national styles" might discern the contrasts between it and the parallel American volume. The British Committee, it proposed, was concerned not so much with the scientific, the methodological, and the contemporary, than with the historical, the philosophical, and the ethical; committee members were unable to "forget that foreign affairs and international relations . . . are in themselves not a closed theoretical system."[40]

Having opened an important discursive space for ethics, resisting the marginalization of the normative, Wight proved a rather cautious moralist. Put another way, his treatment of the ethical problem was, in itself, a construction of politics which began with the possibility— even necessity—of violence, and then held its particular usages up to scrutiny. The claim for Wight's realism is perhaps strongest here, though again the peculiarities of his position bear closer scrutiny.

Wight's formulation of the tension between order and justice owed a great deal to Niebuhr, a disaffected member of the U.S. committee. The main preoccupation of Niebuhr's social ethics during the 1940s and 1950s was the relationship of *love* (the final norm of human relations, but paradoxically the "impossible possibility") to *justice* (the "approximation of brotherhood under conditions of sin"). The latter category was more immediate to politics. While love was harder to relate to social as opposed to individual life, its pull of a higher ideal was necessary lest the provisional structures of justice degenerate into mere order. Niebuhr nonetheless made *order* the third regulating principle in his moral schema. Without an "organizing centre" of power, a government prepared even to use force, relative justice was impossible; yet, order without justice could not endure for long.[41]

It was this tension that Wight found so glaringly absent from Carr and sometimes Butterfield. He described Carr's *Twenty Years' Crisis*, on its reissue in 1946, as "a brilliant, provocative and unsatisfying book," "the one lasting intellectual monument of the policy of appeasement," and not to be read without Leonard Woolf's "deadly reply" in *The War for Peace*.[42] Some years later Wight claimed that Carr had "no views on the irreducible values of our civilization," and that his writing was bereft of the moral resources required to resist evil of the magnitude of Hitler's fascism.[43] As for Butterfield's *Christianity, Diplomacy and War*, a criticism of American moralism in the Cold War, Wight observed that it blurred rather than refined the tension. The history of appeasement had shown how easy it was to forget the victims and the international community as a whole, while seeking to avoid self-righteousness in treating a tyrant or aggressor.[44]

Wight never made clear precisely what he understood by justice or even order. Still less did he attempt any rigorous defense against the epistemological objections to any talk of justice. His justice did not rest on universalist, rationalist foundations, though it intersected with the natural-law tradition that had seemed to him in *Power Politics* a diminishing restraint on European statecraft, but later a source of what he proposed as a rather broad *via media* in political life. The natural law *tradition*, in any case, was an historical artifact belonging to the West—why else should it have mattered to its vitality that the international community was expanded beyond Europe?—and not an immutable or abstract doctrine. Its residue was a certain temper that embodied a sense of the ethical significance of all political action and, once again, a denial of the finality of human institutions (and, for that matter, public opinion). This ethical temper could embolden political leaders to break from traditional thinking as much as it could prompt individuals to dissent from their own government. And it focused attention at that point of tension between what seemed expedient and what was permissible morally, in the way that the just war doctrine put limits around claims of military necessity. Political morality could not be grounded in the Sermon on the Mount; it differed from personal morality "as the moral duties of a trustee are different from those of one who acts on his own behalf." But there could be no complete break in the name of *raison d'etat*. Wight's ethic "upheld the validity of the ethical in the realm of politics." Its "characteristic fruit" was "not so much the dramatic moral veto on political action (though this is always held, as it were, in reserve), as the discovery of an alternative positive policy"—that is, a middle course marked by magnanimity, restraint, and the attainment of greater justice.[45]

INTERNATIONAL THEORY AS DIALOGUE

The commitment to theory in dialogical form arguably is the most definitive, if neglected, feature of Wight's multi-sided orientation. If international theory was, in the end, rumination about human destiny, the alternatives ranged between Kant's teleology of perpetual peace and de Maistre's humanity drowned in blood on the altar of the earth until the end of time. If its ethical core, here and now, was the tension of order and justice, then practical political judgment remained the stuff of argument; it was impoverished when voices on either side succumbed too quickly. And if, contrary to the expectations of social scientists, international politics was not a closed system which yielded knowledge of a cumulative or falsifiable variety, theory was to be found elsewhere in the ongoing conversation among distinct but interwoven traditions of thought.

In each case, as in the framing of any dialogue, Wight's terms served to exclude as much as they appear to broaden. The triadic architecture of his lectures, in particular, drew its categories so tightly in places that they squeezed out persons or movements that caught his interest but fell outside a realist-rationalist-revolutionist matrix. In other places, the contrasts were contrived and anachronistic in their insistence that each "tradition" have a paradigmatic position on each subject. Wight himself expressed similar dissatisfactions near the end of the lectures. There he clarified that his traditions should not be understood as "railroad tracks running parallel into infinity" but, rather, as "streams, with eddies and cross-currents, sometimes interlacing and never for long confined to their own river bed."[46] At best, their interplay is a reciprocal interrogation rooted in a phenomenology of historically constructed positions.

In the dialogue envisioned by Wight, the realist tradition was denied a commanding position and its language of power was historicized. *Power Politics* (1946 and revised editions) gave greatest attention to the practices, images, and language associated with classical realism. But Wight's explorations in *Systems of States* and *Diplomatic Investigations* illustrated that remnants of older traditions—juridical and cosmopolitan—had not been eclipsed. Reformulations of those traditions continued to contend with power-political perspectives, not only within his soul and his texts, but more important in ways that helped modify practice. His analysis of the immense historical changes in the principles of what he called international legitimacy, especially that from dynastic to popular sovereignty,[47] is suggestive of his overall outlook, and, it may be proposed, an instance of "the idea of mankind as a great society whose majority vote can override individual nations."[48]

Wight resorted to dialogical form already during the war to convey something of his own struggles between pacifist and just-war strands of Christianity.[49] He did so again after the war to sketch the ideological complexion of twentieth-century international politics. Writing in Toynbee's multi-volume survey of World War II, he chose to depict

the world in March 1939 partly as a dialogue—a dialogue of the deaf
to be sure—involving the Western Powers, the Axis Powers, and the
Soviet Union.[50] The exercise now seems stilted. The point, nonetheless, was to illustrate something of the gulf that divided the belligerents not only in their "interests" but in the categories by which they
conceived the situation and articulated their respective positions.
Neither war nor international politics generally, to repeat, could be
understood in terms of mere mechanics, that is, apart from actors'
words and the meanings they attached to their actions.

The reader can find, say, in *Power Politics*, passages that correspond to the recurrent, bloodless, Risk-game image of international
politics as a mere succession of hegemonies. Thus:

> The most conspicuous theme in international history . . . is the series
> of efforts, by one power after another, to gain mastery of the states-sys-
> tem—efforts that have been defeated only by a coalition of the majority
> of other powers at the cost of an exhausting general war.[51]

But that sort of sweeping assertion, typically, is qualified in ways that
draw attention back to the language of political conflict. For "a dominant power must be described by purpose as well as by power," that
is, by an appeal—ecclesiastical, ideological, racial—"to some design
of international unity and solidarity." The coalitions which oppose it
likewise resort to speech, to principles: "the liberties of Europe," "the
freedom of the seas," "independence."[52]

In this important sense, Wight's writings amount to more than the
naive empiricism sometimes attributed to them. They suffer, if anything, the fate of Thucydides' *Peloponnesian War*, which in international relations circles tends to be read—or, more likely, taken on
faith—as a description of that recurrent interplay of powers to which
structural realism has now given theoretical rigor. What is neglected,
alongside Thucydides' tragic sensibility, is his preoccupation with
how the war begins and takes its course through the practice of persuasion, until eventually "words lose their meaning" amid the collapse of the institutions and civic commitments that sustained the
ancient Greek "culture of argument."[53] There is likewise a
Thucydidean purpose in Wight's reconstructed interrogations,
whether between liberal democrats, fascists, and Soviet communists
in 1939, or between realists, rationalists, and revolutionists throughout the career of the modern state-system. That purpose is to present

international politics not as the realm of repetition and recurrence, but as the realm of persuasion.[54] Whatever the limits of Wight's own work, the idea of theory as dialogue is open to other interlocutors.[55]

BEYOND POWER POLITICS

The Wight that emerges from the above reading is most amenable to the linguistic turn proposed in this volume, and beyond it to the reacquaintance (acquaintance?) of international politics with the history of ideas, and to the recent revival of interdisciplinary "grand theory" in an interpretive rather than a positivistic mode. His texts provide important foundations for inquiry that proceeds beneath those banners. (In how many other studies of international relations will the reader encounter, alongside Machiavelli, figures such as Pufendorf, Wolff, Gentili, Bolingbroke, for example, or the ideas undergirding the fifteenth-century conciliar movement?) Wight's project, *pace* one of his critics,[56] was precisely not to build a fence around international politics as a discrete, self-contained academic subject. That was the objective, conversely, of those in the U.S. such as Frederick Dunn at Yale and William Fox at Columbia who aspired to disciplinary autonomy and the scientific legitimacy of economics within a circumscribed field of expertise.[57] Given that this orientation essentially triumphed for a generation, at least, it is not surprising that Wight should more often be engaged sympathetically in North America by those self-consciously outside the mainstream of the discipline than by those inside it.[58]

The theological coloration of Wight's formulation of international politics will, of course, be even more inaccessible to many potential readers than what appears as his "classical realism." That coloration might best be understood as a means of dissenting from modernity, and of denying the primacy of the political. The risk of presenting him in such terms at all is that the sense of inaccessibility will be heightened inordinately; but that risk must be set opposite the concern to indicate something of the range and connectedness of his commitments in a context marked by an almost overwhelming sense of uncertainty and crisis. Wight's juxtaposition of time and eternity, for example, may signify yet another mystifying dualism requiring deconstruction, but it was not incompatible with an affirmation of considerable human autonomy and historical indeterminacy in his subsequent writing; if anything, it was the source of that position. The terms that surround his profound suspicion of the twentieth-century state and of the technological impulse that culminates in nuclear weaponry—terms such as idolatry—may again sometimes be too infused with theological assumptions to be appropriable widely. But the critical potential in Wight's conception of international politics is genuine nonetheless, not least in regard to current versions of realism whose historicity comes complete with its own cold, rationalistic world-weariness about "how the world is." Wight's pessimism, by contrast, scarcely merits the name; and his "Olympian detachment" (Bull's phrase) is less obvious than at first glance. For if Wight was not, after the mid-1950s, a prolific writer, he conceived teaching in itself as a form of critical engagement with his own times. As he wrote upon his move to the University of Sussex: "If half of a liberal education in the twentieth century is to gain an understanding of the world we live in, the other half consists in *breaking its influence*, and finding deliverance from the tyranny of the immediate, the novel, and the transitory."[59]

Wight's insistent elevation of the ethical question when it was so out of season in international politics, in both the university and the foreign policy establishment entrusted with waging the Cold War against a threat so great, so iniquitous, as to suspend moral qualms, should not be overlooked in this respect. His study of international politics, in effect, was bound up with the personal and political question of how to live in an era when war and the threat of war pressed so demandingly on human relations. A generation later, moral argument still infuses the definitive issues of international politics: nuclear rivalry, humanitarian intervention, North-South disparity, environmental conservation, and so on. Wight's formulation of the ethical question as a tension of order and justice is neither the only one nor is it free of difficulties. We may want to ask whether this tension, too, should be historicized and delimited to the (passing?) epoch of power politics and the fragmentation of the state-system, or whether justice itself, to follow Alasdair MacIntyre, may have different meanings embedded in different traditions of thought.[60] That said, Wight's formulation does more than capture the conventional poles of argument and the political ambiguity surrounding contemporary conflicts. It requires an account from moralists and partisans of stability alike. It preserves sites of ethical judgment outside of the state and the category of national interest.

Finally, by casting international politics as the realm of persuasion involving a plurality of discourses, and by denying any strict division between participant and academic observer, Wight offers a way out of the totalizing claims of scientific realism to understand its subject. He historicizes its language. He challenges its assumption that there is nothing more for which to hope than a recurrent order on the brink of disorder. And he invites readers to consider the possibilities of languages other than, or beyond, that of power politics that can break its influence and describe alternative futures which are free nonetheless of false expectations.

NOTES

1. Martin Wight, *Power Politics*, Looking Forward Pamphlet no. 8 (London: Royal Institute of International Affairs, 1946), 66. All references are to Wight except where otherwise noted.
2. *International Theory: The Three Traditions*, eds. Gabriele Wight and Brian Porter (Leicester: Leicester University Press, 1991), 15. This text represents Wight's lectures at the London School of Economics in the 1950s.
3. Georg Schwarzenberger, Preface to *Power Politics*, 2d ed. (London: Stevens & Son, 1951). Extracts from Wight's essay of the same name can be found in several of the anthologies assembled in support of the teaching of international politics in American universities in the postwar era.
4. "Why is There no International Theory?" in *Diplomatic Investigations*, eds. Herbert Butterfield and Martin Wight (London: George Allen and Unwin, 1966), 26, 33.
5. Michael Nicholson, "The Enigma of Martin Wight," *Review of International Studies* 7 (1981): 21. Among the "friendly" characterizations of Wight as pessimist, see Hedley Bull, "Martin Wight and the Theory of International Relations," *British Journal of International Studies* 2 (1976): 101-16; and Brian Porter, "Patterns of Thought and Practice: Martin Wight's 'International Theory,'" in *The Reason of States*, ed. Michael Donelan (London: George Allen and Unwin, 1978).
6. Richard Ashley, "The Poverty of Neo-Realism," *International Organization* 38 (1984): 225-86.
7. "An Anatomy of International Thought" [1960], *Review of International Studies* 13 (1987): 227. The likeliest objection to treating Wight as a realist can be anticipated from those who consider him a Grotian, after the seventeenth-century Dutch jurist, or a rationalist. While such a claim is certainly defensible, it might be debated whether the two alternatives are subsumed under what in British circles is denoted as the classical tradition, with its focus on inter-state relations. More important, it might be asked whether Wight's influence in defining the field according to three (now reified) "traditions" has lent realism, fixed on

one side, an air of permanence and an inordinate role in setting the questions.

8. See, e.g, "Why is There no International Theory?" 33.

9. Robert H. Jackson, "Martin Wight, International Theory, and the Good Life," *Millennium* 19 (1990): 261-72.

10. R. B. J. Walker, "Security, Sovereignty and the Challenge of World Politics," *Alternatives* 15 (1990): 11. Walker gives Wight a perceptive, critical reading in *Inside/Outside: International Relations as Political Theory* (Cambridge: Cambridge University Press, 1993), chap. 2. I have chosen, however, to quote Walker on Machiavelli, to read Wight as a "source of critical opportunity," not as legitimation of closure or reification (31).

11. See Hans Morgenthau, "The Intellectual and Political Functions of a Theory of International Relations" [1961], reprinted in *Politics in the Twentieth Century*, vol. 1 (Chicago: University of Chicago Press, 1962), 62-78. But Morgenthau, in a review of *Diplomatic Investigations*, also advised that the insights found in Wight's two major essays alone should be set "against the theoretical propositions of any number of volumes on behaviorism, systems analysis, game theory, decision-making, and so forth." *Political Science Quarterly* 82 (1967): 462.

12. "Why is There no International Theory?" 20, 26, 33.

13. "Brutus in Foreign Policy: The Memoirs of Sir Anthony Eden," *International Affairs* 36 (1960): 302.

14. Kenneth Waltz, *Theory of International Politics* (New York: Random House, 1979), 66: "The texture of international politics remains highly constant, patterns recur and events repeat themselves endlessly."

15. *Power Politics*, 7-11, passim.

16. Ibid., 45.

17. *Systems of States,* Hedley Bull, ed. (Leicester: Leicester University Press, 1977), chap. 5.

18. "War and International Politics" (BBC Third Programme), *The Listener*, 54 (13 October 1955): 585.

19. *Power Politics*, 62.

20. Ibid., 32. Wight's claim here is reminiscent of the analysis of Bismarck's intervention in the French civil war made by Karl Marx, who is hardly vulnerable to the charge of idealism. But Wight doubtless did tend in the opposite direction, if short of the "extreme" doctrine, which he ascribed to Collingwood, that "the historian's job is nothing but the reenactment of past thought." See "What Makes A Good Historian?" (BBC Third Programme), *The Listener* 53 (17 February 1955): 283; and also his review of *The Idea of History,* by R. G. Collingwood, *International Affairs* 23 (1947): 575-77.

21. *Power Politics*, eds. Hedley Bull and Carsten Holbraad (Harmondsworth: Penguin/Royal Institute of International Affairs, 1978), 81.

22. *Systems of States*, 183, 192. See also chaps. 2-3.
23. "Western Values in International Relations," in *Diplomatic Investigations*, 130-31.
24. "Christian Pacifism," *Theology* 33 (July 1936): 31.
25. "Russia, the Church and the West," *Ecumenical Review* 1 (autumn 1948): 25-45. Wight was a member of the editorial board of the *Review* from its founding until 1955. For a fuller treatment, see my "The 'Augustinian Moment' in International Politics: Niebuhr, Butterfield, Wight and the Reclaiming of a Tradition," *International Politics Research Papers* No. 10 (Aberystwyth, UK: Department of International Politics, University College of Wales, 1991).
26. Nicholson, "The Enigma of Martin Wight," 22.
27. "The World Churches," *The Observer*, 22 August 1948, 4. See also his favorable review of *Christianity and Civilization* by Emil Brunner, "Reason and Revelation," *The Observer*, 17 October 1948, 3.
28. "Russia, the Church and the West," 30.
29. Ibid., passim, 28, 41, 43. Wight's 1940 application for status as a conscientious objector, likewise, called the war "the convulsion of a civilization that has forsaken its Christian origins," and a "divine judgment" for a "corporate Sin" independent of country or religion. Quoted in Hedley Bull's introduction to *Systems of States*, 4.
30. Herbert Butterfield, *Christianity and History* (London: G. Bell & Sons, 1949), 29, 105. See too Wight's review, "History's Theme," *The Observer*, 23 October 1949, 7; and, "History and Judgement: Butterfield, Niebuhr & the Technical Historian," *The Frontier* 1 (August 1950): 301-14.
31. *International Theory*, 6.
32. "Written in Anger," review of *The Lie About the West*, by Douglas Jerrold, *The Observer*, 18 April 1954, 7; and the similar review in *International Affairs* 30 (1954): 352-53. Wight also contributed twice to the heated debate that continued in the letters column of the *Times Literary Supplement* from April through June 1954.
33. Reinhold Niebuhr, *The Nature and Destiny of Man*, vol. 2, *Human Destiny* (New York: Charles Scribner's Sons, 1943), 123, 155; *Faith and History* (New York: Charles Scribner's Sons, 1949), 19.
34. "History and Judgement," 306-7.
35. See, e.g., the review of *Politics and Culture in International History*, by Adda Bozeman, *International Affairs* 38 (1962): 228-29. His suspicion of Toynbee's grand narrative might also be noted here.
36. "Why is There no International Theory?" 32. Similar themes can be found in "History's Theme," 7, and "Tract for the Nuclear Age," review of *Peace and War*, by Raymond Aron, *The Observer*, 23 April 1967, 30. See, also, his description of history as imagination, architecture, and reflection upon the culture within which it is written, in "What Makes a Good Historian?" 283-84.

37. "Sarawak," *The New Statesman and Nation* 31 (8 June 1946): 413-14.
38. Bull, introduction to *Systems of States*, 14-15.
39. Judith Shklar, *After Utopia: The Decline of Political Faith* (Princeton: Princeton University Press, 1957), ix.
40. "Introduction to Diplomatic Investigations," 12-13. Cf. William T. R. Fox, ed., *Theoretical Aspects of International Relations* (Notre Dame: University of Notre Dame Press, 1959).
41. Niebuhr, *The Nature and Destiny of Man*, vol. 2, esp. 246-58. Niebuhr applied these ideas to postwar international politics in *Discerning the Signs of the Times* (New York: Charles Scribner's Sons, 1946). See Wight's enthusiastic review in *International Affairs* 23 (1947): 558-59.
42. "The Realist's Utopia," review of *The Twenty Years' Crisis*, by E. H. Carr, *The Observer*, 21 July 1946, 3.
43. "Problems of Mass Democracy," review of *The New Society*, by E. H. Carr, *The Observer*, 23 September 1951, 7. See also the remarks on Carr in *International Theory*, 16-17. That Carr was not part of the British committee is not surprising in light of Wight's views.
44. "Morals and Warfare," review of Christianity, *Diplomacy and War*, by Herbert Butterfield, *The Observer*, 16 August 1953, 7. In a preface to the second edition, written shortly after Wight's review appeared, Butterfield pointedly denied that the exercise of charity implied any blurring of moral standards or a denial of evil (London: Epworth Press, 1953), viii.
45. "Western Values," 123-24. Wight's own pacifism, in a sense, was such a veto, but he did not present it as a political option. His *Power Politics* made the argument that morality, and especially Anglo-American moralism, could not be disentangled from considerations of power and security. Already during the war, he had accepted that force could be an instrument of justice; but he had also invoked for himself the notion of "vocational pacifism," a distinction of medieval monastic origin which accepted that not all Christians could, or ought to, live by the Gospel's counsels of perfection. See "War and the Christian Conscience," *Haileyburian*, c. 1940-41 (copy in possession of the author). Strong echoes of the same position can be found in his later essay on Western values. Here, while pacifism or any individual's defiance of the state on the basis of some higher loyalty was a conscientious objection to the political, even for the good of that realm, the Campaign for Nuclear Disarmament's anti-nuclear campaign was rather an "ill-considered alternative within the realm of the political, . . . one of the heads of the many-headed beast" (122). The renunciation of force ought to be the renunciation of politics.

Wight's late apocalyptic (and, notice, anti-statist) flourish may again leave a misleading impression with regard to his own position on nuclear weapons. He was, if anything, strikingly silent on the matter. Certainly he did not match Butterfield's call for unilateral nuclear disarmament by the end of the 1950s, which he once honored with the ambiguous adjective, "sentimental." But Wight, who had interpreted the atomic bomb as the definitive symbol of human pride, did set out a critical position early in the nuclear age. He saved his most stinging comments for church statements that showed excessive caution or inconsistency in applying just war principles. In one case he accused the authors of censuring, in hindsight, obliteration bombing and the destruction of Hiroshima and Nagasaki, while morally permitting not only "the manufacture of the atomic bomb as a powerful deterrent, which all history shows to be nonsense," but also its potential use in retaliation. At the very least, he did not want the churches giving sanction to nuclear weapons. See Wight's review of *The Church and the Atom: A Study of the Moral and Theological Aspects of Peace and War*, report of a commission of the Archbishops of Canterbury and York, *International Affairs* 25 (1949) 74; also, e.g., his review of both *The Era of Atomic Power*, report of a commission of the British Council of Churches, and a Quaker reply, *International Affairs* 23 (1947): 568-69.

46. *International Theory*, 266. See my review in *International Journal* 48 (1993): 561-66.

47. *Systems of States*, chap. 6. Wight's interest in international legitimacy might well have been prompted partly by a concern to counter his LSE colleague Charles Manning's argument for non-interference in South Africa's "internal affairs" on the basis of traditional doctrines said to undergird international society. I have seen no concrete evidence, however, to support this conjecture.

48. "An Anatomy of International Thought," 226.

49. "War and the Christian Conscience" (see note 45 above).

50. "The Balance of Power," in Arnold Toynbee, ed., *The World in March 1939* (London: Oxford University Press/Royal Institute of International Affairs, 1952), 508-31.

51. *Power Politics*, rev. ed., 30.

52. Ibid., 36-37.

53. James Boyd White, *When Words Lose their Meaning* (Chicago: University of Chicago Press, 1984), chap. 3.

54. Stanley Hoffmann, rather similarly, once described international politics as becoming an "arena of persuasion, more or less coercive," and as "a contest of active perceptions competing for the privilege of defining reality." Quoted in Ralph Pettman, *International Politics* (Melbourne: Longman, 1991), 153. Hoffmann, however, has not made the idea a determining feature of his work.

55. See, e.g., James N. Rosenau, *Global Voices: Dialogues in International Relations* (Boulder, Colo.: Westview Press, 1993).

56. Roy Jones, "The English School of International Relations: The Case for Closure," *Review of International Studies* 7 (1981): 1-13.

57. See, e.g., Dunn's proposed delimitation of the discipline in "The Scope of International Relations," *World Politics* 1 (1948): 144. Cf. Wight's reluctance to grant that the study of international politics was a legitimate branch of academic specialization. "Tract for the Nuclear Age," 30.

58. See, in addition to Ashley, "The Poverty of Neorealism," James der Derian, *On Diplomacy: A Genealogy of Western Estrangement* (Oxford: Basil Blackwell, 1987), especially at 3-5, 32-33, 46.

59. "European Studies," in David Daiches, ed., *The Idea of a New University* (London: Andre Deutsch, 1964), 105 (my emphasis).

60. Alasdair MacIntyre, *Whose Justice? Which Rationality?* (Notre Dame: University of Notre Dame Press, 1988). The question about the historicity of Wight's formulation corresponds to Andrew Linklater's moral tension between the obligations of citizenship and humanity as fundamental to the experience of the modern state-system. See "Men and Citizens in International Relations," *Review of International Studies* 7 (1981): 23-37.

G. THOMAS GOODNIGHT

HANS J. MORGENTHAU *IN DEFENSE* OF THE *NATIONAL INTEREST*

ON RHETORIC, REALISM, AND THE PUBLIC SPHERE

The dramatic ending of the Second World War—the obliteration of Hiroshima and Nagasaki, the revelation of the holocaust, the establishment of the United Nations, and the transformation of the Soviet Union from wartime ally to global competitor—challenged prevailing precepts and practices of international relations. Abjuring the traditional language of diplomacy, elite and public policy discourses of the 1940s were spoken within the horizons of global necessities and apocalyptic fears. A Soviet atomic test in 1949 yet again disrupted the contexts of international relations. "In truth, the first atomic explosion on Russian soil has shattered American foreign policy as it has evolved since 1945," Hans Morganthau wrote. "Now we need a new foreign policy, based on a new balance of power."[1]

This essay is a critical reconstruction of Hans J. Morgenthau's *In Defense of the National Interest* as an argument that draws upon the strategic resources of the rhetorical tradition to craft a moderating discourse for negotiating the exigencies of the nuclear age. At one level, the rhetorical quality of his work is easily enough described. *In Defense of the National Interest* deploys arguments of praise and blame to fashion an indictment of the Truman administration and a defense of the traditional arts of diplomacy. The book is more than a period polemic, however. Like other important discourses that have significantly reshaped and animated public discussion in the United States— Michael Harrington's *The Other America*, Rachel Carson's *The Silent Spring*, Upton Sinclair's *The Jungle*, Harriet Beecher Stowe's *Uncle Tom's Cabin*—Morgenthau spoke to the issues of the day in such a way as to critique, alter, and expand significantly the terms and concomitant grounds upon which policies are formed and justified publicly.[2] Robert Osgood noted the effectiveness of this strategy when he observed that while "Morgenthau's message was shocking to the orthodox formulators and justifiers of American foreign policy" of the day, his views "on the imperatives of security and the balance of power became so much a part of orthodoxy as to cease to be controversial."[3] How did he do it? And, of what enduring significance is his achievement?

Morgenthau, along with other realists writing in the 1950s, has been credited with "rhetorical brilliance" in articulating a position that "swept the field in the United States," but thus far scholars have either extended or critiqued his work only as philosophical doctrine or social scientific theory.[4] Analysts agree that Morgenthau deftly deployed the resources of realism to contest alternative views of foreign policy in the post-war era. The connections between realism and strands of strategic argument well-known within the rhetorical tradition, however, have remained unexamined. It is my contention that some of Morgenthau's more significant contributions, the relevance of his work to present policy discussion, and the general strengths and limits of realism as an orientation of international relations can be extended productively by reconstructive criticism that examines the work from the perspective of a rhetoric that recuperates the public sphere.[5]

The rhetorical tradition itself is an unsteady, successive constellation of controversies, stemming from the debates of the Greek Enlightenment in the fourth century B.C.E. At its beginning are the practices of speech in the *agora*, the contests for adherence producing *dissoi-logoi*, truths in opposition, that could be settled only in public debate. These contested practices of civic life were taken up into the philosophical discussions of the Greek Enlightenment. Thus, what were debates of the classical public sphere among politicians and statesmen became refigured, abstracted, and passed on in the West as controversies among philosophers and advisors over the relationships of theory and practice, choice and conduct, persuasion and judgment, force and influence.

In contemporary discussions, realism is rarely read from the standpoint of the rhetorical tradition. Realism is usually contrasted with idealism and said to be a distinct theoretical or philosophical orientation.[6] As Paul Seabury notes:

> In philosophy, realism and idealism are opposite modes of viewing the nature of things. Realism is a tendency to regard things as they actually are and to accept them as such. Idealism is a habit of idealizing, a tendency to represent things in ideal form or to aspire toward such ideal form as things might take.

In the theory and practice of American foreign policy, these two philosophical concepts take on unique, concrete form. They refer to opposite modes of *perceiving* the nature of, and the possibilities in, the international system or society of nations. They also refer to opposite controlling *principles* of foreign policy.[7]

Seabury is correct to a point. The language of realism does constitute a framework of identification and provide a basis for loose theoretical alignment; however, it should not be overlooked that realism is also, and perhaps more fundamentally, a form of engaging argument. Thus, realists may be identified not so much by consistent philosophical principles as by characteristic inventional strategies that oppose all orientations, theoretical and otherwise, that would read history, interpret action, measure choice, or advise policy from a position outside the political realm.

Constructions of the public sphere vary a good deal among realists, too; but, preeminent within the tradition is the Aristotelian notion that civic deliberation resides at the conjunction of politics, ethics, and prudential judgment. This synthesis is reoccupied and renewed from time to time by rhetors who grapple with contemporary contexts, alternative orientations, and the complicated legacy of realism itself. Thus, as a form of argument, realism characteristically: (1) secures its modes of persuasion in (re)reading historical events as paradigms of conduct and action that contextualize present choice, (2) draws upon distinctive strategies to critique alternative grounds and practices of discursive production, and (3) explains and indicts poor policy as a departure from, or distortion of, norms grounded in history and imminent in the discourse practices of the public sphere. Insofar as *In Defense of the National Interest* strives to both renew realism as an alternative foreign policy discourse and assail prevailing public policy, it offers an opportunity to read the rhetorical reinvention of this tradition at work.[8]

There are two obstacles confronting such a reconstruction. While Morgenthau, in other works, explicitly defended the humanistic tradition, there is little evidence to show that he drew directly from rhetorical theory.[9] Yet, my argument is not that Morgenthau deployed technique to effect persuasion, but that his arguments revitalized a cultural space, the classical political realm, in the interest of coming to terms with a world altered radically by the nuclear age. Thus, his arguments work in a manner Blumenberg suggests when he writes that "after the great conception of each epochal project, the historical process produces its 'reoccupations' as restorations of its continuity."[10]

Even were it possible to show that Morgenthau's argument develops along rhetorical lines that recuperate the public sphere, the objection may be lodged that his rhetoric was part of a different time. The events and the rhetoric of the Cold War may be said to have run their course. But, just as Morgenthau critically re-read key arguments from influential paradigms of the past to speak to present contexts, so we are invited to revisit *In Defense of the National Interest* to examine its principles in light of yet another uncertain epochal shift—the post-Cold War world. In the end, I will argue that Morgenthau's work, read as an exemplar of realist argument, offers what foreign policy scholar Richard Ashley requested: "a model that would preserve classical realism's rich insights into international political practice while at the same time exposing the conditions, limits and potential for change of the tradition in which classical realism is immersed."[11]

The essay proceeds to explicate *In Defense of the National Interest* as Morgenthau (1) moved to recover exemplars of effective practice, (2) defined the present contexts of choice, and (3) weighed competing orientations seeking to encumber the future.

THE PAST: PARADIGMS OF DELIBERATION

As a rhetorical theory of the public sphere, realism traces its classical roots to Aristotle's *Rhetoric*.[12] Aristotle saw public policy as the product of deliberative rhetoric. Foreign policy encompasses topics that require knowledge of the history of foreign affairs and the capacities of self-defense.[13] Public discussion of such topics takes place within the realm of contingent knowledge, where appearances are uncertain, and common choice is to be guided by proofs from probabilities that support alternatives for action.[14] In deliberation, questions of expedience render subordinate questions of justice, although justice itself often figures into practical political questions. The aim of rhetoric is to give effective voice to the truth, and sound rhetorical argument will be more successful than sham counterparts in the long run because argumentation cultivates common judgment, a form of prudential reasoning based upon the evaluation of means and ends in the service of the extended interests of the *polis*.[15] Rhetorical argument, within the Aristotelian tradition, is the art of situated public reasoning. While distinct from scientific proof and dialectical exchange, nonetheless it is theoretically informed in the particular case and occupies a unique juncture at the convergence of politics and ethics.

In Defense of the National Interest begins to reinstitute the possibility of political deliberation by the recovery of a paradigmatic moment of efficacious public argument: Alexander Hamilton's expression of prudent restraint in the face of popular moral pressures to support the revolution in France. According to Morgenthau, Hamilton distilled a complex political question to its essentials: Should the United States intervene on behalf of the revolution? The criteria for deliberation are as plain as they are compelling:

I. Whether the cause of France be truly the cause of Liberty, pursued with justice and humanity, and in a manner likely to crown it with honorable success.

II. Whether the degree of service we could render, by participating in the conflict, was likely to compensate, by its utility to the cause, the evils which would probably flow from it to ourselves.[16]

From this example, the basic precepts of prudent choice are derived: Is the cause really one that we identify with? Is our intervention likely to meet with success? Does the good done compensate for the evils suffered to *us*?

The recovery of a historical paradigm of public discourse creates a place from which a citizen can assess departures from prudent deliberation, thereby setting the context for explanation of failed policy. Morgenthau identifies faulty interpretations of the Monroe Doctrine, for example, as certifying American isolationism rather than as affirming a traditional resolution of issues based upon the principles of sound reasoning. He further indicts John Adams and the notion of "manifest destiny" as conflating practical necessity and moral purpose, thereby supplanting the classical reasoning of the founding period with the use of words as ideological counters. The point of his critique is not the indictment of nineteenth-century American foreign policy. Rather, he hopes to show by way of critical analysis that even when foreign relations meet with success, a legacy of imprudent decision making may result if policies are pursued within a moral rather than a realistic framework.

Sharp shafts are aimed at Wilsonian policy. Whatever the distortions of an age of ideology, the idealizations of Woodrow Wilson demonstrate how policy can become flawed fatally when the right policy is justified by the wrong reasons. Trapped by his own moralizing, Wilson chose to wield American influence not to restore "a new, viable balance of power, but to put an end to the balance of power once and forever."[17] Wilson's utopian ideals induced him to ask for too much change and made him blind to the debilitating consequences of his own inflexibility; thus, the president "returned from Versailles a compromised idealist, an empty-handed statesman, a discredited ally," in short the apotheosis of diplomatic failure.[18] The lesson to be learned is not the personal failure of Wilson, a great but misguided president, but of Wilsonianism as a political doctrine that leaves "moral principles divorced from reality."[19]

The story of Wilson's tragedy stands as a synecdoche for the failure of American foreign policy in the twentieth century. Military might can win wars, but applied to wrong ends, that is constructed within a moral universe of absolutes rather than a rhetorical universe of contingencies, it will fail to win the peace. The distortions of practice are lodged squarely in a "moral" tradition that expresses dissatisfaction with the possible, followed by a failure to grasp the necessary.

THE PRESENT: THE NECESSITIES OF ACTION

The task of recuperating the public sphere requires reconnection with past moments of successful political enactment, and an appraisal of the consequences for departure from the precepts guiding successful policy. Although such argument supplies models for practice, it is incomplete without a formulation of the present that names the situated contexts that invite address. In ordinary times, rhetorical analysis is typically undertaken within the parameters of well-known constraints formed by consensus and division along standing political lines. A political present is delimited by a continuous weaving of the relevant past and the foreseeable future into the situated, urgent policy of an era. In such a context, the art of rhetoric may be reduced to little more than persuasive technique. Occasionally, however, a rhetoric is invented that depicts the present as a radical departure from the past and articulates social and material changes against a reconstituted future horizon. Such a discourse challenges existing practice and presages new alternatives.

In Defense of the National Interest is spun from the uncertain policy choices of the late 1940s; therefore special attention should be accorded to the strategy of naming "the three revolutions of our age" that have caused a break "with the traditions . . . of the West for at least four hundred years."[20] Together these "revolutions" logically deny but rhetorically necessitate the opening of a space for reoccupation of the traditional realm of politics, thereby creating the dynamic of realism that sustained contestatory argument for the nuclear age. Consider the political, technological, and moral revolutions in turn.

The international political system is eclipsed, Morgenthau argues, as a result of the Second World War. The collapse has the following five features: (1) the quantitative expansion of a European invented balance of power politics into territories around the globe, (2) the decentering of Europe as the hub of power politics, (3) the emergence of a bi-polar struggle between superpowers, (4) the disappearance of Great Britain's role as a balancer among competing alliances, and (5) the loss of political authority of Europeans over other nationalities and races. The net result of these political changes is a reduction in the "flexibility" of traditional power politics, which depended upon a center and a periphery to bleed off conflicts. The old-style diplomacy finds less room for maneuver. The moral authority and opportunity requisite to finding common ground for agreement by division with autonomous spheres of influence are diminished because of both the reduction of the number of powerful states and the increased autonomy of post-colonial nations.

Even as the capacity of politics has diminished, the power of technology grows. Advances in communications, transportation, and weapons increase the destructiveness of modern warfare which "is no longer the continuation of diplomacy by other means, an instrument of foreign policy to be used or not used as expediency advises."[21] Atomic warfare is at best a choice between "two kinds of national destruction": the ruin left by aggression or the ruin left by retaliation. Just as technology has made war irrational, so it leaves totalitarian rule secure. "[T]he discrepancy between what a government can do to its citizens and what the citizens can do to their government has become so enormous as to make popular revolution impossible."[22]

Within the gap left by the decline of traditional power politics and the burgeoning power of revolutionary technologies, there emerges "the rise of political religions." Thus, the stakes of foreign policy are increased, even as the assumption of a common interest in survival grows more remote. Locked within the horizons of the "moral revolution," the United States and the Soviet Union head toward a self-made Armageddon.

The "three revolutions" amount to a world that daily becomes a much less manageable and radically more dangerous place. Rhetorically, the strategy works to prompt action by questioning the *telos* of contemporary policy. Once the argument is laid out, it takes little imagination to see where present policies are leading. By depicting exclusive, unacceptable alternatives to the logic of the times— immediate, global preemptive war or ultimate mutual annihilation if atomic war comes—Morgenthau creates pressure for a new basis for foreign policy judgment, a new rhetoric that is grounded in the necessity of political assessment and compromise. Thus, realism contests with, even as it depicts, the realities of a time.

THE FUTURE: A COMPETITION AMONG ORIENTATIONS

The strategy of naming a new age with its own apocalyptic logic provokes a search for alternatives, options that have been formally set in place already by Morgenthau's recovery of the paradigmatic case of Hamilton's prudent construction of foreign policy. While history can serve as a guide, and while depiction of the present can goad to action, rhetorical realism must invent alternative orientations for the future in order to open a space for action. Typically, such a space is opened by pointing out the undesirable qualities of competing discourses. Morgenthau thus attacks the "four intellectual errors of post-war policy" as discursive bases that neither take into account real constraints upon prudent conduct nor address fully the exigencies of the times.

In this section, I will analyze Morgenthau's rhetorical realism in light of the "philosophy of rhetoric" developed by the eighteenth-century theorist George Campbell, who expanded the Aristotelian tradition. Widening the precepts of oratory into the "grand art of communication," Campbell, like Aristotle, measured the success of speech by the end of persuasion, but he argued that rhetoric depended upon adaptations of discourse to the distinctive qualities of the audience—the common exigencies of understanding, imagination, emotion, and will—which together could be brought into harmony and move to action.[23] The failure to address properly any one of these aspects, understanding being chief among them, always results in failed deliberation in the long, if not the short term. In Morgenthau's portrayal of the "four great intellectual errors" of contemporary foreign policy, one finds an indictment of alternative discourses that would detach and exaggerate the grounds of one part of the process of coming to judgment thereby diminishing and distorting the whole. The precepts of a full-throated realism, by contrast, are argued as superior.

Utopianism as a Failure of Understanding

For Campbell, "understanding" is the first prerequisite for any sound rhetoric because rhetoric can be effective only insofar as its proponents ground action in the urgency of a situation rightly appraised.[24] Whatever other embellishments or attractions address might hold, the measure of a successful discourse requires adaptation of the means of speech to the ends of proper judgment.

Morgenthau describes the basic premises that underlay correct understanding of any foreign policy judgment. "Foreign policy, like all politics, is in its essence a struggle for power, waged by sovereign nations for national advantage."[25] Foreign policy is understood correctly as situated action grounded in irreducibly contingent and uncertain questions of choice and conduct. Foreign policy is occasioned as action where the risk of misjudging the intentions of the other can result in either appeasement and aggression or in self-fulfilling fears of aggression and pre-emptive war. In a world where appearances are uncertain, intentions at least partially concealed, allegiances shifting, and the outcome of policy always hanging in the balance, correct understanding should be grounded in as much prudent determination of self-interest as any situation admits.

As wars of the twentieth century became characterized by totalizing aims, measured and bounded understandings of foreign policy gave way, according to Morgenthau, to "utopian moralism." Failure to understand the fundamental nature of foreign policy leads to a substitution of "conspiracy" theories, "especially plausible in a bipolar world." Moral divisions nest policy in moral simplicity rather than address the "complexities and ambiguities" of the real world.[26] If foreign policy is not understood in relation to a pragmatic context of international relations, then policy efforts are bound to follow a cycle of disillusionment. The "utopian, non-political conception of foreign policy as practiced by the United States" is in stark contrast with "the realistic approach its allies take to international problems."[27]

Legalism as Failure of the Imagination

To address the imagination, according to Campbell, is to fashion a place for the understanding to inhabit. To address the audience properly, the rhetor must picture the world with as much fidelity to the whole as is fit for addressing specific occasions. The picture is compelling because it lends emphasis to the "dignity" or gravity of choice the audience confronts. *Dignitas*, itself, is an ancient rhetorical precept that requires the rhetor to represent faithfully the seriousness and consequences of actions under discussion. As a trope, *dignitas* underscores the seriousness of a decision at hand by contrasting the rule-driven, institutionally narrow world of legal regulation with the importance and unpredictability of self-fashioning political actions.[28]

Morgenthau strives to reorient the imagination by bringing to the surface the "fundamental error" of American foreign policy, namely the antithesis of "national interest and moral principles," for, he holds, that "the equation of political moralizing with morality and of political realism with immorality is itself untenable" and an "intellectual error and moral perversion" of the first magnitude.[29] The realization of these premises is brought about by repicturing the world with what is held to be a truer representation of the situation.

The distorted understanding of American foreign policy as a moral drama, Morgenthau contends, leads to a confusing picture of international events as they are mirrored by expectations governing the domestic decision-making processes. "The appeal to moral principles in the international sphere has no concrete universal understanding," he contends, because there is no transnational entity capable of wielding authority. Although appeals to an international community can serve as a pretext for advancing national self-interest, such discourse always plays out a "false dignity" of basically unshared constraints and goals thereby creating the possibility of self-illusion and even "national suicide." Rather, within the context of proper understanding one cannot envision prudently a higher court of appeal than a self-fashioning politics among nations. The "moral dignity of the national interest" requires that one sees international situations from the perspective of public activity rather than from the remote distance of moral principles embodied in legal institutions.

"The legalistic approach, by its very nature, is concerned with isolated cases," Morgenthau concludes, and the world viewed through its lens promulgates an inevitable failure of the imagination. The legalist sees only "the juxtaposition of peace-loving and aggressor nations to that of law-abiding and criminal ones."[30] Thus, situations requiring action become simplified and distorted. "The conflict between the two groups ["Free World" and "Communist Block"], instead of being seen in terms of relative power, is conceived in the absolute terms of peace, law, and order vs. aggression, crime, and anarchy."[31] To imagine international relations in such simplistic terms is to reduce the flexibility and space requisite for negotiation and settling differences. At best, the legalist approach, exemplified in the political gridlock of the United Nations, leaves political action inert. At its worst, legal norms only further entrench disillusionment, as in the failed Yalta accords. Politics can only be successful when an audience sees the perdurable principles of self-interest at work in international events and acknowledges a proper, albeit restricted, place for legal forums within the politics among nations.

Sentimentalism and the Psychology of Form

For Campbell, it is not sufficient to address the understanding and the imagination alone. Persuasion requires attention to moving the passions by articulating the interests of the audience in relation to obtainable and desirable goals. The rhetor motivates the audience by following a psychology of form. Campbell writes:

[I]n order to persuade, there are two things which must be carefully studied by the orator. The first is, to excite some desire or passion in the hearers; the second is to satisfy their judgment that there is a connexion between the action to which he would persuade them, and the gratification of the desire or passion which he excites.[32]

Passion, the mover of action, is bound by the pathetic *and* the argumentative. Passions arouse attention, which understanding and imagination may leave indifferent. Yet, if the audience is to be persuaded to act prudently, the realistic rhetor is self-limited to "the best and most forcible arguments which the nature of the subject admits." Without a convincing argument for the satisfaction of desire, the passions (however much aroused) cannot be satisfied fully. Still, bald appeals to emotion can lead to short-term success for the rhetor; but when "bold affirmations are made to supply the place of reasons" making the plausible convincing, the audience becomes the "prey of quacks and impudent pretenders of every denomination."[33] The duty of the realist rhetorician is to contest popular appeals and remind the audience of the long-term consequences.

Morgenthau names "sentimentalism" that discourse which excites moral principles without attention to the pragmatic course which successful action pursues.

> Whatever the intrinsic nobility of a sentimental approach to foreign policy may be, whatever emotional attraction it may hold for many, its failings as a guide to political action are to be found in the distortion of the political process and in the jeopardy into which it puts the objective, be it moral or political, for which the political action is being undertaken.[34]

Moralistic rhetoric can motivate audiences. When the pathos of moral appeal overmatches practical concerns with the efficacy of policy, bad decisions result—and imprudent conduct invites more of the same.

The Truman Doctrine is presented as a case of a distorted rhetoric. In point of fact, Morgenthau argues not that it was morally improper to aid Greece and Turkey, but that the rhetorical reasoning that supported the intervention created a climate of expectations that could not be satisfied. In order to rouse the public to his cause, Truman "erected a message of salvation to all the world, unlimited in purpose, unlimited in commitments, and limited in its scope only by the needs of those who would benefit."[35] So, by virtue of its invocation of universal moral sentiments, containment became an inflexible principle committing the United States to fights in peripheral areas where it had no essential interests or to the admissions of failure and loss of prestige. "As a guide to political action," Morgenthau writes, the Truman Doctrine "is the victim, as all moral principles must be, of two congenital political weaknesses: the inability to distinguish between what is desirable and what is possible, and the inability to distinguish between what is desirable and what is essential."[36] In short, the Doctrine exaggerates emotional arousal at the expense of occluding from public view the limits of satisfaction. So the lesson: "A foreign policy, to be successful, must be commensurate with the power available to carry it out."[37]

Correct foreign policy requires that prudent choice be articulated in a context in which actions become meaningful and predictable. Argumentation that appraises means and ends relevant to a situation is necessary to constrain the charms of the plausible by a test of probable outcomes. Desire is not enough to create the foundation for success. Considered choices must be made within a defined context. According to Morganthau, "To establish a hierarchical order, an order of priorities among all possible objectives of a nation's foreign policy must be the first step in framing a rational foreign policy. The second step must of necessity be the allocation of the available resources to the objectives chosen, in view of their respective importance to national interest."[38] Morgenthau's principles of correct foreign policy fit seamlessly with Campbell's psychology of form.

Neo-Isolationism and the Failure of Will

The result of the connection of pathos and argument within the boundaries of proper imagination undergirded by right understanding is a resolute will determined to see a course of action through. According to Campbell:

> [That rhetoric which is] the most complex of all, which is calculated to influence the will, and persuade to a certain conduct, is in reality an artful mixture of that which proposes to convince the judgment, and that which interests the passions, its distinguished excellency results from these two the argumentative and pathetic incorporated together. These acting with united force, and, if I may so express myself, in concert, constitute that passionate eviction, that *vehemence* of contention, which is admirably fitted to persuasion, and hath always been regarded as the supreme qualification in an orator.[39]

Such "arguments exciting to resolution and activity" create a "sharpness" in "dissuading" and "persuading"; in short, effective persuasion crafts for an audience the language of engaged public argument.

Interestingly, Morgenthau sees the inflated moral discourses of Cold War struggle as a failure of will. What he brilliantly deduces is that the pre-war policies of American isolationism and post-war containment are different sides of the same coin. He comments that "the attitude of mind which gave rise to [the] isolation [of the twenties and thirties] is by no means dead." Rather, it manifests itself anew in the Cold War crusade which "turns inside out the old isolationism, and approaches the world in a spirit of active participation, provided that participation takes place on its own terms."[40] Neither isolation nor containment offers the determination necessary to act prudently on the international stage because neither commits the United States to the realistic necessities of action and diplomacy.

The failure of American will is rooted in misplaced principles of vehemence. "[T]he belief in our omnipotence arises in part from a historical experience that spared us the memory of some powerful neighbor who threatened the existence of the nation," Morgenthau observes.[41] The "conquering of a continent" has created a frame of mind that exaggerates the "moral might" of the United States and overinflates its sense of national mission. This misguided idealism, born of a unique geographical experience and historical accident, encountered "shock" in the aftermath of the Second World War, when for the first time it was confronted by the Soviet Union, "a wall not erected by nature and not to be scaled at will."[42] The result of an obstacle to international aims that would not yield easily to American policy was not to learn the "limits of our power" but to cling more tightly to the costly "delusion of our omnipotence."[43]

Misdirected idealism constitutes an expensive failure of will because such rhetoric diverts the gaze from honest self-appraisal of means and ends chosen to execute foreign policy, and leads to rationalizing policy failures by scapegoating. Idealistic rhetoric constrains the national ability to engage the enemy at the bargaining table in the pursuit of self-interest, even as it advances a moralism that destroys the middle ground necessary to strive for advantage within the common arena bounded by the shared interest of survival. The neo-isolationists—the "disappointed utopian, legalist, or sentimentalist—lack the will to appraise directly the strength of the enemy, the weaknesses of one's own situation, and the actions requisite to preserve the peace," Morgenthau concludes.[44]

Realism, on the other hand, pursues with vehemence the autonomy of the political realm, a sphere of action that requires resolute judgment in the face of uncertainty, and necessitates unswerving opposition to "the equating of negotiated settlement with the moral approval of the settlement itself, and the equating of a negotiated settlement with appeasement."[45] An administration that forms its policy from expected press reaction, rather than from good reasons, can but enfeeble foreign policy. Weak commitments and debased rhetoric go hand in hand for the Truman administration where, Morgenthau concludes: "[T]he lack of moral determination . . . corrupts both understanding and prudence. It debases understanding into a mere reflection of what

the public opinion 'experts' think the crowd wants; it relegates political prudence to the lowest level of political manipulation."[46]

Either isolationism or globalism, itself a moral withdrawal, con-
fuses the popular course with the prudent one, thereby removing the
resistance to persuasion that validates a rhetoric. Cold War rhetoric is
domestic pandering, and as such, a failure of political will.

The rhetoric of realism is now complete: The nation-state is an
individual actor who speaks within a community of nations, and so
must be every bit in control of its reasons as an individual orator who
addresses an audience. Just as the orator must be prepared to
encounter those whose attitudes range from the indifferent to the hostile, so the nation must act in the midst of a situation where all states
are potential allies and possible enemies. A realist rhetoric of foreign
policy must admit to contingencies, put legal decisions in proper context, restrain hyperbolic moralizing, differentiate between core and
peripheral interests, and steadfastly resist measures that, while popular in domestic politics, remain unsuitable for pursuit of the national
interest in the international arena. In sum, for Morgenthau's statesman "rhetoric is verbalized action, an explanation of deeds done or a
foretaste of deeds to come."[47]

REVIEW AND APPRAISAL

In Defense of the National Interest is a rhetorical argument levelled
against the Truman administration. More than an indictment of the
policies of its time, however, the work constitutes a warning against
any special policy or speculative position that would ground theoretically or represent publicly foreign policy in any context other than
international politics, which itself is an arena for the art of diplomacy.
Diplomacy is bounded by a rhetorical situation where actors must
choose among uncertain alternatives, with probable proof and prudence constraining conduct. The essence of such situated action is an
inescapable risk; on the one hand, misplaced gestures of cooperation
can be read as a lack of power, thereby jeopardizing the peace by
inducing greater aggression based upon false perception of weakness;
on the other hand, measures taken to enhance security may be read as
intentions to conduct conflict, thereby destabilizing the peace through
initiating a spiral of self-fulfilling fears. Thus, realism requires
unflinching argumentation to the merits of decisions based upon the
context of events defined within the public sphere. The book is a cau-

tionary tract that alerts the makers of foreign policy to the dilemmas of alternative discourses that would gainsay realism and purport to outstrip the human condition, itself perennially sustained by cooperation and division.

The attractions of a foreign policy based upon "abstract moralism"—the chief competitor to realism at the time—are many, however. First, moralism panders to the popular preconception that the United States is a special, morally superior nation. Second, it simplifies international policy to a drama of good and evil, thereby creating a basis of identification easily manipulated by associating allies with the good and enemies with evil. Third, the subordination of the political to the moral forms the basis for rhetoric arousing crusades. When crusading energy is spent, calls for isolation follow, continuing the cycle of excess and disillusionment. Fourth, the rhetorics of absolutes create bases for success in domestic politics by providing ready-made explanations for failure while scapegoating those who advocate caution, restraint, and compromise. As George Campbell might have put it, moralism flourishes by trafficking in the realm of the "plausible," thereby obscuring the complex and ambiguous reasons that are to be found by judiciously weighing "probable" evidence and outcomes.

The strategic discourse of the realists of the early 1950s was successful in altering the apocalyptic trajectory of post-war policy. It instantiated different grounds for policy judgment and representation by fashioning an eloquent argument for subordinating the language of ultimates to the more pressing questions of common survival. Morgenthau sustained this rhetorical posture throughout the Cold War, remaining a critic of foreign polices that vitiated the principles of realism, and a theorist who broadened and deepened his reading of history and the humanist tradition.

What contemporary relevance has Morgenthau's recovery of the public sphere? The passing of the Cold War would seem to transform *In Defense of the National Interest* from a timely warning to a work of a different time, a response to an international scene that once more has been changed by revolutions. The epoch-making events of the late 1940s that created the exigency for the renewal of classical realism are now distanced by time and circumstances. Indeed, contemporary foreign policy seems marked by the *absence* of utopian inclinations, absolute faith in international law, the fever of moral crusades, and claims to either isolationism or grand scale, bi-polar struggle.

Although the "three revolutions" of Morgenthau's day seem to have run their course, the disappearance of the Cold War appears to make realism more timely, not less, especially if John Mearsheimer is correct that the shift to a multi-polar world brings on greater violence.[48] And so, this scenario might suggest itself to decision makers. Just as Britain was able to effect a stable balance of power by virtue of its preponderance, the United States occupies now a traditional balancer of power position. Just as Britain was able to fashion a foreign policy based on versions of its self-interest by controlling the seas, so the United States controls the contemporary arena of power mobility, the air. Thus, the 1991 Gulf War, far from being interpreted as the keystone of a new world order, appears (structurally at least) as a traditional balance of power war.

Policy makers trained in realist thinking might find that the contemporary age opens a place for the return of the unfettered pursuit of self-interest based upon systemic understanding of the uses of power. If so, the only "real" questions open would be measurement and application of "assets" to situations at hand. Yet, as Morgenthau himself would engage us in cautionary thinking, it should be remembered that while British policy may have fashioned a long peace in the nineteenth century, the bi-products of a predominant power remaking the world on behalf of its own self-interests were to set the conditions of struggle and turbulence that made the twentieth century a time of turmoil and bloodshed. Thus, to renew Morgenthau's "classical realism" requires not that one extrapolate his arguments as theory or doctrine, but that one work critically to understand the way his discourse developed in context and to adapt his insights to a different time.

Morgenthau's recovery of the public sphere was achieved by (1) rereading paradigmatic moments of civic action, (2) identifying the *telos* of contemporary policy as necessitating moderating alternatives, and (3) interjecting within these horizons a discourse that had resources sufficient to contest alternative, less complete orientations toward action. At the core of this effort was the reoccupation of a traditional cultural form, the classical political sphere—a realm of activity that situates human efforts with deliberation about advantage and survival in the contexts of common choice.

The reoccupation of this position has strengths and weaknesses. Aristotle's own corrective synthesis was built upon a compromise between the improvisation and immediacy of Sophistic argument and the reflection and theoretical development of Plato's reasoning. So,

any argument that would follow in this tradition by striving to con-
join theory and practice is vulnerable to positions that in the name of
realism itself would either collapse theory into pragmatic case formulation of alternatives, or abstract and reduce practice into formalized
system components. No matter how brilliantly constructed, realism as
an affirmative synthesis remains a potentially divided discourse.[49]
Alternatively, the strength of realism resides in its inventional
resources as counterargument that points up the limitations of a
divorced theory and practice of foreign affairs. From a rhetorical
standpoint, the best yield of critical inquiry resides not in extending
realism's theoretical syntheses or policy doctrines but in discussions
that critique alternative orientations, expose distortions within realism's own tradition, and engage contemporary political exigencies.

If we take the tradition seriously and acknowledge that realism is a
product of the human sciences that must sustain an ethical component in the interests of effective practice, for example, then perhaps it
is time with the prospective triumph of "neorealism" to recover a different aspect of the realist tradition, one that would guide an enlarged
sense of purpose and shape an expanded sense of the public sphere.[50]
Ironically, in following the trajectory of Morgenthau's work, the construction of a new foreign policy argument would begin with a critique and reconstruction of the consequences of an overly rationalized
balance of power politics.

Richard Ashley and others have called for the criticism of rationalism and neorealism. Ashley, however, misses the role of rhetoric in
the recovery of the realist enterprise. He grounds his critique on
Jürgen Habermas' differentiation among practical, technical, and
emancipatory interests, finding that each interest serves the cognitive
bases and dialectical operations of realism.[51] "Practical realism is
guided by a practical cognitive interest in sustaining intersubjective
understanding with the context of tradition," he argues. "Technical
realism is guided by a technical cognitive interest in coming to grips
with objective laws so as to expand powers of technical control over
objectified reality."[52] These two components of a realist foreign policy, however, are transcended by an "emancipatory interest" in "self-
reflection" and the "self-formation" of the human species along the
lines of Herz's open-ended dialogue of realism on a global level of
concern.[53] Ashley calls for a "dialogue" that mutually engages the theoretical and the practical in sustained self-criticism of foreign policy
assumptions, but he also concludes that such a discussion is

"unlikely to be persuasive if realist scholars are at base positivist scientists oriented by a technical interest in control."

Morgenthau's enduring contribution is to show that the critique of the reduction of the political realm can be persuasive. A rhetoric of realism can interrupt hegemonic theoretical or practical discourses by rendering apparent the contingencies and risks of choice. Theoretical discourse that purports to outstrip the political can be critiqued by exposing the consequence of subordinating foreign policy to supposedly apolitical realms of discourse. The practices of foreign policy rhetoric can be interrupted by a critical reinterpretation of the unexamined paradigmatic precedent from which such "truths" have veered or been secured. So, Morgenthau's rhetorical realism works much as what Habermas has identified as a proper "strategic" argument that prompts reorientation of discourse into a communicative relationship.[54] For international relations, I would add, such a relationship begins with the recognition of the *dignitas* of communities with diverse histories, interests, and peoples facing common problems and struggling with the challenge of fashioning a viable civic realm.

Like any rhetoric, *In Defense of the National Interest* speaks to its time, and can only be recuperated by a reading that recognizes and critiques its arguments in a wider context. Thus, while Morgenthau's rhetorical opposition was aimed at "idealism" as a prevailing idiom, his position can be redirected also toward the "structuralism" of a neorealist hegemony. The work offers implicit standards of critique for any foreign policy discourse that distorts the political by reducing political action and actors either to "moral abstraction" or to the structurally abstracted and technicized components of systemic process. Such critique is useful in fashioning a viable route to a common civic realm in swiftly shifting post-Cold War contexts. This immanent critique of an important moment in the rhetorical tradition suggests that realism's own renewal depends upon the re-invention of discursive argument that goes "beyond what realism can realistically be expected to address."[55]

Morgenthau's reoccupation of the public sphere draws from a strand of the rhetorical tradition extending from Aristotle to Campbell. This tradition champions rhetoric that strives to distinguish robust realism from impoverished competitors and incomplete imitations. Seen from this perspective, the viability of realism resides neither in its power to strip away constraints in the name of immediate action nor in its capacity to anticipate risk by objective measurement and calculation. Indeed, the hypertrophy of "understanding" itself is a distortion of the "real"—which in the end includes the contingent discourse of human imagination, emotion, and will—all inextricably woven within the discourses of the public realm. "International relations in our period are by their very nature controversial," Hans Morgenthau wrote in 1967.[56] From a rhetorical vantage, the strength of realism resides in its enduring capacity to renew the civic realm and continue the controversy.

NOTES

1. Hans J. Morgenthau, *In Defense of the National Interest: A Critical Examination of American Foreign Policy* (New York: Knopf, 1951), 178.
2. Rachel Carson, *The Silent Spring* (Boston: Houghton Mifflin, 1962); Michael Harrington, *The Other America* (Baltimore: Penguin, 1962); Upton Sinclair, *The Jungle* (New York: Viking Press, 1946); Harriet Beecher Stowe, *Uncle Tom's Cabin* (London: J. Cassel, 1852).
3. Robert E. Osgood, "The Mission of Morgenthau," in *Truth and Tragedy: A Tribute to Hans J. Morgenthau*, eds. Kenneth Thompson and Robert J. Myers (Washington, D.C.: The New Republic Book Co., 1977), 33.
4. Robert O. Keohane, "Realism, Neorealism and the Study of World Politics," *Neorealism and its Critics*, ed. Robert O. Keohane (New York: Columbia University Press, 1986), 9.
5. Morgenthau developed and extended his views in a number of essays and monographs in a variety of fora between 1948 and 1952. See: "The Primacy of the National Interest," *American Scholar* 18 (1949): 207-12; "History's Lesson," *Nation* 171 (16 December 1950): 587-91; "The Mainsprings of American Foreign Policy: The National Interest vs Moral Abstractions," *American Political Science Review* 44 (1950): 833-54; "Power Politics," *Nation* 170 (20 May 1950): 486-87; "Diplomacy's Duty is the Defense of Our Own Interest," *Saturday Evening Post* 224 (11 August 1951): 10; "American Diplomacy: The Dangers of Righteousness," *New Republic* 125 (22 October 1951): 17-19; "What is the National Interest of the United States?" *Annals of the American Academy of Political and Social Sciences* 282 (July 1952): 1-7; "Lessons of World War II's Mistakes: Negotiations and Armed Power Flexibly Combined," *Commentary* 14 (October 1952): 326-33; "Another 'Great Debate': The National Interest of the United States," *American Political Science Review* 46 (1952): 979-81.
6. Keohane, "Realism," 13; Steven Forde, "Classical Realism," in *Traditions of International Ethics*, eds. Terry Nardin and David R. Mapel (Cambridge: Cambridge University Press, 1992), 62-84; Jack Donnelly, "Twentieth Century Realism," *Traditions of International*

Ethics, 85-111; Robert Gilpin, *War and Change in World Politics* (Cambridge: Cambridge University Press, 1981), 93-95.

7. Paul Seabury, "Realism and Idealism," *Encyclopedia of American Foreign Policy: Studies of the Principal Movements and Ideas*, ed. Alexander DeConde (New York: Charles Scribner's Sons, 1978), 856.

8. Morgenthau seems to have integrated into his thinking basic principles of "moral reasoning" characterizing Enlightenment rhetorics. For example, his view of "power" is close to that of eighteenth-century rhetoric. "Power is a psychological relationship in which one man controls certain actions of another man through the influence he exerts over the latter's will. That influence derives from three sources: the expectation of benefits, the fear of disadvantages, the respect or love for men or institutions. It may be exerted through orders, threats, promises, persuasion, the authority or charisma of man or of an office, or a combination of any of the above." "Love and Power," *Commentary* 33 (1962): 249. For a comparison see George Campbell, *The Philosophy of Rhetoric by George Campbell*, ed. Lloyd F. Bitzer (Carbondale, Ill.: Southern Illinois University Press, 1963), 71-98.

9. See for example: Hans J. Morgenthau, *Science: Servant or Master?* (New York: New American Library, 1972). Although Morgenthau worked from a humanistic position, the rhetorical tradition is rarely cited directly in his works.

10. Hans Blumenberg, *The Legitimacy of the Modern Age*, trans. Robert M. Wallace (Cambridge: MIT Press, 1983), 464.

11. Richard K. Ashley, "The Poverty of Neorealism," *Neorealism and Its Critics*, ed. Robert O. Keohane (New York: Columbia University Press, 1986), 297. See also: Richard K. Ashley, "Political Realism and Human Interests," *International Studies Quarterly* 25 (1981): 204-236.

12. Aristotle, *Aristotle on Rhetoric: A Theory of Civic Discourse*, trans. George A. Kennedy (New York: Oxford University Press, 1991), 12.

13. *Rhetoric,* 1359b, 33-39.

14. *Rhetoric,* 1359a, 3-39.

15. *Rhetoric,* 1355a, 2-55.

16. Hamilton qtd. by Morgenthau, *In Defense of the National Interest*, 16-17.

17. *In Defense of the National Interest*, 26.

18. Ibid., 27.

19. Ibid.

20. Ibid., 4.

21. Ibid., 57.

22. Ibid., 59. Morgenthau was more adept at reading the limits of American influence in Asia than he was at reading the consequences of technology which he believed could lead only to affirming totalitarian rule. He did not anticipate, as few did, the role played by information technolo-

gies in penetrating national boundaries. The rhetoric of realism, it seems, outlives its time and is subject to renewals because the discourse frame freezes a present that itself is undermined by change. When change is sufficiently at variance with the announced "realities" of an era, a space is opened up for a recovery of realism. See for example the critique of R. W. Cox, "Social Forces, States and World Orders: Beyond International Relations Theory," *Millennium: Journal of International Studies* 10 (1981): 126-55.

23. For an introduction to Enlightenment rhetorics see: *The Rhetorical Tradition: Readings from Classical Times to the Present*, eds. Patricia Bizzell and Bruce Herzberg (Boston: St. Martin's Press, 1990), 635-896.

24. Campbell, 72-73.

25. *In Defense of the National Interest*, 92-93.

26. Ibid., 94.

27. Ibid., 98.

28. Cicero, *Pro Murena: M.T. Ciceronis Oratio pro L. Murena* (Cambridge: The University Press, 1886).

29. *In Defense of the National Interest*, 33.

30. Ibid., 101.

31. Ibid., 102.

32. Campbell, 77-78.

33. Ibid., 78.

34. *In Defense of the National Interest*, 114.

35. Ibid., 116.

36. Ibid., 117.

37. Ibid., 118.

38. Ibid.

39. Campbell, 4.

40. *In Defense of the National Interest*, 129.

41. Ibid.

42. Ibid., 130.

43. Morgenthau contrasted the "statesman" to the "politician." The former appears as a classical rhetorical figure who unites word and deed in actions taken in the international arena. The latter is a source of equivocation in the interests of domestic popularity. ("The Trouble with Kennedy," *Commentary* 33 [1962]: 51-52).

44. *In Defense of the National Interest*, 135.

45. Ibid., 136.

46. Ibid., 231.

47. "The Trouble with Kennedy," 51-52.

48. John J. Mearsheimer, "Back to the Future: Instability in Europe after the Cold War," *International Security* 14 (1990): 5-56.

49. Gordon A. Craig and Alexander L. George, *Force and Statecraft: Diplomatic Problems of Our Time* (New York: Oxford University Press, 1990), 294-95.
50. Roger L. Shinn, "Realism and Ethics," in *Truth and Tragedy*, 95-103.
51. Jürgen Habermas, *Knowledge and Human Interests*, trans. Jeremy Shapiro (London: Heinemann, 1972). See Jim George and David Campbell, "Patterns of Dissent and the Celebration of Difference: Critical Social Theory and International Relations," *International Studies Quarterly* 34 (1990): 269-93.
52. Ashley, "Political Realism and Human Interests," 204.
53. John H. Herz, "Political Realism Revisited," *International Studies Quarterly* 25 (1981): 182-97.
54. Jürgen Habermas, *The Theory of Communicative Action: Volume II— Lifeworld and System: A Critique of Functionalist Reason*, trans. Thomas McCarthy (Boston: Beacon Press, 1987).
55. Charles W. Kegley, Jr. "The Neoidealist Moment in International Studies? Realist Myths and the New International Realities," *International Studies Quarterly* 37 (1993): 131-46.
56. Hans J. Morgenthau, "Common Sense and Theories of International Relations," *Journal of International Affairs* 21 (1967): 207-14.

III

REWRITING REALIST CONCEPTS

One rewrites in order to improve a text. Sometimes the result is thought to be the better expression of an original meaning; at other times, it extends the idea in a new direction. In any case, textual revision is a process characterized by imperfection, change, negotiation, and fallibility. Traditionally, realism has seemed to be above this process: One identifies the relations of power or suffers the consequences. This attitude is reflected in the standard invocation of the classics of realism, which are seen as equivalent statements of a core doctrine of universal truths. From Thucydides to Machiavelli to Morgenthau, there have been periodic moments when the rest of the world had to be reminded of the harsh realities of power, but realism itself was essentially the same whatever its articulation. Likewise, if the concepts used in theoretical analysis were to be negotiated, that was a question of choosing between the more realistic idea or some normative intrusion into the analytical process. There were times when realism needed to be written, promulgated, and studied, but rewritten, revised, put up for grabs? Never.

Post-realism both rereads and rewrites. Old texts are read anew and texts previously scanted are brought to light, while old concepts also are revised and new ideas are drafted. One consequence of realism's hegemony is that many of the basic concepts of international relations have been articulated in realism's terms. Instead of having realist, institutionalist, Marxist, and other versions of such concepts as sovereignty and security, there are alternative theories working with the same set of realist concepts. Obviously, this linguistic asymmetry is an enormous advantage for the realist, yet no act of writing dominates perfectly. Alternative formulations remain as traces or anomalies. Opportunity awaits the theorist attempting to rewrite the realist concept, a process that ultimately will have to answer both to those who want to survey a wider range of phenomena and to those who liked the familiar map of known terrain.

The authors of the next set of essays have undertaken this ambitious project. By attending to different concepts, they are faced with different problems, but they draw on the basic assumptions of post-realism. The first of these is the linguistic turn itself, that is, the shift from knowledge of reality to understanding of the terms for reality. Whatever is the case, we can only identify it, work with it, and live with it as we name it, describe it, and discuss it. Our language mediates all that we do, it constitutes essential elements of knowledge and action, and it determines our fate as much as do the conditions of nature. Thus, the idea that veridical statements are clear representations of what is outside of language gives way to the idea that any veridical statement is a partial representation also reflecting and incorporating a form of life. The point of inquiry is the same, that is, to discover, explain, and understand what is happening, but the assumption is that these tasks require analysis of the means for their completion.

This focus on discourse ultimately involves consideration not merely of terms and habits of usage, but of the institutions, social structure, and history of the people who have lived with them. It provides a characteristic approach to intervention as well. For discourse, like the texts it manifests, can be revised. Not effortlessly, of course, nor by a single act or even by a single individual. But to the extent that discourse is constitutive, rather than merely a means of description or manipulation, the analysis of discourse can become a means of social change. Thus, another assumption is that the scholar should not be content to observe and explain, but should also engage in critique and reformulation of the discourse of international relations. Instead of writing in a manner that implies the separation of knower and known, the act of rewriting highlights how any claim to know is a mode of participation in the practice it describes. By rewriting the concepts of international relations, the authors of these essays do not mean to suggest that such concepts are merely a literary exercise, but *they do assume that any concept was written from a particular stand-point, within a particular historical moment, and to a particular advantage. The essays do not presume that their words offer a sufficient revision, but they do want to identify alternative versions of the concept and, with that, alternative modes of participation in what is known.*

These essays can be distinguished along an analytical spectrum ranging from central concepts in the lexicon of realism (sovereignty and security), to understated but still crucial concepts in that configuration of terms (prestige and reputation), to a related and confounding concept (nationalism), to a comprehensive bias within the discourse (gender), to a program for rewriting the discourse by comparison with related cultural forms. Taken together, the essays demonstrate how realism is very much a discourse like any other, and that it also depends on very narrow definitions of some terms and on related habits of inattention. The realists' terms can correspond with the reality they value so highly, but they work only through coherence with specific rhetorical and ideological structures. Realism describes what is the case and it denies what also is the case. It produces knowledge and it suppresses knowledge. Any discourse might do the same, of course, but not every discourse need be persistently unreflexive about its own discursive constraints. The point is not to obtain a purified language for international relations but to identify how the prevailing language can be inadequate for the tasks at hand. By rewriting the concepts of international relations, one gains a degree of control over the reality created by language and perhaps thereby an opportunity for better theory and more creative practice.

JEAN BETHKE ELSHTAIN

RETHINKING SOVEREIGNTY

The importance of the concept of sovereignty can hardly be overrated.
It was a formidable tool in the hands of lawyers and politicians, and a
decisive factor in the making of modern Europe.

A.P. d'Entreves
Natural Law

S overeignty is the vote. The union card. The insignia of membership in the club. Less exclusive than it once was, the club now
encompasses much of the globe and those not members at present continue to seek entry, often utilizing rather impolite methods to
that end. Sovereignty remains the "essential qualification for full
membership in international society, or, to express the point more
comprehensively, the qualification which makes a state eligible for
full membership."[1] Sovereignty names an aspiration; serves as a goad
to action; signifies an accomplishment; defines an opposition
(state/society); and encodes a legalistic construction (formal sovereignty).

Why is the discourse of sovereignty so pervasive and so elusive? To
speak to this matter in anything approaching an exhaustive manner
would take many volumes. I propose to scratch the surface of things
only by looking at the contestability of sovereignty as a concept in
order to alert the reader, first, to battles, past and present, surrounding
that concept and, second, to remind the reader of sovereignty's lingering power. As well, I touch on a theme by no means original to me,
sovereignty as a boundary-setting discourse, a way to divide theorizing "domestic politics" from theorizing the state and its "external"
relations.[2] Finally, I suggest ways to move toward a new political discourse of sovereignty that seeks neither the wholesale elimination of

the term nor the reality it helps to constitute but offers, instead, ways to challenge and soften sovereignty's reign. To assume sovereignty uncritically is to assume that our political choices are either cosmos or chaos, order or anarchy. This, indeed, is the way those called "realists" have tended to construe the world of "men and states." But realism, and the theory of sovereignty central to it, is an inherently unstable concept. I begin by pairing thinkers who endorse or criticize sovereignty.

THE CONTESTABILITY OF SOVEREIGNTY

Political theorist Bernard Crick pens a lamentation in *The New Statesman* under the title, "The Curse of Sovereignty."[3] There are, Crick proclaims, crucial differences between power and sovereignty and it is but "vainglorious bluffing which has confused the two and caused shameful deaths." Warming to his topic, Crick lambastes sovereignty as "a greater curse and a source of more conceptual confusion than even Clausewitz's dubious doctrine. For even if one says that something called 'the State' is sovereign, it does not follow that this sovereignty *should* always be used or *can* always be used." As Crick persists in thundering condemnation, coupled with uneasy recall of much of what he has blasted, it becomes clear that he is in a bind that is not his alone but that of many thinkers outraged at abuses of sovereignty (in Crick's case Margaret Thatcher's bellicosity in the Falklands-Malvinas affair) yet unwilling to jettison the idea because if a "whole country is threatened, sovereignty becomes meaningful: as in 1914-18 and 1939-45."

In *The Causes of War* by Michael Howard, we find at one and the same time, a defense of the sovereign nation-state and criticism of its excesses. Howard indicts as tragic an instance of popular sovereignty Crick embraces, namely, the bellicosity of 1914-1918. The "tragedy of 1914," writes Howard, derived from the "later nineteenth century apotheosis of the Nation State, together with the glorification of war which accompanied it." This, for contemporary Europeans, is a "historical curiosity, almost impossible to conceive of today." Searching for the strongest possible intensifiers to score his rhetorical and analytic point against sovereign excess, Howard excoriates "the grotesque and evil exaggerations of militaristic nationalism." He concedes that mistrust of the State is "the beginning of political wisdom." And yet . . . liberal optimism regarding the "reintegration of mankind in new political patterns which will transcend the old 'war system' and make possible perpetual peace" is misplaced as "the Nation State still remains the only mechanism by which the ordinary man and woman achieves some sense, however limited, of participation in, and responsibility for, the ordering of their own societies and the conduct of the affairs of the world."[4] The alternative to the modern nation-state is not a supra-statist order of peaceful integration but a likely dis-integration into militant warring micro-states. Howard need look no further than the tragedy of Bosnia for evidence of the wisdom of a disillusioned realist perspective, his own.

In *The City of God*, St. Augustine writes, "For where can that lust for power in arrogant hearts come to rest until after passing from one office to another, it arrives at *sovereignty? [summum imperium]* There would be no occasion for this continuous progress if ambition were not all-powerful; and the essential context for ambition is a people corrupted by greed and sensuality." The distinctive mark of Roman life as a *civitas terrena,* a city of man, was greed and lust for possession which presumed a right of exploitation. This became a foundation for human relationships, warping and perverting personality, marriage, the family, all things. Augustine writes: "For he who desires the glory of possession would feel that his power were diminished, if he were obliged to share it with any living associate. . . . He cherishes his own manhood."[5] Although Augustine musters a few good words for Roman justice and order, imperfect as they have been, a sometimes scornful critique of the *pax Romana* predominates in his overall narrative. Rome's *imperium* had brought terrible grief to humankind. "Peace and War had a contest in cruelty; and Peace won the prize." The Roman peace "slaughtered the defenseless." Inventing the threat of wicked foreigners to justify their own wickedness, Rome's masters should have erected a statue to honor a new goddess, *"Iniquitas Aliena,"* the evil alien, as She had served them so well. Augustine's ire is meted out against the Roman law of private property, including the absolutism of the *pater familias* who held sway over the household up to and including power of life and death over any and all its members, including his "own" newborn infants. The *dominus* possessed unrestricted property rights, "internally," domestically. Interesting seeds are sown here: absolute dominion over a "domestic" arena is the mark of the sovereign *dominus.* Domestic sovereign absolutism and the terrible reign of Rome both wear a masculinized face. The feminized, the female, requires the masculinized, the male, to be the bearer of the principle of order, both domestically *and* externally, for Augustine also suggests, perhaps more perceptively than he knew, that the iniquitous "alien" takes the form of a feminine force or principle, *aliena,* the unruly external She. Here the feminized representation is the unruly She who disorders.

For David Jayne Hill, onetime United States ambassador to Germany, writing in 1917 and inveighing against the evils of sovereignty, Rome represented a longed-for universalism split apart by hopelessly sullied particularisms. Hill celebrates that which Augustine had so masterfully condemned. For Hill, the *pax Romana* embodies a "universal humanism" established by law, running counter to "the tribalism of primitive European races." In the fifteenth century, "tribalism triumphed." But the time has come for "universal humanism" to "reclaim its own, and reassert the substantial unity of the human races" by revivifying "the splendid postulates of the Roman imperial idea—the essential unity of mankind, the supremacy of law based upon reason and divine command, . . . and the effective organization of peace as a condition of human happiness. . . ." The olive branch of peace embodied in a beautiful image of the Roman imperial idea and ideal is contrasted to the "right of the mailed fist," the *Faustrecht* which led to "so many sovereignties, so many absolute autocrats."[6] A return to peace and to law means back to empire. Sovereignty does not go away in this vision; it is lofted upward. Sovereignty escapes the confines of the nation-state to take residence in the restored temples of the *imperium Romanum* or its twentieth-century equivalent. This reconciliation of universalism and particularism is wholly in favor of universalism, under Western hegemony. Political differences have either melted away or been absorbed within a universalized totality. But who sets the terms for the new universalism, a realist might query? How is such an escape from the perils of state sovereignty to be specified meaningfully in political institutions and life?

Visions of a new and better *pax Romana,* stripped of the unattractive features of dominion, continue to seduce many and various thinkers and political activists. One finds, for example, feminist peace theorists who preach a new religion of universalism by inverting the rankings and evaluations of "old war" theorists of the sort who might hold a soft spot in their hearts for a Roman-style *pax.* That is, they call for a benevolent, feminized peace against a malevolent, masculinized war-system.[7] But "holistic understanding," and a world of transparent harmonies once sovereignty is eliminated, is a vision that itself rests on the very oppositions, hierarchies, and repressions it seeks to displace. If, as Joan Scott has argued, the high politics of wars and states is a "gendered concept, for it establishes its crucial importance and public power, the reasons for and the fact of its highest authority, precisely in its exclusion of women from its work," a totalized version of feminist anti-state discourse functions as the mirror to its diabolical twin.[8] Feminized peace as a gendered concept requires the "masculinized war system" to hold itself intact.

The discourse of state sovereignty makes claims to sovereign identity—"the One is separate from, superior to, and generative of the Many."[9] If that One is a masculinized representation in sovereign discourse, a reversal occurs with much of the peace discourse of feminist universalists. In this latter genre, the One is feminized and this logic of identity prevails over all other terms. The discourse of strong sovereignty in its classic formulation is a discourse of absolute mastery over internal space and independent vulnerability in the external zone of competing sovereignties; the discourse of universalism as embodied in yearnings for Empire or a feminist utopia is a discourse of attunement in which any internal/external divide melts away.

ON THE TRAIL OF SOVEREIGNTY

As we can readily see, sovereignty generates a number of typical problems—mediations of universalism and particularism; definitions of international relations in terms of presence and absence whereby present sovereign states are "primary actors" but the "system itself" is defined by a lack, an absence of sovereignty. This helps us to understand why the choices posed above remain so extreme—either nearly 200 sovereignties vying against one another in a competitive field, or the imperial supercession of sovereignty. A modest project of historic excavation or, better, genealogical reconstruction deepens our appreciation of this stubborn conundrum. Sovereignty is a heroic narrative, a story of the bringing of order and civic peace and unity, on the one hand, and of the necessity of war and state violence, on the other. This narrative gained ascendancy and has held sway as a particular historic configuration, a response to concrete pressures and problems.

In an essay on "The Power and Powerlessness of Women," I argued that power "is indispensible to various ways of thinking—not only about politics but about God and the sacred. Political meanings in the

West got layered over older, mythic understandings, potent images of ritual, taboo, the demonic, the sacred. This is reflected in the OED in which power as a characteristic of political or national strength is declared a 'late use' and one preceded by 'a celestial or spiritual being having control or influence; a divinity.'"[10] This needs fleshing out, for it suggests that claims to earthly *potestas* or power as dominion and rule, constitutive of early modern theories of state sovereignty, are parasitic upon earlier constructions of a singular, sovereign will for much of their force. God's right is coterminous with His sovereign power: it is a right of dominion, rule, possession, "all-pervasive and efficient . . . omnipotent and undefeatable."[11] Human beings are subject to God's sovereign dominion. God's all-pervasive sovereignty misses nothing, attends to everything. This vision of metaphysical realism dependent upon a monistic conception of truth dominated "sovereignty talk" for centuries, laying the basis for the juristic conception of the state.[12] According to Carl Schmitt, the controversial German theorist: "All significant concepts . . . were transferred from theology to the theory of the state, whereby, for example, the omnipotent God became the omnipotent lawgiver . . . the recognition of which is necessary for a sociological consideration of these concepts."[13]

Consider the following: Jean Bodin discussing sovereignty as the *summum imperium,* or that which can neither be delegated nor divided, writes: "Sovereignty is that absolute and perpetual power vested in a commonwealth which in Latin is termed *majestas. . . .* It is the distinguishing mark of the sovereign that he cannot in any way be subject to the commands of another, for it is he who makes law for the subject, abrogates law already made, and amends obsolete law."[14] Hobbes, in chapters 17 and 18 of *The Leviathan,* argues in this way: "The only way to erect such a Common Power . . . is to conferre all their power and strength upon one Man, or upon one Assembly of men, that may reduce all their Wills . . . unto one Will . . . . This is more than Consent, or Concord; it is a reall Unitie of them all, in one and the same Person. . . . This is the Generation of that Great Leviathan, or rather (to speak more reverently) of that Mortall God, to which wee owe under the Immortall God, our peace and defense. . . . And that he carryeth this Person, is called Soveraigne, and said to have Soveraigne Power; and every one besides, his Subject."[15] Hobbes goes on to enumerate the Sovereign's rights which are his powers—to judge all opinions, to name all names, to defend, all as things "necessary to Peace, thereby to prevent Discord and Civill Warre."

Hobbes and Bodin, among others, helped to give "centralizing monarchies the basis they required in legal and political theory." To be sure, they were working from, and appropriating to their own purposes, a body of pre-statist sovereign theory penned by defenders of the papacy as the site of a *plenitudo potestatis,* a plenitude, an untrammeled amplitude, of power. "Much of this was already created for them by papal theory. Certainly, long before this period, Roman imperial doctrine had been used by national kings and territorial princes to justify the overriding of positive laws, and a centralized system of legislation and appointment. Papal doctrine both endorsed this . . . and also supplied something of the more abstract and more generally applicable notion of sovereignty which was to be fully developed in the work of Bodin."[16]

The difference between the earthly enumerated powers, and God's, is that the earthly Sovereign, although untrammeled in his power in the temporal space that is History, is subject to God's grace or punishment. But having taken unto himself all the features of the deity, save personal immortality—although the King-dom is perpetual, hence immortality is in some sense assured—there is precious little constraint, in the worlds of Bodin and Hobbes, on the sovereignty of the absolute *dominus* over a bounded earthly territory, a vast "domestic" space.[17] Explanations for Bodinian and Hobbesian sovereign absolutism fall into two broad categories:

(a) Facing situations of sometimes terrible disorder, with chaos threatening, guaranteed order and civic peace, at whatever price, unsurprisingly takes on the force of an *imprimatur.* The hopeless fragmentation and chaos (in a negative characterization) of medieval Europe—divided as it was into many kingdoms under an overarching if underawing (pardon the neologism) Holy Roman Emperor, with the Pope meddling, too—is the most often cited explanation of the need, having teleological historic force, for sovereign states. The medieval system of rule was "a patchwork of overlapping and incomplete rights of government . . . inextricably superimposed and tangled" with "different juridical instances . . . geographically interwoven and stratified, . . . plural allegiances, asymmetrical suzerainties and anomalous enclaves" abounding.[18] Is this any way to run a continent? Thus the defenders if not the celebrants of the move toward state sovereignty are said to have reasoned. The Thomistic denial of absolute sovereign power to any of the component communities of Christendom, including papacy and empire, gives way to the construction of a perpetual, supreme power, a King's body which could not be dismembered. The Sovereign is the final judge.

(b) The rediscovery "from Roman law of the concept of absolute private property and the simultaneous emergence of mutually exclusive territorial state formations" go together, the great modern classics in political theory being produced in response to a "legitimation crisis," or, another formulation, Rome transmitted the conception of sovereign in the form of the Emperor's *imperium* to the Middle Ages, but this did not really germinate meaningfully until legists, mostly French, crystallized the idea of state sovereignty with discursive and meta-historical justification drawn from one theory of what Rome had, in fact, deeded.[19] One brief example, a statement of Bologna University, famous for its law school, in 1443, updating Roman law to the present moment: "There is one judge, from whom the final decision of cases comes, lest with many judges contending, and no one supreme, litigations would never be finished. Also, no family, no community, no kingdom can remain in its full *status,* unless it has one supreme ruler; because from divisions of heads there easily arises division and schism among the members."[20] The King becomes Emperor in his Kingdom and the formulation *rex imperator in regno suo* is laid on.[21]

The standard narrative, or classical theory, then, holds that sovereignty is indivisible and inalienable. It defines the supreme, the *above* all else. This is, of course, far more than a legal theory or task: it involves civic order, identity, and images of well-being or danger. According to Charles Merriam, sovereignty "finds its source in an original contract and abides permanently in the body politic, the creature of the compact." Sovereignty shifts from King to State, and this State "can no more alienate its sovereignty than a man can alienate his will and remain a man."[22] Rousseau, for example, protects sovereignty in this way through his postulation of the alienability of the general will. The State and sovereignty are united.

Enacted as a politics of terror in the French Revolution, popular sovereignty constituted internal enemies on a par with external foes. The Jacobin Committee of Public Safety, identifying its will with the general will, declared: "Whereas the French people has manifested its will, everyone who is opposed to it is outside its sovereignty; everyone outside the sovereignty is an enemy. . . . Between the people and its enemies, there is nothing in common but the sword."[23] Sovereignty in this scenario explodes its traditional boundary defining function, a world in which the law of external force applies to "foreigners" and justice (with such limiting cases as slaves, for example) pertains among citizens. "Within a country's boundaries no law counts other than that issued by the sovereign, be it prince, parliament or people— no higher law, no imperial law, no divine law, no natural law. There is no appeal to any higher court, no arbiter, avenger or ultimate guardian of peace and justice." This is the legal freedom "of every sovereign country in the regulation of its own *domestic* affairs" [emphasis mine]. People "cling to the magic" of this conception, Arnold Brecht notes wistfully.[24] And this conception can turn upon "the people" themselves should popular sovereign will find among the ranks of the people enemies akin to external hostiles.

Yet those (myself included) who lament the excesses of sovereignty, whether in autocratic or popular forms, cannot do without it: all critiques must take it on as a point of reference, if not a starting point. The least interesting treatments of this theme are those that condemn sovereignty and go on to construct a fantasy world that would come into being were it dissolved altogether. Better, then, to criticize those theories that treat the state and sovereignty as an unproblematic unity. Following the lead of James Tully, one can take matters a step further and link the reigning juridical notion of the state to a legalistic construction of the self. Tully characterizes juridical theorizing as the "dominant ideology" of modern political thought and argues that it contains the following elements. "The state is represented as an independent, territorial monopoly of political power. Political power is the right to kill in order to enforce universal rule of either objective right or subjective rights, such as rights, natural law, common good, tradition, majority will, modernization, or the constitution. Political power is exercised either directly by some sovereign body (monarch, community as a whole, elite) or indirectly by some representative body . . . to whom power is either delegated or alienated by a sovereign power."[25]

The vast majority of "sovereignty analysts" can live with this. Sovereignty triumphed, F. H. Hinsley insists, because it more or less *had* to: the concept was "sooner or later unavoidable" because "men have thought of power in terms of sovereignty," or at least came overwhelmingly to think this way given a "primary need to ensure effective exercise of power, the more so as the growing complexity of the community was serving to emphasize the importance of the state." We have little choice but to stick with sovereignty for one very basic reason: "The internal mechanism of the modern body politic would grind to a halt if the assumption that there was a final and absolute authority within it were to be abandoned. In international practice the existence of a sovereign authority within the separate community is universally recognized as the essential qualification of its membership in the international community."[26] The state is "sovereign in the domestic context" and this sovereignty qualifies it for that agonistic arena, the international system. Harold Laski's qualifiers, articulated in 1921, that the "orthodox theory of sovereignty" in fact coerces the parts "into a unity" and thereby places itself "at the disposal of the social group which, at any given historic moment, happens to dominate the life of the state,"[27] falls out of most accounts of the standard narrative. Sovereignty is reified and one does not, laments Laski, inquire into the purposes for which this particular order is maintained. Indeed, the United States Supreme Court has, from time to time, joined the chorus: "Rules come and go; governments end and forms of government change; but sovereignty survives. A political society cannot endure without a supreme will somewhere. Sovereignty is never held in suspense."[28]

One more brief restatement of the classic theory: (a) internally, sovereignty is power to order a domestic arena, (the word "domestic" implying that such order has already been achieved), (b) externally, sovereign powers exist in a system of at least theoretical independence and equality whose relations are controlled by principles which are the reverse of those which comprise the internal structure of states, on the strong or classical construction of sovereignty. A modified defense creates, or sees, an analogy if not a homology between juridical terms of internal and external rule. Central to the classical account is the notion of "legal subjectivity," drawn from the Romans and lodged in two carriers: the *paterfamilias,* and the force of command or will in law, *jus,* derived from the *populus Romanus* construed as a unified subject. Just as the *paterfamilias* was the "sole, self-determined, and in their sphere sovereign representative(s) of right," so the "multiplicity of equal wills" composed of all multiple "fathers" culminated in a center of "common legal subjectivity," the will or voice of abstract, collective legal personality.[29] Traces of this construction appear in all early modern theories of sovereignty—this despite a recent claim that sovereignty as supreme authority has a historic meaning, now lapsed. "I hesitate to include a fourth meaning, of a husband in relation to his wife, which is as obsolete as meanings get."[30]

Gender disappears in standard defenses of the standard account; nor does it show up in many recent and critical treatments of sovereignty. There is one very large hint that gender has something to do with the classic formulation of sovereignty as a boundary setting discourse of inside/outside, order/chaos, and that is the deployment of the category "domestic" to a politics whenever one's theorizing is framed by the supra-domestic, the inter-national. The domestic arena is peculiarly the arena inhabited by women; it is a particular power-site.[31] The word comes from the Latin, *domesticus, domus,* and it is "of or pertaining to the household or family, as domestic duties." To domesticate is to tame. This suggests that the domestication of the household is a central if untheorized and submerged feature of the discourse of sovereignty. Roman private law of absolute possession and rule was that of the father over his "dependents," his subjects, and, as we have already seen, Roman private law was reinscribed in the laws of sovereign states, in articulating the rights and powers of the sovereign states, in articulating the rights and powers of the sovereign, in the West.

Let me flesh out the preoccupation, indeed the obsession, of sovereign-discoursers with a unified will. There must be one final voice, one final will, brought to bear against cacophony and chaos. As God's will is singular, so must be the Sovereign's. For Bodin, the family lacks perpetual and absolute sovereignty, being a "right ordering of a group of persons owing obedience to the head of a household," but a commonwealth is the right ordering of a number of families by a sovereign power. The two are analogized and within the family, as within the commonwealth, authority is singular and patriarchal. The power, authority, and command a husband has over his wife is "allowed by both divine and positive law to be honourable and right," and the father alone has a "natural right to command," standing as he does in the image of God, the Father of all things. Hobbes gives dominion to both husband and wife but the family lacks sovereignty and is not, for him, a major concern; however, the masculinized face of the Sovereign is retained. This "personalization of sovereign power arose out of a continuation of the arguments from unity and peace. . . . It achieves this purpose by providing a point of resolution for the conflicts arising within a society."[32]

Even liberal theorists who are not preoccupied with sovereignty, and who reject strong dominion theories in the patriarchal tradition, remain concerned with who shall have final say in matters of dispute.

Although the master of the family does not possess legal power of life or death over any member of his family, *pace* Roman law and Bodin, some degree of order is needed and in a case of marital dissension rule "naturally falls to the Man's share as the abler and stronger." Jeremy Bentham, for example, settles competition between man and wife by lodging final say in one party—there cannot be a divided will—and, as the man is almost everywhere the stronger of the two, the final willing belongs to him. This preoccupation with the will and willing and final say is one entry point, then, into the discourse of sovereignty as a gendered enterprise.[33]

Having scratched the surface of this complex matter, I will conclude by offering intimations of fruitful ways to explore the lingering impact of sovereignty on our imaginations and identities. Here are a number of possible directions for fruitful reimagining:

RETHINKING POWER

In my own work, I drew upon Hannah Arendt (as do many current critics of reified images of statist power), noting her attempt to rescue politics from war by separating power from violence. "By conflating the crude instrumentalism of violence with power, defined by Arendt as the human ability to act in concert and to begin anew, we guarantee further loss of space within which authentic empowerment is possible. In this way violence nullifies power and stymies political being."[34] Fine and provocative, as is her insistent use of the metaphor of natality to characterize new and fragile political beginnings. But Arendt is by no means unproblematic. Indeed, when it comes to relations between states, she opts for a Hobbesian war of all against all. We have wars because there is "no final arbiter in international affairs." To be sure, she decries "the sovereignty of the state" as the source of this Hobbesian rule. But that is as far as she goes, despite the fact that she declares the "identification of freedom with sovereignty" to be "perhaps the most pernicious and dangerous consequence of the political equation of freedom and free will," adding that the "famous sovereignty of political bodies has always been an illusion, which, moreover, can be maintained only by instruments of violence, that is, with essentially nonpolitical means." It follows that if men "wish to be free, it is precisely sovereignty they must renounce."[35]

This is a terribly untheorized feature to Arendt's political thought, as is her claim that the Constitution of the United States knows nothing of sovereigns or sovereignty. In making this claim she cites the case *Chisholm v. Georgia*, in which Justice Wilson declared: "To the Constitution of the United States the term sovereign is totally unknown. There is but one place where it could have been used with propriety. [Wilson had the Preamble to the Constitution in mind.] But, even in that place it would not, perhaps, have comported with the delicacy of those, who ordained and established that constitution. They might have announced themselves 'sovereign' people of the United States: But serenely conscious of the fact, they avoided the ostentatious declaration."[36] But nineteen years later, Chief Justice Marshall ostentatiously asserted that: "The jurisdiction of the nation within its own territory is necessarily exclusive and absolute. It is susceptible of no limitation not imposed by itself. Any restriction upon it, deriving validity from an external source, would imply a diminution of its sovereignty to the extent of the restriction . . . ."[37]

Clearly sovereignty is part and parcel of the repertoire of political and juridical concepts in the United States. But the matter is open to contestation. Indeed, Sanford Levinson argues that the United States Constitution features two radically different conceptions of law and the constitution itself: one stresses the constitution as the guarantor of justice; the other, the constitution as an instrument of sovereign will. Specifically, Levinson notes the 1793 case *Prigg v. Pennsylvania* which identified the constitution with "the sovereign will of the people," and declared, in effect, that oppression could be mandated through constitutional forms.[38] Arendt looks at but one version in her eagerness to free the new world from the deadly "sovereign" grip of the old.

Second, the sovereign self as a problematic entity. The sovereign state and the sovereign, autonomous self are linked, so argue a number of contemporary theorists. A few representative examples of this argument must suffice to signal its suggestiveness: "To say that a state is sovereign means that it decides for itself how it will cope with its internal and external problems, including whether or not to seek assistance from others and in doing so to limit its freedom by making commitments to them."[39] And: "It is by virtue of their autonomy, or their capacity to act freely, that *citizens* are constituted as members of a state and as bearers of rights. It is this capacity of the citizen that gives rise to the sovereignty of the state."[40] There is a growing body of feminist work that challenges the predetermined "identity" of the self as sovereign and questions the view of rationality it endorses. But there is an irony in all this, for even as this feminist challenge continues, other aspects of feminist discourse, for example, the dominant argument for abortion as untrammeled choice, shore up the boundaries of self-sovereignty as possession, even claiming property and ownership rights in the self. To some extents and purposes, the sovereign self is problematized, and to others reified, in feminist discourse. This bears further examination.

Although a strong deconstructive route is not the way to go here—it is too thin to sustain a compelling account of political identity—there is plenty of room for examining "the complicity between the sovereign subject and the sovereign state in modern political theory," and indicating that the statist imperatives to which such a theory of political agency is linked may not, over the long run, best serve feminist concerns—concerns that are quotidian in nature and thus fall outside the too-narrow frame of the "sovereign subject as a privileged political agent."[41]

Finally, can we imagine a secure politics *sans* strong sovereignty? Such a politics certainly exists in theory. Indeed, much of the political writing by Central Europeans over the past several decades embraces precisely this possibility. I have in mind those who theorize civil society in opposition to an authoritarian, sovereign state apparatus. The alternative they pose to state-privileging sovereign discourse is *not* a cleaned-up version of Rousseauian popular sovereignty, but something far more subtle. Here the writings of Adam Michnik and Václav Havel are especially important. Theorizing democracy, Michnik seeks to hold tradition and change in tension with one another; to mediate claims of community and individual freedom. His world is a world in "permanent conflict between conservatism and contestation" and if state, in the name of sovereignty, intervenes in favor of one or the other, "pluralism is destroyed."[42] Havel writes of politics as "practical morality . . . humanly measured care for our fellow humans."[43] He downplays sovereignty in favor of civil society as a "domestic" and "international" imperative. A third theorist who has elaborated an alternative to statist versions of sovereignty is a noted Polish philosopher, currently residing in Rome, who has addressed this theme repeatedly, arguing along these lines: "The state is firmly sovereign when it *governs* society and also *serves* the common good of society and allows the nation to realize its own subjectivity, its own identity."[44] The notion of sovereignty here noted is located in neither the state *per se,* nor in some unmediated construction of the sovereign will of the people, but in the various associations of civil society in dialogue with one another as "subjects." This authoritative dialogue, in turn, sustains the state as an entity whose legitimate purpose is to see that rules for civility are followed and the various loci of human social existence, necessary to human dignity and freedom, are protected and served. The co-existence of overlapping, porous entities is assumed. *Rights* inhere in communities and groups, as well as individuals. Thus more power devolves to "mediating institutions" or flows from them than in statist constructions. The self is neither the fully sovereign abstract, legalistic subject *nor* a decentered, fragmented, chameleon-like self.[45] This chastened version of sovereignty is protective of plurality internally and cosmopolitanism externally. The possibility of agreement and alliances is always open. The state is not a hard-shelled, impermeable entity; rather, it exists in an international society in which sovereignty is necessarily limited. States are nested in wider societies, in strategic cultures, if you will. Attunement to *this* stubborn reality lends itself to an analysis at odds with the austere, de-historicized and thoroughly lamentable penchant for formal modeling, for obsessive "numbers crunching," that continues to flourish in the academic study of "IR"—perhaps as a latter-day version of Nero fiddling as Rome burns.

CONCLUSION

The nation-state is a phenomenon that cannot be imagined or legislated out of existence. Needing others to define ourselves, we will remain inside a state/nation centered discourse of war and politics, for better and for worse, so long as states remain the best way we have devised for protecting and sustaining a way of life in common. But we can try to tame and limit the demands of sovereignty; we can, perhaps, move toward what I am tempted to call a post-sovereign politics. I have in mind a politics that shifts the focus of political loyalty and identity from sacrifice (actual or *in situ*) to responsibility. My target is both images of the sovereign self as an unproblematic, unified, sharply boundaried phenomenon as well as the sovereign state in its full-blown, untrammeled instantiation.

Hélène Carère d'Encausse recently argued that attachment to a nation is "an accomplishment of civilized man, not a regression. The nation-state is not a tribal construction. Elements of familialism and tribalism may reverberate and are certain features of any genealogical construction of the modern identity, but they do not dominate."[46] Identification with a national "imagined community" is a complex, many-sided construction. It taps particularism and universalism. Indeed, one might argue it *requires* such, being composed of norma-tively vital aspects of both ethnicity and universal values, organic integration and voluntarism. Human beings require concrete reference groups in order to attain individuality and identity but too complete immersion in such groups limits the boundaries of identity and of identification to fixed familial, tribal, or territorial lines. John A. Armstrong, in a recent piece on "Contemporary Ethnicity," worries that extreme voluntarist individualism leads to the loss of a coherent identity.[47] Statist demands that extract the "last full measure of devo-tion" that most of us would willingly offer to family and dear friends, is a corrective device to our current deracination. That is, modernity denatures non-voluntarist obligations and commitments, then recon-stitutes and abstracts them as mandated blood sacrifice in the name of the collective, a sacrifice of "radical severity," in political theorist George Kateb's words.

Kateb muses interestingly on the question of sacrifice as a man-dated obligation. According to Kateb, no one has a moral obligation to die; hence, conscription is illegitimate. One *may* sacrifice oneself for a "child or a defenseless loved one" but to construe this possibility in contractual terms is "to cheapen it." Kateb detects a perhaps unavoid-able conundrum in modern universalistically cast constitutional republics: on the one hand, and in light of individualist construals, the social group is not idolized; the collective is not sacralized. This makes possible, or should, the free-flow of "self-sacrificing love" toward particular individuals or groups. On the other hand, a "man-dated obligation to die" emerges with greatest force "only in an indi-vidualist moral universe" in which persons have been stripped of ties of great robustness and insistency to particular others. Kateb's argu-ment tends in this direction and leaves us suspended in a political and moral universe in which sacrifice is legally mandated, yes, but the legitimacy of such demands is ongoingly challenged.[48] The demand and the challenge are both reactions to a strongly individual-ist social order.

What Kateb gestures toward is an ethic of responsibility by contrast to what I have called a will-to-sacrifice. An ethic of responsibility means one is answerable, accountable to another, for something; one is liable to be called to account. One is also a being, capable of fulfilling an obligation or trust; reliable; trustworthy. This presumes, indeed requires, a particular construction of what Charles Taylor calls "the modern identity," one constituted in and through the notion of self-responsible freedom.[49] Softening the demands of the iron grip, sovereignty=sacrifice, does *not* mean so loosening the bonds of reason that the self flies off in all directions and can find no good reason to prefer *this* to *that* and can hear in such notions as "responsibility" only a dour and crabby moralism.

The final words shall be Havel's, for he is currently *primus inter pares* in articulating a non-sovereign ethic that retains a strong understanding of accountability:

> The problem of human identity remains at the center of my thinking about human affairs. . . . As you must have noticed from my letters, the importance of the notion of human responsibility has grown in my meditations. It has begun to appear with increasing clarity, as that fundamental point from which all identity grows and by which it stands or falls; it is the foundation, the root, the center of gravity, the constructional principle or axis of identity, something like the "idea" that determines its degree and type. It is the mortar binding it together, and when the moral dries out, identity too begins irreversibly to crumble and fall apart. (That is why I wrote you that the secret of man is the secret of his responsibility.)[50]

NOTES

1. Alan James, *Sovereign Statehood: The Basis of International Society* (London: George Allen and Unwin, 1986), 7.

2. This requires introducing gendered representations explicitly, for such representations proliferate in the story of sovereignty as a heroic saga, the bringing of order to a "domestic space." Let me add that there is no full-blown feminist alternative to sovereignty discourse—not unless one wishes to indulge in millenarian flights of fancy—but a recasting and rethinking that may yield alternative performance requirements, that may compel political action in ways at odds with those historically characteristic of sovereign policies, is not only possible but a vital necessity. One must ask whether state independence is so entangled with the modernist project of what Charles Taylor calls "self-responsible freedom and individual rights" that we abandon it at our peril. Sovereignty is a site of political and theoretical contestation, perhaps now more than ever in our bloody century.

3. Bernard Crick, "The Curse of Sovereignty," *The New Statesman*, 14 May 1982, 6-7.

4. Michael Howard, *The Causes of War*, 2d ed. (Cambridge: Harvard University Press, 1984), 28-32.

5. St. Augustine, *The City of God*, ed. David Knowles (Baltimore, Md.: Penguin, 1972), book I, chaps. 31, 42.

6. David Jayne Hill, "The Evils of Sovereignty," in *The State in International Relations*, ed. Richard H. Cox (San Francisco: Chandler Publishing Co., 1965), 81-88.

7. See, e.g., Donna Warnock, "Patriarchy is a Killer: What People Concerned About Peace and Justice Should Know," in *Reweaving the Web of Life*, ed. Pam McAllister (Philadelphia: New World, 1982). See also: Laura Duhan, "Feminism and Peace Theory," in *In the Interest of Peace: A Spectrum of Philosophic Perspectives* (Wakefield, N.H.: Longwood Press, 1990).

8. Joan Wallach Scott, *Gender and the Politics of History* (New York: Columbia University Press, 1988), 48, 49.

9. R. B. J. Walker, "State Sovereignty, Global Civilization, and the Rearticulation of Political Space," *World Order Studies Program Occasional Papers*, No. 18, (Center of International Studies, Princeton University, 1988), 1-48.

10. "The Power and Powerlessness of Women," in *Power Trips and Other Journeys*, ed. Jean Bethke Elshtain (Madison: University of Wisconsin Press, 1990).

11. Reverend John Murray, "A Biblical Theological Study," in *The Sovereignty of God, or the Proceedings of the First American Calvinistic Conference*, ed. Jacob T. Hoogstra (Grand Rapids, Mich.: Zondervan Publishing House, 1939), 25-44.

12. "The rationale of modern sovereignty owes much to the inventive fantasy of philosophers," writes Susan Buck-Morss in her essay, "Democratic Sovereignty: A Contradiction in Terms" (unpub. mss., 8). If she is right, and I think she is, Bodin with Hobbes close on his heels are among the most inventive. Each is implicated in "the birth of 'ideology'. . . the peculiarly modern habit of justifying political acts by reference to abstract, metaphysical ideals." Some may cavil that Hobbes is no metaphysician. This may be so but what Carl Schmitt calls the "decisionist cast" of his thinking remains both personalistic and architectonic. The quote is from Antony Black, *Monarchy and Community: Political Ideas in the Later Conciliar Controversy, 1430-1450* (Cambridge: Cambridge University Press, 1970), 130.

13. Carl Schmitt, *Political Theology: Four Chapters on the Concept of Sovereignty*, trans. George Schwab (Cambridge, Mass.: The MIT Press, 1985), 36.

14. Jean Bodin, *Six Books of the Commonwealth*, trans. M. J. Tooley (New York: Macmillan, 1955), 25-27, 28, 32.

15. Thomas Hobbes, *The Leviathan* (New York: Penguin, 1968), chaps. 17, 18, esp. 227, 236.

16. Black, *Monarchy and Community*, 80, 81.

17. Before Bodin and Hobbes had penned their classics, the peace of Augsburg (1555) had imbedded the principle of *cuius regio-eius religio* in treaty law applicable to German principalities. Luther had unleashed more than he knew, helping to set in motion a theory of self sovereignty that "mirrors the sovereignty of the state." As I have written in *Women and War* (New York: Basic Books, 1987), "Luther prepares the way for the political theology that underlies the emergence of the nation-state. Its full-blown dimensions become more visible in seventeenth-century calls for holy wars, providentially enjoined so that tyranny might be banished and the True Godhead worshiped. . . . Following the excesses of Europe's religious wars, the crusading ethos does not disappear; it regroups, taking shape as the popular bellicism and militarism of the nineteenth century, feeding notions of sovereignty as a secular mimesis of God as ultimate Law Giver whose commandments must be obeyed and whose power to judge is absolute. Similarly, the triumphant state cannot be resisted, nor its will thwarted" (135-36).

18. Perry Anderson, *Lineages of the Absolute State*, (London: NLB, 1974), 20, 23, 26.

19. John Gerard Ruggie, "Continuity and Transformation in the World Polity," in *Neorealism and Its Critics*, ed. Robert Keohane (New York: Columbia University Press, 1986), 131-57, 144; and F. H. Hinsley, *Sovereignty*, 2d ed. (Cambridge: Cambridge University Press, 1986), 45.

20. Cited in Black, 74. See also Walter Ullmann, "The Development of the Medieval Idea of Sovereignty," *English Historical Review*, no. 250 (1949): 1-33.

21. Gaines Post, "Two Notes on Nationalism in the Middle Ages," *Traditio* 9 (1953): 281-320. Raymond Aron wrote in *Peace and War: A Theory of International Relations,* trans. Richard Howard and Annette Baker Fox (New York: Doubleday and Co., 1966): "Absolute sovereignty corresponded to the ambition of kings eager to free themselves from the restriction Church and Empire imposed upon them, medieval residues. At the same time, it permitted condemning the privileges of intermediate bodies: feudal lords, regions, cities, guilds—privileges which no longer had any basis as the sovereign's will was the unique source of rights and duties."

22. Charles E. Merriam, Jr., *History of Sovereignty Since Rousseau: Studies in History, Economics and Public Law*, vol. 12, no. 4 (New York: Columbia University Press, 1900), 33-35.

23. Cited in Francois Furet, *Interpreting the French Revolution*, trans. by Elborg Forster (New York: Cambridge University Press), 53.

24. Arnold Brecht, "Sovereignty," in *War in Our Time*, eds., Hans Speier and Alfred Kahler (New York: W. W. Norton, 1939), 58-78.

25. James Tully, "The Pen is a Mighty Sword: Quentin Skinner's Analysis of Politics," in *Meaning and Context: Quentin Skinner and His Critics*, ed.

Tully (Princeton: Princeton University Press, 1988) 7-25. Russell Hardin, encapsulating the juridical view, notes that what rights are to individuals, sovereignty is to states; that national sovereignty is "merely the external analog of the internal domestic sovereignty." (Hardin, "Popular Sovereignty and International Intervention," unpub. ms., 17.)

26. Hinsley, *Sovereignty*, 17.

27. Harold J. Laski, *The Foundations of Sovereignty and Other Essays* (London: George Allen Unwin, Ltd., 1921), 28-29.

28. *U.S. v. Curtiss-Wright Export Corp.*, 299 U.S. 304 (1936).

29. See Otto Gierke's difficult but valuable discussion in *Otto Gierke: Associations and Law, The Classical and Early Christian Stages*, ed. and trans. by George Heiman (Toronto: University of Toronto Press, 1977), 96-97.

30. William Safire, "Send in Sovereign for Socialist," *New York Times*, 6 January 1991, 7, 10.

31. I am not implying that women are, or ever have been, wholly powerless within the domestic boundary, but they have been engaged in a complex set of mediations that did not take place on an even playing field, so to speak, particularly when the dominant domestic discourse culminated with the terrible *pater familias*, at least in theory. In practice, many Roman fathers appear to have been decent fellows.

32. Black, *Monarch and Community*, 67.

33. For example: a headline during the 1991 Gulf War read: "Bush's Leadership Bends the Nation To His Will." Jeremy Bentham, *The Principles of Morals and Legislation* (New York: Itofner, 1948), 279.

34. "Realism, Just War, and Feminism in a Nuclear Age," *Political Theory* 13, no. 1 (February 1985): 39-57.

35. Hannah Arendt, *Between Past and Future* (New York: Penguin Books, 1980). From the essay, "What is Freedom?" 164-65.

36. *Chisholm v Georgia*, 2 Dallas 419, 454 (1793). See Hannah Arendt, *On Violence* (New York: Harcourt Brace Jovanovich, 1969), 6. The question before the Court in *Chisholm v. Georgia* was: May a citizen of one state sue another state in the federal courts? The answer: Sure. The result: Amendment XI to reverse the decision. Amendment XI reads: "The Judicial power of the United States shall not be construed to extend to any suit in law or equity, commenced or prosecuted against one of the U.S. by Citizens of another State, or by Citizens of Subjects of any Foreign State" (8 January 1798.)

37. *The School Exchange v. M'Faddon*, 11 U.S. [7 Cranch] 116, 136 (1812).

38. Sanford Levinson, *Constitutional Faith* (Princeton: Princeton University Press, 1988), 68-69.

39. Kenneth Waltz, "Political Structures," in *Neorealism and its Critics*, ed. Robert O. Keohane, (New York: Columbia University Press, 1986), 90-91.

40. Marianne Constable, "Sovereignty and Citizenship in American Immigration Law," unpub. ms., 10. One could, of course, reverse this formulation and

argue that sovereign states constitute citizens as self-contained bearers of rights and claimants upon the state in the form of juridically defined entitlements.

41. Kirsti McClure, "Deconstructing Pluralism: Of Subject and Sovereignty on the Cusp of Post-modernity," unpub. mss., 11.

42. Adam Michnik, "Towards a Civil Society: Hopes for a Polish Democracy," *Times Literary Supplement*, 19-25 February 1988, 188, 198-99.

43. *Václav Havel, or Living in Truth*, ed. Jan Vladislav (London: Faber and Faber, 1987).

44. Cited in Timothy Garton Ash, *The Uses of Adversity: Essays on the Fate of Central Europe* (New York: Random House, 1989), 53. From a homily at Jasna Gora in 1983. The Polish philosopher is, of course, Pope John Paul II.

45. One irony of such accounts is that, in the name of loosening things up, one often finds instead a politics that pushed towards an absolutism of "the particular" and this winds up being little different in practice from the absolutism of the juridical subject: both sorts of selves take their "cases to court," so to speak, rather than into democratic dialogue.

46. See Hélène Carère d'Encausse, "Springtime of Nations," *The New Republic*, 21 January 1991, 17-22.

47. John A. Armstrong, "Contemporary Ethnicity: The Moral Dimension in Comparative Perspective," *The Review of Politics* 52 (1990): 166.

48. George Kateb, *The Inner Ocean* (Ithaca: Cornell University Press, 1992).

49. Charles Taylor, *The Malaise of Modernity* (Toronto: Anasi Press, 1991), 117.

50. Václav Havel, *Letters to Olga* (New York: Henry Holt, 1989), 145.

PAUL A. CHILTON

THE MEANING OF *SECURITY*

"And, you all know, security is mortals' chiefest enemy." These are the words of Hecate to the three Witches in *Macbeth*. A modern reader may experience momentary difficulty in constructing a meaning for them, since *security* has come to be regarded in twentieth-century anglophone culture as one of the chiefest goods. Hecate's words are thus paradoxical, unless one is a critic of the security culture itself. Shakespeare and his contemporaries, however, although they had begun to use the word also in something like its modern sense, knew a different meaning based on the word's Latin etymology. *Security* derives from *se* (without) and *cura* (care), whence culpably *care-less* and *careless*. The shift from negative to positive meaning is connected with the transmutations of society in the early modern period, and in particular with the rise of a political culture predicated upon the nation-state. Such semantic genealogies demonstrate the relativity of linguistically encoded concepts. But the crucial synchronic question remains: If *security* no longer means what the Witches meant by it, what *is* its twentieth-century meaning? More precisely, what concepts, images and emotions are activated when speakers and hearers use the word? If the present meaning arises from historical, social, and political change, not merely some arbitrary twists and turns of language, how well will this concept continue to function in a period of dramatic change? Indeed, could the older sense, the lack of care, be a concept that could serve us better?

POLITICAL SCIENCE, LANGUAGE, AND MEANING

If the concept *security* is embedded in language and culture, the initial problem is to disentangle it. How might this be done? Language and meaning have never been far from the concerns of scholars who

193

have pondered the nature of politics. Murray Edelman provides one of the earliest, and most clear-sighted, modern accounts of the centrality of language, meaning, and metaphor in political culture. He sees language as constitutive of realities, and a central element of all symbolic activities. More specifically, he regards "metaphor and myth" as central elements in his meaning-oriented accounts of political culture. To a certain extent, this view of language reflects the linguistic relativism of the tradition of Richard Sapir and Benjamin Lee Whorf. For instance, Edelman asserts that "Language forms are a critical element in the shaping of beliefs; they do so in ways we do not consciously experience and so are nonobvious."[1] His view of metaphor, though formulated in very general terms, is remarkably consistent with the view now adopted in cognitive linguistics:

> Thought is metaphorical and metaphor pervades language, for the unknown, the new, the unclear, and the remote are apprehended by one's perceptions of identities with the familiar. Metaphor, therefore, defines the pattern of perception to which people respond.[2]

Another property noted by Edelman is that metaphor selects certain perceptions and ignores others. The political significance of metaphor for Edelman is that it is an "instrument for shaping political support and opposition and the premises upon which decisions are made."[3] What is at issue are not the rhetorically prominent flourishes of political oratory, but the patterns of thought that are taken for granted in a political culture. Political speech, argues Edelman, "evokes its most compelling cognitions . . . through the metaphoric views it takes for granted rather than those it explicitly asserts."[4] The political significance of metaphor is thus that it is a means for determining the basic attitudes and assumptions that structure decision making.[5]

Edelman's insights have not been applied in the field of international relations and security studies, despite a wealth of work constantly alluding to language in the post-structuralist vein.[6] It would not be entirely true to say that theorists working within orthodox international relations theory have not shown concern, even anxiety, about what the word *security* means or should mean. Indeed those theorists who have sought a thorough understanding of security as a concept have emphasized its intrinsically problematic nature. This puzzlement may have been partly due to the fact that they remained to a greater or lesser degree enmeshed in realist discourse, or to the fact that their understanding of the nature of concepts and language led them to seek too much clarity. Arnold Wolfers, for instance, who in 1945 had been instrumental in a highly influential Brookings Institute study, produced a paper some twenty years later on "national security as an ambiguous symbol."[7] Another twenty years on, in 1983, Barry Buzan's important and innovative inquiry into the field of security makes a similar point. Seeking to steer a course between Realism and Idealism, Buzan notes on the one hand that security is, in the words of W. B. Gallie, an "essentially contested concept," yet on the other, he asks what is the real-world "referent" of the noun *security*, assuming in objectivist fashion that such a "referent" must exist.[8]

Such studies manage to break with neither realist epistemology nor realist political theory. Buzan's organizing framework remains in many respects the neorealist model most clearly and influentially delineated by Kenneth Waltz. In looking for the objective "referent" of the word *security*, his universe of discourse is still structured by Waltz's three-tier model of global politics. The first level is that of the individual "in" the state; the second, is the state itself with its containing and protective perimeters; and the third is the outside world, the domain of the anarchic international system. These elements, the inside, the boundary, and the outside, derive from a powerful and pervasive spatial image, that of an impermeable container, which is omnipresent in the semantics of natural languages and responsible for very many metaphorical expressions encoded in them. What is more, from early modern times to the late twentieth century, the container image lies at the heart of Western political discourse centering on the state, sovereignty, and security.

These considerations suggest that it would be fruitful to pursue Edelman's insights into the importance of language, and in particular of metaphor, in political thinking and political decision making. Linguistic detail is important for three reasons. First, it constitutes our main evidence as to the underlying belief systems that underwrite international political discourse. Secondly, it constitutes, *per se*, the very stuff of political interaction, and therefore needs to be analyzed as precisely that—a form of action. Thirdly, any individual using a particular language will share the particular semantic system of the language with other speakers of that particular language.

This does not mean that the meanings of the language are fixed. By semantic system, I mean the minimal system of meanings shared by speakers, on the basis of which richer and more precise contextual meanings are implied and inferred in the process of communication. It follows that it is necessary to take account of aspects of the particular linguistic (semantic) system, and of aspects of the connected belief systems of the culture, which may influence, more or less unconsciously, conceptualization and interactive habits. Many aspects of linguistic systems contribute to political discourses and the conceptualizations associated with them, but in this chapter I follow Edelman's emphasis on metaphor, although my understanding and analysis of metaphor is based on cognitive linguistics.

My aim is to make explicit the presence of metaphor in the linguistic and cognitive capacities of human speakers who live in polities in which discourse yields, amongst other connected concepts, the concept *security*. In one sense this is the aim of Buzan pursued by other means, namely: "to map the domain of security as an essentially contested concept . . . to define the conceptual sub-structures on which the mass of empirical studies by strategists and others rests."[9]

METAPHOR AND POLITICAL CONCEPTS

Research in cognitive semantics has repeatedly indicated that physical experience appears time and time again as the metaphorical basis of key aspects of meaning, in particular of polysemy and idiomatic expressions. This is an important fact for understanding the current as well as the possible conceptualization of international relations, defense, and security. Polysemous words, idiomatic meanings, and expressions more explicitly presented as metaphors can be understood as systematic, that is not merely arbitrary or random or idiosyncratic transfers of meaning from source domains arising in the peculiar physical and social experiences of humans. The source domains can be thought of as two kinds, although they overlap and of course they vary from culture to culture.[10] The first is bodily experience. The interaction of human bodies with objects in space seems to yield cognitive image-schemas, gestalts, and kinesthetic images. These are the *preconceptual* basis of conceptual and linguistic organization. They are certainly not the *only* factors influencing linguistic and conceptual structure, but as will be seen they provide a revealing way of understanding systems of thought such as the system of realism. The second kind of source domain for metaphorical expressions is cultural experience, stored as stereotypic frames and scripts. Such sources are relative to cultures in a more obvious way than are kinesthetic image schemas. They include such scripts as social rituals, games, and even spatialized frames such as buildings, with associated scripts for entering, visiting, exiting, and leaving. Obvious examples would be the American liking for the baseball metaphor for politics, and the poker metaphor for international competition. Some culture-based metaphors derive from socioeconomic modes of organization. For example, industrial society seems to give rise to a time-is-money metaphor that becomes encoded in the stable core of the lexicon, giving rise to systematic and productive lexical expressions: time can be "bought," "spent," "wasted," "managed," "invested," used "profitably," and so on.

It is fruitful to concentrate on four particular preconceptual structures which combine physical and cultural grounding in various ways. All have historically been used as the source domain for the metaphorical conceptualization of international relations, defense, and security. The first preconceptual image schema is the CONTAINER schema. It has three key elements: interior, boundary, exterior. This schema constitutes the basis for understanding the words *inside* and *outside*, and enters so fundamentally into our conceptual and linguistic systems that we do not normally attend to it. It is found, for instance, in the semantic structuring of domains as diverse as the visual field and social relationships (*come into* view, *go out* of sight, be *in* the picture, *get into* and break *out of* relationships). It is particularly significant for realist political discourse that the CONTAINER schema is closely bound up with the conceptualization of the human body, though there is considerable variation with culture and gender in its particular manifestations. Stereotypically at least, the body is conceptualized as having an inside, an outside, and a surface boundary. The boundary may be defined in terms of the skin envelope, or in terms of personal space, and be salient or non-salient. What is also significant is that the conceptualization of the body can be linked to numerous other schemas and scripts, the most obvious of which are those of disease and growth, which in turn may be linked with other constructs. Diseases are typically imagined as *invading* the body *from outside*, a notion which rests both on the CONTAINER schema and the warfare script. It is by drawing on such a cluster that the metaphor of the "body politic" has given Western political discourse a major framework for conceptualizing the nation-state, and for making inferences in discursive argumentation about intra- and interstate politics.

It is possible to reconstruct the complex systems underlying particular discourses by considering one's native speaker's knowledge of what is "grammatical," or "natural" in the linguistic culture—which is in part also a political culture. The fact that both the state and the human body may be conceptualized as containers provides a particularly cohesive network of potential entailments, which may explain why the prevailing concept of the state is not only affect-loaded but also why it appears to have a quasi-natural, taken-for-granted obviousness in political discourse of the modern period. This fact also explains the persistence and apparent naturalness of treating the state as a unified person in political discourse.

Since metaphors carry with them entailments from the source conceptual schemas and scripts, the body metaphor potentially entails a variety of concepts, including "urges," "remedies" for social "ills," "cancers," "surgical strikes," "incorporation," "decapitation," and the like. Metaphorical inferencing can then take off along well-known lines. For example, if communism is an *invasive organism, contagious sickness*, or *malignant growth*, it may follow that the body politic should be sanitized, or that the spread of disease should be stopped, or the cancer excised. Such inferences take place in the metaphorical domain, but they can be mapped back into the pragmatic domain of political, social, or military action. The CONTAINER schema is also linked with culturally relative cognitive frames, such as houses, forts, walled cities and so on, each of which have with their own variant structural elements and entailments. The conceptual connections between the CONTAINER schema, the body images, and the culturally embedded form of the stronghold help explain the effect of President Reagan's SDI rhetoric. Despite the technological implausibility, the impervious SDI "roof," "shell," or "shield" was a *cognitively* plausible and natural metaphor.[11] Another example is Gorbachev's "European house" metaphor, which in the late 1980s provided a conceptual tool for debate on the future security and political shape of Europe. In this instance the container image provided a concept of a bounded political entity and focused discourse onto the redefining of "Europe." Different understandings of the form and functions of a prototypical Western *house* (a single free-standing family dwelling) compared with the Russian *dom* (multiple apartments under one roof) yielded discrepant political entailments.

Second, the experience of physical connections between objects and between bodies is the basis for a LINK schema. The prototypical case is that of two entities related by physical contiguity or by some physical bond tying them together. An important variant—precisely, as will be seen, for the semantics of *security*—is the case of a mobile or "loose" object fixed or made stable by attachment to an immobile base. The LINK schema is projected metaphorically for concepts of social "bonds," "ties," or "attachments," abstract notions such as causal and other logical "links" and "connections," moral commitments or "obligations" in which one is "tied (down)" to something or "bound" to do something. Such conceptual structures are manifest in divergent ways, both in realist discourse and in discourses constructing notions of international society.

The third schema is the PATH schema, which has an apparent physical basis in the experience of transportation and bipedal motion. It involves structural elements such as starting point (origin), obstacle, destination (endpoint), path, and directedness toward the endpoint. It has a logic of its own, like all image schemas: It presupposes that a destination is in view or in mind, and necessitates that it be reached by passing through certain points or stages along a single continuous track without deviation or obstruction. Additionally, it may be the case that certain cultures, or certain discourses, focus more on one or the other of these elements. Thus, to focus on directedness, a single path and endpoint is to be "goal-oriented"; to focus on endpoint alone might be to be predestined or predetermined; to focus on origin might involve having a mission, that is, being sent by some source of power; to focus on the path and destination while being unsure of the direction gives the concept of quest. PATH provides the basis for abstract concepts such as purpose and political concepts such as past history and future policy. Lexical reflexes are found in expressions such as "road to socialism," "policy goals," "path to peace," "démarche," "rapprochement," and many others. "Security" itself is frequently represented as the goal of a "quest."

In realist discourse, the PATH schema contributes the cluster of images and meanings used to conceptualize states. We have seen that states are metaphorized as bodies, but they are also metaphorized as persons. Since the conceptual frame for persons involves both directional movement and purposiveness, states themselves have attributed to them (or attribute to themselves) both physical movement and goal-led purposes. Further, since states are metaphorized as CONTAINERS, the type of movement entailed is the movement of a perimeter, that is, "expansion," exerting "pressure" on contiguous containers.

The relationship between these conceptual models and the actual behavior of states is complex. It may be that states, or some states, do behave in expansive fashion. It may even be that they do so because the conceptual models enshrined in the prevalent discourse induce them to behave in such a way, and to expect other states to do the same. However, it is not universal and necessary that states behave expansively, whether they use such conceptual systems or not. The problem with the system of thinking that construes and constructs states as expanding purposive bodies is that it generalizes, naturalizes, and legitimizes such expectations.

The fourth important image schema is that of FORCE dynamics. This image schema derives from the physical experience of pressures and resistances, both exerted and received—i.e. from pushing and striking and from being struck or pushed.[12] The most important cases are probably the experience of lateral push and pull, gravitational force, and the experience of balance. Pressures and resistances are experienced along a scale that goes from total blockage to total "giving way." This schema appears to be important across a wide range of linguistic structure, including modality (possibility, necessity, permission).

FORCE images are the basis of common-sense understanding of the movement of physical bodies, but since the Renaissance they have provided the material for understanding and perhaps creating the relations, diplomatic and military, between sovereign states. Metaphors derived from the classical concepts of gravitation, dynamics, hydraulics, and magnetism seem to be centrally involved in political discourses that have over time become stabilized in the lexicon, to the point that their meanings and use are known automatically to socialized native speakers. Lexical stabilization would explain why such conventionalized metaphors appear alike in the discourse of politicians, policy makers, and academic theorists of international relations. However, the expert discourses utilize the metaphors and their entailments more densely, and more inferentially. The metaphorical structuring of the key expert terms is not normally recognized, but becomes evident when they are extracted: *stability, balance of power, alignment, equilibrium, vacuum, attraction, pressure, polarity*, etc.

A special case is the semantic sub-field, central to realist discourse, of "force," "power," and "influence." The concept of "force" depends on projections from the physical FORCE schema and associated concepts of causality. The concepts of "power," and "influence" are frequently understood in discourse in terms of hydraulic force and container schemas. The etymology of "influence" ("in"+"flow") clearly indicates this connection. All three lexical items, with their contestable but clear distinctions in our culture, are linked to elements of the physical FORCE schema. The inherent logic of the hydraulic metaphor has two highly significant entailments. The first is that the fluid ("power" or "influence") exerts constant pressure on containing surfaces, is liable to expand, overflow, spill over, exert pressure on, seep out, and infiltrate into any neighboring containers. The second is that it is necessary in consequence, according to the associated cognitive scripts, to contain the fluid, prevent seepage, stop the spread, stem the tide, hold back the flood, etc. There are of course additional metaphors, coherent with the fluid metaphor, for representing the notion of expanding influence, the best known of which is the "domino" theory—essentially a force dynamics metaphor for cause and effect dependent on simple mechanical images.

Speakers who inhabit anglophone cultures will find many of these metaphors natural, though speakers in other modern cultures will also take them for granted. What is striking is that the metaphors that pervade the lexicon are systematic and productive, not arbitrary and idiosyncratic. This suggests that they are not without consequence in the concrete process of cognition and communication. In the domain of international politics some of the implications may be summarized as follows:

(1) The concepts communicated in the vocabulary of political discourse are derived from the same cognitive sources, and by the same cognitive mechanisms, as concepts in the lexicon as a whole. Consequently, concepts and metaphors used in political discourse appear natural, as in a sense they are. They also appear to be uniquely necessary, which of course they are not.

(2) Conceptual systems, including metaphors, are not isomorphic with some determinate reality "out there." Different linguistic cultures encode different models, and different discourses make different selections and uses from their languages. It is possible to conceptualize and communicate alternative models. Although languages and discourses do not absolutely constrain conceptualization, the accepted or presupposed concepts may appear to be the only possible and natural ones to their users.

(3) Conceptual models, including metaphor, may be a good or a poor fit, functional or dysfunctional for particular circumstances, and the goodness of fit may change as the circumstances change, but just because they have apparent naturalness and are integrated in complex networks of association, existing metaphors will tend to be preferred and to persist.

These observations lead to a bolder hypothesis. The discourse of international relations—in the senses both of the conduct of and the academic inquiry into relations between states—is influenced and limited in practice by the degree to which these models are entrenched, and by the degree to which they are reflexively monitored. Change occurs through change in discourse: in part this involves change in metaphors. Linguistic analysis and discourse analysis thus can play a role in such change.

THE METAPHORICAL BASIS OF SECURITY AND CONTAINMENT

The semantics of the word *security*, as understood by Macbeth's witches, was given, or had once been given, by the etymology of the word. This is no longer the case in modern English. The semantics of the word, and its verbal and adjectival partner *secure*, can be shown to depend very largely on the LINK and CONTAINER image schemas, together with metaphorical extensions. The evidence for this lies in the systematicity of the words' polysemy, their collocations and the idioms with which they are involved. The dependence on particular image schemas anchors them in a nexus of social and political concepts.[13]

Part of the current semantics of *security* has to do with certainty and surety, notions which are expressed as metaphors based on LINK, in the variant that has to do with unstable objects being fixed in one location—that is, "secured" in the sense in which loose objects are "secured" by some physical attachment. Thus, one of the conceptual elements in the understanding of *security* is connected to the absence of motion, to stasis, and more precisely to the physical restraint of undesired motion. Since spatial concepts (in particular PATH) map metaphorically onto time, we are also talking about absence of and prevention of undesired "movement" in time, that is, undesired change: "a security" is a guarantee of a particular state of affairs over time. The frequent collocation of *secure* and *stable* also bears this analysis out with respect to the concept of change. Expressions in

English security discourse such as: "tight security," "slack security," "loose security," etc., also plainly reflect the LINK metaphor, although there is an overlap with the following metaphorical structures.

The most salient modern meanings of *security* seem to be dependent on the structural elements of the CONTAINER schema; the boundary element of the image schema is particularly crucial. If something is *secure*, then no one can get *into* it, or *out* of it: "a secure building," "secure prison," even "secure computer program." The preposition *in*, metaphorical though usually unrecognized as such, is a frequent clue: "*in* the security of their own homes," "secure *in* their beliefs," etc. The fact that the CONTAINER schema has both an inside and an outside orientation is important: containers prevent both movement *in* and movement *out*. Thus we find: "penetration of security" as well as "leaks of security," "security leaks," while a "hole in security" or a "breach in security" can imply movement in either direction.

The boundary element may become metaphorically specific in discourse. Experience of many kinds of protective surfaces is lexically encoded in natural languages: covers, lids, roofs, walls, fences, shells, shields. All these enter metaphorically into military and strategic conceptualizations: "cover troops with fire," "SDI would provide an impenetrable roof" or "shell" or "astrodome," and extended deterrence in Cold War discourse was said to provide a "nuclear umbrella over Europe." Of course, boundary surfaces are not functional if they have holes—whence expressions such as "leaky ABM systems," "window of vulnerability."[14] One of the most crucial boundary metaphors in American defense discourse has been the "security perimeter," which was repeatedly defined and redefined in the course of Cold War foreign policy. The internal logic of the image schema implies that the farther away, and the more distinct your perimeter line, the farther away your enemy (outside the container) is, and, therefore, the more secure (inside the container and usually at its center) you are. This is especially the case if the enemy—the outsider—is conceptualized as being on an inevitable path of expansion in the direction of one's self.

The CONTAINER schema enters the semantic cohesiveness of security discourse in a variety of ways, depending on the local context and purpose. It is linked, for instance, to its semantic opposites, which cluster around the notion of lack of protection, exposure (etymologically, "positioned outside"), vulnerability and danger. Vulnerability is conceptualized as the condition of having no cover, or no impermeable cover, no roof, no walls, or walls with holes in them, etc. The effect of the "window of vulnerability" slogan derived from the fact that it locked naturally into the conceptual system grounded in the CONTAINER schema.

It is arguable that CONTAINER has also been the conceptual motivator for, and/or the main legitimizing instrument of, many arguments and claims in strategic thinking and many choices and research plans in weapons development programs. The hypothesis would be that once aerial bombardment and ICBMs had become technological facts, the notion of physically secure containers, from castles to continents, were irredeemably undermined. Vulnerability concepts become dominant and often exaggerated. At least some of the reasons for this are the affective and cognitive force of the CONTAINER schema, its role in the conceptualization of the body, and its pervasiveness in the semantics of the English lexicon.

If this is the case, there are two implications. One is that the arguments of those who, during the Cold War, argued for nuclear defense shields of one form or another have a naive cognitive plausibility based on the naturalness of CONTAINER. The other implication is that the converse is true of the arguments of those who, like Robert McNamara, argued for minimum deterrence based on "mutual vulnerability"—a cognitively uncomfortable position. How can "security," if it is based on CONTAINER, be also based on vulnerability, CONTAINER's antithesis? The tendency of Cold War security discourse was to oscillate from one position to the other. The result was the cognitive instability of the whole deterrence debate (even before Gorbachev's diplomacy removed the conceptual lynch-pin by removing the enemy).

In the context of American ideology the container concept of security has historically deep roots. The cognitive analysis is consistent with the narrative script tacitly adopted by James Chace and Caleb Carr, who see the American foreign policy tradition as structured around a "quest for absolute security from 1812 to Star Wars," and who describe the SDI proposals as "a return to the goal of an impenetrable shield with which to protect both the perimeter and the homeland."[15] In effect the Chace-Carr hypothesis is that American foreign policy is influenced by a historical memory that produces and reproduces the search for a closed security container. What the cognitive-linguistic analysis does is show how such a historical memory is conceptually based and structured, and how it is concretized in the verbal substance of discourse.

The CONTAINER schema was implicated in security discourse in the years immediately following World War II, and surfaced lexically in the strategy known as "containment." This policy is thought of by realists as a rational response to a threat issuing from inside the Soviet Union. There are, however, other possible interpretations. Deborah Larson, for instance, argues that, while realist theory predicts the clash of the two superpowers, it does not explain the particular form this clash took with the particular Cold War policies that were adopted, and it does not explain the failure to adopt alternative policies, for instance more cooperative policies recognizing Soviet security and other needs. Larson further argues that a cognitive and social psychological approach is required in order to fill this explanation gap.[16] What her account does not fully do, however, is give an account of metaphor, although it constantly comes up against the role of crucial texts and speeches, and certainly acknowledges the role of metaphor and analogy in the evolution of policy concepts.

The word *containment* and the conceptual system in which it was embedded emerged from a climate of uncertainty in the aftermath of World War II. George Kennan, who was chargé d'affaires at the Moscow embassy, was asked to supply an analysis of the Soviet Union after Stalin had delivered an apparently menacing speech in the Supreme Soviet in February 1946. In the summer of 1947 under the pseudonym "X," Kennan gave the policy of containment its name in an article that bore the title "The Sources of Soviet Conduct." These texts—the "X-Article"—drew on ideas already expressed in the "Long Telegram" that Kennan had sent to the State Department. These texts used a covert metaphor, which in fact is deeply implicated in Kennan's argumentation. By inspecting such presuppositions in the semantics of the vocabulary of the Long Telegram and the X-Article it is possible to pinpoint the organizing principles that give the texts their conceptual coherence.

Throughout both documents the assumption is that the Soviet Union is a container-like entity. This underlying conceptual model produces a lexical cohesion based on the opposition of inner and outer. Kennan's premise (derived from the geopolitics of Mackinder and Spykman) is that the Soviets suffer from an "instinctive sense of insecurity" which comes from living "on [a] vast exposed plain," and which in turn leads them both to fear "what would happen if Russians learned about [the] world without and foreigners learned about [the] world within," and to increase military power in order to "guarantee [the] external security of their internally weak regimes." The Soviet personality itself is represented as a container, as obsessively "secretive," and "ignorant of [the] outside world." Since the container schema can be used to frame an objectivist epistemology, according to which "facts" are "out there," and since the subjective "inner" world is treated as irrational, the Soviet personality can also be portrayed as "impervious to logic of reason," subject to "self-hypnotism" and other forms of irrationality.[17] Geopolitical, psychological, and epistemological notions are thus all underpinned by a CONTAINER schema. This conceptual construct permits metaphorical inferences, with serious policy consequences: although rational argument cannot get through to the Soviet Union, it is "highly sensitive to logic of force."[18] The scope for potential inferences in the Long Telegram is considerable, because the telegraphic ellipses mean that discourse connectives (expressing causal or consequential relations, for example) are left to the reader to supply.

With these metaphors is very closely intertwined a second, related, set derived from stereotypic schemas and scripts serving as knowledge bases concerning the body and disease. The supposed Soviet inwardness and resistance to the real outer world is represented as a mental disease. Again the metaphorical entailments are used to suggest policy. Slipping from the Soviet Union to the entire communist "movement," which the Telegram represents as emanating from the center of the Soviet container, Kennan argues:

> We must study it [the communist movement] with same courage, detachment, objectivity, and same determination not to be emotionally provoked or unseated by it, with which [sic] doctor studies unruly and unreasonable individual.

There are further metaphorical connections. Physical diseases are understood as prototypically liable to spread and contaminate, but this property is transferred here to the supposed mental disease of Soviet ideology:

> Much depends on health and vigor of our own society. World communism is like [a] malignant parasite which feeds on diseased tissue.[19]

A third set of images, related to the second by way of the concept of motion out of a containing vessel, is linked to metaphors derived from the FORCE schema, specifically hydraulics and mechanics, and from the PATH schema. The X-Article in particular develops this conceptual network as the basis for its inferences, maintaining a link with the background geographical argument, and with discourses that conceptualize political power as out-flowing and in-flowing substance:

> [The Kremlin's] political action is a fluid stream which moves constantly . . . toward its own goal. Its main concern is to make sure that it has filled every nook and cranny in the basin of world power. But if it finds unassailable barriers in its path, it accepts these philosophically and accommodates itself to them. The main thing is that there should always be pressure, constant unceasing pressure, toward the desired goal.[20]

Now the concept of "containment" flows, as it were, from these metaphorical premises. It is an intrinsic part of the way irrational emotions, instinctive urges, unruly people, infectious diseases and fluids are conventionally conceptualized that they are thought of as in need of being "contained," "held in," in some confining space.[21] Thus the naming of containment is entailed by the metaphorical system, and is dependent on the initial set of premises—principally, that the Soviet power is a liquid projected outward through "channels" exerting pressure on and penetrating the non-communist world, and that the Soviet Union is also a mentally disturbed patient in need of restraint:

> . . . it is clear that the main element of any United States policy toward the Soviet Union must be that of a long-term, patient but firm and vigilant containment of Russian expansive tendencies.[22]

Metaphorical textures of this type are more than mere decoration. They constitute an aprioristic logic: if X is a fluid (or animal, or disease, etc.) then it is entailed that the right policy is to "contain" X. Metaphorical projections may, in some community of speakers, say the epistemic community of policy experts, come to be adopted consensually as reality; but their effect may be to focus too narrowly and obscure other discourses and facts, they may limit thinking, and they may develop a momentum of their own independent of other forms of evidence and reasoning.

Once Kennan's metaphors became established, as they did, in official discourse, they had the effect of obscuring alternative policies, in particular the more "open" and communicative conceptual models that had been used by President Roosevelt and his Secretary of War, Henry L. Stimson. It is true that the Long Telegram does not seem to have directly or indirectly changed the beliefs of President Truman or Secretary of State James Byrnes—but the American State Department did send copies to diplomatic missions around the globe, and Navy Secretary James V. Forrestal, a key architect of the post-World War II national security policy, made the Long Telegram "required reading" for hundreds of military officers. When the Truman administration was faced with persuading congressmen to vote for aid to Greece and Turkey in 1947, it was Dean Acheson's speech, structured around container images and infectious disease metaphors, that turned the tide, and it was this speech that became the basis of the Truman Doctrine speech.

It is true also that Kennan later disavowed the military interpretation of the containment concept. Nonetheless, the point is that the text itself carried the possibility of such interpretations, and that the burgeoning security discourse continued to crystallize around the metaphorical concepts we have identified. The best example of this process is the document known as NSC-68, drafted by Paul Nitze, which is conceptually consistent with the metaphorical structure of the Long Telegram, and which called for massive increases in American military strength.

NSC-68 derives its textual cohesion from the strikingly frequent repetition of a small number of lexical items, a large proportion of which depend on CONTAINER and FORCE schemas. The international environment is represented as a field of magnetic, mechanical, and hydraulic forces, in which two "centers" of power are "polarized," with other entities in the system "gravitating" toward one or the other. Further, the two "centers" are inside containers, generating "power," which builds up "pressure" inside one of the containers, the internally repressive Soviet Union, causing "expansion." It follows, by the logic of the metaphorical entailments, that the United States is a "bulwark of opposition to Soviet expansion," that it must "check" or "block" the "spread," "halt the expansion" and the "drive" of Soviet "dynamism," "apply pressure" or "counter-force" at certain "pressure points," "contain" the Soviet Union's power, and "roll it back." The United States is thus the "obstacle which stands between it and world domination." This set of metaphorical entailments overlaps conceptually with metaphors derived from body, disease, and derangement metaphors, as is the case in Kennan's texts. Thus it is said to be essential that the United States maintain a "healthy" environment, since the Soviet Union is "decadent," "perverted," and contains "seeds of decay." The policy of containment itself continues to be conceived in terms of counter-pressure and resistance to penetration, but also in terms of a wall-like barrier.[23]

The conceptual universe constructed in NSC-68 produced, and/or justified, the strategy of "building up" what was termed "preponderant strength," of increasing armaments at the "center," that is in the United States and Western Europe, while undertaking risky forms of "containment" at the "periphery." It has been argued by some historians that the policies of Acheson and Nitze were out of proportion to the verifiable military threat. If that is so, the plausibility of their discourse needs to be explained further; the cogency of the textually embodied metaphorical concepts is probably part of such an explanation.

CONCEPTUAL SYSTEMS AND CONCEPTUAL CHANGE

The concept of security that is produced in the classic realist texts of the immediate postwar period is clearly dependent on the CONTAINER schema. However, it is equally clear that the compelling nature of the realist discourse is dependent not on one single schema and derived metaphors, but on a densely interconnected network of schemas and metaphors which are not static but have their own inferential dynamics. Viewing this conceptual network in terms of its dense associative clusters, it is evident that the image schema CONTAINER has many connections with the concept of the state, with the concept of security, and with concepts of the human body and the human person, which themselves are used as metaphors for states. Precisely because of its multiple connections in linguistic and conceptual systems, the CONTAINER schema is difficult to make explicit, modify, or replace. It supplies an image, which, once projected into metaphor and exchanged among powerful individuals and groups, makes the state itself appear to be natural. It is in this way that metaphor can contribute to the reification and legitimization of historically produced phenomena.

This is why it is important to attend to the historical changes that led to current semantic systems constituting political culture in the modern period. The CONTAINER schema becomes a crucial political concept in the period from the fifteenth to the seventeenth century, a period in which the discourses of property, land rights, commerce, and political theory evolved. It is one in which the CONTAINER schema is geographically, economically, and socially realized in land-enclosures, as opposed to commons, and in the defining of nation-state borders, as opposed to the overlapping jurisdictions of medieval Europe.[24] It is also the period at which the very words *secure* and *security* shift semantically—from the meanings of Shakespeare's day to the CONTAINER-based concept characteristic of modern social, economic, and political discourses. The concept of the sovereign state elaborated in Hobbes's *Leviathan*, a canonical text for realist epigoni, is cognitively linked to a CONTAINER image. The inherent logic of the image schema, together with FORCE and PATH, preconceptualizes much of Hobbes's discourse, in particular his notion of security. The schema makes it possible to delimit what is internal (self, friendly, integrated) and what is external (other, hostile, anarchic). Likewise, the container schema entails the notion of *control* of passions, emotions, and instincts—that is, the "containing" of aggressiveness. Putting this more abstractly, the political came to be imagined in spatialized terms, and specifically, through the spatial gestalt of the container which grounds the notions (and feelings) of identity and difference, of self and other, sovereign state and anarchic non-state, clearly and distinctly separated by a bounding limit.

The realist thinking system is, however, neither immutable nor absolute. Although it is true that it is anchored in basic meaning-producing image schemas, and entrenched cultural metaphors, these are not the sole conceptual possibilities, and this is not the sole conceptual system that could yield a sense of the "real." In fact, it may be argued, the more the global economy, global migrations, and global communications evolve, the more this system of thought, with its self-contained sovereign states, appears *un*real. The understanding of boundaries is particularly problematic. The point is not that identities and boundaries are irrelevant, unnecessary, or disadvantageous to human living; rather the point is to ask *which* boundaries are desirable and which have negative effects.[25] As communication and various levels of integration increase the permeability of borders, and as these processes further yield overlapping boundaries in a multiplicity of domains, concepts of identity and difference become increasingly important in conflicting political discourses.[26]

In 1989 the official view was that the military and diplomatic posture sustained by the realist world-picture had brought about the end of the Cold War and the collapse of the U.S.S.R. There is no empirical proof or disproof of such claims. It is equally arguable that realist discourse invented, justified, and prolonged the Cold War. What is clear is that the realist conceptual system in fact failed to predict events; to have done so would have been to predict its own demise. Moreover, it is arguable that since the West had lost its Soviet enemy, the perseverance of the conceptual system outlined above continued to be disastrously dysfunctional as far as the physical safety of very large numbers of people was concerned. Thus the Gulf War of 1991 was "successful" only if viewed from the outside as an "external" clash of container-like states resulting from the penetration of one by another. The container perspective obscured the destruction of ordinary Iraqis and Kurds and Marsh Arabs, and left the Iraqi regime in control. The Serbo-Croat war of 1991-92, and the subsequent débâcle, was also influenced by this kind of perspective, since the Balkan conflicts were perceived by many politicians and officials as civil wars and thus as "internal" problems. The realist discourse of sovereign statehood led in divergent but equally damaging directions—on the one hand providing arguments against "intervention" on the ground, which left UN peacekeeping troops powerless, on the other justifying arguments for the sale of weapons to a "sovereign state," which would escalate the violence. NATO, defining its role entirely within the realist system of thought, failed, after 1989, to adjust itself to new discourses of global politics which no longer constructed a unitary alien threat to the west.

Realist and neorealist discourses had produced a complex reified imagery that was taken for a natural state of affairs. The evident strains on it, at once economic, military, and diplomatic, had led to various attempts to generate new security concepts, attempts that were mediated in various channels and fora—the diplomatic moves in the 1980s driven by Gorbachev's "new thinking," the international actions of engaged scientists, physicians, religious leaders, the freeze movement, the European peace movements, special reports of the United Nations, and the publicizing role of independent commissions such as the 1982 Palme Commission and the 1989 Brundtland report.[27] It is, however, by no means clear that the established concept of security, embedded as it is in an intricate network of concepts of the state, of sovereignty, and of the self, can be easily transformed without modifying many other parts of the conceptual system, and ultimately of political and international systems.

Discursive efforts to reorient security thinking produced novel collocations, such as "common security," "comprehensive security," and the Brundtland report's "global commons" and "environmental stress." These expressions arise, and are comprehended, by negating or respecifying the realist container metaphors and force metaphors. Similarly, the expressions "environmental insecurity" and "food security" challenged realist semantics by replacing the realist linkage between security, the military, and the state with concepts relating to basic needs—that is, needs relating to the physical safety and survival of individuals stated in terms of, for example, food provision, shelter, and community.

This discursive endeavor to decouple the conceptual connections, deeply embedded in the discourses of political modernity, between security, state, sovereignty, and military might can be understood as a process of demetaphorization. The decoupling can be thought of as a *vertical* shift from the abstract and often metaphorized level of interstate relations to the more particular and material levels of concern, that also extend the concept of security *horizontally* to include environmental, social, and individual concerns. In terms of the theory of cognition, language, and discourse what is involved here is a reorientation from superordinate categories and metaphorical conceptualization to "basic-level" meanings. The "basic level" is the level at which human cultures (and specialized groups within those cultures) interact physically and socially with their environment producing corresponding conceptual and lexical organization. Categories at this level are more learnable, memorizable, and recognizable: e.g. *tree* may be basic as distinct from sub-categories of tree (deciduous, oak, types of oak) and superordinate types (wood, forest). Concepts that are abstract, remote, or problematic are expressed by metaphorical projection from basic-level experience (a family *tree*).[28] Now, what I have argued in this chapter is that the predominant understanding of the word *security* in the modern period involves a large amount of metaphorical processing. Consequently, the discourses of security, particularly the specialist discourses, tend to obscure basic-level conceptions and perceptions. A discourse of security at the basic level would be quite different from the highly metaphorized realist and neorealist mode.

In some respects the scalar distinctions between basic-level concepts and metaphorical projections corresponds to the neorealists' levels, which separate individuals in society from the supposed anarchy of the remote international environment. However, changes in the concept of security cannot consist just of an isolated switch of "referents," since an entire system of interrelated concepts, metaphors, and metaphorical entailments is involved. Reconceptualizing *security* will involve demetaphorizing the present understanding, but also reformulating the many conceptual and discursive connections with statehood, sovereignty, and war, as well as developing imagery of linkage. Demetaphorization will be part of the refocusing of thinking onto individual bodies and social bodies, their safety and survival, rather than the privileged preservation of sovereign bodies politic. Container images will need to be reformulated in terms of physical safety and shelter, rather than impermeable containment cordons and the fantasies of defensive astrodomes. LINK and PATH schemas require reformulation as communication, community, and transport, rather than paths to permanent stability and quests for ultimate security. *Security* in these transformed senses could be termed *basic security*.

CONCLUSION

Curiously, there is no opposite of the word *security*, in the negative sense in which Shakespeare was able to use it: *insecure* and *insecurity* are antonyms only of the modern sense of *secure* and *security*, as understood in terms of metaphors of protective containers, stability, and fixity.[29] The closest antonym of the older sense would be *care-full* and *care-full-ness*. These words can be understood in the sense of "full of care *for*," "taking good care *of*"—the quality that Hecate knows Macbeth lacks, for he spurns basic bodily dangers and fears. Secure, in the sense of believing in his own invulnerability, he yet seeks security in the modern sense, by an escalation of preemptive violence, which only exposes him to unexpected dangers. Both senses of the word *security* were available to Shakespeare's contemporaries, but modern readers may reread Hecate's words, mindful that her sense of *se-curity* and the Hobbesian *security* have combined in the twentieth century—that failure to have care for the immediate and the basic has coincided with vaulting ambitions to achieve ultimate security by military means,

And, you all know, security
Is mortals' chiefest enemy.

Notes

1. Murray Edelman, *Politics as Symbolic Action* (Chicago: Marham Publishing Company, 1971), 67.
2. Ibid., 67
3. Ibid., 68.
4. Ibid., 69.
5. Ibid., 68.
6. See, for instance, Richard Ashley, "The Poverty of Neorealism" in *Neorealism and Its Critics*, ed. R. O. Keohane (New York: Columbia University Press, 1986); David Campbell, *Writing Security: United States Foreign Policy and the Politics of Identity* (Manchester: Manchester University Press, 1992); Simon Dalby, "American Security Discourse: The Persistence of Geopolitics," *Political Geography Quarterly* 9, no. 2 (1990): 171-88; James Der Derian and Michael J. Shapiro, eds., *International/Intertextual Relations* (Lexington and Toronto: D. C. Heath, 1989); R. B. J. Walker, "The Concept of Security and International Relations Theory," IGCC Working Papers, no. 3, 1987; *One World, Many Worlds: Struggles for a Just World Peace* (Boulder, Colo.: Lynne Rienner; and London: Zed Books, 1988); "On the Spatio-temporal Conditions of Democratic Practice" (unpublished Ms., 1990); *Inside/Outside* (Cambridge: Cambridge University Press, 1993).
7. Arnold Wolfers, "National Security as an Ambiguous Symbol," in *Discord and Collaboration* (Baltimore: Johns Hopkins University Press, 1962), chap. 10.
8. Barry Buzan, *People, States and Fear,* 2d ed. ([1983]; Brighton: Wheatsheaf, 1991); W. B.Gallie, "Essentially Contested Concepts," *Proceedings of the Aristotelian Society*, New Series, 56: 167-98.
9. Buzan, *People, States and Fear*, 14.
10. For this view of concepts and metaphor, see: George Lakoff and Mark Johnson, *Metaphors We Live By* (Chicago: University of Chicago Press, 1980); George Lakoff, "Cognitive Semantics," *Versus* 44-5 (1986): 119-54, and *Women, Fire, and Dangerous Things: What Categories Reveal About the Mind* (Chicago: University of Chicago Press, 1987); Eve Sweetser, *From Etymology to Pragmatics* (Cambridge: Cambridge University Press, 1990).
11. The existence of conceptual connections with "container" is backed up by etymologies: "shield" and "shell" are cognates; the Romans had a siege weapon with a protective roof called a *testudo* (from *testa*, pot or shell, and meaning tortoise); "protect" involves a Latin morpheme meaning "cover" or "envelope."
12. See Mark Johnson, *The Body in the Mind: The Bodily Basis of Meaning, Imagination, and Reason* (Chicago: University of Chicago Press, 1987); Leonard Talmy, "Force Dynamics in Language and Cognition," *Cognitive*

Science 12, no. 1 (1988): 49-100; Sweetser, *From Etymology to Pragmatics.*

13. For a fuller account of the ideas in this section, see Paul A. Chilton, *Security Metaphors: Cold War Discourse from Containment to Common House* (New York: Peter Lang, 1995).

14. For a literary-rhetorical reflection on the "window of vulnerability" argument in the policy community in the 1970s, see Steven Mailloux, *Rhetorical Power* (Ithaca: Cornell University Press, 1989); and for a critical if non-rhetorical approach see Fred Kaplan, *Wizards of Armageddon* (New York: Simon and Schuster, 1983).

15. James Chace and Caleb Carr, *America Invulnerable* (New York: Summit Books, 1988), 307.

16. Deborah Larson, *Origins of Containment* (Princeton: Princeton University Press, 1985).

17. The Chargé in the Soviet Union to the Secretary of State, *Foreign Relations of the United States, 1946*, 6: 699ff. ("The Long Telegram").

18. Ibid., 707.

19. Ibid., 708.

20. "The Sources of Soviet Conduct," *Foreign Affairs* 25 (1946-47): 575.

21. Consider the following examples: "contain the liquid in a sealed flask," "the epidemic has been contained," "she contained her emotions."

22. "Sources of Soviet Conduct," 575.

23. *A Report to the National Security Council by the Executive Secretary on United States Objectives and Programs on National Security*, 14 April 1950 ("NSC-68"), 13-14.

24. On this cf. John Gerard Ruggie, in Keohane, ed. *Neorealism and its Critics*, 142f.; on diplomacy and state-containers, Garrett Mattingly, *Renaissance Diplomacy* (London: Cape, 1955).

25. As Kevin Clements makes strikingly clear, "Transcending National Security: Towards a More Inclusive Conceptualization of National and Global Security," New Views of International Security, Occasional Paper, no. 1, Program on the Analysis and Resolution of Conflicts, Syracuse, New York, 1990, 18-20. See also Joseph A. Camilleri and Jim Falk, *The End of Sovereignty* (Aldershot: Elgar, 1992).

26. In domestic politics an important manifestation of this is the rise of nationalist, racist, and ethnocentric discourses in western Europe as well as in the former territories of the Soviet empire.

27. For a brief summary of these trends see Buzan, *People, States and Fear*, 12-14. Key documents are: *Concepts of Security* (United Nations Department of Disarmament Affairs, Report of the Secretary General, 1986); *Common Security. A Programme for Disarmament*, Report of the Independent Commission on Disarmament and Security Issues under the Chairmanship of Olaf Palme (London: Pan, 1982); World Commission on Environment and Development, *Our Common Future* (Oxford: Oxford University Press, 1987); Richard Ullmann, "Redefining Security," *International Security* 8, no. 1

(1983): 129-53; Mary Kaldor, "Transforming the State: An Alternative Security Concept for Europe" in Bjorn Hettne, *Europe: Dimensions of Peace* (London: Zed Books, 1988); R. B. J. Walker, "The Concept of Security"; *One World, Many Worlds*; Dalby, "American Security Discourse"; Clements, "Transcending National Security."

28. On basic-level categorization, see for instance Eleanor Rosch, "Natural Categories," *Cognitive Psychology* 4 (1973): 328-50, and for a summary, Lakoff, *Women, Fire and Dangerous Things.*

29. In its older etymological sense "secure" already has a negative prefix (*se-, sine-,* "without"). The appearance of "insecure" and "insecurity" shows that awareness of the etymological prefix has disappeared. "Insecure" and "insecurity" seem to come into use in the late 1640s, perhaps under the impact of the English civil wars, which are also the context for Hobbes's argument for Leviathan, the sovereign provider of security.

JENNIFER L. MILLIKEN

METAPHORS OF PRESTIGE AND REPUTATION IN AMERICAN FOREIGN POLICY AND AMERICAN REALISM

During the Vietnam War, the objectives of American policy toward Vietnam centered not on the strategic importance of the "real estate" involved, but on the effects a defeat in Vietnam would have on the United States' prestige in the world and its reputation for keeping its commitments.[1] American policy makers spoke often of these considerations. And they measured American actions in Vietnam against them, weighing the costs in lives and resources of deepening intervention against the costs in prestige and reputation of halting that intervention.[2] If prestige and reputation are, as many claim, the intangible side of power, then in this conflict the intangible weighed more than the tangible. It was an astonishingly heavy load to bear, not least of all for the 58,000 dead Americans and the 2 million dead and 4.5 million wounded Vietnamese.

Recently, talk of prestige and reputation was in the wind again. In the period leading to the Gulf War, wise men of American foreign policy like Henry Kissinger spoke of how the United States had to respond to Iraqi aggression or risk losing prestige. In the immediate afterglow of "victory," much of the public commentary on the war centered on how the United States had "buried" the Vietnam Syndrome, healing national "wounds" and gaining a sense of "pride and unity" lost when the country was humiliated in Vietnam.[3] Along with the announcements of a "national recovery" came claims that "now the world will again listen" when the United States speaks, for in Iraq we "demonstrated to the world that there is really only one superpower these days."[4]

What is this talk of prestige and reputation, such that it can justify one bloody conflict and frame the expected rewards of another? This is the question I take up in this chapter. As briefly outlined in part one of my discussion, prestige and reputation have been sensible and

217

natural objects of concern for American policy makers since at least the early 1950s, and were of central concern during the Vietnam War. Yet, drawing on the Vietnam War case, part two argues that prestige and reputation are social constructions, dependent for their natural-ness on "an extensive and mostly unconscious system of metaphor."[5] As such, the use of prestige and reputation to define state practice deserves critical scrutiny; for what it casts in shadow (e.g., the com-plexities of political and economic situations in other regions) and what it hides (e.g., the death and injury of millions of people).

Realism, the dominant approach of the American discipline of international relations, should in theory give scholars a basis for criti-cal scrutiny. The third part of the essay argues that realism cannot do so. Like policy makers, realist theorists treat prestige and reputation as "facts" of the international system. Also like policy makers, this treatment by realist theorists rests upon an unreflective acceptance of the "metaphorics" of prestige and reputation. The result is that even quite trenchant realist critics of particular American interventions end by making such practices seem reasonable.

PLANNING TO CAST THE SHADOW OF POWER

> To back away from this challenge [the Korean War], in view of our capacity for meeting it, would be highly destructive of the power and prestige of the United States. By prestige I mean the shadow cast by power, which is of great deterrent importance.
>
> Dean Acheson[6]

Concern for prestige and reputation can be found in a wide range of American policy events since World War II, among them the Korean War, the Cuban Missile Crisis, the U.S. invasion of Grenada, and the 1991 Gulf War. Most broadly (and as befitting recent cases), the atten-tion given prestige and reputation can be interpreted as a "credibility obsession" that has infused American policy toward the Third World.[7] More narrowly (and befitting its historical development), this "recurring, compulsive concern about its reputation" may be inter-preted as stemming from American management of its deterrence rela-tionship with the Soviet Union and its allies.[8]

The idea of deterrence through prestige and reputation has typi-cally been articulated through the "domino theory": the notion that if one country in a region were lost to Communism, surrounding countries would soon follow. The domino theory dates back in spirit (if not in name) at least to NSC-68 (April, 1950). NSC-68 put forward an argument based on a narrative of moral and psychological leadership. In it, a first defeat for the United States as the leader of the Free World would cause its allies to doubt U.S. leadership, lose morale, and give in to Communism. As it would for later policy makers, the leadership narrative also worked in reverse. "As we ourselves demonstrate power, confidence, and a sense of moral direction, so those same qualities will be evoked in Western Europe" and other allies like Japan.[9]

Written and spoken through a leadership narrative, prestige and reputation were central in the Johnson administration's policy toward Vietnam. For example, in October 1964 John McNaughton, assistant secretary of defense, wrote in support of a policy of escalating the war by bombing North Vietnam that:

> US aims in SEA[10] are: to help SVN and Laos develop as independent countries; to get DRV to leave its neighbors alone; to protect U.S. power and prestige. . . . It is essential—however badly SEA may go over the next two-four years—that the U.S. emerge as a "good doctor." We must have kept promises, been tough, taken risks, gotten bloodied, and hurt the enemy badly.[11]

McNaughton was pessimistic that any government could manage South Vietnam, or that bombing North Vietnam would stop the Viet Cong. Nonetheless, he supported a bombing program for the image of a "good doctor" it would create. William Bundy, assistant secretary of state, approached bombing in much the same way. Acknowledging that "the domino theory is much too pat," he went on to set out how countries would be "lost" if the U.S. did not undertake a bombing policy. In the immediate area, "the faith of the ROK would be shaken" and "the GRC would feel deserted and alone, with predictable consequences." Outside the area, the U.S.'s allies would come to believe that the U.S. was not "strong and at the same time wise." That impression would in turn "drastically affect our ability to keep the peace and keep the waverers from veering clear over to Communist answers."[12]

If more "hawkish" policy positions in the debate on bombing were based on narratives of leadership and, thus, prestige and reputation, so too were other, more "dovish" policy positions. For example, George Ball, also assistant secretary of state, wrote in October, 1964 against bombing and for a policy seeking a "political solution" in Vietnam. His memorandum begins,

> *Would the clear evidence of our intention to carry out our commitments increase U.S. prestige?* The assumption which has governed our planning has been that the U.S. must successfully stop the extension of Communist power into South Vietnam if its promises are to be given credence. It is argued that failing such an effort our allies around the world would be inclined to doubt our promises and to feel they could no longer safely rely upon American power against Communist aggressive ambitions.

Ball was codifying that U.S. prestige, together with its reputation for keeping its promises, were the main criteria for assessment of Vietnam policy. In making this codification, Ball was seeking to limit American involvement in the war. Yet his case did not challenge the codification as such. Instead, Ball argued from *within the accepted criteria* that "it remains to be proved that in terms of U.S. prestige and our world position" that bombing was the better policy.[13]

The natural importance for "hawks" and "doves" alike of American prestige and reputation was not limited to debate on bombing North Vietnam. Similar discussions recurred in the decision in July 1965 to introduce large scale combat forces into Vietnam, and in later decisions to expand those forces. Sometimes, the reputation to be secured did shift from that of the United States' reputation with its allies to that of the United States' reputation with the Soviet Union. For example, Dean Rusk contributed greatly to the 1965 ground-troops decision with his claim that "the integrity of the U.S. commitment is the principal pillar of peace throughout the world. If that commitment becomes unreliable, the communist world would draw conclusions that would lead to our ruin and almost certainly to a catastrophic war."[14] But, like Ball's critical comments, such shifts took for granted prestige and reputation as objects of American foreign policy.

What, though, are prestige and reputation? Rusk's evocation of these objects draws upon a metaphor ("pillar of peace") that represents one aspect of experience (America's security commitments) in terms of another (the physical structure of a building). McNaughton's evocation does the same, though, for the United States' reputation was represented in terms of the faith people place in a talented surgeon. Such constructs suggest that at least partly, prestige and reputation are objects of metaphor.

METAPHORICS OF THE VIETNAM WAR

In politics as in other fields of practice, metaphors structure how people define (or constitute) phenomena and, therefore, how they act.[15] Consider, for example, the metaphor of "inflation is an adversary," found in statements like "inflation has *robbed* thousands of people of their savings," or "inflation has *attacked* the foundations of the economy." From this understanding, a particular political stance and ways of acting toward inflation are made plausible. A government can declare war on inflation, establish a new chain of command to fight it, and call for sacrifices from the populace. Similarly, the metaphor of "war is a disease" also structures persons' definitions and actions. Based on "war is a disease," a war becomes something vague, subhuman, and unthinking. Consequently, a government can operate (surgical strikes) or, at least, appear to operate (be seen as a "good doctor"). If the disease is too far gone, policy makers may even think and act in terms of halting medication. As George Ball once proposed, the war in Vietnam "is like giving cobalt treatment to a terminal cancer case."[16]

Metaphors like "inflation is an adversary" or "war is a disease" are used in social communication so regularly as to seem "plain talk" about the world. But such metaphors are *not* thereby "plain talk." Through their use, people make *selective distinctions* that, by highlighting some aspects of a phenomenon, downplay and hide other features that could give a different stance. "War is a disease," for example, highlights some aspects of war relating to sickness and health (e.g., the spreading of conflict through the social body, the loss of central functions of a government). At the same time, its use obscures other aspects that could be used to constitute what war is, and hides still others (e.g., the reasons and motives of people engaged in the struggle).

In the Johnson administration's debates about the bombing and ground troop decisions (September 1964-July 1965), "plain talk" metaphors appear in public interviews and speeches by high-level policy makers, making them part of the public justification of the war. Equally, though, such metaphors are found in secret memoranda, meeting notes, and cables by high-level policy makers, making them part of the "inside" planning of the war.[17] Consider, for example,

General Maxwell D. Taylor, then U.S. ambassador to South Vietnam, using a metaphor of physical entities in a secret cable to Dean Rusk about bombing policy.

> From Saigon point of view we cannot view Bien Hoa as merely an improved version of similar past conduct. For the moment, I believe no rpt. no action needs to be considered purely for impact on local morale. However if there is no U.S. reaction, our prestige is going to sag both with friend and enemy.[18]

A physical entity metaphor was also illustrated earlier in Rusk's evocation of the U.S.'s reputation as the "principle pillar of peace." In constructions like these, actions that the U.S. undertakes (or, more frequently, does not undertake) in Vietnam have effects on prestige and reputation akin to those we normally ascribe to corporeal beings and material objects. Like a car or a building, prestige and reputation can be hit and damaged (and presumably, repaired). Like a person or a plant, prestige and reputation can be tied to something and can sag (the reverse, perhaps, of to "stand tall"). And like all manner of material life, these objects can be magnified.[19]

Commerce, a second regular metaphor of Vietnam War policy, can be seen in use in this evaluation of bombing by McGeorge Bundy.

> A reprisal policy—to the extent it demonstrates a U.S. willingness to emphasize this new norm of counter-insurgency—will set a higher price for the future upon all adventures of guerrilla warfare, and should therefore somewhat increase our ability to deter such adventures.[20]

In the metaphor of commerce, what the U.S. does in Vietnam is treated as creating costs or gains in prestige and reputation and related notions of credibility. The cost/gain formulation suggests that American action in Vietnam is a financial transaction, and prestige and reputation the profits gained or lost in the transaction. Certain transactions, in turn, involve greater financial risks (and, perhaps, greater profits) than others: these actions, as the language of "stakes" suggests, are gambles.[21]

A third type of "plain talk" metaphor in Vietnam War policy is that of personal honor. For example:

But if I left that war and let the Communists take over South Vietnam, then I would be seen as a coward and my nation would be seen as an appeaser and we would find it impossible to accomplish anything for anybody anywhere on the entire globe.

U.S. President Lyndon B. Johnson[22]

Underlying President Johnson's discussion of the need to escalate the war with a ground force intervention is an understanding of the United States as a person ("my nation . . . an appeaser"). In such constructions, U.S. actions in Vietnam are treated as occasions for demonstrations of excellence and opportunities for winning and losing personal honor. The treatment is partly reminiscent of seventeenth and eighteenth century aristocratic politics, when any action a prince undertook was "his personal act in which his personal sense of moral obligation revealed itself and in which, therefore, his personal honor was engaged."[23] But the terms that demarcate the reverse of winning and losing in this way—humiliation, embarrassment, weakness, cowardice—are used more in a manner common to twentieth century fears about the loss of male prowess and sexual performance.[24]

Finally, one finds metaphors of position used regularly by policy makers to construct prestige and reputation. For example:

In the final analysis, our influence in Europe depends not merely on defense efforts we are making, but on European confidence in our judgment. If we took action that might be regarded as demonstrating either a lack of judgment or lack of restraint, we would greatly undermine our European position.

George Ball[25]

Position metaphors like Ball's are reminiscent of seventeenth- and eighteenth-century notions of balance of power politics as arrangements or positioning of state spheres. In the twentieth century, a "position" or "standing" of a country can be altered (e.g., "undermined") by how other countries perceive its actions. Thus, from changes in a country's prestige and reputation (as evaluated by other countries) come changes in the balance of power of the international system.[26]

In the Johnson administration's policy debates, metaphors of physical entities, commerce, personal honor, and position were often used in relationship with each other. Thus, for example, the United States could cut its losses (commerce) and cut the damage to its prestige (physical entities). And in an extension of this, the United States could do so under conditions humiliating to the United States (personal honor) and damaging to its international standing (position). This intermixing of metaphors suggests a complex metaphorical coherence in how prestige and reputation were constructed.

To explore this metaphorical coherence, let us first focus on what the different constructions enable: a claim that objects of U.S. prestige and reputation exist and that they are so valuable as to be worth even the risk of having to see a war "clear through at considerable cost in casualties and materiel." These objects are worth so much because of their psychological effects. If the United States should let its prestige and reputation be damaged, its allies will lose confidence in American judgment. Allied faith in the United States will be shaken; their will to resist will be undermined, and they will become less hopeful. Non-aligned countries will see the United States as weak and unwise. The communists, having fulfilled their wish to show others the worthlessness of an American commitment, will be better able to intimidate and more willing to act aggressively.[27]

This narrative is of course that of the United States' moral and psychological leadership. Three assumptions appear to link the metaphors described above, and thus to make the narrative a plausible story about the world. The first is that prestige and reputation are things "out there" in the world of states in a material sense. Both the physical entities and positions constructions obviously draw on such an assumption.

Second, prestige and reputation constructions of physical entities and personal honor are bound together in personifications of the U.S. state. Via use of terms like honor and humiliation, and constructs wherein prestige is observed, measured, judged, etc., the United States is personified as living in a community of states. The status of the United States in this community is important to it, as it would be to any leading citizen.

Third, and following from the above, prestige and reputation are the sort of things that can be quantified and have a value assigned to them. This notion is requisite to commerce constructions, which allow for references to "additional increments of U.S. prestige" (quantification) and "setting a higher price" (assigning value). It also figures in personal honor constructs, though, for example, in the claim John

McNaughton made that United States stakes in South Vietnam were "(70 percent) to avoid a humiliating U.S. defeat (to our reputation as a guarantor)."[28]

The assumptions linking different systemic metaphors of prestige and reputation are not necessary to their construction. In the constitution of reputation in American congressional politics, for example, the reputation of a member of Congress is not a commodity: it cannot be quantified, but instead rests on the qualitative notion of always keeping one's word. Nor does the American policy making construction match the observations of North Vietnamese Premier Pham Van Dong that "the South Vietnamese mercenaries have sacrificed themselves without honor" and "the Americans are not loved, for they commit atrocities." In the latter construction, one had to fight "for the people"—it was not enough to "get bloodied." [29]

But if policy-making assumptions of prestige and reputation, borne in metaphor, do not parallel other political constructions, they do parallel other familiar experiences in American culture of sexuality and health. Sexuality can be bought and sold (commerce). Its meaning is often taken to be phallic, a notion akin to prestige "sagging" and "standing tall" (physical entities). And its signifiers are used to define a person's social position in everyday encounters (position). In addition, male sexual prowess is typically demonstrated on women; similarly, the U.S. was seen by policy makers as demonstrating its strength on countries understood to be dependent, vulnerable, and overemotional. For example, the Republic of Korea "*depends overwhelmingly* on the sure belief the U.S. will act," "the situation in ROK *just isn't strong*, and it could be compounded to a dangerous point by a neutralist, unify-at-any-price *sentiment* that . . . *could be easily aroused.*"[30] Male sexual prowess is demonstrated *to* other men, though; in a similar fashion, it was the aggressive and threatening, yet quite rational communist world which ultimately had to be convinced of the U.S.'s determination.[31]

Now consider the cultural experience of health. Clearly, our assumptions about our bodies involve notions of physical entities that can be damaged, suffer blows, etc. (physical entities). What is less often recognized is that health in Western culture is understood in terms of quantification and value ("the *costs* of smoking," "*adding* years to your life": commerce). Health benefits in the U.S. are still mostly earned in the labor market or purchased from private plans (commerce). And being healthy and fit (or having the image of being healthy and fit) gains people admiration and respect (personal honor). Thus systematic overlaps exist between health in American culture and prestige and reputation in American foreign policy. Those overlaps also extend to portrayals: for example, the U.S. personified by policy makers as a health care provider ("the good doctor") and Vietnam described as a "patient."

Parallels like those between American prestige in the international system and sexuality and health in American culture are in a sense unremarkable, for metaphoric thought allows people to draw on familiar experiences in order to understand the unfamiliar. American policy makers were no exception. Woven into and supporting their attempts to deal with the complexities and abstractions of international relations were more familiar cultural understandings. But perhaps despite these parallels to American culture, policy-makers' constructions were reasonable for international relations. Perhaps, whatever metaphorical expressions, the stance growing out of their understanding of prestige and reputation "captured" the realities of the international system.

Perhaps. But this stance was never really tested in the Vietnam context, much less in other contexts of U.S. intervention. Instead, given their familiar understanding of prestige and reputation, American policy makers assumed that their actions spoke to the political psychology of the community of states. They did so *despite* a lack of evidence, or *evidence to the contrary*.

To begin with, Soviet concepts of deterrence did not emphasize "the importance of reputation and the delicacy of credibility."[32] American policy makers, though, assumed that American actions in Vietnam would "make the U.S. stance with the U.S.S.R. credible." Then there were the U.S.'s European allies. By all accounts, they did not understand American prestige as resting on the U.S. guaranteeing South Vietnam. Instead, they saw the venture as throwing the U.S.'s prestige into doubt. American policy makers, though, remained convinced that European governments would respect the U.S. for its activities, privately if not publicly. Finally, there were the Asian "dominoes." The United States' Asian allies were consistently portrayed by American policy makers as being ready to fall to Communism should the U.S. fail to keep its word. Yet—as policy makers did and then did not recognize—past tests had been "failed" without this result. For example:

Unfortunately, the Thai—who doubted U.S. firmness at the time of the Laos settlement—now have swung to an excessive faith in the U.S. ability to save SVN somehow. Thus if SVN goes bad, we now estimate that the Thai would have little faith in the U.S. whatever we did for them, and would probably recognize Communist China, ask us to leave militarily, and seek to survive by accommodation.

William Bundy[33]

When allies or enemies took a stance of doubting the engagement of American prestige in Vietnam, they must have used a different definition of prestige and reputation from that of American policy makers, at least concerning when prestige and reputation were "at stake." Thus, definitions of prestige and reputation used by American policy makers were selective in setting aside other possible definitions held by representatives of other states. Selective distinctions involved in metaphorical construction, though, do not merely replace other versions of the *same objects*: e.g., reputation as understood by Pham Van Dong, or prestige as understood by the Wilson government in Britain. Metaphorical constructions also select by hiding features that could potentially be used to define *different objects*.

A case in point is the way American policy makers personified the U.S.'s Asian allies. De-emphasized in the evocation of "Asian dominoes" was another possible understanding of regime instability: that instability did not come from a failure of U.S. leadership, but from indigenous social conflict. States may be like persons; they are also structures criss-crossed by class and gender conflicts, ethnic struggle, religious rivalries, etc. engaged in by different groups. When American policy makers constructed their intervention in the name of prestige, the concerns and struggles of those groups were occluded. If, in contrast, they had been the basis for understanding the conflict, other action might have been plausible—for example, negotiating with the National Liberation Front.

Another feature of the situation downplayed by the metaphorics of prestige and reputation was the destructiveness of intervention. Death in those constructions was the death of a state (e.g., South Vietnam, the terminal cancer patient), and intervention by the U.S. was a way to prevent such death and to keep disease from spreading ("good doctor": act in a credible fashion to defend an ally). Such constructions hid the violent deaths of people, and the role of intervention in creating those deaths. If people's lives had been a concern,

American policy would not have been escalatory. It might even have been de-escalatory.

THEORIZING THE IMPRESSION OF POWER

As evidenced by the Vietnam War, prestige and reputation have been objects of great significance in American foreign policy practice. They have been spoken of in debate with great force and passion, and with cool-headed rationality. They have formed part of the foreign policy imaginary, being woven into narratives of American leadership in international relations. Out of this way of speaking and imagining, they have been regularly acted upon in American interventions. Yet, as I have argued, these are highly problematic objects of state action: constructed in American culture out of a stance toward international relations resting on questionable simplifications and occlusions.

What does international relations theory have to say to this problem? While I will amend this later, the immediate answer is: very little. Stanley Hoffmann has sketched the history of the discipline in the United States as being intertwined with the Cold War and American policy makers' concerns to have an "intellectual compass" for "exorcis[ing] isolationism," "rationaliz[ing] the accumulation of power," and the like.[34] Hoffmann suggests that realism, the dominant disciplinary approach, has provided this intellectual compass in three successive waves: a first wave in the 1950s of traditional realist work, a second wave from the late 1950s into the 1960s of strategic theory, and a third, more recent wave of international economic relations.[35] Whatever wave, prestige and reputation have been part of the intellectual compass. Theoretical use of these objects has overlapped substantially with policy-making definitions, most obviously in the case of second wave strategic theory, but also in first and third wave writing. The result has been that the realist stance has been too near that of American policy makers to enable a truly critical understanding.

Let us begin with the preeminent first wave theorist, Hans Morgenthau. Morgenthau wrote and revised his now-classic work, *Politics Among Nations*, through the early years of the Cold War: first edition, 1947, second edition, 1954, third edition, 1960. The work took concerns which preoccupy American policy makers and abstracted and generalized them into historical laws. That means that *Politics Among Nations* was not for contemporary policy makers a first education in realism, so much as realism was an intellectual frame for American policy. But for others—for example, would-be American policy makers, the "interested public," and their educators—*Politics Among Nations* was something of a first education. And what it taught (and teaches) was how to understand ongoing American foreign policy practice in terms of a realist "rational essence" of international relations.[36]

Morgenthau's construction of prestige is a good example of this dynamic. Following American policy makers, Morgenthau linked prestige to the Cold War "struggle for the minds of men."[37] But unlike them, Morgenthau generalized that struggle to the history of international relations. From Spartan imperialism to the German attack on the Soviet Union in the Second World War, prestige was a factor in aggression by states.[38] Conversely, prestige also featured in deterrence in the Roman Empire through British hegemony in Europe in the nineteenth century and American hegemony in Latin America in the twentieth century.[39]

Morgenthau based his historical reading on an understanding of prestige as the psychological "image" nations hold of other nations' "power positions on the international scene."[40] That image influences the power evaluations nations make in preparing their foreign policy, and hence the actions they undertake. Nations will therefore typically seek to control their international image. Image-control is done through a "policy of prestige": seeking through diplomatic ceremonial, shows of military force (including intervention), foreign aid, and other instruments to "impress other nations" with one's own power.[41]

For Morgenthau, success or failure in a policy of prestige ties together seemingly disparate historical contexts. For example, if a nation has an image of another nation as being unwilling or unable to wage war ("low reputation for military power"), an attack is likely to follow. The Japanese came to attack the U.S. at Pearl Harbor based on such an image of the U.S.; it was *the U.S.'s mistake.*[42] If, in contrast, a nation makes itself appear strong militarily ("reputation for unchallengeable power") and selective in its use of power ("reputation for self-restraint"), other nations are less likely to challenge it. Creation of that image was part of the policy of imperial Rome; for a long time, it secured the Empire against sustained revolts.[43]

The advice that emerges for American policy is that in the Cold War struggle, too, the U.S. should seek a reputation for power tempered by self-restraint. Such advice recalls William Bundy advising in

1964 that the U.S. should seek in Vietnam to appear "strong and at the same time wise."[44] The resemblance is hardly an identity: Morgenthau was a vocal critic of the position of Bundy and others that an image of strength and wisdom could be achieved through deepening intervention in Vietnam. Morgenthau's criticism comes from his argument that prestige should never be sought for "its own sake," but always as a means of contributing to national interests of "substance," e.g., territorial defense and security zones.[45] But neither is the resemblance accidental: Morgenthau's understanding of prestige overlaps with American policy definitions and their metaphorical systems. These overlaps mean that although Morgenthau (and others educated by *Politics Among Nations*) might be critical of specific prestige policies, there is little room in vocabulary or imagination for a stance questioning a policy of prestige in general.

Like American policy makers in their constructions, in Morgenthau's writings states are quasi-human subjects. They hold images of each other; these images rest upon evaluations states make. Also like American policy makers, Morgenthau expected that such images can be manipulated by the U.S., and that image-control is "an indispensable element of a rational foreign policy."[46] Morgenthau did not construe the United States as the leader of the free world (American policy makers' version of the leadership narrative), so much as the world's superpower governor. But a governance identity brings nuance, not a radically different construction. Morgenthau assumed that allies are kept as willing supporters of a governing state by demonstrations of strength coupled with moderation. He also assumed that intervention is a policy instrument for looking strong and moderate.

Further, in his famous account of the balance of power, Morgenthau's construction shares policy makers' metaphor of position. In Morgenthau's understanding, the balance would not be overturned if a country like Vietnam were "lost" to the United States. But his historical examples instruct that neither would the United States' position be strengthened. "[W]hen little Finland seemed able to hold its own against the Russian giant," for example, Soviet military prestige sank to such a low that the German general staff was convinced to attack.[47] Although not the domino theory, that account is one of prestige failure leading to deterrence failure.

In the support it gives in principle to a policy of prestige, to the link between it and deterrence, and to its enactment through intervention,

Morgenthau's first wave realism accepts and therefore cannot challenge basic assumptions of American prestige practices. That limited stance is all the more apparent in second wave realism. The theorization of prestige and reputation that strategic theory uses is written mainly in the idiom of commerce: costs and benefits, assets, state acts that have a quantifiable value. That understanding of prestige and reputation does not merely give general support to prestige policy; it creates a stance in which deterring communist states depends on intervening in places like Vietnam.

To trace out this understanding, consider Thomas Schelling's strategic theory, one of the major works of the second wave of realism. Schelling approached deterrence as a strategy "game" in which the outcome depends on what each participant expects the other to do, and how each consequently calculates its "payoffs." That approach makes deterrence a matter of whether a deterring state can influence its opponent's expectations. As Schelling demonstrated, an opponent's expectations are not so easy to influence, especially if the threats a state makes are also "costly" to it (e.g., lives lost) and it is seen to have freedom of action not to bear such costs.[48] Thus a central problem for deterrence becomes the problem of making credible threats.

Schelling's solutions to the credibility problem include techniques for a deterring state to restrict its freedom of action (e.g., soldiers as "trip-wires") and for making itself impervious to the costs of acting on a threat (e.g., pre-programming a nuclear reprisal). A state may also make itself appear irrational (announce conflicting policies), thereby increasing expectations it might also "irrationally" bear heavy costs.[49] At the core of such solutions, though, is the use of reputation as a deterrent: from a deterring state's previous act(s), arise expectations by the state being deterred that a threat is real. For Schelling, the importance of reputation (or "prestige") lies in the way that all a state's "commitments" (deterrent acts) are interdependent. Not meeting a commitment therefore does not merely affect expectations about the next threat a state makes, or its more important ones, but *all current and future threats.*[50]

Applied to the United States, Schelling's understanding has some familiar consequences, made possible through familiar metaphors. The United States cannot easily get out of commitments, because when it was seen to do this in the past, "it cost us something."[51] The United States "saves" states (versus, for example, people); and it does so to "save face" for the United States.[52] The U.S. should deeply value its reputation with the Soviet Union. Indeed, "Soviet expectations about the behavior of the United States are one of the most valuable assets we possess in world affairs."[53] This could be Robert McNamara or Dean Rusk speaking, and not merely because of the conclusions, but also because of the assumption of a position within the U.S. state ("we," "our assets") and the metaphorical system used to reach the conclusions: an anarchic system of states, like companies in a free market, rationally calculating costs, targeting competitors' lines, and guarding their market-share. Schelling may not have approved of Vietnam policy; his understanding of prestige and reputation, though, gives no grounds for thinking it was a bad business decision.

One of the hallmarks of second wave realism is said to be its willingness to look dispassionately at the use of force in American foreign policy. Third wave realism, in turn, is said to have learned from Vietnam that force may not be quite so useful, an insight encouraging it in its attention to economic issues in an interdependent world. Even if third wave realists are more doubtful about force, though, they have not undone the realist acceptance of prestige and reputation as objects of state action. Rather, they have rejected aspects of the second wave stance, only to recuperate that of the first wave.

Consider the criticism Hoffmann (a self-styled third wave realist) has made of Vietnam policy making. In one of his more trenchant commentaries, Hoffmann describes American policy as having "radically flawed premises." The war was fought against an enemy with "literally unlimited" interests and support, which meant that victory would require "massive involvement"; but that involvement was ruled out because the U.S. had only limited "real interests" in South Vietnam.[54] The U.S. nonetheless continued to fight the war, though, because of the value placed on prestige and reputation (or "credibility" as Hoffmann calls it). Of this, Hoffmann says:

> [W]as there not something absurd and self-defeating about grand displays of force and tenacity justified not by the intrinsic importance of the stakes in Vietnam, but by the notion that in an age of deterrence (which is a gamble on credibility) and of contests of will, each confrontation becomes a test of our global credibility, of our resolve everywhere?[55]

However "absurd" the belief "that even tests for limited stakes have unlimited importance because of credibility," the U.S., as Hoffmann sees it, clung to this justification and to the hope it could "save South

Vietnam" through "nation-building" because "if we confessed the meagerness of our interests in Vietnam, then we were doomed to lose."[56] The result was a "moral disaster": a "bloodbath" in Vietnam and Cambodia unmitigated ethically by the U.S.'s "good intentions."[57]

Hoffmann's criticisms about Vietnam are strong. But for all their bite, they leave the absurdity and the "hubris" unexplained. How did successive American administrations come to be "impaled . . . on the stupid-heroic horn of our own dilemma," i.e.: fighting for global credibility when "real interests" did not make the fight worthwhile?[58] That question is unexplored by Hoffmann (and, indeed, the notion of tragedy implied in "hubris" forecloses the need for explanation). A partial explanation can be found in the way that *prior to* Vietnam, prestige and reputation had come to be valued in American foreign policy discourse, so that a psychology of American leadership based on prestige and reputation had become part of the American policy imaginary. Hoffmann does not question or challenge that more general context. Rather, much like George Ball's insider's dissent, Hoffmann's criticisms *assume* it.

The continued acceptance of prestige and reputation as policy criteria emerges most clearly in the conclusion of Hoffmann's critique, which draws general "errors" from Vietnam policy making. Two of the errors involved how the U.S. maintained its credibility. First, "[w]e weakened our own credibility by asserting that our failure to do the impossible in Vietnam affected our capabilities to do the possible and necessary elsewhere." This "error" is also projected by Ball. Projecting it assumes prestige and reputation are a valid basis for American foreign policy. Second, "[i]f our global credibility was involved . . . it was also because we insisted on seeing in Hanoi an arm of international communism, one head of a single multiheaded hydra."[59] Again, the existence or even the importance of maintaining the object of credibility is not at issue, but rather what makes the United States credible.

CONCLUSION

Hoffmann is hardly alone in his taken-for-granted construction of prestige and reputation (*qua* credibility): these objects are frequent visitors in third wave realism. Sometimes they are used as part of the descriptive underbrush of international relations, referred to in passing. Sometimes, they are featured prominently.[60]

234 JENNIFER L. MILLIKEN

Whether as "mere" description or developed theoretical concept, this continuing reference to prestige and reputation should be questioned. As the Vietnam War case makes clear, serious issues of empirical confirmation of claims about prestige and reputation exist. And as the Vietnam War case also makes clear, realist definitions of prestige and reputation give an inadequate basis for criticizing policies of intervention and escalation.

Realist scholarship is quite unreflective about the metaphorics of prestige and reputation examined here. This limits their critical capability and range of alternatives. A social constructivist view, by contrast, can support a critical understanding of international relations that is open to alternative possibilities of state action.

NOTES

1. I would like to thank Elisabeth Binder, Keith Krause, Diana Saco, and the editors of this volume for their comments on earlier drafts of this chapter.
2. The term dominating policy discussion by the end of the Vietnam War was "credibility," and it is this term that scholars have tended to use to characterize American policy (e.g., Stanley Hoffmann, *Primacy or World Order: American Foreign Policy Since the Cold War* [New York: McGraw-Hill, 1980], Seymour Hersch, *The Price of Power: Kissinger in the Nixon White House* [New York: Summit Books, 1983], Gabriel Kolko, *Confronting the Third World* [New York: Pantheon Books, 1988]). But in 1964-65, the period I examine most closely, prestige and reputation (used together or separately) were the dominant terms. To be more historically accurate, I follow this usage here. Note, though, that accompanying the use of prestige and reputation was a network of other terms, including credibility, standing, humiliation, saving face, and image.
3. Peter Applebombe, "At Home, War Healed Several Wounds," *New York Times*, 4 March 1991.
4. Craig Whitney, "The Next Step will be Building a Solid Future on the Shifting Sands," *New York Times*, 3 March 1991.
5. George Lakoff, "Metaphor and War: the Metaphor System Used to Justify War in the Gulf," (Unpublished Ms., 1991), 1.
6. Dean Acheson, *Present at the Creation: My Years in the State Department* (New York: W. W. Norton & Co., 1969), 528.
7. Kolko, *Confronting the Third World*, 293.
8. Patrick Morgan, "Saving Face for the Sake of Deterrence," in *Psychology and Deterrence*, eds. Robert Jervis, Richard Lebow, and Janice Gross Stein (Baltimore: Johns Hopkins University Press, 1985), 136.

9. *Foreign Relations of the United States, 1950,* vol. 1, *National Security Policy* (Washington, D.C.: U.S. Government Publications, 1984), 240, 255.

10. Abbreviations used in this and subsequent quotations include the following: DRV: Democratic Republic of [North] Vietnam; GRC: Taiwan; GVN: Government of [South] Vietnam; NLF: National Liberation Front; NATO: North Atlantic Treaty Organization; NVN: North Vietnam; ROK: Republic of [South] Korea; SEA: Southeast Asia; SVN: South Vietnam; VC: Viet Cong.

11. John McNaughton, "Aims and Options in Southeast Asia," 13 October 1964; *Pentagon Papers. Senator Gravel edition,* vol. 3 (Boston: Beacon Press, 1971), 580-83.

12. William Bundy, "The Choices We Face in Southeast Asia," 19 October 1964, Lyndon Baines Johnson Presidential Library (hereafter cited as LBJ); William Bundy manuscript, 17-16 to 17-25.

13. George Ball, Memorandum, 5 October 1964; *The Atlantic,* July 1972, 33-49.

14. Dean Rusk, "Viet-Nam." 1 July 1965. LBJ. NSF/VN/Box 20/Vol. 37/410. For histories that support the point about continued reliance on prestige and reputation arguments, see, for example, George Kahin, *Intervention: How America Became Involved in Vietnam* (New York: Alfred A. Knopf, 1986); William Conrad Gibbons, *The U.S. Government and the Vietnam War: Executive and Legislative Roles and Relationships,* 2 vols. (Princeton: Princeton University Press, 1986); Gabriel Kolko, *The Anatomy of a War: Vietnam, the United States, and the Modern Historical Experience* (New York: Pantheon, 1985); and Wallace Thies, *When Governments Collide: Coersion and Diplomacy in the Vietnam Conflict* (Berkeley: University of California Press, 1988). For a discourse analysis of the decision to commit ground forces that is also supportive, see David Sylvan and Hayward Alker, "Foreign Policy as Tragedy: Sending 100,000 troops to Vietnam." Paper presented at the XIVth World Congress of International Political Science Association, July 1988, Washington, D.C.

15. The constructive power of metaphor is addressed in some depth in other contributions to this volume, especially Paul Chilton's essay. My work draws upon sources shared by Chilton, especially George Lakoff and Mark Johnson, *Metaphors We Live By* (Chicago: University of Chicago Press, 1980) and George Lakoff, *Women, Fire and Dangerous Things: What Categories Reveal About the Mind* (Chicago: University of Chicago Press, 1987). Like Chilton, I combine this more cognitively oriented work with a social constructionist focus. A source for that aspect has been Norman Fairclough, *Language and Power* (New York: Longman, 1989).

16. George Ball, 21 July 1965. Comments made during a meeting with the president, 21 July 1965, LBJ Meeting notes file.

17. Due to space limitations, I can give only limited illustrations of systemic metaphors in use in the Johnson administration's bombing and ground troop decisions. I cite about forty documents here that are relevant; the original study for the essay was based on a data set of three hundred documents for

the period September 1964-July 1965. For information about and references for the latter, please contact the author.

18. Maxwell D. Taylor, Cable, 2 November 1964. LBJ NSF/VN/Box 10/Vol. 21/49.

19. See, among others: George Ball, Memorandum, 5 October 1964; John McNaughton, "Observations Re South Vietnam After Khanh's Re-Coup," 27 January 1965. *Pentagon Papers. Senator Gravel edition,* 3: 686-87; Senator McGee, reply to Senator Church in U.S. Senate debate on Vietnam, 17 February 1965. Quoted in William Conrad Gibson, vol. 2, 1986. 131-33; John McNaughton, "A Preliminary Shot at an Outline," 10 March 1965. LBJ NSF/VN/Box 15/Vol. 31/978; Chester Cooper and James Thomson, "Memorandum for Mr. Bundy," 29 June 1965. LBJ NSF/VN/Box 18/Vol. 35/355; and Ambassador Martin (Thailand), Cable 2201, 30 June 1965. LBJ NSF/VN/Box 45-46/Vol. 66/5.

20. McGeorge Bundy, "A Policy of Sustained Reprisal." 7 February 1965, *Pentagon Papers. Senator Gravel edition,* 3: 687-91.

21. See also: Robert Johnson, "War Termination in Vietnam," 11 February 1965. LBJ NSF/NSC History, Deployment of Forces; Senator McGee, reply to Senator Church, 17 February 1965: Meeting of President Johnson with General Eisenhower, 17 February 1965. LBJ Meeting notes file. McGeorge Bundy handwritten notes; James Thomson, "The Vietnam Crisis: One Dove's Lament," 19 February 1965, LBJ NSF/NSC History, Deployment of Forces; Ambassador Rice (Hong Kong), letter to William Bundy, 24 June 1965. LBJ NSF/VN/History, Deployment of Forces; and George Ball, "A Compromise Solution in Vietnam," 1 July 1965, *Pentagon Papers. Senator Gravel edition,* 4: 615-19.

22. President Johnson, early 1965 interview. From Doris Kearns, *Lyndon Johnson and the American Dream* (New York: Alfred A. Knopf, 1965), 252-53.

23. Hans Morgenthau, *Politics Among Nations,* 3d ed. ([1947]; New York: Alfred A. Knopf, 1960), 248.

24. See: George Ball, Memorandum, 5 October 1964; John McNaughton, "Aims and Options in Southeast Asia," 13 October 1964; William Bundy and John McNaughton, "Summary of Courses of Action in Southeast Asia," 21 November 1964, *Pentagon Papers. Senator Gravel edition,* 3: 659-60; McGeorge Bundy handwritten meeting notes of meeting with the President, 9 March 1965. LBJ Meeting Notes File; McGeorge Bundy, "The Demonologists Look at the Noise from Hanoi, Peking and Moscow," 20 April 1965. LBJ Troops/Vol 41/Box 3/44a; John McNaughton, "Analysis and Options for SVN," 13 July 1965. LBJ NSF/VN/Vol. 37/Box 20/216a and; Robert McNamara, "Recommendations of Additional Deployments to Vietnam," 20 July 1965. LBJ NSF/VN/Vol. 74-75/Box 12/501.

25. George Ball, Memorandum, 5 October 1964.

26. See: William Bundy and John McNaughton, "Summary of Courses of Action in Southeast Asia," 21 November 1964, *Pentagon Papers. Senator Gravel edi-*

tion 3: 659-60; Robert McNamara, Statement before the Armed Services Committee, 18 February 1965, *New York Times*, p. 1, 19 February 1965; Ambassador Bohlen (France), Cable, 1 March 1965. LBJ NSF/VN/Box 14/Vol. 30/147e; and Robert McNamara, off-the-record interview with Arthur Krock, 22 April 1965. Papers of Arthur Krock, Princeton University Library.

27. *Fighting war*: Robert McNamara, "Recommendations of Additional Deployments to Vietnam," 20 July 1965. *Faith shaken*: Robert McNamara, Off-the-record interview with Arthur Krock, 22 April 1965. *Less hopeful*: William Bundy, speech before the Washington Chamber of Commerce. *Congressional Record: Senate*, 1 March 1965: 3786-89; *Intimidate*: William Bundy, "South Vietnam Courses of Action," 23 January 1965. LBJ NSF/VN/Box 18/Vol. 35/606; *WWIII*: Dean Rusk, "Viet-Nam," 1 July 1965.

28. *Increments*: Ambassador Rice (Hong Kong), letter to William Bundy, 24 June 1965. Higher Price: McGeorge Bundy, "A Policy of Sustained Reprisal," 7 February 1965. *Humiliation*: John McNaughton, "A Preliminary Shot at an Outline," 10 March 1965. The figure was McNaughton's calculation, which he offered to McNamara without explanation of how it had been derived.

29. *The Pentagon Papers. Senator Gravel edition,* 3: 521-22.

30. William Bundy, "The Choices We Face In Southeast Asia," 19 October 1964.

31. The partial exceptions to this were the European states, although they too were understood as being vulnerable and somewhat prone to emotionality. For a discourse analysis of the gendered and partly eroticized nature of American bombing policy, see Jennifer Milliken and David Sylvan, "Soft Targets, Hard Bodies and Chic Theories: U.S. Bombing Policy in Indochina." Paper presented at the XVIIth World Congress of IPSA, July 1991 Buenos Aires. For a discussion of gendered and other social constructions of "otherness" in the more general context of the international hierarchy of First World/Third World states, see Roxanne Doty, "The Social Construction of Contemporary International Hierarchy" (Ph.D. diss., University of Minnesota, 1991).

32. Patrick Morgan, 1985, 143.

33. *Credibility with the Soviets*: Dean Rusk, comments made in Meeting with the President, 21 July 1965; John McNaughton, "Annex-Plan of Action for SVN," 24 March 1965, *Pentagon Papers. Senator Gravel edition* 4: 695-702; and Dean Rusk, "Viet-Nam," 1 July 1965. *Respect in private*: William Bundy, "The Choices We Face in Southeast Asia," 19 October 1964; and Robert McNamara, off-the-record interview with Arthur Krock, 22 April 1965. *Asian dominoes*: (among others) George Ball, Memorandum, 5 October 1964; William Bundy, "The Choices We Face in Southeast Asia," 19 October 1964; John McNaughton, "Observations re South Vietnam after the Khanh Re-Coup," 4 January 1965; Meeting of President Johnson with General Eisenhower, 17 February 1965; Robert McNamara, off-the-record interview with Arthur Krock, 22 April 1965; and Ambassador Rice (Hong Kong), letter to William Bundy, 24 June 1965.

34. Stanley Hoffmann, *Janus and Minerva: Essays in the Theory and Practice of International Politics* (Boulder Colo.: Westview Press, 1987), 10.
35. Ibid., 11.
36. Morgenthau, 7.
37. Ibid., 81.
38. Ibid., 84-85, 419.
39. Ibid., 80-82, 163.
40. Ibid., 73, 79.
41. Ibid., 80.
42. Ibid., 83.
43. Ibid., 81.
44. William Bundy, "The Choices We Face in Southeast Asia," 19 October 1964.
45. Morgenthau, 79. Even here, though, the question remains as to how one defines such things. American policy makers, after all, considered South Vietnam part of their security zone.
46. Ibid., 80.
47. Ibid., 84-85.
48. Thomas C. Schelling, *The Strategy of Conflict* ([1960]; Cambridge: Harvard University Press, 1980), 39-43.
49. Thomas C. Schelling, *Arms and Influence* (New Haven: Yale University Press, 1966).
50. Ibid., 55-59.
51. Ibid., 63.
52. Ibid., 124.
53. Ibid., 125.
54. Stanley Hoffmann, *Primacy or World Order: American Foreign Policy Since the Cold War* (New York: McGraw-Hill Book Company, 1980), 24-25.
55. Ibid., 24.
56. Ibid.
57. Ibid., 25.
58. Ibid.
59. Ibid., 26.
60. For examples of descriptive use, see: Stephen Krasner, *Defending the National Interest: Raw Materials Investments and U.S. Foreign Policy* (Princeton: Princeton University Press, 1978), 275; and Kalevi Holsti, *Peace and War: Armed Conflicts and International Order, 1648-1991* (Oxford: Oxford University Press, 1991), 18-19. Works with strong theoretical emphasis include: Robert Jervis, *The Logic of Images in International Relations* ([1970]; Princeton: Princeton University Press, 1989); Robert Gilpin, *War & Change in World Politics* (Cambridge: Cambridge University Press, 1981); and Barry Nalebuff, "Rational Deterrence in an Imperfect World," *World Politics* 43, no. 3 (1991): 313-35.

Yosef Lapid

Nationalism and Realist Discourses of International Relations

> There is an inverse relationship between the importance of nationalism in
> the modern world and the amount of scholarly attention it has received.
>
> Ernest Gellner[1]

In the post-Cold War era, nationalism has finally come to be recognized as probably the most explosive political force of our century. However, this belated recognition—forced upon us by dramatic historical events such as the implosion of the Soviet Union, the reunification of Germany, and the violent disintegration of Yugoslavia—in no way eliminates the need to reexamine the reasons behind the sustained failure of most Western social sciences to generate serious theoretical interest in a foremost historical phenomenon.[2] For the neglect-of-nationalism-problem has resulted in "the most striking example of a general failure among experts to anticipate social developments."[3] And in the absence of a sober effort to face up to the cross-paradigmatic and cross-disciplinary scope of the "neglect-problem," we risk stumbling into an equally frustrating situation, in which voluminous new literatures continue to be associated with a remarkable poverty of theoretical understanding.[4]

As a discipline, international relations hardly deviates from this embarrassing pattern.[5] And yet, that realism somehow partakes in this "neglect-of-nationalism-problem" may seem, at first, quite remarkable. For what is the subject-matter of realist discourses, one may ask, if not *nation*-states, *national*-power, *national*-interest, *national*-security, inter*national* relations and so on? Is it possible that realism—a tradition that subscribes to an ontology of conflictual group fragmentation—has somehow failed to pay attention to that category of distinction (i.e., the "national") which in the modern world "has tended to determine the size and shape of political units"?[6]

Furthermore, to the extent that realism is a discourse on war and survival, it is even more difficult to fathom how realist scholars could have possibly avoided the national factor. For from the very beginning the principle of nationalism was closely linked, both in theory and practice, with the idea of war. In brief, to the extent that one takes seriously the realist consensus concerning ontology (conflictual group fragmentation) and problematique (survival/war), few phenomena, if any, should have had greater *prima facie* relevance than nationalism.

Such considerations notwithstanding, nationalism is, or so I posit, among the phenomena overlooked or discounted by recent realist discourses. The problem seems deeply rooted in the intellectual foundations of the realist tradition. It is already evident, for instance, in Hobbes's *Leviathan* which, as Richard Helgerson pointed out, "belongs not to a discourse of the nation but to a discourse of the state."[7] My argument suggests, however, that this problem has been aggravated by recent neorealist efforts to systematize the insights of classical realism into a more "scientific" format.

Affirming that nationalism is not a phenomenon that international relations scholarly discourses can currently afford to ignore, the analysis unpacks the discursive neorealist logic that can be held largely responsible for the postulated "neglect-of-nationalism" problem. The immediate objective is to facilitate a better understanding of why, where, and how we might fruitfully engage in a productive rethinking of the neorealist vocabulary and assumptive framework concerning nationalism in the post-Cold War era.

In pursuing this objective, I shall pay some attention to the role of rhetoric in social scientific research. In tune with the orientation of this volume, I approach both nationalism and the realist tradition as discursive languages—rather than as "essentialist" categories or "positive" theories. Three related considerations render "taking language seriously" particularly promising in this case. First, whatever else it may be, nationalism is also a potent *performative discourse* that aims "to impose the legitimate definition of the divisions of the social world and, thereby, to *make and unmake groups*."[8] In "the act of social magic" achieved by performative discourses, language and rhetoric become productive forces that "may *contribute to producing* what they apparently describe or designate."[9] Recognizing the import of language in the social construction of reality offers a way to break the gag of essentialist categories which continue to suffocate the study of nationalism.

Second, as a near hegemonic—and (would-be) "scientific" discourse—neorealism participates in vigorous "struggles over classification." These are struggles over "the power of imposing a vision of the social world through principles of division."[10] Such struggles take place in both scientific and political domains, and their outcomes have long-lasting symbolic effects. The interesting question here is not whether scholarly discourses get dragged into such struggles—for, as astutely pointed out by Bourdieu, they invariably do—but whether they assume a *critical* or *complicitous* attitude toward a given principle of social "division."[11] International relations realist discourses, in particular, are vulnerable to the charge of being "discursive accomplices of a state-centric mode of authority."[12] Paying closer attention to linguistic/rhetorical moves is hence essential to any effort to transform "problem-solving" approaches—which take prevailing social frameworks for action as "immutable" or "given"—into more reflexive critical discourses.[13]

This last clarification takes us directly to the third consideration concerning a "linguistic turn." There seems to be a solid consensus among critics of the dominant tradition, that neorealist and classical realist discourses do not differ significantly as far as their complicitous attitude toward nationalism as a principle of social division is concerned. According to this view, "the realist account of international politics relies heavily on the image of nation-states as idealized political communities. The ideal is fundamental to the logical structure and coherence of both classical and structural realism."[14] Challenging this view, this chapter demonstrates that there are significant differences between classical realism and neorealism in both the nature and the degree of their putative "complicity" with the nationalist world-view. Although undeniably open to a "first-degree-complicity-charge" with nationalism, neorealism subscribes to an exceedingly narrow definition of the "national" principle of division which collapses critical distinctions between nation and state and nationalism and sovereignty. To a far greater extent than classical realism, neorealism insists on sovereignty and territoriality as statist—as opposed to "national"—principles of social division and global political organization. Insofar as the distinctions between nation and state and nationalism and sovereignty continue to ascend and to consolidate—as they have done in recent years—we may be in for a serious rethinking of the relationship between neorealism and nationalism as properly defined.

The argument is presented in four consecutive stages. First, I establish a point of departure by addressing the substantial presence of nationalism on the agenda of classical realism. Next, I explore the steps involved in the Waltzian recasting of classical realism as neorealism, touching upon rhetorical elements which may have facilitated the ascendence of neorealism to a dominant discourse status in international relations. The third step traces the lamentable "exit" of nationalism from the recent international relations theoretical enterprise, back to one of its origins in the dense theoretical "logic" entailed by Waltzian neorealism. The fourth and final section suggests that the "exit" of nationalism from the neorealist agenda is contingent and transcendable, as opposed to inherent and immutable. Along with other perspectives, the realist tradition has much to offer to a post-neorealist discourse on nationalism.

ONCE UPON A TIME . . .

The conspicuous vanishing of the "national" from the realist agenda is a recent development. Without postulating a fallen golden age of realist scholarship on nationalism, the national phenomenon has, in the past, captured the sustained attention of classical realist thinkers such as Edward H. Carr, Hans J. Morgenthau, John H. Herz, and many others. His embarrassing 1945 prediction concerning the imminent demise of the nation-state notwithstanding, Carr offered an insightful historical analysis of nationalism. Three widely differing views of the "nation" were conjured to challenge the core neorealist belief that inter-national relations "have remained more or less unchanged through the past three or four centuries."[15] Also, Carr's anticipation of a dual (i.e. internal and external) challenge "to the nation as the final and acceptable unit of international organization" seems anything but dated in the current global situation.[16]

Nationalism also played an important role in John Herz's life-long project to construct an acceptable idealism/realism synthesis.[17] Herz built his political realism on a structural "constellation" described as the "security dilemma." This dilemma arises whenever "ultimate power units" (city-states, tribes, nation-states, empires, etc.,) interact without a superior authority to control them. We are told that "power considerations have always ruled 'inter-national' relationships *whatever units constituted the basic units of such relations*"[18] It is hence hardly surprising that the fulfillment of national aspirations "often means nothing but a sudden awakening of the 'sense of power and security' and corresponding policies of power competition."[19]

Morgenthau engaged the "paradoxes" of modern nationalism on multiple levels.[20] At the psychological level, his understanding of nationalism is colored by his Hobbesian premise of an innate human urge for power. In his "biological" version of political realism, nations express the potent transference of power impulses from the individual to the state. Nationalism is fueled by the irrational human need to bestow loyalties on more enduring entities. National publics are therefore depicted by Morgenthau as instinctively aggressive, though capable of control by responsible leadership.[21]

Morgenthau's view of nationalism as a principle of global political organization is equally pessimistic. The historical evidence reveals "the insufficient, self-contradictory, and self-defeating nature of nationalism as the exclusive principle of international order."[22] Following the logic of his realist theory, Morgenthau stipulates that nationalism is "a principle of disintegration and fragmentation, which is prevented from issuing in anarchy not by its own logic but by the political power which . . . puts a halt to its realization at a certain point."[23]

Morgenthau differentiates also between traditional forms of nationalism and the new phenomenon of nationalistic universalism. Traditional nationalists operate on a premise, not shared by Morgenthau himself, that in a society of "satisfied" nation-states, national survival could be secured by the observance of the principle of self-determination. Traditional nationalism may result nonetheless in two types of conflict behavior: conflicts between a nationality and an alien master, and conflicts between national groups over respective spheres of dominion.[24]

Nationalistic universalism is however far more intractable. It resembles a religious crusade promoting a single moral system for the entire world. It was first launched by Woodrow Wilson's war to make the world safe for democracy. It was carried to new heights by Hitler's aggressive totalitarianism. And during the Cold War nationalistic universalism was energetically pursued by both the Soviet Union and the United States.

The combination of universal nationalism and nuclear technology has raised the specter of anarchy and universal destruction. Morgenthau insists, however, that it is nowhere preordained that "nation-states" should constitute the permanent political units of international life. To the contrary, "the contemporary connection between interest and the nation state is a product of history, and is . . . bound to disappear in the course of history."[25]

A comprehensive analysis of nationalism in classical realism is beyond the scope of this essay. We can conclude, however, that nationalism does figure prominently on the agenda of classical realism. At minimum, we have seen: (1) a dual understanding of nationalism as: (a) an expression of an enduring human need, and (b) a modern principle of global political order (Morgenthau); (2) a recognition that nationalism operates in both "domestic" and "global" political arenas, which, incidentally, are constructed as based on similar principles, structures, and processes (Morgenthau, Carr, Herz); (3) an explicit realization that there are no "preordained" units—not even the nation-state—in international relations (Morgenthau) and hence an affirmation of the need to determine empirically "what are . . . the basic units of ultimate power in the inter-national field"[26]; (4) a challenge to the postulate of continuity in international relations, based on historically changing definitions of the "nation" (Carr); and (5) a recognition of the promise held by a new realist/idealist synthesis for a more comprehensive account of nationalism in international relations theory (Herz).

This condensed depiction of classical realism suggests that the reliance of classical realism on the nation-state as an idealized political community is tempered by a keen recognition that there are no "permanent units" in history. To the extent that a "complicitous" relationship can be nonetheless postulated between classical realism and the national principle of division, it must be of a hedged and flexible kind. For ultimately classical realism subscribes to a historically contingent ontology involving constant flux and epochal transformations. As pointed out by Berki, Ashley, Walker, and others, classical realism does acknowledge the critical role played by human understandings and practices in the production of social reality.

The situation is, however, quite different with respect to neorealism. Whereas traditional realists treated the nation-state as an ideal or as an aspiration, Waltz simply appropriates it as a reality and as a safe premise for neorealist theorizing. Herein lies a qualitative difference between classical realism and neorealism regarding their respective "complicity" with the national/statist principle of social division.

Kenneth Waltz sets out, as noted, to recast the realist tradition into a more scientific format. As pointed out by Alexander and Colomy, theoretical activities of this kind (i.e., elaboration, revision, and reconstruction) are frequently encountered in scientific discourses.[27] Scholarly traditions "may be enriched and elevated by these processes of theoretical change; they may be also impoverished and simplified, robbed of their sophistication and denuded of some of their most powerful intellectual sustenance."[28] I shall posit that with respect to nationalism, the recasting of classical realism into (Waltzian) neorealism, fits into the latter category.

ENTER NEOREALISM

Prior to continuing with the main argument, I should offer some clarifications concerning Waltz's influential reformulation of classical realism. According to Waltz, classical realism was left "beyond the theoretical pale" by even its most theoretically self-conscious proponents—i.e. Raymond Aron and Hans Morgenthau.[29] Waltz's self-declared mission was therefore to bring realism and international relations theory "within the theoretical pale."[30]

The essential steps in this ambitious project can be briefly enumerated. Neorealism begins with the isolation of international relations as a distinct and intellectually coherent field of inquiry. It continues with a tightly reasoned elaboration of the basic ideas of system, structure, and units. "By depicting an international political system as a whole, with structural and unit levels at once distinct and connected," explains Waltz, "neorealism establishes the autonomy of international politics and thus makes a theory about it possible."[31]

Waltz insists that the "idea that international politics can be thought of as a system with a precisely defined structure is neorealism's most fundamental departure from traditional realism."[32] He does mention, however, three further changes referring respectively to: (1) a shift to structural explanations, (2) a focus on "structural logic" as opposed to "human nature" accounts, and (3) an approach to "units" (sovereign states) as "functionally similar," with differences among them defined exclusively in terms of capabilities.

These amendments result in a structural "logic" that identifies "self-help" and "power politics" as constitutive features of world politics.[33] Waltz constructed this "logic" in the following discursive sequence: "First, he divided the universe of system into structure and unit levels. Second, he took structure to represent the system level of analysis. Third, he defined structure in highly restrictive terms."[34] The result was an effective equation of the international system level of analysis with a narrow definition of structure, and a wholesale banishment of phenomena, including nationalism, to the unit level.

Whereas an adequate understanding of neorealist theory requires a solid grasp of Waltz's departures from classical realism, an insight into the ascendence of his theory to a dominant discourse status in international relations requires an appreciation of his rhetorical strategy. As pointed out by Lawrence Prelli, scientific rhetoric is strategically created with a view to securing acceptance as scientifically reasonable by a special kind of audience. It is based on a particular kind of "topical logic."[35] Discursive strategies are particularly important when major theoretical elaboration, revisions, or reconstructions—such as those proposed by Kenneth Waltz—are being contemplated.

Waltz is explicit about the scope of his departures from classical realism. In terms of rhetorical strategy he relies on two highly effective "topoi" for delineating "legitimate" scientific modifications. These are: (1) the topos of continuity in science and (2) the topos of progress and truth in science.[36] When scholars acknowledge—as Waltz does with respect to classical realism—the relative validity of the views they wish to supercede, the topos of continuity helps them defend their proposed modifications without upsetting the stability of the addressed scholarly community. This is certainly the case with Waltz's depiction of the relation between classical realism and neorealism.[37] However, when Waltz claims radical discontinuity—in terms of "scientific" credentials—for his "new" realism, he does so under the topos of progress and truth in science.[38]

Be that as it may, in recent years a realization has crystallized that "Waltz seems prepared to abandon a massive area of political reality in the international system in order to hang onto [his] definitional nicety."[39] That this is a mistake leading to a massive loss of insight with respect to nationalism, is the burden of our argument in the next section.

Exit Nationalism

"If social science had shaped the modern world," says Raymond Grew, "nationalism would not be the troubling force it is today."[40] One can certainly say that much with respect to neorealism. The world of international politics—as constructed by Waltz's neorealist discourse—rigorously erases the theoretical relevance left for the "national" category. In fact, his *Theory of International Politics* (1989)—generally acknowledged as the "exemplar" for neorealism— even lacks a separate index entry for "nationalism."[41]

Prior to pursuing the discursive etiology of this remarkable omission, it may be helpful to delimit the term "nationalism" as used in this study. We differentiate between two empirically inter-related, but analytically distinct, meanings: (1) nationalism as a normative "blueprint" for global political organization, and (2) nationalism as a sociological/behavioral "fact."[42] In its first connotation, nationalism is a "theory of legitimacy" (Gellner); a "theory of self-determination" (Cobban); a "core doctrine" (Berry); a "global political programme" (Hobsbawm); or a "generative order for geopolitical organization" (Portugali).[43] All of the above equate nationalism with a modern way of constructing (or imagining) the world which designates the "nation-state" as the archetypical polity at the global level.[44]And, according to many, it is "by far the most potent ideology in the world."[45]

Nationalism so defined is, however, a recent development. The French Revolution (1789)—not the Peace of Westphalia (1648)—is the earliest point of reference for its appearance as a fully articulated blueprint for global political order.[46] It follows that any theoretical discourse that would take seriously the temporal unfolding of global structures and international orders must consider both 1648 and 1789 as highly significant (epoch-creating) "moments."[47] In different ways, both "moments" may hold keys as to how historically evolving structures, and institutions, result in new principles of division, involving novel conceptions of identity and political community.[48]

In its second connotation, nationalism need not detain us in great detail. It refers to active political movements seeking to defend or to advance the interests of respective ("real" or "constructed") national entities. In this "sociological" sense, there have been "nations" and "states" long before 1789. But in the absence of a coherent nation-state "blueprint," the mere presence of such entities did not result in the explosive pattern of global division associated with modern nationalism.[49]

We can return now to our main theme concerning the forced "exit" of nationalism from the neorealist discourse. Keeping in mind our two understandings of nationalism, the ensuing critique consists of two basic arguments: (1) With respect to nationalism as a "generative blueprint," the realist tradition was reduced by Waltzian neorealism to a posture of virtual silence. (2) Neorealism does offer some limited discursive tools for engaging the national phenomenon at the sociological level. Both arguments affirm, however, the secondary role ascribed to the "national" by the neorealist discourse and both stand in need of further elaboration.

Starting with our second line of criticism, we recall that neorealism sets up international relations as a coherent field of inquiry by firmly isolating it from the domestic arena. Pursuing the implications of this ontological gambit the "national" falls squarely within the domestic/hierarchic/unit-level domain of Waltz's bifurcated political universe. We recall furthermore that for "theory-building" purposes, neorealism axiomatically discounts all aspects of the domestic arena except those related to (state) power and capabilities. It follows that situating the "national" within a domestic "control-of-capabilities" matrix is the only way in which neorealism allows nationalism to affect significant outcomes at the global level. However, monitoring the ways in which nationalism fragments, augments, and/or dilutes the power base of extant sovereign states cannot possibly mature into a comprehensive theorization of the "national" in international relations. Ultimately, the neorealist logic relegates nationalism—along with all other domestic factors—to a "second order force" in world politics.[50]

More important perhaps—because of largely self-imposed restrictions—neorealism, in its Waltzian formulation, cannot easily expand its discursive horizon to include "constitutional" (as opposed to "distributional") ramifications of contemporary nationalism. The programming of neorealism to explain continuity and change in distributional terms—which may have been an asset during the Cold War—seems particularly disabling in the midst of a new "epoch-creating moment." For extreme measures of fluidity are now experienced at all levels, and they seem to extend to the "constitutional" underpinnings of our global political order.[51]

These observations take us back to the first line of criticism of the neorealist account of nationalism. To reiterate, the charge is that—with respect to nationalism as a generative blueprint—neorealism is reduced to a posture of discursive silence. This silence is, to some extent, the product of Waltz's acknowledged departures from classical realism. In other words, the moves taken by Waltz to bring international politics "within the theoretical pale," can be shown to have had the unintended effect of pushing the "national" further beyond the reach of the neorealist discourse.

A comprehensive substantiation of this charge would involve a detailed, ontological and epistemological, scrutiny of Waltz's reworking of realist ideas on system, structure, and units. For our present purposes, suffice it to say that having banished nationalism to the "hierarchic" component of the political universe, Waltz fortifies his discursive "domestication" of nationalism by: (1) endorsing a highly restrictive definition of international "structure," and (2) equating the entire system-level of analysis with this severely truncated structural construct.

As noted already, Waltz insists that in his "new" realism "structural and unit levels (are) at once distinct and connected."[52] However, by depicting units as given and "functionally similar" entities—and by minimizing the relevance of "non-structural" factors at the systemic level of analysis—Waltz leaves us with only one set of variables (i.e. capabilities) able of mediating structures and units in international politics. But, as noted, "distributional" variables are singularly ill-suited to capture "constitutional" ramifications of modern nationalism.[53]

The problem can be further elucidated from still a different angle. Conceptualizing nationalism as a "generative blueprint" involves an ontological position which sees *all* social action—regardless of whether it occurs under "hierarchy" or under "anarchy"—as dependent on pre-existing rules and conventions.[54] Insofar as nationalism indeed "generates" recurrent quests of "national congruence" (nation-building, self-determination, separatism, irredentism, etc.), it does so as a meaning-producing doctrine, not as a hidden physical structure operating behind the back of unsuspecting agents (i.e., "nations" and "states"). This ontological position is, however, largely incompatible with the "positional ontology" which grounds the neorealist construct of "structure." For Waltz's "generative structure" operates through (mechanical) acts of "arrangement," which highlight the *unintended* results of systemic organization.[55]

It follows that in order to be able to incorporate the "generative" aspects of nationalism, neorealism must either (1) expand its definition of "structure" to include "actor differentiation" (Ruggie) and normative webs of meaning (Kratochwil) or, alternatively, (2) incorporate constitutive rules and shared webs of meaning—such as nationalism—as perhaps "non-structural," but still consequential, factors operating at the global polity level.[56] However, as long as Waltz and his followers continue to resist such extensive reformulations, nationalism—as a global-level generative blueprint—will be effectively blocked from the neorealist discourse. And such a blockage can only seriously cripple the neorealist ability to explain major developments occurring at the epicenter of its declared domain of scholarly interest.

CONCLUSIONS

What are the wider implications of this analysis? Are the revealed flaws in neorealism inherent and immutable, or are they contingent and transcendable? Is one to proceed in the direction of elaborating and revising neorealism? Or is one better advised to move to a radically different discourse?

We have seen that—in its Waltzian version—neorealism is no guide for the perplexed in matters "national." The neorealist discourse bolts nationalism to the domestic arena, thus blocking the possibility of seeing the "national" as a "first-order force" in international relations; it blurs distinctions between "nation" and "state" at the unit level, thus making it difficult, or redundant, to seek a non-tautological relationship between "nation" and "state"[57]; it casts nationalism in "distributional" as opposed to "constitutional" terms, thus blurring the distinction between "nationalism" and "sovereignty" at the systemic/historical level; and it emphasizes continuity over change, thus depriving nationalism of transformative—as opposed to reproductive—ramifications.

In its dash for positivist scientific respectability, neorealism has lost much of the sophistication displayed by classical realism toward modern nationalism.[58] The open-ended ontology of classical realism—with respect to "basic units of ultimate power"—was replaced by a neorealist insistence on the sovereign state as the "ontological given" for international relations theorizing.[59] All that presumably matters in international politics—i.e. "anarchy," "self help," "balancing of power," "security dilemma," "rationality," etc.,—is traced back by neorealist accounts to actions and co-actions of such pre-existing "ontological givens."

Those who would follow rigorously the neorealist "logic," are bound to marvel at the expanding sense of international relations puzzlement concerning nationalism. They are likely to dismiss as nonsensical the notion that "we are stuck with the reality of international relations: not inter-*state* relations but inter*national* relations."[60] And they will be unfazed by the insistence that "there really does exist an *international system*, with nations as constituent elements rather than states."[61]

Indeed, recent transformations notwithstanding, neorealist proponents seem unshaken in their conviction that "actors can only be understood in the context of a system composed of sovereign states."[62]

In view of these charges, it is possible that some of those interested in restoring nationalism to theoretical respectability in international relations will opt to keep their distance from realism in general and neorealism in particular. This is, of course, a legitimate reaction. Personally, my preference would be in favor of an engaged multi-paradigmatic dialogue with realist discourses contributing their share to a serious disciplinary rethinking of nationalism. At least three considerations support my inclination. To begin with, nationalism itself should greatly benefit from further elucidation in realist terms. In many ways, the national phenomenon seems glove fitted for realist analysis. And as noted, in the past, realist scholars have substantively contributed to a better understanding of nationalism. To the extent that current realist discourses can rekindle a sustained interest in the "national" problem, we may justifiably look forward to a new round of sound realist contributions on nationalism.

Secondly, realist discourses—neorealism in particular—could also benefit from greater attention to the national factor in international relations. As a scholarly discourse, neorealism reflects the *sancta simplicitas* of the Cold War. That world is no longer with us, and neorealism itself now faces the difficult challenge of becoming more "realistic." Addressing the nuanced complexities of the national problem could help neorealism in this difficult task. For as aptly pointed out by Professor Hinsley some twenty years ago, "to wrestle with the problem of nationalism is to realize the full complexity of international relations."[63] So rather than deepening the frequently deplored neorealist complicitous relation with reified state-centrism, greater attention to contemporary nationalism may end up fostering a more critical neorealist "vision" of the "national" principle of division.

And finally, nationalism is likely in the foreseeable future to confront policy makers with exceedingly difficult challenges. Whether we like it or not, realist and neorealist scholars are the most likely to serve in influential policy advising positions. In lieu of a critical reconsideration of the realist fund of knowledge on nationalism, such advisers are bound to arrive at rather simplistic policy prescriptions. For these reasons, realist discourses in general, and neorealism in particular, should be involved in a serious rethinking of nationalism in the post-Cold War era.[64]

Notes

1. E. Gellner, *Nations and Nationalism* (Oxford: Billing and Sons, 1983), 753.
2. Nickos Poulantzas portrayed the nation as "the blind spot in the social sciences today." Joshua A. Fishman refered to nationalism as "the elephant that western social theory overlooked." A. D. Smith presented the sociology/nationalism encounter as "a sad catalog of neglect and missed opportunities." J. A. Agnew conceded that there is no geography of nationalism. K. E. Schwab testified that "most psychologists refuse to take national identity seriously as a legitimate problem for research." J. Spencer acknowledged that anthropology "has made only a limited contribution to the study of nationalism." And G. Graham admitted that the "subject of nationalism is not one on which political philosophers have dwelt very much."
3. R. Jalali and S. M. Lipset, "Racial and Ethnic Conflicts: A Global Perspective," *Political Science Quarterly* 107 (1992-93): 585.
4. See, W. Kymilcka, "Misunderstanding Nationalism" in *Dissent* (winter, 1995): 131-37.
5. Invoking the proverbial elephant and the blind men metaphor, Ernest Haas reported that, as of 1986, the "elephant" (i.e. nationalism) "lumbers around without doing much useful work." See, "What Is Nationalism and Why Should We Study It?" *International Organization* 40, no. 3 (1986): 708. See also Yosef Lapid and Friedrich Kratochwil "Revisiting the 'National': Towards an Identity-Agenda in Neorealism?" in their co-edited volume, *The Return of Culture and Identity in IR Theory* (Denver: Lynne Rienner, 1995).
6. R. N. Berki, *On Political Realism* (London: J. M. Dent & Sons, 1981), 37.
7. R. Helgerson, *Forms of Nationhood* (Chicago: University of Chicago Press, 1992), 295.
8. P. Bourdieu, *Language and Symbolic Power* (Cambridge, Mass: Harvard University Press, 1991), 221.
9. Ibid., 220.
10. Ibid.
11 Ibid., 225.
12. M. J. Shapiro, "Moral Geographies and the Ethics of Post-Sovereignty," *Public Culture* 6 (1994): 480.
13. M. Hoffman, "Agency, Identity and Intervention" in *Political Theory, International Relations and the Ethics of Intervention*, eds. I. Forbes and M. Hoffman (London: St. Martins Press, 1993), 196.
14. C. Reus-Smit, "Realist and Resistance Utopias" *Millennium* 21, no. 1 (1992): 14.
15. E. H. Carr, *Nationalism and After* (New York, Macmillan, 1945), 1.
16. Ibid., 38. See also E. Gellner, "Nationalism Reconsidered and E. H. Carr," *Review of International Studies* 18 (1992): 285-93.

17. J. H. Herz, *Political Realism and Political Idealism* (Chicago: University of Chicago Press, 1951).

18. Ibid., 76 (emphasis added).

19. Ibid. As he proceeded with his realist/idealist synthesis, Herz articulated the need to go beyond an "undiluted" power and security dilemma in explanations of international politics. And by keeping nationalism at the center of attention, he offered valuable hints as to how one might retrofit contemporary nationalism into such a realist/idealist synthesis. Interestingly enough, Herz extended the applicability of this realist survival/security model to minorities and other "out-groups" relations. See, Ibid, 189-200.

20. H. J. Morgenthau, *Politics Among Nations*, 4th ed. (New York: Knopf, 1967).

21. W. Bloom, *Personal Identity, National Identity, and International Relations* (Cambridge: Cambridge University Press, 1990), 77.

22. H. J. Morgenthau, "The Paradoxes of Nationalism," *The Yale Review* 46 (1957): 484.

23. Ibid.

24. Ibid.

25 G. Russell, *Hans J. Morgenthau* (Baton Rouge: Louisiana State University Press, 1990), 224.

26. Herz, *Political Realism and Political Idealism*, 224.

27. J. C. Alexander and P. Colomy, "Neofunctionalism Today: Reconstructing a Theoretical Tradition" in *Frontiers of Social Theory*, ed. George Ritzer (New York: Columbia University Press, 1990), 43.

28. Ibid.

29. K. N. Waltz, "Realist Thought and Neorealist Theory," *Journal of International Affairs* 44, no. 1 (1991): 24.

30. Ibid., 29.

31. Ibid.

32. Ibid., 30.

33. For an insightful critique of this "logic"—based on a "costructivist" approach to social theorizing—see A. Wendt, "Anarchy is What States Make of It: The Social Construction of Power Poltics" *International Organization* 46, no. 2 (1992): 391-425.

34. B. Buzan, C. Jones, and R. Little, *The Logic of Anarchy* (New York: Columbia University Press, 1993), 31.

35. L. J. Prelli, *A Rhetoric of Science* (Madison: University of Wisconsin Press, 1989), ix.

36. K. S. Zagacki and W. Keith, "Rhetoric, Topoi, and Scientific Revolutions," *Philosophy and Rhetoric* 25, no. 1 (1992): 77-95.

37. Waltz, "Realist Thought and Neorealist Theory."

38. Effective scientific rhetoric is only one of the explanations for the ascendance of neorealism as a highly persuasive discourse in international relations. Many other factors—intellectual and social and internal and

external—need to combine in a comprehensive account. See, George Ritzer, *Metatheorizing in Sociology* (Lexington, Mass.: Lexington Books, 1991), 1-14.

39. Buzan, Jones, and Little, *The Logic of Anarchy*, 52.

40. R. Grew, "Editorial Foreword," *Comparative Studies in Society and History* 1-2 (1992):1.

41. The existing entry for "nations"—which refers readers to "domestic political structures"; "hierarchic systems and structures"; "states"; and "units"—accurately marks the receding contours of the "national" on its forced exit from the neorealist discourse. See, K. N. Waltz, *Theory of International Politics* (Reading, Mass.: Addison-Wesley, 1979), 247. It is both noteworthy and consistent with our thesis that Waltz's previous classic *Man, the State, and War* (1959) had index entries for nationalism and nationality as "cause of war" and as "basis of peace"(258).

42. This "fact" vs. "norm" distinction with respect to "nationalism" duplicates a parallel distinction with reference to "sovereignty" in the work of John Ruggie and Robert Jackson. My argument stipulates that both sovereignty and nationalism must figure prominently in any historical mapping of key "constitutional mechanisms" in modern international relations. See, F. V. Kratochwil, *Rules, Norms, and Decisions* (Cambridge: Cambridge University Press, 1989).

43. See, E. Gellner, *Nations and Nationalism* (Oxford: Billing and Sons, 1983); A. Cobban, *The Nation State and National Self-Determination* (New York: Thomas Y. Crowell Co., 1969); C. J. Berry, "Nations and Norms," *The Review of Politics* 43, no. 1 (1981): 75-87; and Y. Portugali, "Nationalism, Social Theory and the Israeli/Palestinian Case," in *Nationalism, Self-determination and Political Geography*, eds. Ronald John Johnson, David B. Knight and Eleonore Kofman (London: Croom Helm, 1988), 151-65.

44. B. Anderson, *Imagined Communities* (London: Verso Editions, 1983).

45. D. Miller, "Nationalism" in *The Blackwell Encyclopedia of Political Thought* (Oxford: Basil Blackwell Inc., 1987), 352.

46. See, H. Bull, "The Importance of Grotius in the Study of International Relations" in *Hugo Grotius and International Relations*, H. Bull, et al., eds. (Oxford: Clarendon Press, 1990), 65-94. The Westphalian "moment" marks the crystallization of an inter-state order based on the novel principle of territorial sovereignty. On the other hand, "The critical moment in the history of nationality was when the hitherto distinguishable, if not entirely separate, ideas of cultural nation and political state moved together, and merged in one single idea." Cobban, *The Nation State and National Self-Determination*, 109.

47. "Epoch-creating moments" are well-defined by Istvan Bibo as "great moments of fluidity which are sudden turning points for eras that have become stagnant or unchanging in direction. Such historical moments can point to new directions valid for a long time to come." Arguably, we are cur-

rently in the midst of such a "moment."

48. For a recent example of a book which targets the relationship between sovereignty and changing conceptions of political community—but avoids in-depth treatment of the equally important problem of nationalism and changing conceptions of political community, see R. B. J. Walker and S. H. Mendlovitz, eds., *Contending Sovereignties* (Boulder, Colo.: Lynne Rienner Publishers, 1990).

49. We still have scant idea what the world of politics would look like if the "nation-state" blueprint were to be transcended by some novel organizational pattern. But we can be reasonably sure that—in a "sociological" sense—both "nations" and "states" would still figure prominently in such a world.

50. J. Mearsheimer, "Back to the Future," *International Security* 15, no. 1 (1990): 5-56.

51. What constitutes a proper political unit—i.e. at what level of inclusiveness should the social contract of the next millennium be drafted?—has surfaced as the key question. While distributions of capabilities and balances of power seem largely irrelevant to this question, nationalism and the quest for identity should play a central role in the quest for a new principle of social division.

52. Waltz, "Realist Thought and Neorealist Theory," 29.

53. The interesting implications of ethnonationalism, for instance, are not to be gauged at the level of capabilities or of changing numbers of sovereignties in the system. The truly important question concerning non-sovereign forms of nationalism is not whether they will be able to close their "sovereignty gap" (some will and many will not), but whether they have the potential to durably situate themselves in innovative ways vis-a-vis sovereignty itself. For it is here that we may be already witnessing a subtle recalibration of the institutional shadows cast respectively by 1648 and 1789. See, J. Mayall, *Nationalism and International Society* (Cambridge: Cambridge University Press, 1990).

54. D. Dessler, "What's at Stake in the Agent-Structure Debate?" *International Organizations* 43, no. 3 (1989): 441-73.

55. Ibid.

56. Some of the discursive tools for such purposes are already available under terms such as "process" (Keohane and Nye); "dynamic density" (Ruggie); "interaction capacity" (Buzan). Some critics lump these terms together under the "liberal factor" rubric, and suggest that this is the weakest part in current efforts to come up with a new realist/liberalist synthesis. However, discourse analysis suggests caution with respect to "non-structural" accounts of nationalism. For the term "structure" empowers what it designates. It is hence questionable whether it is possible to elevate nationalism to a "first-order factor" in international relations without designating it a "structural" element.

57. See, H. Wiberg, "States and Nations as Challenges to Peace Research," *Journal of Peace Research* 28, no. 4 (1991): 337-43.

58. J. L. Gaddis, "The Cold War's End Dramatizes the Failure of Political Theory," *The Chronicle of Higher Education,* 22 July 1992, A44; D. Puchala,"Woe to the Orphans of the Scientific Revolution," *Journal of International Affairs* 44, no. 1 (1990): 59-80.

59. S. D. Krasner, "Realism, Imperialism, and Democracy," *Political Theory* 20, no. 1 (1992): 39.

60. Howard, "Ideology and International Relations," 9.

61. B. B. Hughes, *Continuity and Change in World Politics* (Englewood Cliffs, N.J.: Prentice Hall, 1991), 199.

62. Krasner, "Realism, Imperialism, and Democracy," 39.

63. F. H. Hinsley, *Nationalism and the International System* (London: Hodder and Stoughton, 1973), 182.

64. See Lapid and Kratochwil, "Revisiting the 'National.'"

V. SPIKE PETERSON

THE GENDER OF RHETORIC, REASON, AND REALISM

This chapter argues that moving beyond realism—to post-realism—requires moving beyond the gender-blindness of conventional accounts.[1] My argument weaves together areas of inquiry that are usually treated in isolation. Intellectual developments associated with the rise of systematic inquiry in ancient Greece—marked by the shift from rhetoric to philosophy and its foundational dichotomies of reason over affect, mind over body—comprise one area of inquiry. Another is the study of historical-political developments—the shift to centralized authority and its dichotomies of public over private, civilized over "other"—within which Western science and political theory "emerged." A third area of inquiry is feminist scholarship that identifies Western philosophy and science as masculinist (privileging that which is associated with maleness over that which is associated with femaleness) and androcentric (taking male ways of being and knowing—as constituted under conditions of gender hierarchy—as the putatively human norm). A final area encompasses feminist critiques of state formation as institutionalizing and legitimating gender (and other) hierarchies and, specifically, as "naturalizing" the dichotomy of male-female "difference" that has excluded women (and others associated with the feminine) from intellectual and political power.

These areas of inquiry have generated extensive literatures that are complex and often controversial. My objective in this paper is less to explicate these literatures than to draw linkages between them.[2] It is these linkages that expose the centrality of gender in states and ideologies (in political and intellectual developments) and, therefore, the importance of feminist perspectives in refiguring realism. The core of my argument is that, historically, the following were mutually constituted (interdependent) processes: the institutionalization and naturalization of sexual difference and gender hierarchy in state making, the dichotomizing pursuit of transcendent reason in Western philosophy, and the articulation of androcentric realism in Western political theory. Moreover, this mutuality is not "simply" a conceptual linkage (e.g., between symbolic constructions of masculinity, rationality, power, and sovereignty) but a historical, empirical, and "structural" linkage that is visible through a feminist lens on state making and its ideological productions. Therefore, attempts to rethink realism must also engage a rethinking of gender relations and state orders.[3]

I first consider the importance of examining gender and of focusing on early, rather than modern, state formation. I then turn to the significance of specifically Athenian state making and tell a gender-sensitive story of rhetoric, reason, and realism in the Athenian context. Implications of this story for refiguring realism are considered in the final section.

THE SIGNIFICANCE OF GENDER

I focus on gender because this is where realism is most exclusionary. It must be underscored that gender is not only about women: it is about masculinity and femininity as a dichotomy that structures the identities, discursive practices, and material conditions of *all* men and women. Neither is feminism limited to documenting women's exclusion from and/or trivialization within malestream accounts. While analyses that "add women" and privilege their ways of knowing and being are valuable as "corrective" contributions, the transformative power of feminist critiques lies in understanding gender as a theoretical category, not only an empirical marker.[4]

From this perspective, gender and its effects are pervasive (in our ways of being and ways of knowing) and their exclusion from theoretical projects renders such projects structurally biased and therefore systemically flawed. In particular, feminists argue that the oppositional terms of male-female and masculine-feminine are not symmetrical but, like other Western dichotomies, the first term is accorded primacy and dominance.[5] As a consequence, characteristics identified closely with hegemonic masculinity (e.g., reason, agency, autonomy, freedom, transcendence) are privileged over those associated with femininity (e.g., emotion, passivity, interdependence, necessity, contingency). Finally, feminists locate masculinism at the "roots of Western epistemology, even Western culture itself" and argue that

"the fundamental dichotomies" between subject-object, rational-irra-
tional, culture-nature, and reason-emotion are all derived from the
basic male/masculine-female/feminine "hierarchy that is central to
patriarchal thought and society."[6]

Feminists are thus arguing that gender hierarchy is not coincidental to but in a significant sense constitutive of Western philosophy's
objectivist metaphysics and its corollary expressions of instrumental
reason, binary logic, and positivist science. Insofar as objectivist metaphysics marks the turning point from rhetoric to reason, this paper
focuses on the institutionalization of that metaphysics, the hierarchical dichotomies it constituted, and their effects on the theory and
practice of realism.

THE SIGNIFICANCE OF EARLY STATE MAKING

I focus on early state making because this is where "the human
story" took a decisive turn marked by profound "intellectual" and
"political" transformations. In terms of belief systems, state making
involved new questions about the nature of "man," his relationships to
"others," and his relationship to the known world. Historically this
meant the displacement of "fatalistic" world views wherein the natural
order and social order are unified and individual "will," "human
agency," and sovereign subject(ivitie)s were not intelligible constructs.

> So long as the world was one in which no agentic imperative was think-
> able, human beings resigned themselves to fatalism and saw the world
> through a prism of magical thinking in which capricious forces might,
> at best, be placated or tricked . . . .[7]

State making then marked a shift to awareness of human efficacy and
a new story of reflective and responsible subjects who "take action"
and acquire some measure of "control" over their reality.

In terms of socio-political organization, states were formed
"against" existing social orders; they marked a shift from corporate,
kin-based communities to the *institutionalization* of centralized
authority, gender and other stratification (based on the exploitation of
reproductive and productive labor), organized warfare, and justificatory ideologies. Resistance to early centralization was widespread and
long lasting but did not prevent states from becoming the dominant
form of social organization.[8] Key to this transition was the positive

feedback loop that amplified centralized political (and ideological) authority:

> There are multiple roads to statehood . . . .[but] once a society begins to evolve more centralized and more permanent authority structures, the political realm itself becomes an increasingly powerful determinant of change . . . . feed[ing] back to all the sociocultural features to make them fit more closely in its overall pattern.[9]

The point here is that coercive power alone tells us little about state making: the centralization of political authority requires not only economic and military power but also the centralization of ideological authority. Hence, culture and ideology are key to ensuring the "success" of states (both in terms of legitimating hierarchical rule and effectively reproducing justificatory ideologies) as states manipulate symbols, discursive practices, and ideological productions to mask their coercive power and effectuate indirect rule. In short, successful state making requires making states—and their oppressive dynamics—seem natural and even desirable.

Gender relations are central to these processes because state making marks the institutionalization of patriarchal relations that oppress women "as a group" even as they codify differences and competition *among* women. To the considerable extent that state making *depends on* the reproductive and productive labor of women, ideologies that de-politicize gender hierarchy are inextricable from the politics and discursive practices of centralized authority.[10] With state formation then, the exploitation of women and their exclusion from "public" authority and status is enforced by the power of the state and the *reproduction* of gender hierarchy is enabled by centralized "authorization" of particular masculinist ideologies.

In early states these revolutionary transformations have not yet been "naturalized," which is one effect of their institutionalization. Thus, an examination of early states reveals gender hierarchy, its attendant essentializing of dichotomized "gender difference," and the exclusion of women from political and ideological authority as historically contingent social constructions. More important, it exposes these constructions as not coincidental to but constitutive elements of consolidating and reproducing state systems.

In other words, states *depend* on the subordination of women (and others) and their exclusion from political and ideological authority.

Women cannot simply be included—as refiguring post-realism requires—without dramatically reconfiguring state orders. Conversely, as today's realities force a rethinking of states, the latter must include a rethinking of gender.

THE SIGNIFICANCE OF THE ATHENIAN CONTEXT

I focus on the Athenian context because this is where the realist narrative, which is also the scientific narrative, begins. It marks the turn from rhetoric to philosophy and realism; from skepticism to the Western codification of a binary metaphysics (mind-body, subject-object, culture-nature) and a binary politics (public-private, insider-outsider, civilized-Other).

The inadequacy of international relations theories of the state[11] is exacerbated by neglect of the Athenian *polis*: not only because modern states replicate many of its features, but because Athenian texts established constructions of authority, identity, politics, security, and public-private spheres that profoundly shaped and continue to discipline Western political theory and practice. This is not to equate Greek city-states with modern European states or to deny the systemic effects, for example, of religious traditions, individualism, and industrialization on the context of modern state formation. It is to suggest that greater attention to early state making generally, and the Athenian *polis* specifically, would expand our understanding of modern states, with implications for refiguring realism.

The realist narrative constructs Thucydides as "the first writer in the realist tradition as well as the founding father of the international relations discipline."[12] Subsequent realists have (selectively) drawn on his work as well as other ancient and classical sources of philosophy. Thucydides was able to "begin" the tradition of realism in part because he wrote during the "beginning" of the Western tradition of centralized authority (state making). While we honor his insights on the nature of war, we pay little attention to the context of state making within which he wrote and which shaped his thinking. By examining the work of the first realist *in context*, we are able to see it not only as "political theory" but historically and in relation to linguistic, socio-cultural, and economic developments.

Not coincidentally, this context included the "beginning" of systematic inquiry: the development of philosophy as objectivist metaphysics. By embracing the linguistic turn, post-realists chal-

262 V. SPIKE PETERSON

lenge objectivist claims, which are especially prominent in neorealism.[13] Insofar as refiguring realism entails moving beyond objectivism, we do so more effectively by situating the latter not only in relation to the revival of science in the modern era but the early institutionalization of this metaphysics in ancient Greece and in the context of state making. As G. E. R. Lloyd argues in regard to the emergence of states and science in Greece, "political experience" and "speculative thought" appear to be not just analogous developments but "two aspects [two stories?] of the same development."[14]

Thus, examining realism in its earliest context informs our understanding of both state making processes and the epistemological "roots" of realism. The former is relevant to theorizing states and making sense of transformations in today's "real world" and the latter is relevant to constructing a post-realism that fully addresses critiques of positivism. Moreover, the *interaction* of these dimensions is particularly clear in the Athenian context, an insight we would do well to highlight in analyzing today's turbulent context.

Because of the availability of materials and scholarly interest in ancient and classical Greece, we know a great deal about this interaction and, especially, the gender dynamics of the transition to rationalist philosophy and to political authority based on elite male citizenship. Ancient and classical texts suggest how female-identified principles (matrilineal kinship, maternal potency, women's sexuality) were domesticated in the transition to patriarchal states. In Cantarella's words,

> . . . history of the female condition in antiquity . . . allows identification
> of the moment when a practice of discrimination of centuries' duration
> was rationalized and presented for the first time as necessary,
> inevitable, and eternal. It was during the centuries of the Greek *polis*
> that the assertion of the "difference" between men and women was cod-
> ified.[15]

Thus, an examination of Athenian state making reveals essentialized sex difference as historically contingent but constitutively central to the Western tradition of political and ideological authority. Again, masculine agency and activities in the public sphere *depended* on a feminized and denigrated but nonetheless essential private sphere.

THE ATHENIAN STORY THROUGH A GENDERED LENS

Expanding agricultural, commercial, and military activities marked the economic and political environment of Greek state formation, with attendant population pressure, land hunger, and recurring debt crises.[16] In the seventh and sixth centuries B.C.E., the increasing wealth of a middle class and impoverishment of non-propertied citizens and small farmers led to demands for land redistribution and debt cancellation. The Athenian "answer" to political and economic turbulence was to further erode aristocratic kinship as the basis of social organization in favor of citizenship based on the property claims of individual households.[17]

The patriarchal *oikos* became the primary socioeconomic and political unit, upon which the state depended, and which the state protected to ensure an economically stable and substantial middle class based in household production. This simultaneously instituted and promoted a model of household "families"[18] that was distinguished from a public/political sphere. Propertied men acquired status, authority, and resources as patriarchal heads-of-households and as participants in the newly prestigious public sphere. This was at the expense of women, who lost a variety of status, authority, and resource claims by being identified exclusively as biological and social reproducers in the now subordinated "private" sphere.

Political and economic changes both shaped and were shaped by the intellectual turbulence of the times. In the fifth century B.C.E., Herodotus, "father of history," and Thucydides "father of realism," wrote secular narratives depicting, respectively, the Persian and Pelopponesian wars. But Herodotus' history went beyond military matters to describe the immense variety of customs and social organization in the known world. The issue of cultural relativism raised by knowledge of "other" societies was an important source of Greek reflection on the relationship between particulars and universals. Similarly, in recounting the Peloponnesian War, Thucydides sought more than a record of military engagements. He examined the significance of specific events in order to understand the nature of war and power relations more generally (though he excludes domestic power relations[19]). These historians were only two of the ancient thinkers struggling with the question of how to distinguish the particular and contingent from the universal and unchanging. While they asked the question in terms of historical events and their underlying causes, others asked the question in terms of "natural events" and how to understand change and permanence.

The itinerant sophists pursued this question in regard to the meaning of politics. They explored the separation of nature or *physis* (the realm of necessity and unchanging laws) from convention or *nomos* (the realm of the particular as distinctively political). To be a successful—that is, persuasive—speaker in the assembly and law courts required knowing the conventions—necessarily particular to each *polis*—and applying them appropriately. In this sense, the sophists were relativists; they "denied the possibility of absolute and immutable knowledge," advancing instead a "consensualist theory of truth."[20] Rhetoric here refers to "the different ways of achieving assent in different, particular audiences."[21]

The sophistic belief that "man is the measure of all things" supported democratic rather than oligarchic politics in the sense that qualities deemed necessary for political participation could be learned rather than inherited.[22] In promoting democracy, sophistic instruction focused on the "process of verbal communication between men and between groups of men which made the democracy workable."[23] To sophists, the absence of universals implied that arguments must be settled not by a process of calculation based upon foundational axioms, but by "the giving of *good reasons* to one's audience, particular reasons as to why they should, in that situation, assent to one's claims."[24]

But the Athenian "answer" we inherited, in response to this intellectual turbulence, rejected the sophistic, rhetorical tradition in favor of a foundational philosophy that informed realist political theory. Plato was hostile to the new forms of sophistic instruction and critical of existing political arrangements. Rather than democratic political community engaged in rhetorical debates, Plato sought reforms promoting "disinterested philosophical dialectic."[25] Political leadership was not to be entrusted to an assembly of corrupt speakers but to "philosopher-kings" who ruled by reason alone and were not distracted by private needs, desires, or emotional attachments. Platonic philosophy ostensibly excluded rhetoric and sophistic methods, positing instead "another world of intellectual objects, the Forms, accessible to reason alone and not to the senses."[26]

What is striking about this depiction is the extent to which Plato's denouncement of rhetoric and celebration of reason was politically motivated. The "answer" he developed was dramatically shaped by the preferences (desires) he had, in the context of intellectual and political turbulence in which he lived and thought. Through our Enlightenment filters we tend to separate philosophy and politics, but they were not separate in Plato's time (and are not separate in ours). Plato sought foundations that would ensure the certainty of absolute truth, thus resisting skepticism, and the stability of the political order, thus resisting tyranny, anarchy, and/or radical democracy. His masculinist philosophy and political theory was intended to displace rhetoric and presumably avoid the problematic sociopolitical issues raised by the latter's relativism. Of course, rhetorical dimensions of communication were not eliminated but continued to shape discursive practices. Plato masked his own use of rhetoric by casting his "answers" as starkly distinguished from and definitively superior to the competing—primarily sophistic—formulations. In Winton and Garnsey's words, "The conflict between rhetoric and philosophy was resolved by the creation of a society whose basis is philosophy, in which rhetoric can have no role."[27]

By examining Western philosophy in the context of state making and its ideological transformations, the political dimensions of that philosophy come into focus. We are reminded that intellectual questions were not pursued independent of political questions but shaped by them. Plato's "answer" claimed universality but was particular; it was one among others and has come to look like the "rational" and "most accurate" answer because it successfully constituted itself as such. It did so in part by claiming that "real knowledge" was attainable because man could discern the systematic correspondence of thought to "unchanging subject-matter."[28] What marked man—as philosopher and political agent—was the uniqueness of his abstract reasoning, his capacity for *transcending the material world of necessity and contingency: the world of women, "Others," and nature.* In short, public sphere activities (politics!) simultaneously *depended upon* private sphere activities and defined "rational man" and "political actor" as *the exclusion* of that which is associated with the feminine. Henceforth, women qua "woman" were not only denied access to public sphere activities but were condemned to inferiority by immutable association with qualities that *contradicted* rational thought and political action—the most valuable ways of being and doing in the new "Western tradition."

Discussion

I have argued that reason and realism displaced sophistic rhetoric and became the Western "answer" to the political and intellectual turbulence of Athenian state making. This answer tells a particular story from a particular vantage point. By claiming universality, however, it denies its particularity and by claiming to be realistic, it denies "other" vantage points and alternative stories. Specifically, it excludes the power relations of gender from all constructions of politics. Women, private sphere activities, *and private sphere morality* are categorically separated from a conception of politics that is applied internally as well as externally.

In the context of European state making, modern realists adopted this particular story and reproduced its erasures. In Christine Sylvester's words, "international relations theorists [came] to accept unquestioningly the stories pretheorists told about the separability in space and in morality of public and private spheres."[29]

In the sixteenth century, Machiavelli drew upon ancient Greek writings as he analyzed events in Italy, where conflicts among city-states were not dissimilar to those of the Hellenic world. His public sphere was an exclusively male domain of power politics. This contrasted starkly with the private sphere of feminine softness and sentimentality. The latter was less a haven than a source of danger and limitation, ever threatening to man's pursuit of *virtu*. In Wendy Brown's words, "*Fortuna* and female power not only conspire to undo men but are also the very things man is acting against, in an effort to master, control or escape."[30]

Hobbes was also familiar with ancient political theory and his political philosophy was also formed in a turbulent context. His radical nominalism was at odds with Athenian perspectives but it served him well in rendering women and private sphere activities invisible. His depiction of the state of nature became the discipline's model of pre-state and inter-state anarchy and provided the central problematique of international relations. But it is a model fixated on male behavior in a context of perpetual conflict in which all societal ordering is erased. Hobbes' abstract man "is a creature who is self-possessed and radically solitary . . . whose relations with others are either contractual or unavoidably violent."[31]

What realists, ancient and modern, share is a story of the world that presupposes exclusively male behavior and vantage point. This bias frames the discipline in particular (and partial) ways, including: an understanding of "human" nature as atomistic, autonomous, and power-seeking; the state of nature as anarchic (categorically asocial conditions preceding or outside of the rational ordering of states); the patriarchal state as primary, as legitimate defender of the collective's security and as pursuing national interests through instrumental reason; the public sphere/politics as objective, rational, freedom-seeking, and realistic, thus, definitively separate from private sphere attachment, affect, necessity, and moral principles; and the security dilemma as the relentless pursuit of power politics as the "only" rational strategy in a context of perpetual competition and conflict. In this story, there are "men" but no mothers, states but no prior social orders, reason and power but no emotional engagement, public politics but no private power relations, governments but no households, and state security but no global society. Gender and its power relations are invisible.

A feminist post-realism takes history and context more seriously, asks where the women (and Others) are, and sees relations where realism sees oppositional dichotomies, and interdependence where realism sees autonomy. It tells a different story of anarchy, sovereign individuals, states, public and private spheres, politics, and security.

From a feminist perspective, the lack of society and socialization in the state of nature (or under conditions of anarchy) is a less than coherent and manifestly ahistorical story. Individual humans are biologically incapable of surviving in the absence of social relations and cooperation. To deny this fundamental fact, and the primacy of cooperation it entails, is to tell a profoundly unrealistic story of human life. An irreducible basis of nurturance ought to be the most obvious "given" of the human condition—and would more likely be the story told if mothers were the author(itie)s. To insist on this nurturance is not, however, to deny conflict but to situate conflict in the larger context of actually existing cooperative social relations and simultaneously in a discursive context: a world of meanings, arguments, and arguers. Thus, it looks for interactions between conflict and consensus, and between material necessity and rhetorical practice. It also shifts our understanding of what is "natural" (read inevitable and not, therefore, political), which permits us to see the denial of this cooperation as a politically motivated interpretation. Finally, it prompts us to change the international relations question from: "How is cooperation possible?" to "How is cooperation manifested in specific contexts, including that of international politics?"

The latter question invites a historical, not mythical, story of state making. Quite simply, states did not emerge out of chaos or anarchy but out of other forms of social organization (however unstable and elusive those forms may appear during turbulent periods). Failure to take those other forms seriously impoverishes not only our understanding of states and state making but also our knowledge of alternatives to states as we know them—knowledge perhaps especially important in the current context of state transformations. The historical story of state making reminds us that centralization was resisted and the success of states was neither natural, immutable, nor necessarily "good."

From a feminist post-realist perspective, states mark the institutionalization and legitimation of social hierarchies in which the autonomy and social adulthood of women "as a group" was sacrificed in favor of group survival based on male-defined needs and dominated by elite men. To ignore the oppressive consequences of state making is to deny the reality of most of the state's "subjects." It is to exclude from political analysis the power required to impose, legitimize, and reproduce systemic inequalities. It is also to accept acritically the state's legitimating claim that it represents the will of the entire society.[32]

Through a feminist lens, the state is gendered and its gender is masculine. The maleness of the state is due in large part to the conventional dichotomy of private and public and the construction of the public sphere and politics as exclusively masculine. In the realist story, women and the activities of the private sphere are outside of politics and must be prevented from contaminating the public sphere, which is a domain of free, rational agents. As abstractions, women are primarily excluded by associating them with the denigrated private sphere and denying them the rationality that marks "man" as the highest animal. Concretely, women have been (and continue to be) excluded from political power by limiting citizenship to those who are property owners and/or who perform military duty. Even when formal barriers are removed, patterns of gender hierarchy prevent women's *de facto* equality in political power.

As the editors of this volume point out, for realists, the public sphere is autonomous and politics are paramount. There is an important linkage here: the atomistic conception of "unrelated" men, the autonomy of the public sphere, and the sovereignty of states are conceptually and structurally interdependent. They all presuppose the categorical exclusion of private sphere (and other contextual) realities: nurturance, socialization, emotional commitments, normative rules, embodied reproduction, and socially necessary labor. They all privilege the idea of (male) agents who are unconstrained by private moralities or personal attachments and who employ instrumental reason to pursue power. Why? Because "That's the way it [read human nature/Plato, the nature of politics/Aristotle, the security dilemma/Thucydides] is." The linkage exposed here is discursively drawn in the context of establishing and legitimating particular forms of "human" (read ruling) agency: "rational man," "political agent," and "state sovereignty" are mutually constituted in the process of centralizing hierarchical authority in Western state forms.

The public-private dichotomy structures external as well as internal relations.[33] Because the public/state is masculine and categorically separate from the private sphere, international relations treats the latter as irrelevant: the discipline is definitively about relations between, not within, states; and private sphere activities (domestic in both senses) are excluded from analyses. Because reason and political order are masculine, their absence in inter-state relations renders anarchy feminine (in the sense of disorder, uncertainty, and uncontrollable passions): principles of justice, fairness, and progress that characterize civil society are deemed inappropriate and even dangerous where rule by brute force prevails.[34] Finally, because the dichotomy is so naturalized in Western thought, its extensive effects are taken for granted and we rarely consider how it reproduces and reinforces oppositional separations at the expense of recognizing interdependence.

The identification of human agency with male reason and the latter's construction as antithetical to "woman" was a condition of defining sovereign rational man and establishing his distance from "Others," including "outsiders." This exclusionary definition is key to both the construction of philosophy and political theory. The oppositional lens featured in objectivist and realist accounts magnifies and legitimizes self-other, us-them, aggressive-passive, insider-outsider, and protector-protected dichotomies.[35]

Here the question of "who we are" is resolved in a particular way. Reasoning man was the highest form of life and specifically required the *polis* for his realization.[36] By insisting on and legitimating the particular political order of the *polis*, the Greeks denied the possibility of political solidarity with those outside of this order as well as with the disenfranchised within it. Read through this lens, the security dilemma becomes a "given" and the state becomes the "answer" for providing security.[37]

But feminists and Others ask, "Whose security is achieved by the state system?" Insofar as states are predicated upon unequal distribution of material and authoritative resources internally and violence or its threat externally,[38] they reproduce and even legitimate structural violence and the insecurity this poses for the majority of the planet.[39] Thus, while Western philosophy and political theory were innovative, cultivating a spirit of greater control over man's world and articulating a concept of abstract equality, they in fact were and remain powerful legitimators and reproducers of reason and rule by the numerically few.

Although realism has never represented an accurate "story of the world" (no story can make that claim), the representation it reifies has concrete effects. On one hand, the mind-body dichotomy at the core of Western philosophy constitutes ways of knowing that privilege a disembodied and disembedded reason. The cost of pursuing certainty over ambiguity is a tendency toward ahistorical, decontextual, and acritical accounts. Through this lens, the interaction of multiple realities is masked and the attraction of short-term oversimplifications is magnified. On the other hand, the public-private dichotomy at the core of political theory constitutes ways of doing that privilege the identities and activities of some at the expense of others. The cost of identifying politics exclusively with the public sphere is a tendency toward elite and instrumentalist accounts. Through this lens—exemplified in realist accounts—the reality of socially necessary labor and how symbolic and material power are reproduced is obscured.

Through an objectivist and realist lens that takes "sovereign rational man," competition, gender dichotomy, and social hierarchies as "naturally given," a variety of questions cannot be asked and critical challenges cannot be raised. Against objectivism, the embedded and embodied reality of concepts and practices is obscured. Against "realism," normative questions appear irrelevant or pointless, multiple realities are rendered invisible, and alternative visions appear necessarily utopian. In both, the actual direction of dependencies is inverted. We "forget" that abstractions require a material medium, that the pursuit of reason requires an emotional commitment, that elites are sustained by the production activities of non-elites, and that public sphere activities rely on effective domestic maintenance and reproduction. We "forget" that all views are from somewhere particular and contingent and no single view from everywhere is possible.

Gender is at work here because the exclusion of "the feminine" is foundational to realist constructions of rational man, political agency, and state sovereignty. Historically, realism flourished during periods of turbulence, articulated by those seeking stability, certainty, and (their corollary:) increased control/domination. Realism is now being challenged in the midst of the political turbulence of changing states and the intellectual turbulence of changing epistemologies that we identify as post-modernity. Shifting gender relations were key to earlier transformations, as they are in the present context. Today's nationalist struggles, critical social movements, religious fundamentalisms, democratic mobilizations, peace initiatives, human rights, ecological attitudes, welfare-state crises, development policies, and restructured labor forces cannot be realistically analyzed without attending to gender. And today's multiple and fluid identities, contradictions between public and private moralities, post-positivist epistemologies, critiques of rationalism, realism, and humanism, and post-realist pursuit of rhetorical strategies cannot be adequately addressed without attending to gender. In Philip Windsor's words, "Contemporary history and contemporary philosophical undertakings mean that any reconciliation of the public and the private, the intellectual and the emotional, the considerations of morality with those of contingency, depend crucially on a re-examination of Western values and schemata—not least as they are determined by the relations between women and men."[40]

International relations discourse has conventionally been derived from what some men have done, what questions they asked, and what answers they generated, having consulted exclusively with each other. As a consequence, international relations theories—including neorealism, liberal-institutionalism, structuralism, and postmodernism—fail to take seriously both how gender affects our knowledge claims about international "reality" and how international processes have gender-differentiated effects.[41] Advocates of a post-realism seek a "radical inclusiveness" that acknowledges realist insights and moves beyond them to generate more adequate languages for today's realities. From a feminist perspective, post-realism must also move beyond the masculinism pervading international relations discourse and practice. Ultimately, this involves challenging not only patriarchal but related racist, capitalist, heterosexist, imperialist, and nationalist oppressions that underpin the world "as we currently reproduce it."

In short, post-realism must move beyond the discourse of objectivist dichotomies *and* the social relations of structural violence constituted by the historical state system. The ideological legitimation of state orders replaced the complexity and relativism of sophistic rhetoric with the ostensible certainty of reason and the competitive social relations of realism. A new rhetoric, or post-realism, must address the challenge of moving beyond Western philosophy's construction of reason and gender hierarchy at the core of states and Western political theory.

NOTES

1. I am echoing Sandra Whitworth's demand (*Feminism and International Relations* [London: Macmillan, 1994], x) that IR theorists—including post-realists—move beyond pseudo-inclusion: "Numerous anthologies are including a feminist chapter, but most of the work that appears throughout the rest of those anthologies seems unfamiliar with, and unaffected by, feminist scholarship."

2. Only authors specifically referred to are cited in this chapter. For references to work underpinning this argument see my "An Archeology of Domination: Historicizing Gender and Class in Early Western State Formation," (Ph.D. diss., The American University, 1988); "Introduction" and "Security and Sovereign States: What Is at Stake in Taking Feminism Seriously?" in *Gendered States: Feminist (Re)Visions of International Relations Theory*, ed. V. Spike Peterson (Boulder, Colo.: Lynne Rienner Publishers, 1992).

3. Changes in states are recognized as contemporary political transformations that IR theorists must address. Changes in gender relations (e.g., shifting divisions of labor, reproductive rights and technologies, feminization of poverty, welfare state crises, etc.) are also important contemporary issues but remain invisible in conventional—gender-blind—accounts.

4. On the sex-gender distinction and feminist theory, see, for example, Linda Nicholson, ed., *Feminism/Postmodernism* (New York: Routledge, 1990); Judith Butler, *Gender Trouble* (New York: Routledge, 1989); Judith Butler and Joan W. Scott, eds., *Feminists Theorize the Political* (New York: Routledge, 1992); C. T. Mohanty, A. Russo, and L. Torres, eds., *Third World Women and the Politics of Feminism* (Bloomington: Indiana University Press, 1991).

5. Jacques Derrida, *Of Grammatology*, trans. G. C. Spivak (Baltimore: Johns Hopkins University Press, 1976); Richard Ashley, "Living on Borderlines," in *International/Intertextual Relations*, ed. James Der Derian and Michael J. Shapiro (Lexington, Mass.: Lexington Books, 1989).

6. Susan J. Hekman, *Gender and Knowledge: Elements of a Postmodern Feminism* (Cambridge, Mass.: Polity Press, 1990), 68. On feminist critiques of rationalism and science, see also Sandra Harding, *Whose Science? Whose Knowledge?* (Ithaca, N.Y.: Cornell University Press, 1991); Evelyn Fox Keller, *Reflections on Gender and Science* (New Haven, Conn.: Yale University Press, 1985); Louise M. Antony and Charlotte Witt, eds., *A Mind of One's Own* (Boulder, Colo: Westview Press, 1993).

7. Jean B. Elshtain, *Public Man, Private Woman* (Princeton, N.J.: Princeton University Press, 1981), 13-14.

8. Michael Michael, *The Sources of Social Power*, vol. 1 (Cambridge: Cambridge University Press, 1986).

9. Ronald Cohen, "Introduction," in *Origins of the State*, eds. Ronald Cohen and Elman R. Service (Philadelphia: Institute for the Study of Human Issues, 1978), 8.

10. Feminist critiques of state making are extensive; the following is a brief summary of relevant points. Male groups cannot reproduce themselves without controlling the sexual reproduction of women (to ensure biological reproduction within the group) and the socialization of children (to ensure culturally appropriate values and loyalties to the group). Jill Vickers ("At His Mother's Knee: Sex/Gender and the Construction of National Identities," in *Women and Men*, ed. G. H. Nemiroff [Toronto: Fitzhenry & Whiteside, 1990], 483) argued that the patriarchal organization of sex/gender is one (but not the only) way that men (who lack a materially "certain" blood tie) "construct enduring forms of social organization, group cohesion and identity." In Zillah Eisenstein's words, patriarchy "expresses the struggle to control women's options in order to keep their role as childbearers and rearers primary" (*The Radical Future of Liberal Feminism* [Boston: Northeastern University Press, 1981], 16). To the extent that women are excluded from defining group interests and compelled to comply with male-defined needs, their autonomy is limited. So excluded, women are at the same time denied the status of social adulthood (read political agency, sovereign subjectivity) attached to group decision makers. In effect, the continuity of the group is secured by limiting the autonomy, equality, and authority of the group's physical and social reproducers and reproduction—conventionally ignored as private sphere activity—"is revealed as the most political activity" (Vickers, "At His Mother's Knee," 482).

11. Yale H. Ferguson and Richard W. Mansbach, *The Elusive Quest: Theory and International Politics* (Columbia: University of South Carolina Press, 1987).

12. Paul R. Viotti and Mark V. Kauppi, *International Relations Theory: Realism, Pluralism, Globalism* (New York: Macmillan, 1987), 34.

13. Richard Ashley, "The Poverty of Neorealism," *International Organization* 38, no. 2 (1984): 225-86.

14. G. E. R. Lloyd, *Magic, Reason and Experience* (Cambridge: Cambridge University Press, 1979), 249.

15. Eva Cantarella, *Pandora's Daughters* (Baltimore: Johns Hopkins University Press, 1987), 179. Similarly, in regard to the insider-outsider dichotomy of orientalism that is conventionally associated with modernity, Shiraz Dossa ("Political Philosophy and Orientalism: The Classical Origins of a Discourse," *Alternatives* 12, no. 3 [1987]: 343) identifies ancient political philosophy, especially that of Plato and Aristotle, as the "moment" that "spawned and fixed the idea of the Orient as negation."

16. Michael Grant, *The Rise of the Greeks,* chap. 2, (New York: Charles Scribner's Sons, 1988).

17. The lawmaker Solon set up wealth, not birth, as the qualification for citizenship and his inheritance laws freed household property from clan, i.e., kin-based, control. Cleisthenes' secular reforms (ca. 508 B.C.E.) established the principle of location, not clan, which registered citizens on the basis of affiliation with a *deme*, the local community (whether ancient or newly created).

18. That is, the "family" as we think of it does not exist prior to but is constituted by state formation processes that alter political and re/productive structures, marking a shift from kinship as a principle of societal organization to kinship as household co-residence of immediate "blood" relations.

19. Rebecca Grant, "The Sources of Gender Bias in International Relations Theory," in *Gender and International Relations*, eds. Rebecca Grant and Kathleen Newland (Bloomington: Indiana University Press, 1991).

20. Richard Harvey Brown, "Theories of Rhetoric and the Rhetorics of Theory," *Social Research* 50 (spring 1983): 135.

21. John Shotter, "Rhetoric and the Recovery of Civil Society," *Economy and Society* 18, no. 2 (May 1989): 155.

22. Lloyd, *Magic, Reason*, 244n. 73; R. I. Winton and Peter Garnsey, II, "Political Theory," in *The Legacy of Greece: A New Appraisal*, ed. M. I. Finley (Oxford and New York: Oxford University Press, 1984), 41.

23. Eric A. Havelock, *The Liberal Temper in Greek Politics* (New Haven and London: Yale University Press, 1964), 156.

24. Shotter, "Rhetoric," 155 (emphasis in original).

25. Winton and Garnsey, "Political Theory," 42.

26. Bernard Williams, "Philosophy," in *The Legacy of Greece: A New Appraisal*, ed. M. I. Finley (Oxford and New York: Oxford University Press, 1984), 209.

27. Winton and Garnsey, "Political Theory," 47.

28. Williams, "Philosophy," 231-32.

29. Christine Sylvester, *Feminist Theory and International Relations in a Postmodern Era* (Cambridge: Cambridge University Press, 1994), 83.

30. Wendy Brown, *Manhood and Politics* (Totowa, N.J.: Rowman and Littlefield, 1988), 89.

31. Christine Di Stefano, *Configurations of Masculinity* (Ithaca, N.Y.: Cornell University Press, 1991), 104.

32. See Grant, "Sources of Gender Bias," 14-17.

33. V. Spike Peterson, "The Politics of Identity and Gendered Nationalism," in *Foreign Policy Analysis*, ed. L. Neack, P. J. Haney, and J. A. K. Hey (Englewood Cliffs, N.J.: Prentice-Hall, forthcoming), 12-18.

34. Anne Sisson Runyan and V. Spike Peterson, "The Radical Future of Realism: Feminist Subversions of IR Theory," *Alternatives* 16, no. 1 (1991): 67-106.

35. The latter are institutionalized in protection rackets: creating a threat and then charging for protection against it. Charles Tilly argued that nation-states engage in such rackets by creating a system of mutually threatening centralized governments and charging citizens taxes and military service to support effective defense of state boundaries. See "War Making and State Making as Organized Crime," in *Bringing the State Back In*, eds. P. B. Evans, D. Rueschemeyer, and T. Skocpol (Cambridge: Cambridge University Press, 1985). Feminists have similarly identified marriage as a protection racket: under conditions of systemic male violence, women are forced to seek pro-tection—from generalized male violence—by disadvantageous marriages to particular men. See Anne Sisson Runyan, "Gender Relations and the Politics of Protection," *Peace Review* 2 (fall 1990): 28-31. Of course, it is not a coinci-dence that marriage rackets are a feature of states. And the insidiousness of all protection rackets is that the need for protection is "real" though seeking it effectively reproduces the threatening system (Peterson, "Security and Sovereign States").

36. Winton and Garnsey, "Political Theory"; M. I. Finley, *Politics in the Ancient World* (Cambridge: Cambridge University Press, 1991).

37. Richard Ashley, "Untying the Sovereign State," *Millennium* 17, no. 2 (1988): 227-62.

38. Ashley, "Untying."

39. Peterson, "Security and Sovereign States"; Simon Dalby, "Security, Modernity, Ecology: The Dilemmas of Post Cold War Security Discourse," *Alternatives* 17 (1992): 95-133.

40. Philip Windsor, "Women and International Relations: What's the Problem?" *Millennium* 17, no. 3 (1988): 453.

41. On feminist IR, see, for example, Grant and Newland, *Gender and International Relations*; J. Ann Tickner, *Gender in International Relations* (New York: Columbia University Press, 1992); Christine Sylvester, *Feminist Theory*; Peterson, *Gendered States*; V. Spike Peterson and Anne Sisson Runyan, *Global Gender Issues* (Boulder, Colo.: Westview Press, 1993); Marysia Zalweski and Jane Parpart, eds., *Feminism, Maculinity and Power in IR* (Boulder, Colo.: Westview Press, forthcoming).

JAMES DER DERIAN

A REINTERPRETATION OF REALISM
GENEALOGY, SEMIOLOGY, DROMOLOGY

"Everyone is a Realist nowadays, and the term in this sense needs no argument."

Martin Wight, *International Theory*

"Things are going to slide in all directions Won't be nothing Nothing you can measure anymore."

Leonard Cohen, "The Future"

Realism. Historical, social, philosophical, political, economic, artistic, cinematic, literary, legal realism. Machiavellian, Hobbesian, Rousseauian, Hegelian, Weberian, Kissingerian realism. Optimist, pessimist, fatalist realism. Naive, vulgar, magical realism. Technical, practical, empirical realism. Classical and scientific realism. Structural, structurationist, poststructuralist realism. Minimalist, maximalist, fundamentalist, potentialist realism. Positivist, post-positivist, liberal, neoliberal institutionalist, radical, radical interpretivist realism. Critical, nuclear, epistemic realism. Sur-, super-, photo-, anti-, neo-, post-realism. And now at your local malls and supermarket check-outs, hyper-realism.

Clearly, realism comes in many flavors, and everyone has their favorite. Yet in international relations the meaning of realism is more often than not presented as uniform, self-evident, and transparent—even by those critics who in debates great and not-so-great have questioned its historical relevance, political function, or heuristic value.[1] Cast from idealism's failure to stop Hitlerism, congealed by the bipolar exigencies of the Cold War, rigidified by a disciplinary scholasticism, modern realism for a *longue durée* came in one flavor only, a vanilla "traditional." True, a neapolitan neorealism, celebrating the colors of progress, parsimony, and microeconomic method, emerged from the theory doldrums of the 1970s. But against the backdrop of a multiplicity of extra-disciplinary realisms, the purported differences between traditional realism and neorealism, for which so much ink and not a few drops of figurative blood have been spilled, appear as so much hair-splitting. Indeed, when measured against the amount of literal blood-letting that has been done in realism's name, the debate over the differences seems obscenely academic.

So why yet another essay on realism? Arguments could be made that there remain gaps in our knowledge of the subject, or that there is always some new phenomenon or experience against which the claims of realism must be tested. These arguments, made in the service of a research program or a particular problematic of realism, are certainly sound and sometimes persuasive.[2] But I do not intend to rehearse or to rely on them. Instead, this essay applies the alternative approaches of genealogy, semiology, and dromology to realism as a first step toward a critical pluralism, that is, a productive, interpretive response to the plurality of texts in international relations.

First, to reinterpret realism is to step backward, look wider, and dig deeper, not to excavate some reality that has been lost or lurks beneath the surface of things, but to lay bare persistent myths of a reality that can be transcribed by a school of thought and yet still claim to speak for itself. As I have argued in previous cases, a genealogy is the most appropriate way to begin such a task.[3] A genealogy calls into question the immaculate origins, essential identities, and deep structures of realism, revealing the metaphorical and mythical beginnings of a uniform realism while producing through interpretation several realisms that never "figure" in the international relations official story. What Bertolt Brecht said of the study of realism in literature equally applies to our own field of inquiry: "Realism is an issue not only for literature: it is a major political, philosophical and practical issue and must be handled and explained as such—as a matter of general human interest."[4]

Second, a *semiology* is needed, in the sense of a study of realism as a symptom of a more general condition of late modernity, in which an old order is dying and a new one not yet constituted. To the ear of the other, this might have the sound of a Marxian dialectic, a linguistic structuralism, or a metaphysical eschatology. In intent if not in fact a semiology is an *anti*-metaphysical, pragmatic investigation of realism's reliance on an archaic sign-system in which words mirror objects and theory is independent of the reality it represents. The subsidiary purpose is to show how this para-philosophical conceit has disabled realism's power to interpret as well as manage the current disorder of things.[5]

A semiology, then, provides a method for a study of the interdependent mix of power, meaning, and morality that makes up realism. In *The Twilight of the Idols*, Nietzsche exposed this link with a harsh clarity:

> To this extent moral judgment is never to be taken literally: as such it never contains anything but nonsense. But as semeiotics it remains of incalculable value: it reveals, to the informed man at least, the most precious realities of cultures and inner worlds which did not know enough to "understand" themselves. Morality is merely "sign" language, merely symptomatology; one must already know what it is about to derive profit from it.[6]

He is equally blunt about the potentially radical effects of a semiological inquiry: "I fear we are not getting rid of God because we still believe in grammar . . ."[7] His fear applies as well to this investigation: disturbing the apodictic link between a positivist theory of realism and a correspondence philosophy of language, it cannot be construed as merely an academic exercise—which perhaps is one more reason why the international relations academy has kept semiology at a distance.[8] The dual imperative of securing the state and international relations theory from anything more threatening than incremental change has placed a premium on "traditional" approaches. A semiology disturbs this naturalized order, not out of a faddish desire for innovation, but out of a suspicion that there are high moral costs attached to the kinds of inertial systems of thought that become institutionalized in high politics and higher learning.[9]

Third, a dromology of realism is required, in Paul Virilio's sense of a study of the science or logic of speed, because the representational principle described above which underpins realism has itself increasingly become undermined by the ascendency of temporality over spatiality in world politics.[10] Elsewhere I have identified this as the "(s)pace problematic" of international relations, where the displacement of geopolitics by chronopolitics makes a nation-state security founded on the stasis of a fixed identity and impermeable territory increasingly difficult to maintain.[11] In turn, the multifarious effects of speed compound the need for a semiology of realism: the instantaneity of communication, the ubiquity of the image, the flow of capital, the videographic speed of war have made reality a transitory, technologically contingent phenomenon.[12]

In a world in which speed is not just the measure but the end of progress, tendencies and flows, arrivals and departures, all forms of movement come to govern and devalue both the immobile object and objectivity itself. *Real* estate, in the dual sense of transparent and immovable property, loses out to *irreal* representations which are infinitely transferable. In short, the dromocratic machine colonizes reality and its "reflective" mediation, realism. With a casual hyperbole Paul Virilio freeze-frames this imperialism of movement:

> It's clear that we are currently in a period of substitutions. One generation of reality is in the process of substituting itself for another and is still uncertain about how to represent itself. And we have to understand that it is very much connected to real-time images. It's not a problem of the configuration or the semiotics of the image, but a problem of the temporality of the image.[13]

In the current age of speed, surveillance, and simulation, genealogy, semiology, and dromology provide new deconstructive tools *and* antidiplomatic strategies to reinterpret realism.[14] This essay, then, is doubly prodomal, a sign of both the heightened anxiety and trammeled hope that appear when the mirror of an old order cracks and we must remember, reimagine, and if possible, reconstruct a new image of our self-identity.

THE SCHOOL(YARD) OF REALISM: GET REAL, GO FIGURE

How do genealogy, semiology, and dromology differ from past efforts to interpret realism? First, they offer new perspectives on realism in a period of rapid change. The failure of realism to anticipate or to explain the end of the Cold War, and its willingness in gravelly baritones to rationalize the violence that ensued in Nagorno-Karabakh, Bosnia, Somalia, and elsewhere, can be studied as signs of how the very inability of realism to represent and decelerate change *necessitates* the rationalization and ethical cleansing of violence. This is not a reiteration of the question whether realism reflects or belatedly rationalizes the harsh realities of an anarchical system. Nor is it a rehash of the realist-idealist debate of the 1930s. To be sure, some similarities—most explicitly in the Balkans and no less so in the Baltic—do cry out for a comparative appraisal of what states and international institutions must do to manage the post-Cold War better than the inter-war period. But first an intellectual effort is needed to demythologize the antinomies of realism that have from its beginnings constituted and so confounded international relations.[15]

The three approaches that make up a critical pluralism continue the refiguring of realism begun by Richard Ashley, Rob Walker, Nicholas Rengger, Fredrich Kratochwil, Nicholas Onuf, Alexander Wendt as well as the editors of this book and a new generation of international relations thinkers.[16] This school, if it could be called such, differs from previous ones because it interprets realism as an ongoing discursive struggle that cuts across the traditional theory-practice, idealist-realist, and other synchronic and scholastic antinomies of world politics. It gives notice of how realism in its universalist philosophical form and particularist state application has figuratively *and* literally helped to constitute the discordant world it purports to describe.[17] In other words, the scholars of this school do not seek to repudiate realism: they seek instead to dismantle a variety of epistemic privileges by which one form of realism dominates contesting forms.[18]

A critical pluralist approach to realism should not, however, be mistaken as one more policing action, to substitute a new disciplinary gaze for realism's para-philosophical guise. There is nothing to be gained by positing some "new," purer form of realism in opposition to older, corrupted ones. My aim, as perverse and colonial as it may sound, is to deconstruct realism in order to save it. This is an attempt to open up the hermeneutic circle, to enlarge the interpretive community, to break out of the prison-house of a reductive vocabulary that has so attenuated the ethico-political dimension of realism. The intent is to flood the protected marketplace of international relations theory with a multiplicity of realisms, devalue its proprietary origins, and in the process break its traditional dependency upon an evil, utopian, or merely irrational other to maintain a pure identity. We might just then be able to reinterpret the value of realism in a period of rapid systemic change.

As I have said, others have already begun to pursue this line of inquiry. But at this point perhaps it would be a mistake to call the refiguring of realism a debate between uniform schools of thought. So far, it has been more of a scrap in a school yard with slogans instead of theory filling the air; as I see it, with a "get real" crowd on one side and the "go figure" on the other. Nonetheless, for the sake of exposition it might be useful to pretend that these two groups exist as coherent discursive communities.

On the one hand (ready to curl into the fist), the "get real" group first domesticates an internal order and constructs an anarchical external one with stories of the recurrence and repetition of struggles for power, enjoining us, in circular fashion, to prepare for the worst if we do not maintain a realist perspective and global engagement. Recent statements from two arch-realists capture this discursive antinomy of order and anarchy. The first is from the national security advisor to former President George Bush, Brent Scowcroft:

> The last time the world was in a roughly analogous situation was in 1919. At that time, there were no great, global threats apparent to American interests. . . . Though we couldn't see where the threat was coming from in 1919, the U.S. nourished the seeds of World War II by disengaging.[19]

The other is from Zbigniew Brzezinski, who held the same office earlier in the Carter administration:

> In some respects the post-Cold War situation in the Far East is reminiscent of Europe prior to World War I. In light of that, continued American involvement in the Far East remains a necessary stabilizing factor.[20]

This world view has been reproduced and legitimized in think tanks, mid-level foreign policy and intelligence bureaucracies, centers for international studies, and international financial and corporate institutions.[21] But the technicians of realism are able less and less to resort to a resistant history or a fragmenting commonsense to make their prescriptions. Their preferred rapid-response philosophy for accelerating new world disorders has become the hyperrealist simulation. In this technical manner realism is reproduced in international relations, ranging from the computer simulation of worst-case scenarios to the serialization of the war game after-action reviews.

On the other hand (with pen as sword), the figuration crowd advocates a more reflective, rhetorically conscious attitude toward a rapidly shifting, highly ambiguous, heavily mediated international politics. They challenge the axiomatic, positivist conception of the real that assumes an object for every name, the authority of every referent. They disabuse the realist use of historical analogy to domesticate contingency, citing not just new, non-analogous configurations of power but also new modes of representing them, such as simulations, CNN, faxes, camcorders, and the like. They understand realism as a powerful, performative script which now more than ever must be reinterpreted and refigured for a changed world.

How the script is figuratively conceived, how it uses and is used by literary tropes, historical analogues, technical reproduction, and spectacular staging, is considered to be as "real" and important a factor as any "literal" or "material" reality. For the figurative realist, "theory" and "story" rejoin in their common Greek and Indo-European root, *weid*: a "vision" that gives us knowledge of the world. In every script a stage is set, actors cast, and a vision inscribed. Whether an audience will come to the show depends on much more than a particular script's ability to copy reality. The verisimilitude which empowers realism depends upon a dramatic and rhetorical bag of tricks that are socially and performatively produced.[22] Hence, our understanding of the power of realism requires an equally if not excessively performative *description* of its current figurations, in the sense of a critical distancing from present vocabularies and canonistic readings that might engender not just a new perspective but open up the possibility for a variety of new realisms.

THE MEANING OF BEGINNINGS, THE NAMING OF NAMES

Where might a genealogy begin? First, by de-familiarizing the most familiar beginnings.

"What do we mean by realism?" The question triggers a mix of familiar phrases, such as "states," "struggle for power," "human nature," "international anarchy," "balance of power," and "security dilemma." Sometimes for pedigree, German words like *Realpolitik* or the American malapropism "geopolitics" are thrown in, along with a quote or two from Thucydides, Hobbes, Machiavelli, or Morgenthau. Sometimes explicitly but more often implicitly, onto-theological foundations for realism are presented as natural laws, as in the Augustinian dogma that evil is real and pervasive, or its Benthamite secularization that all humans are reducible to self-optimizing units. And finally, adding veridical power to the common epistemic model is the Rankean fiat—often cross-dressed by the neorealists as a scientific truth—that a realist depicts things as they really are, rather than as an idealist might wish them to be, or worse, a textualist might interpret them into being. Thus credentialed, authors can get down to the business of defending their particular realism as the arch-method for the field.

But what happens—as seems to be the case to this observer—when the "we" fragments, "realism" takes on prefixes and goes plural, the meaning of meaning itself is up for grabs? A stop-gap solution is to supplement the definitional gambit with a facile gesture. The international relations theorist, mindful of a creeping pluralism, will note the "essentially contested" nature of realism—duly backed up with a footnote to W. B. Gallie or W. E. Connolly—and then get down to business as usual, that is, using realism as the best language to reflect a selfsame phenomenon. This amounts to an intellectual plea of *nolo contendere*: in exchange for not contesting the charge that the meaning of realism is contestable, the international relations "perp" gets off easy, to then turn around and commit worse epistemological crimes. In honor of the most notorious benefactor of nolo contendere in recent American legal history, we might call this the "Spiro-ette effect" in international relations.

This is only one of many rhetorical moves that shore up the identity of an epistemic realism based on difference.[23] What form might an alternative script take? The first act would have to go to the medieval nominalists, for they, not the idealists, were the first to present the philosophical antinomies which gave rise to a realist school of thought. Medieval scholar Friedrich Heer sets the apocalyptic scene for the arrival of nominalism in the beginning of the fourteenth century:

> Stagnation, the shock to Christendom, national antagonisms, social arrogance and exclusiveness all found their reflection in the intellectual and spiritual life of the time. This was the period when nominalism triumphantly invaded the universities and theology, a victory for those who would sharply distinguish faith from knowledge, spirit from matter, God from man, and the natural from the supernatural; this philosophy, like mysticism, was expressive of the doubts and despair which troubled the age. Both nominalism and mysticism were attempts at building inner kingdoms of the mind and soul whilst outside the peoples of Europe remained locked in a state of permanent civil war.[24]

William of Ockham (1300-1349?), one of many thinkers nominated for the dubious position of "father of modern thought," is most closely identified with the origins of nominalism—to such an extent that it often went by the name of "Ockhamism." A Franciscan who attacked the stupidity of the Inquisitors, the avarice of the theology professors, and the lust for power of the Pope—and spent some time in papal custody for his good efforts—Ockham matched his radical theological views with a highly individualist philosophy. Writing against the dominant Thomist doctrine that words stood for universals which reflected the order of the cosmos, he put forward the "democratic" thesis that universal or abstract terms were mere conveniences of language, existing in name only. There were no universal meanings authorized by God, only temporal understandings reached through dialogue and agreed upon by the majority. Hence, there is no absolute guarantee, as claimed by the realists, that there is a physical reality that corresponds to particular terms. From this reinterpretation of language some drew radical conclusions: much of the Bible was a fictional naming-game, and although God probably did exist, he had become a very remote "other" who no longer had much to do with human affairs. According to Heer, Ockham was "excommunicated in 1328, conquered Paris with his nominalism about 1340, and from there it spread to the German universities."[25]

Can one not detect in this doctrine of the late Middle Ages an echo of a representational battle going on in the late Modern Ages? The "death of the author," "logocentrism," "undecidability," "indeterminacy"—the bellwether words of postmodernism—all have the tintinnabulation of a latter-day nominalism in them. And the problematical relationship of words to objects was certainly front-and-center in the seminal encounter of idealism and realism in international relations. In *The Twenty Years' Crisis*, E. H. Carr located the weakness of the League of Nation idealists in their slippery use of language. He approvingly quoted Bertrand Russell—"Metaphysicians, like savages are apt to imagine a magical connexion between words and things"— to lead his attack on the "metaphysicians of Geneva" who "found it difficult to believe that an accumulation of ingenious texts prohibiting war was not a barrier against war itself."[26]

The injunction that words mean what they say and say what they mean is the core-principle of realism—and its greatest aporia, or inherent contradiction in its international relations adaptation. For without a central authority, without a Leviathan of language, who is to legislate meaning in world politics? As long as there was a commonly accepted diplomatic culture and a "natural" hegemony or balance of power, the question did not arise in any significant way. But when power and culture fragments, diffuses, and accelerates, there is more dissonance than harmony in realism. To paraphrase Frederick the Great: discourse without power is like an orchestra without a score. Or in the trope that opened this essay—without a hegemonic script, realism begins to resemble an absurdist play.

HETEROREALISM

Better, some might think, an absurdist play than a three-ring circus. This would seem to be the view of those feeling buffeted by the winds of change who would seek to close the disciplinary shutters against new intellectual challenges. The illiberal attitude of neoliberal institutionalism toward postmodernist feminism, and the insecurity of security studies toward poststructuralism fit the bill.[27] I do not wish to rehearse this (so far) non-debate. I note it only as part of a necessary academic exercise, in the hope that a discursive space can be opened and maintained for the start of a dialogue that would make these defensive reactions—including, of course, this one—unnecessary. Instead, I wish to re-introduce the antinomies and prototypes of realism that never seem to "figure" in the reductive identity of realism in international relations. This just might help us to construct a form of "heterorealism" that can imagine, constitute, and help to manage many new world orders.

If nominalism represents the first act of the lost script of realism, then it is the literary and artistic creeds of realism that make up the second and third. It might seem ironic that realism as a school of thought should be resurrected in the eighteenth century in the fictional form of the novel. It was also expedient: Britain's censorial Licensing Act of 1737 encouraged the intellectual talents of the day to turn to the novel as a relatively safe conduit for social satire. Writers like Daniel Defoe and Henry Fielding were described as "realists" because of their detailed depiction of everyday life, the drawing of characters from the lower classes and outlaw fringe, and the use of an easy and familiar language. For the modern purist who considers the "docudrama" an affront to truth and good taste, a reading of Defoe's *Journal of the Plague Years* (1722), or Fielding's *Tom Jones* (1749) is suggested. Both are considerably more "realistic," that is, superior in verisimilitude, than the "factual" accounts of the day (such as Samuel Pepys' account of the 1665 London plague). The same was thought by Marx and Engels of the greatest literary realist,

Honoré de Balzac, who considered himself a scientific historian first and a novelist second.[28] And in his influential *Studies in European Realism*, the marxist scholar Georg Lukács lauded Balzac's "profound comprehension of the contradictorily progressive character of capitalist development" and, then, after noting that "the great realist of France found worthy heirs only in Russia," claimed that "It is not by chance that Lenin . . . formulated the Marxist view of the principles of true realism in connection with Tolstoy."[29]

In painting a similar battle was being played out, with realism once again defined by a dominating antinomy. The first salvo, "The Realist Manifesto," written by the painter Gustave Courbet against the classicist affectations of the Salon, self-consciously eschews eloquence and rhetorical flourishes for a spare and neutral style that is meant, one can surmise, to convey authenticity and—realism:

> The title of Realist was thrust upon me just as the title of Romantic was imposed upon the men of 1830. Titles have never given a true idea of things: it were otherwise, the works would be unnecessary. I have studied, outside of any system and without prejudice, the art of the ancients and the art of the moderns. I no more wanted to imitate the one than to copy the other; nor, furthermore, was it my intention to attain the trivial goal of art for art's sake. No! I simply wanted to draw forth from a complete acquaintance with tradition the reasoned and independent consciousness of my own individuality. To know in order to be able to create, that was my idea. . . . in short, to create living art—this is my goal.[30]

As a school of thought and movement of painting, realism was once again born from its critics. The best appreciation of this birth that I have located is the strange mix of respect, confusion, and ridicule that fills the letter of the French writer Champfleury to George Sand. A lengthy excerpt is warranted, both for its seminal remarks and its relevance for a later debate in international relations between neorealism and its critics:

> If I write you this letter, Madame, it is because of the lively curiosity, full of good faith, that you have shown for a doctrine which takes shape from day to day and which has its representatives in all the arts. A hyper-romantic German musician, Mr. Wagner, whose works are unknown in Paris, has received extraordinary maltreatment in the musical journals, by M. Fetis who accuses the new composer of being tainted

288 JAMES DER DERIAN

with *Realism*. All those who put forward new aspirations are called *Realists*. We shall surely see realistic doctors, realistic chemists, realistic manufacturers, realistic historians. M. Courbet is a realist; I am a realist: since the critics says so, I let them say it. But, to my great shame, I confess that I have never studied the code containing the laws according to which the first comer is allowed to produce realistic works.

The name horrifies me by its pedantic ending; I am afraid of schools as of the cholera and my greatest joy is to encounter clear-cut personalities. That is why, in my opinion, M. Courbet is a new man. With ten intelligent people, one could get to the bottom of the question of *Realism*; with this mob of ignorant people, envious, powerless, critical, all one gets is words. I will not define Realism for you, Madame: I do not know where it comes from, and where it goes, what it is . . . .[31]

What is the point of this historical run through the various beginnings of realism? First, realism, which presents itself as a superior representation of reality, has displayed a wide range of rhetorical and figurative styles, cultural values, and philosophical tendencies. Whether it was used to refer to a doctrine of the material world, to "things as they really are," or to an artistic or literary movement, the variations and interpretations of realism have been conditioned by the tradition against which a particular form of realism emerges. For instance, in France the realist novel was heavily materialist, evolving from the anti-romantic, sociological forms of Balzac and the Goncourt brothers, to the deterministic, practically Darwinistic naturalism of Zola. In England, realism missed the naturalist turn, preferring to explore a moral landscape rather than document a mechanistic universe, as best exemplified in the work of Dickens and George Eliot. A similar range of differences can also be traced in the variety of paintings, from Gustave Courbet to today's Chuck Close, which have been categorized under the rubric of "realist."

What generalizations can we make of this long history of realism, in its passage from counter-hegemonic force to a dominant discourse? It emerges from the struggle against nominalism in the late medieval ages; against capitalism and romanticism in the nineteenth century; and against idealism in the twentieth. Judging from the diversity and complexity of its historical opposition, it seems absurd to try to attach a fixed identity to realism, as has been the tendency in international relations. This is a lesson learned early by one of the greatest students of realism, Martin Wight—a lesson seemingly lost on many of the neorealists:

Statesmen act under various pressures, and appeal with varying degrees of sincerity to various principles. It is for those who study international relations to judge their actions, which means judging the validity of their ethical principles. This is not a process of scientific analysis; it is more akin to literary criticism.[32]

Unless, of course, the very function—and paradox—of realism is to reappear when uncertainty rises, when the link between referent and object becomes too attenuated, when the mirror of nature cracks: that is, in times like our own, when a less accessible and more unstable reality shows its face. We need, then, to consider the possibility that the power of "realism" lies not in its immanence but in its distance from reality, from the realities of contingency, ambiguity, and indeterminacy that realism tries to keep at bay. This is why I believe we must turn to the doctor of reality, Nietzsche, to understand the power and persistence of realism in irreal times.

A NIETZSCHEAN READING OF REALISM

I rely on Nietzsche for this purpose, both because his genealogical approach is a powerful investigatory tool, and because no one has more deeply charted the figurative and literal power of realism. Not, of course, the realism per se of international relations, but the primordial form of natural, fundamental, or rational realism underlying it, that which holds there is a physical world independent of its perception or representation. In *The Wanderer and his Shadow* he challenged the fundamental realist belief that the naming of something reveals its independent existence:

> The word and the concept are the most obvious reason why we believe in this isolation of groups of actions: we do not merely *designate* things by them, we originally believe that through them we grasp what is true in things. Through words and concepts we are now continually tempted to think of things as being simpler than they are, as separated from one another, as indivisible, each existing in and for itself. There is a philosophical mythology concealed in language . . . .[33]

In the *Twilight of the Idols* he exposed the origins of this mythology: "Language belongs in its origins to the age of the most rudimentary form of psychology; we find ourselves in the midst of a rude fetishism when we call to mind the basic presuppositions of the metaphysics of language—which is to say, *reason.*"[34] From its earliest moments reason had noble aims, but soon took on the characteristics of the forces which gave rise to it:

> If one needs to make a tyrant of reason, as Socrates did, then there must exist no little danger of something else playing the tyrant. Rationality was at that time divined as a *saviour*; neither Socrates nor his "invalids" were free to be rational or not, as they wished—it was *de rigueur*, it was their *last* expedient. The fanaticism with which the whole of Greek thought throws itself at rationality betrays a state of emergency: one was in peril, one had only one choice: either to perish or—be *absurdly rational* . . . .[35]

The result is that "the 'real world' has been constructed out of the contradiction to the actual world: an apparent world indeed, in so far as it is no more than a *moral-optical* illusion."[36] This is not to say that neither Nietzsche nor his latter-day proponents have taken an idealist position; rather, he is intent on dismantling the oppositional relationship with idealism from which realism derives its power and meaning. For it is within this destructive co-dependency that humanity takes revenge on life now and holds out for a better life later. In this modern condition the morality of idealism has little appeal and a limited power. This is made clear by his preamble to a passage quoted earlier in this essay:

> Moral judgement belongs, as does religious judgement, to a level of ignorance at which even the concept of the real, the distinction between the real and the imaginary, is lacking: so that at such a level "truth" denotes nothing but things which we today call "imaginings." To this extent moral judgement is never to be taken literally: as such it never contains anything but nonsense. But as *semeiotics* it remains of incalculable value: it reveals, to the informed man at least, the most precious realities of cultures and inner worlds which did not *know* enough to "understand" themselves. Morality is merely sign-language, merely symptomatology; one must already know *what* it is about to derive profit from it.[37]

Nietzsche leaves the reader with no doubts about the disease lurking behind the symptoms: "To divide the world into a 'real' and an 'apparent' world, whether in the manner of Christianity or in the manner of Kant (which is, after all, that of a cunning Christian)—is only a suggestion of decadence—a symptom of declining life . . . ."[38]

From Hegel to Spengler, Kennedy to Fukuyama (and yes, from Gilpin to Mearscheimer) realists of various stripes have attempted to survey the future through the lens of historical and philosophical experience. Have they, however, "understood" the "moral-optical illusion" from which they view the world and envision a knowledge of it? I think not, and I think a genealogy of a forefather of realism can help us to understand why.

THE GHOST OF THUCYDIDES

There is of course no original realism to discover. But just as America needs its Columbus and "founding fathers" to mythicize and legitimize the best and worst of its history, international relations needs its seminal—they never seem to be "embryonic"—figures like Thucydides, Machiavelli, Hobbes, Weber, and so on. Robert Gilpin is most famous for giving voice and a disciplinary force to this sentiment ("Everything—well, almost everything—that the new realists find intriguing . . . can be found in the *History of the Peloponnesian War*"[39]), but it has often been repeated, either implicitly in the assumption of a self-reproducing "tradition" of realism, or explicitly in the neorealist notion of a scientific accumulation of knowledge.

In North American international relations there seem to be only two periods worthy of historical study in any detail, from which the origins and lessons of realism are then drawn and defended. The first is the Peloponnesian War, the second is the Cold War (which, some will admit, requires a smattering of knowledge of World War II). That both histories should be ideologically adducible for a contemporary balance of power, with the United States in the role of hegemonic balancer is of no passing interest—but not the subject of this genealogy.[40] What is of interest is how the battle over Thucydides' shroud revealed new fissures in the monolithic facade of realism, and helped to reconstitute new forms of realism.

I have neither the desire nor the space to reproduce all of the skirmishes that have made up this discursive struggle. Probably the most skillful and compact treatment of the debate came from Michael Doyle, who surveyed the field and argued that Thucydides the "Minimalist Realist" wins out over the contending claimants, the "Fundamentalist" and "Structuralist Realists."[41] Like many others in the field, Doyle exerted most of his intellectual efforts on a choice between parsimonious schools of thought rather than an appreciation of the interpretive forces that give rise to a plurality of meaning in Thucydides' text. Nonetheless, he ended on a useful cautionary note: "Paternity suits tend to be messy."[42]

Of more significance is the growing literature which treats Thucydides as a historically-situated thinker who acquired a transhistorical power for realism because of his skillful use of rhetoric and dramatic constructions. First out on this new interpretive form was Hayward Alker's "The Dialectical Logic of Thucydides' Melian Dialogue."[43] Alker used Nicholas Rescher's formalization of dialectics and Kenneth Burke's dramaturgical approach to present the case that the lessons of Thucydides are acquired and reinterpreted through an endless political argumentation.

This reclamation of Thucydides from formal modelers and structuralist neorealists was further advanced by Daniel Garst's "Thucydides and Neorealism."[44] In this essay Thucydides appears as a friendly ghost of political realism, not tortured—as those proto-scientists, the alchemists, tried to "torture" lead into gold—into the family-line of neorealism. Rather than claim some "true" version of Thucydides as Author-God of realism, Garst considered him as "a contested terrain for realist and critical approaches to international relations theory."[45] By focusing on the highest rhetorical moments of The Peloponnesian War, the speeches and debates, Garst produced new insights into the relationship of discourse and hegemony. He historicized and opened the hermeneutic circle of realism without diluting its analytical power for our own times.

The latest, and certainly the strangest transfiguration of Thucydides, appears in a new book on the 1991 Gulf War by the British philosopher Christopher Norris, Uncritical Theory: Postmodernism, Intellectuals, and the Gulf War.[46] Before the start of the war, French social critic Jean Baudrillard published an article in the London Guardian, "The Reality Gulf," in which he argued that the Gulf War (as paraphrased by Norris) "would never happen, existing as it did only as a figment of mass-media simulation, war-games rhetoric or imaginary scenarios which exceeded all the limits of real-world, factual possibility."[47] At the end of the Gulf War he reiterated and defended his position in a provocatively entitled article in La Libération, "The Gulf War Has Not Taken Place."[48] This was to be understood as a "virtual" engagement, unlike any prior war. According to Baudrillard:

The true belligerents are those who thrive on the ideology of the truth of this war, despite the fact that the war itself exerts its ravages on another level, through faking, through hyperreality, the simulacrum, through all those strategies of psychological deterrence that make play with facts and images, with the precession of the virtual over the real, of virtual time over real time, and the inexorable confusion between the two.[49]

Ignorant of, or perhaps choosing to ignore the ironic element of Baudrillard's critique, Christopher Norris took severe umbrage from these articles, and dashed off a polemic that drew from Derrida, Foucault, Lyotard, and others to refute what he took to be the excessive and flip postmodernism of Baudrillard. More important is who he channeled for an alternative—realist as opposed to hyperrealist—interpretation of the Gulf War: yes, the ghost of Thucydides. Or rather the magical figure in J. Fisher Solomon's 1988 book, *Discourse and Reference in the Nuclear Ages*, who offered the hermeneutic key for understanding the perpetual war without referents—nuclear deterrence—through a "potentialist realism."[50]

Where this interpretive tug-of-war with Thucydides will end, I am not sure. But since it is the semiology of realism which concerns me, in the dual sense of a study of the symptoms of a disease and the sign-system of a powerful discourse, it perhaps is best to end with Nietzsche's take on the matter, one that contains, I believe, a particular poignancy for contemporary realism:

My recreation, my preference, my *cure* from all Platonism has always been Thucydides. *Thucydides* and, perhaps, Machiavelli's *Principe* are most closely related to myself by the unconditional will not to gull oneself and to see reason in *reality*—not in "reason," still less in "morality" . . . One must turn him over line by line and read his hidden thoughts. *Sophist culture*, by which I mean *realist culture*, attains in him its perfect expression . . . *Courage* in face of reality ultimately distinguishes such natures as Thucydides and Plato: Plato is a coward in face of reality—consequently he flees into the ideal; Thucydides has himself under control—consequently he retains control over things. . . .[51]

THE ENDLESS JOURNEY OF REALISM

As we have seen, there is a general consensus that realism in international relations was first articulated in its modern form by E. H. Carr in his 1939 polemic, *The Twenty Years' Crisis*. Adopting a de-Marxified historical materialism, Carr took on the inter-war idealists who were, according to Carr, in the grip of a Benthamite utilitarianism and a *laissez-faire* political economy. As I have simplified Carr's rich account, this caused the leaders of the time to mistake aspiration for analysis, appease when they should have confronted Hitlerism, and make possible if not certain the coming of the Second World War. If Carr provided the indictment against idealism, the horrors of totalitarianism and genocide delivered the verdict and sentence. This story of idealism's culpability, drowning out a well-documented contemporary argument made by A. J. P. Taylor that appeasement was the most realist of all possible options in the 1930s, became the historical *Ur*-text for traditional realists.[52]

It was not, however, the intent of this essay to challenge Carr's thesis, nor his reliance on a caricature of idealists that now makes the most notorious critics of realism seem magnanimous.[53] The aim of genealogy, semiology, and dromology is to understand how realism was reinterpreted and transfigured into a variety of forms. One took the form of a sea change, as when Carr's and the emergent English school of realism was refigured as it traveled from Britain to the United States. Realism dropped the Augustinian language of providence and sin which was used by the Christians Herbert Butterfield and Martin Wight (and to a lesser extent by Carr who had been more under the influence of Marx than Reinhold Niebuhr, despite some claims to the contrary).[54] Realism as a counter-narrative was quick to take on new ideological baggage, with Cold War realists seeing in Stalin what the idealists had failed to discern in Hitler. Under the pressure of the behavioralist turn of the American discipline, and the allure of policy relevancy, it also began to take on a scientific identity, although cautiously and self-consciously at first. In *Politics Among Nations* Morgenthau could assert that "politics, like society in general, is governed by objective laws," but then turn around in a sympathetic review of Martin Wight's work to criticize contemporary efforts "to reduce international relations to a system of abstract propositions with a predictive function."[55] The path of scientization that realism took is most evident in the work of Kenneth Waltz, who moved in *Man, the State and War* (1959) from the heavily qualified conclusions that he drew from the game theory of von Neumann and Morgenstern, to a complete endorsement of microeconomic theory in *Theory of International Politics* (1979).[56]

There have been recurrent attempts to restore some flesh and blood to realism, most notably by Kenneth Thompson and a small but impressive group acting as torch-bearers for political realism.[57] But for the most part the dominant story of realism in North American international relations has been one of a sanitized reduction to minimalism, and a dialogue of the deaf between opposing schools. To borrow from literary examples of realism, it is as if the field moved from Honoré de Balzac's *La Comédie Humaine* to Bret Easton Ellis' *Less than Zero*. Richard Bernstein provides, I believe, the best advice for when theory reaches such an impasse:

> We can never escape the real practical possibility that we may fail to understand "alien" traditions and the ways in which they are incommensurable with the traditions to which we belong . . . But the response to the threat of this practical failure—which can sometimes be tragic—should be an ethical one, i.e., to assume the responsibility to listen carefully, to use our linguistic, emotional, and cognitive imagination to grasp what is being expressed and said in "alien traditions." We must do this in a way where we resist the dual temptations of *either* facilely assimilating what others are saying to our own categories and language without doing justice to what is genuinely different and may be incommensurable *or* simply dismissing what the "other" is saying as incoherent nonsense. We must also resist the double danger of imperialistic colonization and inauthentic exoticism—what is sometimes called "going native."[58]

However, there are signs, discernible in the recent efforts to reinterpret Thucydides and other classical realist texts, of the approach of what could be called a *Ulyssesian* realism.[59] It is "Ulyssesian" in two senses. The Homeric sense captures the quintessential qualities of early North American realism. Even more so than in Europe, which had a long pre-history of a historical realism, realism in America emerged in opposition to a legalist-moralist tradition. The "founding fathers"—men like Reinhold Niebuhr, Walter Lippmann, Hans Morgenthau, and George Kennan—were Machiavellian, to the extent that they openly recognized the paramountcy of power in both domestic and international affairs. They were not, however, willing to subordinate their principles to the pressing demands of the prince or to the passing desires of the public. They were "Ulyssesian realists" in the sense that early in their careers they had heard and survived the siren calls of power, wandered and been tested in the wilderness, and then returned to warn the public of grave dangers: of "technocratic illusions" (Niebuhr), "a new feudalism" (Morgenthau), and "the sophisticated mathematics of destruction in which we have been entangled" (Kennan).[60] Most of them challenged conventional wisdom with nuanced positions of opposition at critical moments in American politics: Niebuhr criticized area bombing in World War II, Lippmann took on McCarthyism in the 1950s, Morgenthau early on came out against the Vietnam War, and Kennan opposed the Reagan arms build-up in the 1980s.

But another dimension is needed to equip the Ulyssesian realist for the journey into late modern times, for we have passed from heroic and epic to technocratic and hyperreal forms of governance. Despite the best efforts of its earliest practitioners, realism was scrubbed clean of its original theologico-ethical rhetoric of tragedy and providence, justice and order, and neutralized by a nascent social science in search of a value-free discourse. In Homeric terms, the gift of knowledge took on a strictly academic exchange-value; its sacrificial powers of symbolic communication were lost. Subsequently, the public philosophy of realism was handed back to the (Second) Cold War ideologues.

Now more than ever reality requires a new script: one that can match in representational power the demands of a new spatio-temporal matrix that can fit the world onto a single microchip and disappear it in a nanosecond; that can find a new language for a multipolar, multicultural, deterritorialized world politics; and most important, that can imagine not an end to history but alternatives to the present. A realism stuck in the empirical prison of things as they really are encourages a denial and resentment toward things as they truly differ, for it is the will to reduce the other to the same and historical differences to objective laws that builds the traditionalist foundation of realism and divides the actual from the possible. Needed in its place is a critical realism that can recognize the tenuity of its singular reach, the instability of its antinomic foundations, and the necessity of an irreality beyond it. In short, recognition rather than colonization of the other.

But a critical and pluralist realism must be pragmatic as well, if it is to recognize the danger from others beyond recognition. Whether mythically, naturally, or socially constructed, monsters can have violent effects. Here the other Ulysses' encounter with the cyclops Polyphemous instructs. When asked his name by his captor, Ulysses word-plays and replies "Nobody" (*Outis*). Later, after using further guile to blind the cyclops, he makes good his escape when Polyphemous, helpless and in pain, shouts to his tribe that "Nobody" is getting away. At the most dangerous moments, Ulysses eschews any notion of universal dangers for the singularity of each threat, and chooses cunning—and punning—over brute force as his first and final options. The first lesson of a Ulyssesian realism is that it is better to be Nobody than to be reduced—or to reduce others—to a fungible (or, worse, edible) thing.

The second lesson comes from an all-together similar *Ulysses*, which reveals the hole at the center of realism:

> His (Bloom's) logical conclusion, having weighed the matter and allow-ing for possible error?
>
> That it was not a heaventree, not a heavengrot, not a heavenbeast, not a heavenman. That it was a Utopia, there being no known method from the known to the unknown: an infinity renderable equally finite by the suppositious apposition of one or more bodies equally of the same and of different magnitudes: a mobility of illusory forms immobilised in space, remobilised in air: a past which possibly had ceased to exist as a present before its probable spectators had entered actual present existence.[61]

The final lesson of both Ulysses is, fittingly, a paradox: realism in late modernity requires counter-myths, not new essentialist truths. Without the reality of a universal subject (no-body), an immobile cen-ter (no-where), or a fungible power (no-thing), in short, without the surety of a selfsame, sovereign identity, realism requires an affirma-tive leap into the imaginary. The endgame of *Ulysses*, to ask and to will a yes from the other, represents the true beginning and just desti-nation of realism. Otherwise we will not be.

NOTES

1. Some of the more notable signposts of this debate include: Reinhold Niebuhr, *Moral Man and Immoral Society: A Study in Ethics and Politics* (New York: Scribners, 1932); E. H. Carr, *The Twenty Years' Crisis: 1919-1939* (London: Macmillan, 1939); Hans Morgenthau, *Politics Among Nations: The Struggle for Power and Peace* (New York: Knopf, 1948); John Herz, *Political Realism and Political Idealism* (Chicago: University of Chicago Press, 1951); H. Bull, "International Theory: The Case for a Classicial Approach," *World*

Politics (April 1966): 361-77; and J. David Singer, "The Incompleat Theorist: Insight Without Evidence," *Contending Approaches to International Politics* (Princeton: Princeton University Press, 1969), 63-86.

Two narrative reviews of the seminal figures of realism offer more insights than most analytical accounts: Michael J. Smith, *Realist Thought from Weber to Kissinger* (Baton Rouge: Louisiana State University Press, 1986); and Joel H. Rosenthal, *Righteous Realists: Political Realism, Responsible Power, and American Culture in the Nuclear Age* (Baton Rouge: Louisiana State University Press, 1991).

For a range of "post-realist" perspectives see: Richard Ashley, "Political Realism and Human Interests," *International Studies Quarterly* 25 (spring 1981): 204-36, and "The Poverty of Neo-Realism," *International Organization* 38 (spring 1984): 225-86; R. B. J. Walker, "Realism, Change, and International Political Theory," *International Studies Quarterly* 31 (March 1987): 65-86; Anders Stephanson, *Kennan and the Art of Foreign Policy* (Cambridge, Mass.: Harvard University Press, 1989); Friedrich Kratochwil, *Rules, Norms and Decisions: On the Conditions of Practical and Legal Reasoning in International Relations and Domestic Affairs* (Cambridge: Cambridge University Press, 1989); and Roger Epp, "Power Politics and the Civitas Terrena: The Augustinian Sources of Anglo-American Thought in International Relations" (Ph.D. diss., Kingston Ontario: Queen's University, 1990).

2. For a sample of internal critiques, see Robert Keohane, "Realism, Neorealism, and the Study of World Politics," in Keohane, ed., *Neorealism and Its Critics* (New York: Columbia University Press, 1986), 1-26; Alexander Wendt, "Anarchy is What States Make of It," *International Organization* 46 (spring 1992): 391-425; and Barry Buzan, Charles Jones, and Richard Little, *The Logic of Anarchy: Neorealism to Structural Realism* (New York: Columbia University Press, 1993).

3. See James Der Derian, *On Diplomacy: A Genealogy of Western Estrangement* (Oxford: Blackwell, 1987); and "The Value of Security: Hobbes, Marx, Nietzsche and Baudrillard," in *The Political Subject of Violence*, eds. David Campbell and Michael Dillon (Manchester and New York: Manchester University Press, 1993).

4. Bertolt Brecht, quoted by Sandy Petrey, *Realism and Revolution: Balzac, Stendhal, Zola and the Performances of History* (Ithaca: Cornell University Press, 1988), xii.

5. I characterize the current assumptions of realism in international relations as "para-philosophical" because they take on the dress (say, as Serbian para-military forces pose as a legitimate army) of a uniform realism without any intellectual engagement with the debates (especially of the last two decades) that have surrounded a mitotic body of thought. My particular point of purchase against the tradition is extrinsic and poststructuralist, and can be tracked from Wittgenstein and Austin to Barthes and Derrida (see below). But there

has been another tributary (among others) of thought closer to the mainstream of philosophical realism that poses just as serious an internal challenge to many of the positivist as well as political assumptions of international relations realism—one, I might add, that has suffered just as serious neglect in the field. I refer to post-marxist theorizing about the relationship of realism to idealism, materialism, and empiricism. For instance, the interwar period produced a series of rich, aesthetic antinomies, most notably between Bertolt Brecht's agitprop expressionism and Georg Lukács' essentialist formalism, and Walter Benjamin's romantic subjectivism and Theodor Adorno's psychoanalytic modernism, all of which in one form or another held up realism as a means to cut through false consciousness, "defetishize" a reified reality, and provide a commonality of purpose and action. The emergence of the "Frankfurt School" as well as the post-marxist phenomenological and structuralist critiques of Jean-Paul Sartre and Louis Althusser attest to a diversity of realisms that have been ignored until quite recently by international relations theory. For a review of how some of these thinkers influenced debates over realism, see Frederic Jameson, *Marxism and Form: Twentieth Century Dialectical Theories of Literature* (Princeton, N.J.: Princeton University Press, 1971); and Roy Bashkar, *Reclaiming Reality: A Critical Introduction to Contemporary Philosophy* (London: Verso, 1989). For arguments endorsing their significance for international relations, see V. Kubalkova and A.A. Cruickshank; John Maclean, "Marxism and International Relations: A Strange Case of Mutual Neglect," *Millennium* 17 (summer 1988): 295-320; Mark Hoffman, "Critical Theory and the Inter-Paradigm Debate," *Millennium* 17 (summer 1987): 231-50; and Jim George and David Campbell, "Patterns of Dissent and the Celebration of Difference: Critical Social Theory and International Relations," *International Studies Quarterly* 34 (1990): 269-93.

6. Friedrich Nietzsche, *Twilight of the Idols*, trans. R. J. Hollingdale (Middlesex, England: Penguin, 1968), 55.

7. Ibid., 38.

8. I cite Nietzsche and use the term "semiology" here to provide a broad description of the "linguistic turn," that is, the various theoretical reactions to the loss of a pivotal center of meaning that has taken the form of structuralism, structurationism, or poststructuralism. Although they remain in the shadows (largely because their visage—not to mention verbiage—is not overly appreciated in international relations discourse), two thinkers along with Nietzsche guide this semiology: Roland Barthes and Jacques Derrida. Particularly useful are two essays which engage historical and linguistic forms of realism: Barthes' *S/Z* (New York: Farvar, Strauss and Giroux, 1974), which takes apart line-by-line Balzac's *Sarrasine*—and many of the tenets of representational realism with it—and Derrida's *Limited, Inc a b c . . .* (Baltimore, Md.: Johns Hopkins University Press, 1977), which pushes beyond the limit the radical implications of J. L. Austin's speech-act theory through a critical, often polemical engagement with the philosopher of lan-

guage, John Searle. An especially useful bridging text between speech-act theory and later applications of structuralist and poststructuralist theories of representation is Sandy Petrey's *Realism and Revolution*.

9. Semiology may be more resistant than other approaches to this inertia but it is not immune, as Roland Barthes, whose own career moved from a structural semiotics to an artful semiology, made amply clear in an interview:

> [I] could say, however, that the present problem consists in disengaging semiology from the repetition to which it is has already fallen prey. We must produce something new in semiology, not merely to be original, but because it is necessary to consider the theoretical problem of repetition . . . to pursue a general and systematic enterprise, polyvalent, multidimensional, the fissuration of the symbolic and its discourse in the West.

See "Interview: A Conversation with Roland Barthes," *Signs of the Times* (1971), reprinted in *The Grain of the Voice* (New York: Hill and Wang, 1985), 129.

10. See Paul Virilio, *Pure War* (New York: Semiotext(e), 1983); *Speed and Politics* (New York: Semiotext(e), 1986); *War and Cinema: The Logistics of Perception* (New York: Verso, 1989). A trivial but telling recent example of the primacy of time over space (and what fills that space) is the lead-in commentary on President Clinton's inaugural address: the three major networks and PBS put the emphasis on its 14-minute brevity.

11. See "The (S)pace of International Relations: Speed, Simulation, and Surveillance," *International Studies Quarterly* 34 (1990): 295-310.

12. This mood and need was captured in a remark by Tom Brokaw, quoted in "Being Whatever it Takes to Win Election," Michael Kelly, *New York Times* (23 August 1992): 295-310.

> The news cycle has become a 24-hour-a-day thing, and it moves very fast all the time now. What happens is that a fragment of information, true or false, gets sucked into the cycle early in the morning, and once it gets into the cycle it gets whipped around to the point that it has gravitas by the end of the day. And, unfortunately, people are so busy chasing that fragment of information that they treat it as a fact, forgetting about whether it is true or not.

13. Paul Virilio, interview, from *Art and Philosophy* (Milan, Italy: Giancarlo Politi Editore, 1991), 142.

14. For an explanation of the dangers and opportunities presented by the new "antidiplomacy," see James Der Derian, *Antidiplomacy: Spies, Terror, Speed and War* (Oxford: Basil Blackwell, 1992).

15. The problem of defining "realism" and "idealism" in international relations will be dealt with below. But at the starting gate it might be helpful to have some minimal, generic definitions. "Realism" in general refers to a belief or doctrine that a physical world exists as a reality independent of how we might perceive or conceive of it. "Idealism" is used here in the sense of the

unity of intelligence and external reality in an idea, a metaphysical tradition that stretches from Augustine to Hegel to Marx. Of course the confusion between realism and idealism pre-dates current epistemological debates. We shall see how in our field it surfaces in E. H. Carr, who drew distinctions between a "scientific" (i.e. marxoid materialist) realism and a "utopian" (i.e. Benthamite utilitarian) idealism. It is not a stretch to argue that Carr would find much of today's neorealism—especially its reliance on a warmed-over utilitarianism—to be idealist. See below and E. H. Carr, *The Twenty Years' Crisis: 1919-1939*, 5-30.

16. See note 1.

17. Indeed, a good way to separate a hard-core realist from the rest of the international relations pack is to ask whether the re-evaluation of realism is a cause or effect of its *Destruktion* as a self-evident concept and unified school of thought. "*Destruktion*" can be read in the Heideggerian sense of "de-structuring" a term to retrieve its pre-metaphysical meaning; or it can be read simply (and less usefully) as the "destruction" of a monological "Realism." For those wishing an elaboration of the first reading, see Hans-Georg Gadamer, "*Destruktion* and Deconstruction," *Dialogue and Deconstruction*, ed. D. P. Michelfelder and R. E. Palmer (Albany: State University of New York Press, 1989), 102-13.

18. Obviously it is possible and non-contradictory to be, in the manner of Hegel for example, both a philosophical idealist and a political realist. But since Hegel's failure to achieve a "final solution" for the synthesis of both in a philosophy of totality, interpretive philosophers ranging from Thomas Kuhn and Alasdair MacIntyre to Michel Foucault and Jacques Derrida have argued that realism and idealism share more similarities than differences. They are both part of a rationalist tradition that no longer enjoys a natural *universality*. In effect, the whole idealist-realist debate has become in philosophical circles something of a side-show for the much more critical issue of a paradigmatic incommensurability opening up in Western philosophy, where the validity of fundamental truth claims of both idealists and realists have been called into question. In simple terms (that sacrifice the nuance and complexity of the issue), the contest between realists and idealists has been subsumed by a much larger battle between the Enlightenment project— in Richard Rorty's words, the "Cartesian-Lockean-Kantian tradition"— and post-empiricist and poststructuralist philosophy in which neither side seems to share the same standards of rationality, values, language itself. Or rather, one side assumes universal standards for both, while the other denies any for either. This essay notes but does not intend to enter this fray. Needless to say, I believe there is much be gained in international relations theory—and in our understandings of world politics—by joining this debate. For a further exposition of the darker side-effects of the Enlightenment project (including Hegel's "final solution"), see Zygmunt Bauman, *Modernity and the Holocaust* (Cambridge Mass.: Polity Press, 1989); and Richard J. Bernstein, "The Incommensurability and Otherness Revisited," *The New*

Constellation: The Ethical-Political Horizons of Modernity/Postmodernity (Cambridge, Mass.: MIT Press, 1992); and Richard Rorty, *Philosophy and the Mirror of Nature* (Princeton: Princeton University Press, 1979).

19. Brent Scowcroft, "America Can't Afford to Turn Inward," *New Perspective Quarterly* (summer 1992): 7.

20. Zbigniew Brzezinski, "Selective Commitment," *New Perspective Quarterly* (summer 1992): 15.

21. The continued hegemony of realism in international relations has been noted by many with differing attitudes and approaches to the subject. See for instance: Stanley Hoffmann, "An American Social Science: International Relations," *Daedalus* (summer 1977): 41-60; Hedley Bull, "The Theory of International Politics," *The Aberystwyth Papers: International Politics, 1919-1969* (London: RIIS, 1972), 38-39; Robert Keohane and Joseph Nye, *Power and Interdependence* (Boston: Little, Brown, 1977); John Vasquez, *The Power of Power Politics: A Critique* (New Brunswick, N.J.: 1983); Hayward Alker and Thomas Biersteker, "The Dialectics of World Order: Notes for a Future Archaeologist of International *Savoire Faire*," *International Studies Quarterly* 28 (June 1984): 121-42; Richard Ashley, "The Poverty of Neo-Realism"; William Olson and Nicolas Onuf, "The Growth of a Discipline Reviewed," in *International Relations: British and American Perspectives*, ed. Steve Smith (Oxford: Blackwell, 1985); and Yale Ferguson and Richard Mansbach, *The Elusive Quest: Theory and International Politics* (Columbia: University of South Carolina Press, 1988).

22. The view that norms, values, "truth" itself are produced through language has been part of a long debate that ranges from Wittgenstein and Austin to Barthes and Derrida. That this debate should still be ignored in international relations, and worse, contested in ignorance (with a few notable exceptions) of the most important texts, is the equivalent of maintaining a Ptolemaic view of the universe in the physical sciences.

23. The best compendium of those differences remains *Neorealism and its Critics*, ed. Robert Keohane, but for a remarkably lucid view from above the fray, see Richard Little, "Structuralism and Neo-Realism," in *International Relations: A Handbook of Current Theory*, eds. Margot Light and A. J. R. Groom (London: Frances Pinter, 1985), 74-89. For a more critical and complex view of the dependency of epistemic realism upon difference, see William Connolly, *Identity\Difference*, 36-63; and David Campbell, *Writing Security*, 1-15.

24. Friedrich Heer, *The Medieval World: Europe 1100-1350* (London: Weidenfeld and Nicolson, 1961), 26.

25. Ibid., 277.

26. Carr, *Twenty Years' Crisis*, 30.

27. See Der Derian, *Antidiplomacy*, 1-15.

28. See *Marx and Engels on Literature and Art*, ed. L. Baxandall and S. Morawski (St. Louis, Mo.: Telos Press, 1973), 30-32, 115-16, 150.

29. Georg Lukács, *Studies in European Realism* (New York: Grossert and Dunlap, 1964), 13. See also Lukács' *Essays on Realism* (Cambridge, Mass.: MIT Press, 1981).

30. *Realism and Tradition in Art, 1848-1900: Sources and Documents*, ed. Linda Nochlin (Englewood Cliffs, N.J.: Prentice Hall, 1966), 33-34.

31. Ibid., 38-39.

32. Martin Wight, *International Theory: The Three Traditions*, eds. Gabriele Wight and Brian Porter (London and Leicester: Leicester University Press, 1991), 258. Wight went on to list over a dozen novels that should be essential reading for every student of international relations.

33. Nietzsche, *The Wanderer and his Shadow*, 11.

34. Nietzsche, *Twilight of the Idols*, 38.

35 Ibid., 33.

36. Ibid., 39.

37. Ibid., 55.

38. Ibid.

39. Robert Gilpin, "The Richness of the Tradition of Political Realism," *Neorealism and Its Critics*, 308.

40. This interpretation has been persuasively argued by Justin Rosenberg, "What's the matter with Realism," *Review of International Studies* 16 (October 1990): 285-304.

41. See Michael Doyle, "Thucydidean Realism," *Review of International Studies* 16 (July 1990): 223-37.

42. Ibid., 237.

43. Hayward Alker, Jr., "The Dialectical Logic of Thucydides' Melian Dialogue," *American Political Science Review* 82 (September 1988): 805-20.

44. Daniel Garst, "Thucydides and Neorealism," *International Studies Quarterly* 33 (March 1989): 3-28.

45. Ibid., 3.

46. Christopher Norris, *Uncritical Theory: Postmodernism, Intellectuals, and the Gulf War* (London: Lawrence and Wishart, 1992).

47. Ibid., 11.

48. Jean Baudrillard, "The Gulf War Has Not Taken Place," *The Guardian* (29 March 1991).

49. Ibid., 193.

50. J. Fisher Solomon, *Discourse and Reference in the Nuclear Age* (Norman Okla.: University of Oklahoma Press, 1988).

51. *Twilight of the Idols*, 106-7.]

52. See A. J. P. Taylor, *The Origins of the Second World War* (New York: Atheneum, 1962).

53. On the reductionist interpretation of idealism, see David Long, "J. A. Hobson and Idealism in International Relations," *Review of International Studies* 17 (July 1991): 285-304.

54. For a fuller account of the influence of British realists on their American counterparts, see Epp, "Power Politics and the Civitas Terrena: The Augustinian Sources of Anglo-American Thought in International Relations."

55. *Politics among Nations*, 4; "The Intellectual and Political Functions of Theory," in *Truth and Power* (New York: Praeger Publishers, 1970), 251.

56. See *Man, the State, and War* (New York: Columbia University Press, 1959); and *Theory of International Politics* (Reading, Mass.: Addison-Wesley, 1979).

57. See Alberto Coll, *The Wisdom of Statecraft*; Smith, *Realist Thought from Weber to Kissinger*; and Rosenthal, *Righteous Realists*. Another exception would be *The Logic of Anarchy* by Barry Buzan, Charles Jones, and Richard Little, who construct a revisionist theory of neorealism that is much more complex and historical than Waltz's.

58. R. J. Bernstein, *The New Constellation: The Ethical-Political Horizons of Modernity/Postmodernity* (Cambridge, Mass.: MIT Press, 1992), 65-66.

59. This construction of a "Ulyssesian realism" is inspired by but not faithful to interpretations from the *Dialectic of Enlightenment* by Theodor Adorno and Max Horkheimer, and "Ulysses Gramophone: Hear Say Yes in Joyce" by Jacques Derrida. See in particular the new translation of Adorno by Robert Hullot-Kentor of the second chapter, "Odysseus or Myth and Enlightenment," *New German Critique* 50 (summer 1992): 109-42; and the translation of Derrida by Tina Kendall and Shari Benstock, in *A Derrida Reader: Between the Blinds*, ed. Peggy Kamuf (New York: Columbia University Press, 1991), 571-98.

60. See *Righteous Realists*, 118, 135, 160.

61. James Joyce, *Ulysses* (New York: Random House, 1986), 575

IV
REWRITING FOREIGN
POLICY

From the perspective of realism, writing policy is the least of the tasks of statecraft. Action, not words, is the credo, and written statements are incidental accoutrements/or means of deception/or the hallmark of institutions that lack the force to back up their pronouncements. Once again, however, the realist is caught unaware. As the essays in this section demonstrate, foreign policy is a mixture of manifold practices of composition. Whether dependent on unacknowledged texts, or extending cultural practices of racial labeling into state action, or reinscribing the general text of modernity on indigenous peoples, or constructing a common narrative through practical deliberation, the decision makers in international affairs are enmeshed in rhetoric. Moreover, their decisions often turn on rhetorical skill. Therefore, the assessment of a policy requires determining the persuasive disposition of the forum, practice, discourse, or audience shaping the key decisions, as well as the verbal artistry of individual actors. This does not remove the need for an assessment of forces, but it does identify how limited such an assessment can be.

To paraphrase Kenneth Burke, the analyst of international relations needs to know what to look for and what to look out for. The following essays bring the general orientation of this volume into the art of application, and so they begin by looking for the discursive context in which foreign policy decisions are made. One can still see a world of states calculating forces to maintain equilibrium, but within that *one also sees how decisions are shaped as well by their discursive locale, and how other locales are seen or not seen at all because of what is said or not said about them. One learns to look for the means by which place is constructed in the language of policy and to look out for hyperbolic definitions of place which can become conduits to human slaughter. One can look for the characteristics of a delibera-tive process that produces well-reasoned policies and look out for those ways in which that process is likely to break down or be circum-vented. Although the analysis of discourse begins with a plethora of texts and many opportunities for distraction, ultimately it can pay for itself by identifying the hidden costs of business as usual.*

By taking this perspective on the construction of international rela-tions, one becomes sensitive to both large-scale and localized con-straints on foreign policy. On the one hand, large-scale processes of cultural formation such as imperialism and modernization can be tracked through their instantiation in the language, and logic, of diplomatic argument. (The realist can see these processes, of course, but cannot account for them comprehensively, that is, independently of national interest and state action.) On the other hand, local ("domestic") influences on foreign policy can be identified in terms of their specific means of deliberation and influence. (Again, the realist knows they exist, but generally sees them as impediments to state action rather than as constitutive processes of policy formation.) More important, perhaps, is the related tendency in these essays to redefine the idea of constraint in a manner more consistent with creative pol-icy formation. The analysis of discursive constraints can reveal how some things thought to be natural or inevitable are subject to choice and negotiation, and how some things not thought about at all are arbitrary but powerful limitations on statecraft, and how some things thought to be incidental or marginal factors can become the means for rethinking one's entire strategy.

The following essays suggest that there are several lessons to be learned from incorporating these considerations into the analysis of international relations. For one, foreign policy is made in a number of settings, and interpreted (and supported or resisted) even more broadly. The rhetorical turn may simplify some things but it also points to additional complexity. Executive and legislative roles, elite and public forums, political, economic, and cultural interests, and other elements of "domestic" politics are active influences in the dis-courses of foreign policy. Second, decision making that is relatively univocal has a strong tendency to become unrealistic. (It also has a strong capability for organizing those who use it, which is why it occurs and prevails in the first place.) This attention to how any dominant discourse can become counterproductive counsels against decision making that is shielded from public accountability, as some realists prefer, or against any other undue valorization of executive authority. As the last essay in this section argues, effective foreign policy is more likely to result from a process that allows a wide range of interested parties to have a hand in its formulation.

Thus, the rhetorical turn takes us to the classical concept of prudence. Realists and post-realists alike can agree on the need not only for realistic policy but also for realistic language and mutually expedient negotiations. The crucial step now is to recognize that prudence is to be found within interpretation and through advocacy, processes that require not only analytical skill and political discipline but also imagination and a sense of fallibility.

DAVID J. SYLVAN AND STEPHEN J. MAJESKI

RHETORICS OF PLACE CHARACTERISTICS IN HIGH-LEVEL U.S. FOREIGN POLICY MAKING

At the Yalta Conference, in February 1945, Roosevelt and Stalin briefly discussed Indochina and the role that the French should play therein after the world war ended. During their colloquy, "the President said that the Indochinese were people of small stature, like the Javanese and Burmese, and were not warlike."[1] Five years later, Roosevelt's successor approved an official policy statement in which those Indochinese fighting against the French were described as "a determined adversary who manufactures effective arms locally . . . and who was, and is able, to disrupt and harass almost any area within Vietnam . . . at will."[2] In the space of that five years, the Indochinese had, effectively, become different people for U.S. government officials, with consequences for U.S. policy that are still being felt today. This article is about that transformation.[3]

Our argument will be in three parts. First, we will develop a position on U.S. foreign policy making about war and diplomacy in the Cold War era. This position is centered around the notion of foreign policy making as a distinctive culture constituted by certain descriptive and argumentative practices; to a significant degree, research on those practices will focus on particular rhetorical devices. Second, we will turn to a discussion of documents pertaining to Vietnam and Indochina. Our concern here is to elucidate how these words came to signify particular places appropriate, under certain circumstances, as destinations for U.S. combat troops. Finally, we shall consider the issue of codification: how particular aspects of reasoning about places can be formalized and abstracted as systematic claims or maxims (e.g., "realism") about international relations. Those maxims, of course, can take on a life of their own; we shall briefly look at this phenomenon as well.

Background: The Culture of U.S. Foreign Policy Making

We begin with the view that U.S. foreign policy making is a culture. What this means in theoretical terms we shall specify below; however, it is worth noting at the outset that the claim is both theoretically derived, stemming from a particular research program, and empirically grounded, arising from studies we have made of U.S. foreign policy making about Vietnam and Laos in the early and middle 1960s.[4]

Although these studies are limited in time and place, we believe that our claim has a more general validity: both to other periods of U.S. foreign policy making (at least after World War II) and, with appropriate modifications, to the foreign policy making of other states as well. The historical discussions in this paper are a first, small step in the direction of the first kind of generalization.

First, some observations. U.S. foreign policy making about war and diplomacy is, at the highest level, the province of a small group of individuals. (Until recently, these individuals were almost exclusively white males; while we do not, *a priori,* claim that this racial and gender identity outweighs other attributes such as social class, we would note that, in subtle but important ways, U.S. foreign policy making culture is marked by that identity.)[5] Although there is nothing fixed about these matters, the group does not usually consist of more than five individuals; at times, we are dealing with just two persons. Thus, in both the Kennedy and Johnson administrations, foreign policy making at the highest levels involved the president, the national security adviser, the secretary of defense, and one or two other persons (for Johnson, the secretary of state and occasionally the under secretary of state; for Kennedy, the attorney general). By contrast, high-level foreign policy making in the Truman administration involved mostly the president, the secretary of state, and either the under secretary of state or the secretary of defense; in the Eisenhower administration, policy making was the province simply of the president and the secretary of state. Of course, it should be kept in mind that, over the course of any given administration, the positions mentioned above may be, and usually are, occupied by more than one person. Moreover, as even this brief listing should make clear, there is nothing statutory about foreign policy making: other than the president (or, as in the Reagan administration, a surrogate), no particular office need be represented or, conversely, excluded, from high-level foreign policy making. As a corollary, certain meetings may include considerably more than five or six persons (e.g., the 21-25 July 1965 meetings about Vietnam; the 25-30 June 1950 Blair House meetings about Korea), yet only a small number of those participants are in fact high-level policy makers.

When we speak of high-level policy making, we of course imply the existence of lower levels as well. What is distinctive about the top level is that participants at all levels agree that higher level policy makers are the ones to whom the broadest and most serious problems are referred. We use this formulation deliberately, since policy making is not simply a process of decision making, as the standard political science terminology would have it. Policy making also involves the formulation of recommendations among which decisions are made; moreover, policy making includes analyses and characterizations that define particular issues and demarcate their contours. In this respect, high-level policy makers enjoy a considerably greater degree of autonomy relative to the bureaucracy than conventional accounts of bureaucratic politics and cybernetic processes would credit. We regularly observe top officials producing broad, abstract documents which stand apart from, or go well beyond, the views of the bureaucracy. A classic example is provided by Dean Acheson on 26 June 1950, writing by himself a statement that defined Korea as a place in which the U.S. had to go to war:

> He wanted time to be alone and to dictate. We were called in [three hours later] and he read to us a paper he had produced, which was the first draft of the statement finally issued by the President, and which was not significantly changed by the time it finally appeared, the following day . . . the course actually taken by this Government was not something pressed upon [Acheson] by the military leaders, but rather something arrived at by himself, in solitary deliberation.[6]

Whatever their legal authority may be, high-level policy makers are such by virtue of their explicit adherence to the policies that the group is making or has recently made. Individuals who dissent on many issues or for any significant period of time do not remain in the group: they are marginalized, excluded from meetings, or fired; alternatively, they resign, feeling that their usefulness is at an end. Such individuals' places may subsequently be taken by others, who continue to espouse faith in the group's policies. Cases in point are the resignation of Robert McNamara as secretary of defense and the earlier return of Walt Rostow from bureaucratic Siberia as national security adviser; both changes were due to the positions these men expressed on the Vietnam War.[7] Another example is George Ball, supposedly the house dissident in the Johnson administration. In fact, Ball's arguments against escalation shared many of the same premises as those of other high-level policy makers and his specific concerns were largely accepted as valid by other members of the group.[8] When Ball lost out definitively, his resignation followed shortly.

We referred above to explicit adherence. It must be said that this adherence (or, should the case arise, dissent) is expressed within the group. Although rumors abound regarding the positions which particular individuals take and although the general outlines of policy are fairly quickly disseminated within the relevant bureaucracies, policy making about war and diplomacy is a remarkably secretive and undemocratic activity. Journalists who count themselves as in the know are often deliberately misled by their confidential sources,[9] while Congress is frequently lied to, given partial information on policy, and often communicated with only long after the fact. Acheson's dictum that "the flatulent bombast of our public utterances will lead no one but fools" may not quite be correct but does express a preference for secrecy and a cynical contempt for democracy that are widespread among high-level policy makers.[10] The secret decisions (prior to the 1990 congressional elections) by Bush and his associates to go to war against Iraq are a recent, post-Cold War example of this same tendency.

In short, high-level policy making is the province of a small, largely autonomous, normatively cohesive, and secretive group of persons. Small wonder, then, that we can characterize that group as sharing a culture, the culture of high-level policy making about war and diplomacy. That culture is constituted as a recognizable whole by dint of relations among certain distinctive features. First, and most generally, the culture is a problem-solving one. Policy is made about what are considered to be problems; policy making revolves around discussions about the specific nature of certain problems and how those problems might plausibly be solved. To be sure, these discussions may appear highly abstruse or focused on long-range problems, but for individuals who make high-level policy, there is a world of difference between such matters and idle or academic "speculation": the former are the stuff of their identity in the culture; the latter are no more relevant to the culture than a work of art or poetry would be.

Second, problem solving involves three activities: formulating recommendations, choosing among recommendations, and reopening
debate. Individuals put forward or associate themselves with recommendations; these in turn consist of claims that particular problems
exist and that those problems can be solved by engaging in certain
courses of action designed to accomplish certain goals. After several
recommendations have been advanced, one recommendation is
adopted as the new policy; at least some of the time, it may be implemented at a lower level. Often, implementation is difficult and so recommendations may then be put forward about how problems in
implementation might be solved. More generally, a particular issue
can always be reopened for debate because the problems that motivated policy can plausibly be deemed to have changed: certain details
of the situation can be said to be different (for better or worse) than
was previously the case and hence to demand different solutions. In
this way, policies change over time.

At the core of any recommendation, any decision, and any move
to reopen debate are situation descriptions. Problems are situations
considered as actually or potentially undesirable; solutions are situations considered as involving the elimination or amelioration of
problems. Each of the three aspects of problem solving thus involves
the juxtaposition of two (or more) situations: recommendations, as
arguments about how a problem (e.g., a weak ally) and a solution
(e.g., sending military advisers) are closely linked; decisions, as
(minimally) agreement among members of the culture that certain
recommendations (e.g., to withdraw) do not adequately link problems and solutions; and recommendations that reopen debate, as
arguments that the situation has changed (thereby necessitating new
solutions to altered problems). When we speak of situations, we
should not imagine that these present themselves immediately to
the eye. Rather, situations are constructed linguistically, by means
of descriptions. For example, on 19 January 1961, Eisenhower told
Kennedy that "the evidence was clear that Communist China and
North Vietnam were determined to destroy the independence of
Laos" and that Kong Le "was a lost soul and wholly irretrievable."
Kennedy, describing the situation as "serious" and possibly
"approaching a climax," was then told by Eisenhower that "the
entire proceeding was extremely confused."[11] This example, totally
anodyne in character, indicates just how nuances in wording can
construct situations as quite different from each other. Eisenhower

urged Kennedy to prepare to intervene militarily; Kennedy, though, employed less apocalyptic language and, some months later, opted for a neutralization policy. Both men presumably were drawing upon reports from other officials and "the field"; such reports, of course, were themselves situation descriptions; and so forth, all the way down.[12]

In general, high-level foreign policy-making officials are skilled at the use of language. Many write elegant and vivid prose; others have a knack for oral expression. This is hardly surprising, given that one of the principal tasks of policy makers is to persuade others to accept their situation descriptions as reasonable and as displaying good fit between problem and solution. Accordingly, we find considerable emphasis on various rhetorical devices pertaining to what Chaim Perelman[13]calls the "structure of reality": claims that a particular situation description is "realistic," "pragmatic," or "judicious," while those of another recommendation are "exaggerated," "unduly pessimistic," or "not a real solution to the problem." Of course, as Perelman points out, action is not necessarily the same as intellectual agreement: policy makers need not have the same structure of thought in order to agree on accepting, rejecting, or at least listening seriously to a particular recommendation. The point of policy rhetoric, like that of most other kinds, is to command assent, not necessarily to change thoughts.[14] Individuals can end up agreeing with a particular policy position for any number of private reasons: political ambition, memories of childhood traumas, a need for cognitive consistency; they cannot, however, vocalize these concerns without running the risk of losing membership in the group. A cabinet officer cannot say that he agrees with a certain argument because he always hated his father. Instead, he has to put forward problem-solving descriptions to explain his position.

This does not mean that policy makers are hypocrites, at least no more so than other persons in the public eye. Although high-level officials often conceal or falsify their activities, their public utterances are remarkably similar to their private ones in both language and tone. Consider, for instance, NSC 68, a document that Truman demanded be kept secret and tightly guarded: its authors spend considerable time quoting from the Declaration of Independence and the Constitution in ways that Aristotle would certainly call epideictic.[15] Acheson himself, he of the contemptuous attitude toward "flatulent bombast," made innumerable private or confidential statements in which the U.S. and its military allies are casually described as "free and equal" in the face of totalitarian aggression.[16] For all practical purposes, policy makers are true believers.

Paradoxically, then, the secrecy of high-level policy makers gets undercut by their public utterances. To be sure, important details will routinely be concealed or falsified. Yet the speeches, press conferences, and other public statements of high-level policy makers are remarkably informative—at least for interpretively skilled audiences. Bureaucrats are given significant policy guidance by such statements; senators, newspaper reporters, and other interested parties use the statements to decipher formally secret decisions. We might say that "Kremlinology" has a White House analogue.

Our argument so far is that high-level policy involves a rhetoric of problem solving built up out of situation descriptions. The question now becomes what these descriptions are about. If, as is the case in our research, the concern is with questions of war and diplomacy, then descriptions will be about whether wars should be fought in a given place and, if so, how they should be conducted there.[17] Situations, then, pertain to places:[18] certain places will be deemed to involve a commitment of some sort or to be important enough to fight for; others will be characterized as not enjoying a U.S. commitment or being hopeless to fight in. Places, however, are unlikely to be redescribed anywhere near as often as are situations. Instead, because policy makers "know" about them already and because there is nothing "new" about them, place characteristics are considered relatively fixed, so much so that references to them are often implicit or ritually explicit (e.g., at the beginning of major policy statements). In this way, places come to be apprehended as having certain physical qualities[19] and as being lived in by certain types of people.

Studying the construction of place characteristics thus offers the possibility of shedding light on what is among the most important and the most overlooked of research topics in the making of foreign policy about war and diplomacy. What region is a country in? What resources are found in a given place? What kind of people live in a particular area? What are the salient topographical features of a given locale? The answers to these questions are constructed rhetorically, not read off of some universal encyclopedia. They rarely change; they are right underneath our noses; all the more reason to study them as they emerge from the pens and mouths of high-level policy makers.

FOREGROUND: THE CONSTRUCTION OF PLACE CHARACTERISTICS

The arguments above, though empirically grounded, are couched at a high-level of abstraction. Places, however, like situation descriptions, are built from details. Thus, to abduce the categories from which to put forward a theory about place characteristics, we shall need to start with a particular case or set of cases. Given our interest in U.S. foreign policy making about Vietnam, we shall look at just how that place emerges as a location which U.S. officials will later deem worthy of a war.

In the first years after World War II, Indochina is considered a place that at one point belonged to France. After the Potsdam conference, Truman informs Chiang Kai-shek that "for operational purposes it is desirable to include that portion of French Indo-China lying south of 10 degrees north latitude in the Southeast Asia Command. This arrangement would leave in the China Theater that part of Indo-China which covers the flank of projected Chinese operations in China." A year and a half later, this characterization still holds: Indochina is still a place that was once French, but within which other forces might establish a "Communist-dominated, Moscow-Oriented state."[20] Indochina, though, has no political or strategic wholeness: it can be divided into parts by external or internal forces.

By mid-1947, Indochina is still not much more defined. A cable from the secretary of state refers vaguely to Indochina and places it in "southern Asia"; Indochina seems to contain "Vietnam territory (e.g., establishment Cochinese REP, occupation southern Annam and Moi Plateau, and Dalat plan French-dominated Federation to which Vietnam would be subservient)." Again, we have bits and pieces; on the other hand, the area is inhabited by "newly autonomous peoples . . . Vietnamese [who] will for indefinite period require French material and technical assistance and enlightened political guidance which can be provided only by nation steeped like France in democratic tradition and confirmed in respect human liberties and worth individual."[21]

The next year sees important changes. As communist armies defeat Kuomintang forces in China, situations are described in more serious terms. In September, the undersecretary of state worries about a "rapid increase of Communist activity which has taken place in southeast Asia early this year." Southeast Asia, it turns out, now includes "Burma, Malaya, Indochina and Indonesia." This tells us where Indochina is located, but not yet what kind of place it is. To begin answering that question, we turn to a policy statement of the same month, entitled "Indochina," which lays out an immediate objective (to terminate hostilities in a way satisfactory to the French and the Vietnamese peoples) and several long-term objectives: "to eliminate so far as possible Communist influence in Indochina and to see installed a self-governing nationalist state which will be friendly to the US . . . and patterned upon our conception of a democratic state"; to foster association of Indochinese peoples with western powers, particularly France; to raise the standard of living so as to reduce receptivity to "totalitarian influences"; and to "prevent undue Chinese penetration and subsequent influence in Indochina so that the peoples of Indochina will not be hampered in their natural developments by the pressure of an alien people and alien interests."[22] Here we have Indochina as a place inhabited by several peoples and susceptible to Chinese penetration and influence. There are still relatively few internal contours (Vietnam is now deemed to have three parts: Cochinchina, Annam, and Tonkin; Indochina is now divided into Vietnam, Cambodia, and Laos), economic features are largely unspecified, and there is not a word of the topographical discussions which later will become so prominent. Indochina is thus a place, or a set of places, which is largely of interest because it is threatened by Vietnamese communists and Chinese (communist) influence. As of yet, there is no claim that Indochina is particularly important to the United States or that there is any basis for a U.S. commitment.

This, too, changes. As the Kuomintang withdraw from the mainland of China, the tone mounts regarding Indochina. In May, 1949, the State Department "considers no effort shld be spared by FR, other Western powers, and non-Commie Asian nations to assure [Bao Dai] experiment best chance succeeding." This "consideration" is still not a commitment but it is clearly moving in that direction: later in the cable, there is discussion of the prospect of recognizing Bao Dai's government and "complying with any request by such Govt for US arms and econ assistance." Less than two weeks later, Chinese pressure is linked to an early ancestor of the domino theory: "while Vietnam out of reach Soviet army it will doubtless be by no means out of reach Chi Commie hatchet men and armed forces"; this could affect "other South Asian govts who stand in most immed danger from Commie conquest Indochina."[23] Indochina is now in the process of being constructed as a fence, or buffer, between communist regimes to the north and noncommunist states to the south.

This characteristic permits Indochina to be a place to which containment logic can be applied. In June, the secretary of defense requests that the National Security Council staff study how to apply containment in Asia as a whole. In July, the deputy under secretary of state calls for "a program of action" on East Asia, including aid for Indochina "to help seal off [the] China border and prevent the spread of Communism into Southeast Asia." Acheson responds favorably, stating that "it is a fundamental decision of American policy that the U.S. does not intend to permit further extension of Communist domination on the Continent of Asia or in the Southeast Asian area."[24]

A full-scale policy review then starts, resulting in NSC 48. (During the review period, the Soviet Union explodes an atomic bomb.) This document assiduously builds up Indochina as a place with all the attributes one might expect of a strategically important location. "The extension of communist authority in China represents a grievous political defeat for us; if southeast Asia also is swept by communism we shall have suffered a major political rout the repercussions of which will be felt throughout the rest of the world, especially in the Middle East and in a then critically exposed Australia." Asia as a whole has strategic value to the United States: keeping it noncommunist denies its power resources, particularly manpower, to the Soviet Union; moreover, "Asia is a source of numerous raw materials, principally tin and natural rubber, which are of strategic importance to the United States." The conclusion of the study is that the U.S. should "support non-Communist forces in taking the initiative in Asia . . . and be prepared to help within our means to meet such threats by providing political, economic, and military assistance and advice where clearly needed to supplement the resistance of the other governments in and out of the area which are more directly concerned."[25]

Policy making now moves quickly. A State Department working group adds more details to the characterization, claiming that:

> Unavoidably, the United States is, together with France, committed in Indochina. That is, failure of the French Bao Dai "experiment" would mean the communization of Indochina. It is Bao Dai (or a similar anticommunist successor) or Ho Chi Minh (or a similar communist successor); there is no other alternative. The choice confronting the United States is to support the French in Indochina or face the extension of Communism over the remainder of the continental area of Southeast Asia and, possibly, farther westward. We then would be obliged to

make staggering investments in those areas and in that part of Southeast
Asia remaining outside Communist domination or withdraw to a much-
contracted Pacific line. It would seem a case of "Penny wise, Pound
foolish" to deny support to the French in Indochina.[26]

That is, Indochina is now a place in which the U.S. is committed even
though it has not as of yet recognized the Bao Dai government or provided military or economic aid (the working group recommends military aid). The U.S. is committed because of where Indochina is and
when the insurgency is taking place (after the communist victory in
China and, most recently, after Ho Chi Minh's provisional government has been recognized by China and the Soviet Union).

On 2 February 1950, Acheson recommends that Truman recognize
the Bao Dai government, along with counterparts in Laos and
Cambodia. The next day, Truman agrees. Several weeks later, a new
NSC report is presented exclusively about Indochina. This mostly
repeats by now familiar arguments with, as one might expect, heightened emphasis given the focus on Indochina alone. We now learn that
Indochina is "the area [of Southeast Asia] most immediately threatened. It is the only area adjacent to communist China which contains
a large European army, which along with native troops is now in
armed conflict with the forces of communist aggression." With this
French-led army, we start to fill in the blanks about what kind of
place Indochina is on the inside: it contains not only communists but
European and "native" anti-communists. Here we find the nucleus of
a future state that could be assisted to defend itself, providing that
things have not gone too far. Hence, it "is important to United States
security interests that all practicable measures be taken to prevent further communist expansion in Southeast Asia. Indochina is a key area
of Southeast Asia and is under immediate threat"; State and Defense
should work together on a program to protect U.S. security interests
in Indochina.[27]

On 9 March, Acheson requests that Truman grant a joint State-
Defense request to provide military aid for Indochina. The memorandum repeats language from earlier documents, although it adds a new
wrinkle: Indochina is the kind of place, because of its border with
China, in which an invasion can be disguised as a nationalist guerrilla
movement.[28] Aficionados of Vietnam war justifications will recognize
in this reasoning subsequent arguments about the "Ho Chi Minh
trail."

The Joint Chiefs of Staff are a bit slow to grasp the State Department's contouring of Indochina. In mid-April, they submit a report referring to Indochina as simply one part in a larger (and strategically vital, of course) Southeast Asia. Within a few days, though, the military is back in line with the argument that "from the military point of view, the key area in Southeast Asia for stopping the spread of communism, is Indo-China."[29]

Thus, within a relatively short period of time, Indochina is constructed as a place of great strategic importance, inhabited by peoples who might be willing to fight against communism, and to which the United States has a commitment. That commitment deepens over the next year, as the Korean War brings major increases in economic and military aid, study missions, government liaison offices of various sorts, new NSC reports, and a gradual thickening of the U.S. presence in Indochina. Yet for all this activity, no one is quite sure what would happen if push comes to shove. In May of 1950, the chargé at Saigon complains that Indochina "may still be in the Twilight zone" in which "we would not know what to do in case of attack"; even after the outbreak of the Korean War, we find an official in the Southeast Asia Affairs Division complaining that State Department officers are still "accustomed to deriding any expressions of concern over the suppression of nationalist movements in Asia as being the result of a preoccupation with the 'patter of naked brown feet' (a patter which I should think would by now have drummed its way into the hearing even of people in Paris)."[30]

The problem for people who want to send in the cavalry is that Indochina has been defined in primarily external terms. Internal characteristics are much hazier: there are too many peoples, too much confusion between communists and anti-colonialists, too vaguely defined a state (French? Indochinese? Vietnamese?). What then are U.S. troops to do "inside"? This internal formlessness of Indochina is precisely the principal argument against Dulles's intervention proposals in the spring of 1954.[31] Only later, with the departure of the French, the advent of the Diem government, and the setting up of an externally and internally well-defined South Vietnamese state, is a structured place (not just a location) finally constituted to which a U.S. commitment can in fact take the form of large scale ground combat with American troops.

This is not to say that the Truman administration's construction of Indochina is unimportant from the standpoint of later policy. Quite the contrary: had it not been for the construction of Indochina as a strategically vital location, worth hundreds of millions of dollars in military aid, it is dubious that the French would have been able to hold on as long as they did in Indochina or that the U.S. would have intervened politically as it did in 1954-56. The Viet Minh would more than likely have come to power in all of Vietnam (and perhaps the rest of Indochina) in the early 1950s; the war, with its million Vietnamese lives lost, might never have taken place. In short, the contouring of Indochina that took place in 1948-50 was necessary, even if not sufficient, to bring about the Kennedy and Johnson escalations more than a decade later.

This analysis permits two theoretical observations. One is how difficult it is to define a place. It appears, at a minimum, that places are far more nested (regions, states, sections), far more complex (peoples, history, borders), and far more subtle (locations, internal features) than the situation descriptions to which our previous research has accustomed us. Yet precisely because places seem both so commonsensical and so much in the background, policy makers rarely set down all the interconnections of their constructions.[32] The second observation pertains to the fragmented nature of changes in place characteristics over time (a phenomenon we have underplayed above). Precisely because of the subtle and yet apparently banal nature of the way in which place characteristics appear to many policy makers, it is quite possible for different individuals or organizations to go on characterizing a place as noticeably different from their colleagues' characterizations. Even though deviant situation descriptions are winnowed out in the policy making process, multiple place characteristics can, at least for a time, continue to exist.[33] Certainly the Pentagon's logistical notion of place is radically different from that of the State Department; although most generals are not high-level policy makers, we can well imagine that their superiors who do fall into this category may matter of factly employ their characterizations. This is a matter for further investigation.

HIGH GROUND: CODIFICATION AND INTERNATIONAL RELATIONS THEORY

The picture of place characterization that emerges from the above analysis is paradoxical. On the one hand, places are constructed as such more slowly and hesitatingly than are situations. On the other hand, as apparently common-sensical claims, there is little or no explicit disagreement about how to characterize a particular place. We thus have a fragmented and uneven process but not an overtly argumentative one. Given that high-level policy making is organized around explicitly competing arguments, this is a curious finding. How to explain it?

Let us recall that place characterization occurs in the context of problem solving. High-level policy makers are engaged in a process of formulating problems and solutions in such a way that other members of the culture accept certain situation descriptions as fitting together while rejecting others as not fitting. Characterizing places explicitly is an adjunct—arguably a necessary one—to this problem solving; it is not, however, an end in itself. Claims that Indochina is near some other place or has certain raw materials are made in order to persuade others to accept or reject a particular pairing of problem and solution. If, however, these claims were in some way problematic or violated the common sense of the culture, they would not be rhetorically useful for problem-solving. Hence, it is precisely their culturally obvious (albeit incoherent or perhaps contradictory) nature that leads them on occasion to be invoked.

A "fact" that "everyone knows" is most useful rhetorically if it has not already been enunciated many times.[34] Quite apart, then, from their role in providing the "about" of situation descriptions (this was our major emphasis above), place characteristics are of greatest persuasive importance early in the policy making process regarding a given issue. We should expect—as in fact we find—that place characteristics flourish precisely in the first stages of policy making; later on, they are made explicit more rarely: in major set-piece policy statements (e.g., guidance for the bureaucracy or the public), for example, or if a new group takes over in high-level policy making.

Place characteristics are rhetorically useful not only when they are first uttered but when they are stated in a canonical or codified fashion. Even the most banal-seeming statements can appear urgent or compelling if they are couched as general observations *cum* rules of international relations or as painfully learned maxims of foreign policy. Again, this does not mean that those who make these statements are hypocrites; on the contrary, such rules or maxims may be their own hard-won lessons. We thus have no reason to doubt the sincerity with which claims such as the following were made:

Question whether Ho as much nationalist as Commie is irrelevant. All Stalinists in colonial areas are nationalists. With achievement natl aims (i.e., independence) their objective necessarily becomes subordination state to Commie purposes and ruthless extermination not only opposition groups but all elements suspected even slightest deviation. On basis examples eastern Eur it must be assumed such wld be goal Ho and men his stamp if included Baodai Govt.

Similarly, there is no reason to assume that references to the "balance of power," the "translation of . . . power potential into military strength," or "political pressure" gained from dealing "with Asiatic peoples who are traditionally submissive to power when effectively applied" are boilerplate with which no one really agrees.[35] Quite the contrary.

Codification, as a rhetorical device in the context of foreign policy making, has two notable features. One we have already alluded to: practicality. A moralistic-sounding statement such as "[w]ithout allies and associates the leader is just an adventurer like Genghis Khan" is useful in a particular problem-solving context (here, arguing that a certain course of action will not solve a given problem).[36] The second aspect of codification is its detailed quality. No matter how general or abstract rules or maxims about specific places may appear to be, they are always tied to a specific policy-making moment. "Lessons" of "Munich" or "Pearl Harbor" are different depending on whether policy makers are discussing Greece and Turkey in 1947, Korea in 1950, Vietnam in 1965, or Iraq in 1990.[37] This polyvalence is evident even when place names are used in purely iconic form: "we don't want another Vietnam," for instance, means something quite different when discussing U.S. Marines in Lebanon and the C. I. A. in Nicaragua—even if in both cases the speaker is the same. Hence, there are infinitely many "lessons" that can be codified from the place characteristics of any historical event; however the broad outlines may be constructed, they emerge only through the details of a policy-making context.

The practicality and detail of place characteristic codifications in policy making distinguish them sharply from codifications employed by scholars of international relations. Nowhere among even the most "policy-relevant" of theorists do we find a problem-solving focus remotely as sharp as among policy makers; nor do even the most subtle theoretical arguments compare in nuance with the place character-

324 DAVID J. SYLVAN AND STEPHEN J. MAJESKI

istic "lessons" routinely adduced by policy makers. Even scholars with a deep appreciation for what "statesmen" do tend to formulate their theoretical positions in a fashion that could not be used for problem solving in the practical and detailed fashion of foreign policy making culture. Compare, for instance, Morgenthau's conception of "status quo" and "imperial" powers with Kennan's Long Telegram: the latter is incomparably more pointed and contextually shaded.

In and of itself, this difference should not come as a great surprise. Certainly we expect scholarship to be less practical—at least immediately so—than policy work; we also know that scholars of a theoretical bent try to abstract from details while policy makers cannot afford that luxury. Still, it is worth emphasizing the difference because of the way in which a particular scholarly research programme has tended to represent its theoretical and empirical arguments. We refer here, of course, to "realism" as the term is understood in the field of international relations research. The "new realists," we are told, "like their classical forebears, study international practice and theorize about it in part to add to the list of 'do's and don'ts' formulated by Thucydides, Morgenthau, and others. The new realists thus continue a tradition that political theorists call 'advice to princes.'"[38] In light of the above discussion, though, such advice bears more than a passing resemblance to that proffered by Polonius to another prince.

Still, even if policy makers do not listen closely, or at all, to what realists say (a state of affairs ruefully admitted by Gilpin), they nonetheless may be said to imbibe realist arguments as part of a general approach to their daily activities.[39] This is a variant of Keynes's famous dictum about the influence of long-dead scribblers on practical men of affairs; the problem with it is that, in practice, it tends to mean very little. No doubt policy makers are predisposed to think that states are important, or wars to be expected, or power a critical component of international relations. However, such statements by themselves are hardly evidence that realist doctrines are used in policy making, since one could find similar statements even among classic "idealists" such as Norman Angell or Arnold Toynbee.[40] What do such statements mean? That policy makers ought to disregard reporting on nonstate movements such as guerrilla forces or (for a nonmilitary example) Buddhist monks? Of course not, since we know that policy makers attend carefully to such reports. Or perhaps the statements mean that war is inevitable and that it is pointless to think about diplomatic routes toward peace. This too is incorrect, since

however much high-level officials may be "hardball" in their orientation, they spend a great deal of time on diplomacy and on finding
ways not to fight. As that quintessential "realist," E. H. Carr, has written, "[t]he impossibility of being a consistent and thorough-going realist is one of the most certain and most curious lessons of political
science. Consistent realism excludes four things which appear to be
essential ingredients of all effective political thinking: a finite goal, an
emotional appeal, a right of moral judgment, and a ground for
action."[41]

Realism thus looks quite unrealistic as a way of capturing how policy-making culture works. Yet for many scholars, the connection
between the two is axiomatic. How can this be? Perhaps the answer is
that realism must be understood on its own rhetorical ground. If writers such as Gilpin can think of themselves as giving advice to princes,
we might wish to ask whom they are actually advising. Not princes, it
appears, but those who read realist works. This suggestion, though,
points to a different rhetorical study, outside the bounds of this paper.
For the time being, the power vacuums and regional hegemons of policy-making work will have to be understood in terms other than the
rhetoric of realism.

NOTES

1. Memorandum of conversation, 8 February 1945, 3:45 P.M., reprinted in
   United States Department of Defense, *United States-Vietnam Relations,
   1945-1967* (Washington, D.C.: U.S. Government Printing Office, 1971), bk. 7,
   V.B.1., 59. This is the public Defense Department edition of the *Pentagon
   Papers*, hereafter cited as *PP*, DoD ed.
2. NSC 64, "The Position of the United States with Respect to Indochina," in
   U.S. Department of State, *Foreign Relations of the United States, 1950* [here-
   after cited as *FRUS, 1950*] (Washington, D.C.: U.S. Government Printing
   Office, 1976-80), 6:745. NSC 64 was circulated on 27 February 1950 and
   approved by Truman on 24 April 1950.
3. Thanks to Jennifer Milliken and the editors of this volume for their comments on earlier drafts of this paper.
4. The relevant studies are David J. Sylvan and Stephen J. Majeski,
   *Constructing the Inevitable: U.S. Foreign Policy Making and the Vietnam
   War* (forthcoming), chaps. 3, 5, 7. Details of our data creation procedures
   may be found in David J. Sylvan, Stephen J. Majeski, and Jennifer L.
   Milliken, "Theoretical Categories and Data Construction in Computational
   Models of Foreign Policy," in *Artificial Intelligence and International*

Politics, ed. Valerie M. Hudson (Boulder, Colo.: Westview, 1991), 327-46; our approach to theory building and model construction is laid out in Stephen J. Majeski and David J. Sylvan, "Modeling Theories of Constitutive Relations in Politics," (typescript, 1994).

5. In recent years, various studies have begun focusing on race and gender in the foreign policy making of various states. See, to begin with, Roxanne Lynn Doty, "The Social Construction of Contemporary International Hierarchy," (Ph.D. diss., University of Minnesota, 1991); Jennifer L. Milliken and David J. Sylvan, "Soft Bodies, Hard Targets, and Chic Theories: U.S. Bombing Policy in Indochina" (paper presented at the World Congress of the International Political Science Association, Buenos Aires, July 1991); and Jutta Eleonore Weldes, "Constructing National Interests: The Logic of U.S. National Security in the Post-War Era," (Ph.D. diss., University of Minnesota, 1993).

6. George Kennan, in Acheson Seminars (at Princeton), transcript of 13-14 February 1954; quoted in Bruce Cumings, *The Roaring of the Cataract, 1947-1950*, vol. 2 of *The Origins of the Korean War* (Princeton: Princeton University Press, 1990), 627.

7. It is, of course, profoundly ironic that McNamara's replacement (Clark Clifford), chosen by Johnson because McNamara was too "dovish," was in fact a dissenter on the war whose arguments helped turn around Johnson's policy of escalation.

8. David J. Sylvan and Hayward R. Alker, Jr., "Foreign Policy as Tragedy: Sending 100,000 Troops to Vietnam" (paper presented at the World Congress of the International Political Science Association, Washington, D.C., August 1988). See also Hayward R. Alker, Jr. and David J. Sylvan, "Some Contributions of Discourse Analysis to Political Science," *Kosmopolis* 24, no. 3 (1994): 5-25.

9. Example: the Kennedy administration's leaks about the Taylor-Rostow mission to South Vietnam in November 1961, when the actual recommendations and decisions were portrayed in the press in terms practically opposite their true nature. Journalists also have a long history of complicity with high-level policy makers, allowing themselves to serve as mouthpieces (e.g., James Reston for Dean Acheson) or even censuring stories that might otherwise prove embarrassing (e.g., the *New York Times* on the Bay of Pigs invasion).

10. Quotation from *FRUS, 1950,* 1:394.

11. Exchange in *PP*, DoD, ed., 10:1361-64.

12. Jennifer L. Milliken, "A Grammar of State Action: U.S. Policymakers' Social Construction of the Korean War" (Ph.D. diss., University of Minnesota, 1994), chap. 6. Cf. W. Lance Bennett, "Political Scenarios and the Nature of Politics," *Philosophy and Rhetoric* 8 (1975): 23-42.

13. Chaim Perelman, *The Realm of Rhetoric*, trans. William Kluback (Notre Dame: University of Notre Dame Press, 1982).

14. In this respect, Perelman seems (ibid., 13) to have shifted position somewhat from his earlier, co-authored, work, there, we find a focus on "the mind's adherence to the theses presented for its assent." Ch. Perelman and L. Olbrechts-Tyteca, *The New Rhetoric: A Treatise on Argumentation*, trans. John Wilkinson and Purcell Weaver (Notre Dame: University of Notre Dame Press, 1969), 4. Cf. Kenneth Burke, *A Rhetoric of Motives* (1950; reprint, Berkeley: University of California Press, 1969), 42, 54, on rhetoric as action-inducing and on opinion as "in the moral order of action."

15. Quotations from Declaration of Independence and Constitution in *FRUS, 1950*, 1:238 and passim. Truman probably wanted the document kept secret because of its economic and budgetary implications, though his original order about secrecy stemmed from concerns about Soviet atomic weapons (in *FRUS, 1950*, 1:142). Regarding epideictic rhetoric, see Aristotle, *Rhetoric*, Loeb Classical Library (1926), 1.9.40: "for epideictic speakers, [the] subject is actions which are not disputed, so that all that remains to be done is to attribute beauty and importance to them." Perelman and Olbrechts-Tyteca in fact attempt to rehabilitate epideictic rhetoric, pointing to its political importance (*New Rhetoric*, 49-51). For the "action" implications of ancient Greek epideictic orations, see Nicole Loraux, *The Invention of Athens: The Funeral Oration in the Classical City*, trans. Alan Sheridan (Cambridge: Harvard University Press, 1986); one might well doubt whether a "pure" epi-deictic (or, for that matter, deliberative or forensic) speech could exist as such.

16. Quotation from *FRUS, 1950*, 1:394. Perhaps the most interesting references to "freedom" are in his 1947 cables written during the formulation of the Truman Doctrine (the "creation," in the words of Acheson's memoirs).

17. Arguably, places are relevant in certain other types of foreign policy making (e.g., decolonization issues; membership in particular international or supra-national organizations), but we do not know how common these are. Economic and environmental policy making, for example, may be geo-graphic in focus but may also be about issues that are not tied to particular places. If there is a distinction, perhaps it has to do with matters of rule or empire.

18. Situations occasionally pertain to times—e.g., "now is not the time to fight"—but statements of this sort presume a consideration of policy with respect to a particular place (e.g., Laos).

19. Gearóid Ó Tuathail, "Foreign Policy and the Hyperreal: The Reagan Administration and the Scripting of 'South Africa,'" in *Writing Worlds: Discourse, Texts, and Metaphors in the Representation of Landscape*, ed. Trevor J. Barnes and James S. Duncan (London: Routledge, 1992), 155-75.

20. Truman to Hurley, 1 August 1945, *PP*, DoD, ed., 8:44; Acheson to Moffat, 5 December 1946, ibid., 8:85. The latter cable was drafted by Charleton Ogburn, Jr. of the Division of Southeast Asia Affairs and Woodruff Wallner of the Division of Western Europe Affairs.

21. Marshall to Paris embassy, 13 May 1947, *PP*, DoD, ed., 8:100-102. This cable, too, was drafted by Ogburn, though not with any Western Europe Affairs Division clearance. Note the routine use of epideictic rhetoric.

22. Lovett to Saigon consul, 22 September 1948, *PP*, DoD, ed., 8:141-2; Department of State, "Policy Statement: Indochina," 27 September 1948, ibid., 8:143-9.

23. Acheson to Saigon consul, 10 May 1949, *PP*, DoD, ed., 8:190-2; Acheson to Hanoi consul, 20 May 1949, ibid., 8:196-9. Ogburn drafted both cables.

24. Johnson to Souers, "United States Policy Toward Asia," *PP*, DoD, ed., 8:218; Rusk to Acheson, "US Policy and Action in Asia," 16 July 1949, quoted in Cumings, *Roaring of the Cataract*, 162; Acheson to Jessup, 18 July 1949, quoted in ibid. Interestingly, these statements were made immediately after U.S. forces were, under Pentagon pressure, withdrawn from Korea.

25. NSC 48/1, "The Position of the United States With Respect to Asia," 23 December 1949, *PP*, DoD, ed., 8:226-64; ibid., 8:266-72. The latter reference contains the slightly revised conclusions of the report; in this form, it was approved by the National Security Council on 29 December.

26. "Military Aid for Indochina," 1 February 1950, *FRUS, 1950*, 6:711-5.

27. NSC 64, "The Position of the United States With Respect to Indochina," 27 February 1950, *FRUS, 1950*, 6:744-7. The report was approved by Truman on 24 April.

28. "Allocation of Funds to Provide Military Assistance to Thailand and Indochina Under Section 303 of the Mutual Defense Assistance Act," *FRUS, 1950*, 6:40-4. Truman approved the request the next day.

29. Johnson to Acheson, 14 April 1950, *FRUS, 1950*, 6:780-1; Lemnitzer to Bruce, "Military Assistance for Indo-China," 19 April 1950, ibid, 6:787-9. In the Johnson memo, the Chiefs suggested that military aid be augmented by economic aid, "psychological programs," and "special covert operations." Acheson requested economic aid for Indochina on 17 April and Truman granted the request on 1 May.

30. Gullion to Acheson, 6 May 1950, *FRUS, 1950*, 6:802-9; Ogburn to Rusk, "Latest Proposals for Indochina," 18 August 1950, ibid., 6:862-4.

31. See William Conrad Gibbons, *The U.S. Government and the Vietnam War: Executive and Legislative Roles and Relationships* (Princeton: Princeton University Press, 1987), vol. 1, chap. 4, for a good discussion of the various attempts by Dulles, Vice President Nixon, and Admiral Radford (chairman of the Joint Chiefs of Staff) to get U.S. military intervention approved. See also the reference by General Ridgway, as part of his topographical and logistical briefings, to the "additional grave complication of a large native population, in thousands of villages, most of which are about evenly divided between friendly and hostile." "Memorandum for Record," 17 May 1954, quoted in ibid., 237.

32. Because the historical argument in this paper is, of necessity, based on the Truman administration; and because we lack systematic access to high-level

primary sources for that administration (this is a matter of logistics: the materials are scattered across the Truman Library, the National Archives, and numerous collections of papers) such as we have enjoyed for the Kennedy and Johnson administrations, it is conceivable that our claim about the sketchiness of place characteristic constructions might end up being modified. Nonetheless, the *FRUS* volumes (and, to a lesser degree, the *Pentagon Papers*) do contain a number of high-level materials; they strongly support the common-sensical and background aspect of places for high-level policy makers.

33. Note that different place characteristics can emerge even when the same metaphors are employed (e.g., "flank"; "vital" region).

34. Cf. Aristotle, *Rhetoric*, 1.2.21 on the usefulness of choosing highly specific *topoi*. Perelman and Olbrechts-Tyteca perhaps overemphasize the benefits of "triteness" in *topoi*: see *New Rhetoric*.

35. Acheson to Hanoi consul, 20 May 1949, *PP*, DoD ed., 8:196 (drafted by Ogburn); NSC 48/1 (see n. 25 above), 228, 254, 239.

36. Statement made by Eisenhower, opposing unilateral employment of U.S. ground combat forces in Indochina, 28 April 1954. Minutes of NSC meeting quoted in Gibbons, *Vietnam War*, 219.

37. It is particularly interesting to compare the use of the Munich analogy by Truman and Johnson, as the latter arguably was modeling his statements after those of the former. Nonetheless, Johnson's Munich differs in several respects from Truman's. For example, Johnson's Munich is one in which a "guardian" is confronted by the spectre of "surrender" in the face of "growing might" and "grasping ambition"; Truman's Munich has none of these characteristics. *Public Papers of the Presidents of the United States: Lyndon B. Johnson, 1965* (Washington, D.C.: U.S. Government Printing Office, 1966), 2:794; *Public Papers of the Presidents of the United States: Harry S. Truman, 1950* (Washington, D.C.: U.S. Government Printing Office, 1965), 742. Interestingly, none of Truman's speeches or public statements in 1947 dealing with the "Truman Doctrine" mention Munich.

38. Robert G. Gilpin, "The Richness of the Tradition of Political Realism," in *Neorealism and Its Critics*, ed. Robert O. Keohane (New York: Columbia University Press, 1986), 320.

39. Ibid., 321; Robert O. Keohane, "Realism, Neorealism and the Study of World Politics," in Keohane, ed., *Neorealism and Its Critics*, 3-4.

40. On the importance of specificity with regard to codified rules about war and peace, see Aristotle, *Rhetoric*, 1.4.9-10.

41. E. H. Carr, *The Twenty Years' Crisis, 1919-1939: An Introduction to the Study of International Relations*, 2d ed., (1946; reprint, London: Macmillan, 1981), 89.

ROXANNE LYNN DOTY

THE LOGIC OF *DIFFÉRANCE* IN INTERNATIONAL RELATIONS
U.S. COLONIZATION OF THE PHILIPPINES

The relationship of the Western peoples to the inferior races, with
which they have come into contact in the course of the expansion they
have undergone, is one of the most interesting subjects in history.[1]

T he categories "western peoples" and "inferior races" to which the
above quotation refers have undergone several transformations
over the past century. Just as these categories were once accepted
as natural, the contemporary categories of "first world/third world,"
"core/periphery," "developed/underdeveloped," "modern/tradi-
tional," and "North/South" are widely regarded in international relations as neutral and unproblematic. They function as a pre-conceptual
frame within which relations among countries so classified can be
analyzed. This is true of a variety of approaches that differ radically
in other ways, yet share these same classificatory schemes. The
approach taken in this study suggests that relations among countries
classified as "North/South" and among peoples previously classified
as "Western peoples" and "inferior races" have functioned as occasions for the construction of identities. Identities, in this study, are
not presumed to exist prior to the discursive practices surrounding
particular issues. Rather, various issues have provided the contexts
within which identities have been constructed.

This study takes particular issue with neorealism which implicitly
suggests an understanding of language and power that precludes the
posing and examination of questions regarding the discursive construction of identities. Defining the essence of international relations
as the rationally calculated pursuit of national interests by unitary
state actors, neorealism regards itself as having captured the enduring
elements and fundamental truths of global political life. While neorealist research programs have devoted precious little attention to

North/South relations, the studies that do exist focus on differential power configurations and the pursuit of self interest by state actors. The issue of identity construction is considered irrelevant.[2]

The empirical case examined in this study suggests that, contrary to the assumptions of neorealism, questions of identity are as central to policy makers as are calculations of power and national interest. This is not to suggest that calculations of power and national interest are unimportant. Rather, it is to suggest that identities precede and help to define interests. For example, in order to have interests that are global in nature, a country must first have an identity as a global power. Identities determine whether one will be permitted to articulate one's own interests and whether that articulation will be taken seriously. To focus solely upon interest defined as the accumulation of power and to assume that identity construction is an already accomplished fact, results in an inadequate understanding of international relations and leaves us with a rather narrow understanding of power. Neorealism gives analytic priority to a kind of power that operates on and through given subjects inhabiting a taken-for-granted world. To do so elides other forms of power that are implicated in the very construction of worlds and their inhabitants. Therefore, a post-realist study needs to politicize the ways in which difference, a key component in identity construction, has been articulated on a global scale. My analysis focuses on an early and fiercely debated foreign policy decision that inaugurated the U.S. as a colonial power, the U.S. colonization of the Philippines at the turn of the century. Regarding language as *productive*, I suggest that the division of the world into what is now referred to as "North/South" (and was once referred to as "Western peoples" and "inferior races") is a function of a particular discursive logic that socially constructs different kinds of subjects and relationships between them.

The discursive practices embedded in the debates and commentaries surrounding the U.S. decision to colonize the Philippines exemplify the social construction of international identities in one specific historical instance of "North/South" relations. These practices constructed a world in which subjects were inscribed with particular qualities that made certain policies and courses of action rather unremarkable. The discursive practices I examine in this study are from a variety of sources ranging from official/government texts to those of scholars, non-academic writers, travel writers, and anti-imperialists. They suggest that realist explanations are incomplete in an important sense. Imperialism did not result in all cases where imbalances of power existed. Though the United States arguably had the capabilities to do so, colonizing Spain after the Spanish-American War was never seriously contemplated as a possibility. Power differentials were not the only nor necessarily the most important factor making colonization possible. Rather, as I suggest below, colonial relationships have a distinctly social logic by which actors construct themselves and others and the "reality" that makes practices such as colonialism possible. At the beginning of the Spanish-American War the absorption of an entire archipelago in the "Orient" was unthinkable. Over a relatively short period of time, however, "knowledge," "truth(s)," and identities were constructed such that this action came to be not only thinkable but necessary.

In exploring this question, I use a "textual" approach which stresses the productive nature of language.[3] Neorealism brings with it an implicit theory of language in which it is regarded as reflective of rather than constitutive of "reality" and the possibilities "reality" holds. In contrast, a textual approach suggests that subjects, objects, and practices are not brute facts. In fixing names to things we establish their existence and their relationships to other things. What subjects and objects *are* to us depends upon their representation in language. An analysis of the debates over annexation of the Philippines demonstrates that discursive practices were central rather than epiphenomenal to the production of international possibilities.

Focusing on language or discourse permits us to conceive of imperial relationships as processes of constructing "knowledge" about those being colonized as well as those doing the colonizing. It is a process that constructs the sovereign as well as the non-sovereign. Such a conceptualization suggests that social actors are not given prior to practices, but rather are socially produced and reproduced by practice(s). Such a conceptualization also suggests that imperialism is a social or cultural practice in which power and knowledge cross in complex ways. In the following sections I examine how international identities were constructed by drawing upon certain presuppositions regarding race and gender and how these identities made colonization possible. In my concluding section I suggest that Derrida's concept of *différance* is useful in elucidating how differences were constructed in this particular case and how they may continue to be constructed.

THE WHITE MAN'S BURDEN

In 1899 Rudyard Kipling wrote the now well-known poem, "The White Man's Burden." This poem was a call for the United States to assume the kind of responsibilities embodied in British colonial rule. "Take up the White Man's burden. Send forth the best ye breed." Kipling's words were published in *McClure's Magazine* shortly before final action on the Paris Peace Treaty by which the Philippines were formally annexed by the United States. U.S. Senator Benjamin Tillman recited the poem in full during the Senate debates on Philippine annexation.[4] How the "white man's burden option" came to be regarded as the only viable course of action for the United States involved a complex interplay between race and gender as well as the invocation of parental and animal analogies whereby the essence of the Filipino was constructed as the opposite or other to "American manhood." Not to colonize the Philippines was represented as an affront to "American manhood."

Tropes of inferiority work in both subtle and not so subtle ways. How signifiers such as race and gender come into play is contingent and variable. For example, Susan Jeffords has suggested that gender, in specific situations, has worked to overcome/erase racial difference and construct a masculine bond.[5] In contrast, this particular case suggests that gendered and racialized "other(s)" complemented one another and enabled the construction of American manhood. Race and gender worked together to construct a distinctly American version of the white man who was simultaneously differentiated from and yet bonded to his British/European counterpart. Analogies to children and animals were also fundamental to this construction. Filipinos were alternatively regarded as children or animal-like, both opposites to "man."

Victory at Manila Bay presented the possibility of the United States becoming a colonial power, a possibility which, at one level, if realized would go against all for which the U.S. ostensibly stood. To some, this possibility threatened to cause the U.S. to "forget what we are and for what we stand."[6] At the same time, *not* to annex the Philippines presented the equally grave possibility that the United States would cease to be a place "where a man can stand up by virtue of his manhood and say I am a man."[7] If the United States did not act upon this opportunity to take the Philippines, the rest of the world might come to regard it as "so effeminate that we are incompetent to colonize, to develop, and to govern territorial possessions."[8]

American manhood, as these excerpts illustrate, was linked with the ability and willingness to annex, to colonize, to take what "men" implicitly had the right, by virtue of their manhood, to take. The Philippine Islands and their inhabitants were symbolic means by which American manhood could be reproduced. The act of colonizing was an affirmation of manhood. Although not wishing to be like their rapacious British/European counterparts, to simply let this opportunity slip away would be tantamount to announcing to the world one's impotence. The Philippines were simply there for the taking, prizes to be lost, won, and passed among the victors. Professor Dean C. Worcester of the University of Michigan, member of President McKinley's First Philippine Commission, suggested that the Spanish in the Philippines had "lost much of their virility" and for the United States to withdraw from the islands "would stultify ourselves in the eyes of the world."[9]

Still, "taking the Philippines" could not be represented as brutal and forceful rape of a defenseless victim. Unlike Spain, whose colonial rule was maintained through the inspiration of fear, U.S. rule would be based upon love and sympathy. "That the America's conception of the moral duties attaching to conquest will be very different to theirs can hardly be a subject of doubt."[10] The distinctly American version of manhood enabled the United States to carry out civilizing missions that would be different from those of Europe. It thereby became the duty of the United States to annex the Philippines to prevent them from becoming the "spoil of other nations." The United States could colonize without resorting to the harsh and repressive colonial methods of Europe. The difficult and noble task of restoring "peace and order in those islands" and giving "their people an opportunity for self-government and for freedom under the protecting shield of the United States" were tasks that "American civilization and American manhood were up to."[11]

Opponents of colonization also focused on its implications for American manhood. American manhood was threatened by the possibility of becoming more like the colonizing powers of Europe, giving way to the "lust for imperial splendor" and corrupting the integrity of the United States. American manhood was inextricably linked to the integrity of the American republic. "The glory of the American Republic is that it is the embodiment of American manhood."[12] As the debates indicate, however, American manhood could lead to conflicting conclusions as to the appropriate course of action. The dilemma of whether to colonize or not to colonize could not be resolved by invoking gendered identities alone. Nancy Stephan suggests that the "lower races" have represented the female type of the human species and females have represented the "lower races" of gender.[13] United States' colonial discourse supports this suggestion. Racialized constructions of identity supplemented gender and pointed increasingly toward a duty, an obligation to colonize.

THE WHITE MAN'S BURDEN

American manhood was supplemented by the binary oppositions of advanced/superior and backward/inferior races. Being a White Man involved a relation of superior to inferior and was a form of power and authority over non-whites.[14] It was a way of distinguishing self from other. The racial classifications found in the U.S. colonial discourse carried with them the implicit identification of the "lower" races with sub-orders of humanity. Both opponents and advocates of colonization drew upon racialized oppositions. Anti-imperialist Andrew Carnegie, believed that "contact of the superior race with the inferior race demoralizes both." Antiimperialist David Starr Jordan concurred. "Wherever we have inferior and dependent races within our borders today, we have a political problem."[15] In the end, "race" played a pivotal role in making the act of conquest possible. The words of Senator Albert Beveridge echoed Kipling's theme.

> We will not renounce our part in the mission of our race, trustees under God, of the civilization of the world. And we will move forward to our work, not howling out regrets like slaves whipped to their burdens, but with gratitude for a task worthy of our strength and thanksgiving to Almighty God that He has marked us as his chosen people, henceforth to lead in the regeneration of the world.[16]

While there existed differences in opinion as to whether the U.S. should colonize the Philippines, all parties to the debates shared the presupposition that the non-white Filipinos were inferior to the white race. This consensus added to the United States' dilemma. One alternative to colonization was the incorporation of the Philippines into the territory of the United States. Racial difference was fundamental to those who opposed incorporation. For example, Senator Augustus Turner, who opposed annexation, argued that acquisition of the

Philippines would either lead to a situation of tyranny and slavery of the Filipino population by the U.S., a situation that would "corrupt the integrity of our people," or to a situation of universal miscegenation:

> . . . it would do such violence to our blood, to the history and traditions of our race, and would leave such frightful results in mongrelizing our citizenship, that the advocates of the new movement in favor of a greater America prefer the alternative risk of debauching our institutions rather than do that, by an assimilating miscegenation which will certainly impoverish and debilitate our citizenship.[17]

The possibility of an equal status for Filipinos was unthinkable because they were regarded as essentially different kinds of human beings. Carl Schurz, a prominent antiimperialist, was also opposed to incorporating the Philippines into the United States; it would be impossible to Americanize the Philippines:

> Whatever we may do for their improvement, the people of the Spanish Antilles will remain in overwhelming numerical predominance, Spanish Creole and negroes, and the people of the Philippines, Filipinos, Malays, Tagals, and so on—some of them quite clever in their way, but the vast majority utterly alien to us, not only in origin and language, but in habits, traditions, ways of thinking, principles, ambitions—in short, in most things that are of the greatest importance in human intercourse and especially in political cooperation.[18]

Incorporating the Philippines then, would either result in (1) two kinds of Americans; the first enjoying the privileges of taking part in the government, the second being ruled by the first, a situation which would be a violation of the Declaration of Independence as well as of the civic virtue the United States prided itself upon, or (2) a mongrelization of U.S. citizens.

Whitelaw Reid was the publisher of the *New York Tribune* and an American member of the Hispanic-American Commission that met in Paris to negotiate an end to the Spanish-American War and a settlement regarding the Philippine Islands. In September of 1898 his article, "The Territory With Which We Are Threatened," appeared in *Century Magazine*. It attracted universal attention. The territory with which the U.S. was threatened was the Philippines. The reason they posed a threat sprang from the fear that ultimately they might be admitted into the Union as a State. Reid asserted that there was no more urgent public duty than to resist the concession of such a possibility. Admission into the Union would constitute "a degeneration and degradation of the homogeneous, continental Republic of our pride too preposterous for the contemplation of serious and intelligent men."[19]

Race like gender, though, could lead to different conclusions regarding annexation of the Philippines. It was when parent/child and animal analogies were linked with gendered and racialized identities that colonization became the only reasonable course of action. In the words of President McKinley, "There was nothing left to do but take them all and educate the Filipinos and uplift and civilize them."[20]

THE WHITE MAN'S BURDEN

Sander Gilman has suggested that categories such as "sexuality," "race," and "illness" have at various points in history overlapped and supplemented one another.[21] United States' colonial discourse suggests also the significance of attributes linked with children and animals. White male identity was not only constructed vis-à-vis its gendered and racialized other, but also vis-à-vis its childlike and uncivilized/animal-like other. It was these attributes that were essential to making colonization possible. Filipino identity was constructed as "other" to white American manhood, which was presumed to be inherently civilized, rational, and humane. By invoking analogies to children and animals, and linking them with racial and gendered identities, both the American "self" and the Filipino "other" were constructed in such a manner that colonization was not only made possible, but as McKinley's words suggest, was the only reasonable course of action.

Filipino identity moved between two poles, both closer to nature than the "rational" American white man. When more benignly portrayed, the Filipino was childlike, lacking the kind of rationality generally attributed to adults. The Filipino was impulsive, imitative, and lacking any reflection as to the consequences of actions.

> The Filipino, like most Orientals, is a good imitator, but having no initiative genius, he is not efficient in anything. He has no attachment

for any occupation in particular. Today he will be at the plough, tomor-
row a coachman, a collector of accounts, a valet, a sailor, and so on; or
he will suddenly renounce social trammels in pursuit of lawless
vagabondage. The native never looks ahead; he is never anxious about
the future; but if left to himself, he will do all sorts of imprudent things,
from sheer want of reflection on the consequences, when as he puts it,
"his head is hot" from excitement due to any cause.

Less benignly portrayed, the Filipino identity was in many ways
more akin to an animal than to a human being.

So long as he gets his good and fair treatment, and his stipulated
wages paid in advance, he is content to act as a general utility man. If
not pressed too hard, he will follow his superior like a faithful dog.
Even over mud and swamp, a native is almost as sure-footed as a goat
on the brink of a quarry. I have frequently been carried for miles in a
hammock by four natives and relays through morassy districts too dangerous to travel on horseback. They are great adepts at climbing wherever it is possible for a human being to scale a height; like monkeys,
they hold as much with their feet as with their hands; they ride any
horse barebacked without fear; they are utterly careless about jumping
into the sea among the sharks, which sometimes they will intentionally
attack with knives, and I never knew a native who could not swim.[22]

The animal analogy was not confined to travel writers such as John
Foreman. Senator Henry Cabot Lodge, an expansionist who argued in
favor of United States' annexation and the subsequent suppression of
the Philippine insurrection, suggested that "A native family feeds; it
does not breakfast or dine, it feeds. A wooden bowl of rice with perhaps a little meat stewed in with it, is put on the floor; the entire family squats around it; the fingers are used to convey the food into the
mouth. I have never seen any Filipino eat otherwise."[23] Filipinos were
positioned in a relation of similarity to dogs, monkeys, and other animals that "feed" rather than "dine." They were rendered specimens
subject to observation, analysis, and judgment by the commanding
gaze of the West.

These constructions rendered the Filipinos incapable of self-government and in need of guidance, tutoring, and uplifting. The shifting
between child and animal analogies made possible a wide range of
practices. At a fundamental level, Filipino identity was such that they

were not capable of articulating their own interests. The obligation thus fell to the United States "to do for the Filipinos more and better than the mass of people can ask or think."[24] They must be "willingly or unwillingly brought into the light." Protests on the part of the Filipinos that they had won their independence from Spain and that the United States had no jurisdiction over the Philippines could thus be ignored. The parent/child analogies pointed insistently toward tutoring and guidance. The uncivilized animal analogies enabled the use of force and violence to accomplish this noble task. "These alien people, the Mohammedans, these people accustomed to revolution, and to blood and to disorder" would compel the U.S. to use cruelty: "nothing but the strong hand, nothing but cruelty, nothing but the iron rule will enable us to maintain that dominion."[25] The justifications for the control of others and the use of force to do so were located in the inherent nature of those "others." John Barrett, U.S. minister to Siam, suggested that "the Asiatic appears to best advantage in lands which are dependent on some strong European government. Although civilization may not always seem to help him, it does far better by him when dispensed through forceful foreign hands than when caught in a haphazard way through his own agency."[26] U.S. Senator Augustus Bacon argued that "Only with the sword and gun can millions of semicivilized be kept in subjection."[27]

Identities so constructed rendered defensible and necessary practices that otherwise would have been deemed reprehensible. The United States could remain benevolent and civilized while engaging in the brutal subjugation of a distant population. The hierarchical classification of human beings implied different inherent rights attached to those human beings.

Only certain kinds of subjects could serve as the basis for territories and peoples that would be recognized as sovereign. The identity of subjects determined their status in the international system, i.e., sovereign or dependent. The attributes attached to the subjects were also attached to geographical space, thus constructing the United States and the Philippines as particular kinds of subjects, creating certain possibilities and precluding others.

FIELD OF POSSIBILITIES

The classifications discussed above functioned to differentiate subjects, simultaneously positioning them vis-à-vis one another, and thereby creating certain possibilities. Important policy implications followed. Some courses of action were made possible and others impossible; a "field of possibilities" was created.

On the one hand the Philippines were made annexable or colonizable. Even those who opposed annexation participated in a construction of the Filipino that made such a course of action possible. The use of physical force was made possible and indeed justified in advance. The Filipino was constructed as the kind of subject who often mistook kindness for weakness. One of the reasons that Bacon opposed annexation was that the U.S. would be forced to go against its most cherished principles and resort to force. The reason for this was that the Filipinos would not understand conciliation, "nothing but the strong hand, nothing but cruelty, nothing but the iron rule will enable us to maintain that dominion."[28] Travel writer Foreman also suggested that non-European races did not understand acts of generosity. Stanford's David Starr Jordan had suggested that only brute forces could hold certain peoples to industry and order.

The same discursive practices concomitantly created certain impossibilities, insofar as certain courses of action did not enter into the realm of conceivable possibilities. The Philippines would not be left alone to handle their own affairs, command their own resources, or engage in diplomatic relations with other countries. On the world stage, the Philippines were not international actors. In contrast to approaches such as neorealism which take sovereign states as given, this analysis illustrates how sovereignty itself gets constructed and linked with other attributes, thus constituting particular kinds of international subjects.

Discursive practices constructed both "sovereign" and "colonizable" identities. The intertextual nature of this analysis lends support to the assertion that a particular "regime of truth" was widely accepted. A deconstructive reading of the texts also suggests that the terms that constituted the subject identities and the relationships among different subjects had no inherent meaning. For example, the term "civilized" did not inherently *refer* to a way of being in the world. There was no intrinsic meaning to being "civilized." One could argue that "civilized" pointed to or referred to subjects who were "lovers of liberty" as these texts implied. But, "lovers of liberty" itself had no intrinsic meaning that would permit it to unproblematically and naturally characterize certain subjects. Certainly, the Filipinos considered themselves "lovers of liberty." We could try to

point to an "empirical" state of affairs that would be indicative of subjects who were "lovers of liberty," perhaps the absence of slavery.
Such a meaning however, would mean that the United States was not
civilized until 1865. Even if we could reach agreement on this meaning, there would remain the problem that "slavery" itself has no
intrinsic meaning. We could say that "slavery" refers to the absence of
"freedom," but then to what does "freedom" refer? Certainly, after
annexation the Philippines were not free. Are we to assume that by
implication this meant that the U.S. was not civilized since the U.S.
was the reason the Philippines were not free? We could go on indefinitely with this case. My point, however, is that the content of the
terms I have been referring to in this case as well as the other terms
examined in this study acquired their "positivity" only in relation to
other terms.

The concept of *différance* is useful here. Derrida has used this term
to describe the play of difference in language: "every concept is
inscribed in a chain or in a system within which it refers to the other,
to other concepts, by means of the systematic play of differences.
Such a play, *différance*, is thus no longer simply a concept, but rather
the possibility of conceptuality, of a conceptual process and system in
general."[29] *Différance* then is the very possibility of meaning. One
sense of this term indicates *difference*. As discussed above, the attributes attached to the subjects of these texts acquired meaning only by
virtue of *differing* from other attributes, civilized/uncivilized, enlight-
ened/despotic. Another sense of *différance* is that of *deferring*, which
refers to the fact that meanings are never fixed or stable, i.e., signi-
fieds become signifiers in an endless signifying chain. The circulation
of signs defers the moment in which we can encounter the thing
itself.[30] In the above texts, what the terms ultimately referred to could
be endlessly deferred. The fact that meanings were widely taken to be
fixed, at least temporarily, is indicative of the inextricable link
between power and "knowledge" or power and "truth." This link, in
effect, stops the signifying chain and permits meaning to become naturalized, taken for granted. It thus makes possible certain practices
that are consistent with these meanings.

How were meanings naturalized? Each of the oppositions
depended upon a point of differentiation, a point where civilized
became differentiated from uncivilized. This differentiation was made
possible by a dominant signifier. This dominant signifier may be
thought of as the center of the discursive structure, which both makes

the structure itself possible and limits its play. It is the point where the substitution of signifiers is no longer possible.[31] What was this dominant signifier, the center of this discursive structure? I would suggest that a distinctly American version of "white man" was the dominant signifier in these texts. The terms "civilized," "enlightened," "lovers of liberty," "benevolent," and so on became fused and came to rest with "white man" while the opposites, such as uncivilized and unenlightened came to rest with the "non-white other." "White man" was the reference point in relation to which the oppositional distinctions could be posited. "White man" was given transcendental status, implicitly understood to exist outside of the discursive system instead of itself being constructed by that system. However, as suggested above, a deconstructive reading of these texts calls this status into question. This analysis suggests that "white man" was itself a discursive construction, whose meaning depended upon its opposite.

In one sense the "findings" of this study are quite unremarkable. It is not that surprising to find that U.S. foreign policy discourse at the turn of the century was racist. Still, the ideas, values, "reality" instantiated in this discourse facilitated the practices that led to the deaths of over one million Filipinos. Contrary to what neorealism would suggest, my analysis illustrates that these things were not epiphenomal. Interestingly, and perhaps somewhat ironically, this analysis is not entirely incompatible with a neorealist analysis. Neorealists would likely claim that the United States was merely doing what came naturally. "Where gross imbalances of power exist, and where the means of transportation permit the export of goods and of the instruments of rule, the more capable people ordinarily exert a considerable influence over those less able to produce surpluses."[32] What neorealism ignores, though, is that calculations of national interest and the use of military and/or economic power take place within a social context, a world consisting of subjects, objects, and relationships. It is the constructing of social contexts, the making of worlds that neorealism either ignores or takes as epiphenomal. United States' colonial discourse suggests this world making was central to enabling this particular foreign policy practice. This case suggests that if we want to understand possibilities for international relations more generally, it is important to examine the processes that construct the "reality" upon which such relations are based. Although the categories and specific oppositional elements present in this study may not constitute our current "reality," it is possible that the underlying logic has remained quite similar. For example, we could speculate that "white man" had been supplanted by "developed nation." This logic permits a general symbolic economy by which the "other" is constructed as the different and deferred "self." This has been particularly significant in the construction of possibilities for that aspect of international relations known as "North/South relations." Discussions of a new, post-cold war world order have for the most part been silent on North/South relations. Studies along the lines suggested here are important for assessing the alternative possibilities for this aspect of international relations.

NOTES

1. Benjamin Kidd, *Control of the Tropics* (New York: Charles Scribner's Sons, 1898), 56.
2. Two prominent studies on North/South relations that are illustrative of the realist approach are Stephen Krasner, *Structural Conflict: The Third World Against Global Liberalism.* (Berkeley: University of California Press, 1985) and Robert W. Tucker, *The Inequality of Nations* (New York: Basic Books, Inc., 1977).
3. Michael J. Shapiro, "Textualizing Global Politics," in Shapiro and James Der Derian, eds., *International/Intertextual Relations* (Lexington, Mass.: Lexington Books, 1989) provided an excellent discussion of what is entailed in such an approach. See also Roxanne Lynn Doty, "Foreign Policy As Social Construction: A Post-Positivist Analysis of U.S. Counterinsurgency in the Philippines," *International Studies Quarterly* 37, no. 3 (1993): 297-320.
4. *Congressional Records,* 55th Congress, 3d sess., 1898-1899: 1531-32.
5. Susan Jeffords, *The Remasculinization of America—Gender and the Vietnam War* (Bloomington and Indianapolis: Indiana University Press, 1989).
6. David Starr Jordan, *Imperial Democracy* (New York: D. Appleton and Company, 1901), 41.
7. George Hoar, *Congressional Records,* 55th Congress, 3d sess., 1898-1899: 496.
8. George Hoar and David Nelson, *Congressional Records,* 55th Congress, 3d sess., 1898-1899: 496 and 834.
9. Richard Drinnon, *Facing West: The Metaphysics of Indian Hating and Empire Building* (Minneapolis: University of Minnesota Press, 1980).
10. John Foreman, *The Philippine Islands* (New York: Charles Scribner's Sons, 1899).
11. Henry Cabot Lodge, *Congressional Records,* 55th Congress, 3d sess., 1898-1899: 834.

12. Whitelaw Reid, *Problems of Expansion as Considered in Papers and Addresses* (New York: The Century Co., 1900), 14.
13. Nancy Leys Stephan, "Race and Gender: The Role of Analogy in Science" in *Anatomy of Racism*, ed. David Goldberg (Minneapolis: University of Minnesota Press, 1990).
14. Edward Said, *Orientalism* (New York: Vintage Books, 1979).
15. Jordan, *Imperial Democracy*, 32.
16. Albert Beveridge, *Congressional Records*, 56th Congress, 1st sess., 6 January 1900.
17. Augustus Turner, *Congressional Records*, 55th Congress, 3d. sess., 1898-1899: 785.
18. Carl Schurz, "American Imperialism," in *Republic or Empire—The Philippine Question*, ed. William Jennings Bryan (Chicago: The Independence Company, 1899).
19. Reid, *Problems of Expansion*, 14.
20. H.W. Brands, *Bound to Empire—The United States and the Philippines* (New York: Oxford University Press, 1992), 25.
21. Sander Gilman, *Difference and Pathology: Stereotypes of Sexuality, Race, and Madness* (Ithaca and London: Cornell University Press, 1985).
22. Foreman, *The Philippine Islands*, 182-89.
23. Henry Cabot Lodge, *Congressional Records*, 56th Congress, 1st sess., 7 March 1900: 2632.
24. Marion Wilcox, "The Filipino's Vain Hope of Independence," *North American Review* 171 (1900): 333-47.
25. Jehu Bacon, *Congressional Records*, 18 January 1899, 55th Congress, 3d sess., 1898-1899: 638.
26. John Barrett, "America in the Pacific and Far East," *Harpers* (June-November 1899): 919.
27. Bacon, *Congressional Records*, 1898-1899: 738.
28. Ibid.
29. Jacques Derrida, "*Différance*," in *Margins of Philosophy*, trans. Alan Bass (Chicago: University of Chicago Press, 1968), 11.
30. Ibid., 9.
31. Jacques Derrida, "Structure, Sign, and Play in the Discourse of the Human Sciences," in *Writing and Difference*, trans. by Alan Bass (Chicago: University of Chicago Press, 1978), 279.
32. Kenneth Waltz, *Theory of International Politics* (Reading, Mass.: Addison-Wesley, 1979), 26.

FRANKE WILMER

INDIGENOUS PEOPLES, MARGINAL SITES, AND THE CHANGING CONTEXT OF WORLD POLITICS

Seneca historian John Mohawk tells a story of a phone call he received while he was editor of *Akwesasne Notes*.[1] The phone rang at 3 A.M. At the other end was a very excited voice yelling into the receiver "Please help us! You must help us quickly! They are going to wake up the lizard and we will *all* die!"

John rubbed his eyes, and realized upon waking more fully that this middle-of-the-night caller spoke English with a strange, non-European but British accent. "Wait a minute, calm down now. Who is this and *where are you calling from?*" John asked. He learned that the caller was an Aboriginal Australian who had heard of *Akwesasne Notes'* involvement in international indigenous issues. A mining company, it seemed, was about to begin drilling on Aboriginal sacred land. According to Aboriginal oral tradition, a huge sleeping lizard lived beneath the earth in that area. All of "us"—human beings, animals, trees and the entire natural world we live in—are in the lizard's dream. If the lizard awakens, the dream will cease to exist.

Aboriginal oral tradition represents a version of reality that provides the context and meaning of Aboriginal life. Another version of reality—let us call it the western scientific narrative—might refer to large uranium deposits in the area to be drilled. A voice within that narrative, let us say the ecologist, argues for prohibitions against drilling in that area so as not to release nuclear reactive materials into the atmosphere and water systems, which may well poison all of "us" by working its way through the food chain.[2] In this case it seems that there is one reality but two different ways of knowing it. It would also appear that aboriginal oral tradition, thousands of years old, contained some important knowledge that the western scientific tradition did not contain until within the last few decades.

The problem with realism is that it validates only one interpretation of reality, or, said differently, it validates only one way of experi-
encing reality, denying the validity of others. According to the
realists' version of reality, international relations consists of relations
among nation states seeking power to influence the international distribution of values. Power, according to realists, is the ability to exert
control over people, resources, territory, and value-allocating institutions. "Sovereignty"—the inviolability of jurisdictional boundaries
and the freedom of governments to behave arbitrarily and without
restraint—is the organizing principle of world (dis)order, which can
be more accurately described in terms of international anarchy.

Another version of reality is that international relations consists of
relations among nation states, indigenous nations, and other transnational and international non-state actors. These actors engage in global
discourse, bargaining over the inclusion of a variety of values to be
allocated internationally. Although sovereignty is an illusive concept,
states clearly participate in world order on the basis of sovereign
equality, subject to certain restraints; for example, the use of force in
relations among states is prohibited. The concept of "human rights"—
rights that individuals and groups may assert against unrestrained and
arbitrary uses of government power—provides an organizing principle
for world order. These human rights include not only political freedoms and due process, but the right of individuals to exist within and
pursue a distinct path of cultural evolution. According to the alternative version, human beings can coexist within the limits of the natural
world, but they cannot, ultimately, control it. Power is the ability to
give and sustain life and to enhance life-giving capabilities. And there
are certainly many, many other versions of reality. There may be as
many as four thousand distinct ethnic groups, each representing a
unique path of cultural evolution with its own unique universe of cultural context and meaning, or "version of reality."[3]

Is it not increasingly apparent, in light of the multicultural composition of our cities, our nation states, and our world society, that we
must find a way to coexist in tolerance of many versions of reality?
This does not necessarily conflict with global and national civic discourse and the various degrees of normative agreement such discourse facilitates. Anthropologist Ken Taylor, whom I interviewed
while he was executive director of Survival International, spoke of his
experience with a South American Yanomamo community in the
1970s.[4] He described the Yanomamo practice of roaming as they har-

vested the rainforest for food and how a particular community might host representatives or scouts from other Yanomamo communities. The various Yanomamo communities were understood as having local cultural variations, and when entertaining these visitors, the Yanomamo had developed a short phrase to refer to communications impasses caused by cultural differences. It means something like "I cannot understand this aspect of your behavior because it comes from a difference in your culture and I simply accept the difference." This prevented a breakdown of communication and any unnecessary conflict or hostility that might otherwise follow from intercultural differences. We might consider the "invention" of this phrase (which in my own language I have never been able to reduce to less than twenty words), as a kind of social technology. I use the term "technology" as the application of knowledge to solve problems. In this case, the problem is a social or communicative problem.

The need to restructure global and national political orders, both cognitively and substantively, in a matter compatible with the coexistence of multiple and diverse world views and identities is increasingly imperative. In light of this, a concept such as the Yanomamo word for accepting "the impossibility of some aspects of intercultural communication" would represent a tremendous breakthrough. Once international relations and other fields of social science drop the assumption that indigenous peoples represent some "primitive" or "earlier" stage of western development, they become open to admitting of the possibility that something truly important and valuable can be *learned* from indigenous peoples. Indigenous peoples' technologies—social, environmental, or political—will never be taken seriously within the realist paradigm.

INTERNATIONAL INDIGENOUS ACTIVISM

The United Nations Commission on Human Rights Sub-Commission on Prevention of Discrimination and Protection of Minorities Working Group on Indigenous Populations met for the twelfth year in 1994 to continue their work toward developing a draft declaration on the rights of indigenous peoples. In attendance were ten organizations of indigenous peoples with U.N. observer status,[5] eighty-four other indigenous peoples' nations and organizations, observers from twenty-nine nation states and a host of other interested international non-governmental organizations.

Can realism account for the articulation of common interests and political activism among a global alliance of two million indigenous people of the Cordillera region of the Philippines, one million Mapuche in Chile, 600,000 tribal people of the Chittagong hill tracts in Bangladesh, three and one-half million North American native people, 50,000 Kuna living east of the Panama Canal, one million "Small Peoples of the Soviet North,"[6] and the approximately two hundred ninety-five million other indigenous people spread throughout the world?

A realist perspective on international politics does not address the possibility of collective action and normative conflicts for at least two reasons. First, realism focuses on the state, associations and relationships among states, and the influence of non-state actors *on* states, but not on the normative basis of world order itself. Second, the relevant processes are either limited to those involving state-to-state relations or, at best, the formation of regimes as intervening variables in interstate relations. The *context* of international relations is either assumed to remain relatively fixed, to change very little and very slowly, or to be irrelevant.

According to realist thinking, unarmed indigenous peoples, whose claims to economic resources have been routinely superseded by those of modernizing states for five centuries, should not be capable of influencing the global distribution of power and values. Among groups engaged in international activism, indigenous peoples have the least control over any significant international power resources. They fight few "hot wars," and even when they do, they do so with the poorest, least technologically advanced weapons.[7] Indeed, they do not even possess the most fundamental international political "resource" that at least affords peoples of the Third World a seat at the table of world politics—internationally recognized sovereignty. Although indigenous peoples make up a majority of the population in Bolivia, Guatemala, and East Malaysia, they do not control the political institutions of any state. Because they have no way of coercively influencing the international allocation of values, the experience of indigenous peoples is perceived to be marginal to the study of international relations from the perspective of the realist paradigm.

Yet it is precisely because the influence of indigenous activism is anomalous to realism that it ought to be taken seriously. Politics is about power, and power is about the use of resources to influence. The international indigenous movement draws attention to the use of persuasive, rhetorical and symbolic power, yet the realist paradigm has primarily focused on military and economic resources used to obtain, maintain, and redistribute power on a global scale. The influence of indigenous voices on the rhetoric of international discourse is evidenced, among other things, by the fact that terms denying the moral competence of indigenous peoples—"backward," "uncivilized," or "primitive," for instance—are falling into disuse.

Armed with the power of protest, direct action, and moral suasion, indigenous activists and advocates have an impressive record of using these symbolic forms of power to influence international actors. For example:

- A number of national governments reported to the United Nations Working Group on Indigenous Peoples in 1991 on constitutional and legislative reforms implemented in order to recognize the rights and special status of indigenous peoples.[8]
- The Australian government has committed itself to negotiate a treaty—the first ever—with the country's Aboriginal people.[9]
- Multilateral development banks have withdrawn support from ongoing projects in response to the political activism of indigenous groups affected by the projects.
- The World Bank issued guidelines to consider the impact of development projects on indigenous peoples.[10]
- The International Labor Organization revised a convention to eliminate its paternalistic tone toward indigenous peoples.[11]
- The Mohawk Nation has established a permanent delegation in Europe.
- A lawsuit was filed in New York in 1993 against Texaco for its disregard for the impact of oil exploration on the indigenous peoples and the ecosystem of the Ecuadorian Oriente. As a result, Texaco has pulled out of the area, estimating that the legal costs render the investment too costly.[12]
- An alliance among the James Bay Cree, Inuit of northern Quebec, and environmental and indigenous activists in the United States and Canada has successfully defeated plans for a $50 million Canadian hydroelectric power project.

Because the demands of indigenous peoples have relied almost exclusively on the weight of moral suasion, their arguments are essentially normative. The politics of indigenous activism is, therefore, a classic struggle between the least powerful (indigenous groups) and the most powerful (industrialized nations) over normative issues, played out in international fora.

More important, the least powerful have been able to extract concessions and compromises from the most powerful actors. According to the realist view of world politics, this should not be happening. As actors of vastly unequal coercive power engage in a discourse over issues pertaining to the allocation of values, the arena of world politics seems much less anarchic and more like normal politics in a civic community. To account for these developments, we need a model of world politics that refers to the role of rhetoric in the formulation and transformation of international norms.

MARGINAL SITES AND INTERPRETIVE PARADIGMS IN THE STUDY OF INTERNATIONAL RELATIONS

A series of articles appearing in 1990 pointed to the existence of "marginal sites" of politically significant experience; sites existing on the "margin" of the prevailing paradigm directing the study of "international relations."[13] These sites are unconnected to the "bounded territoriality" of states central to the realist paradigm. These are sites where the distribution of power is embedded in internalized meanings; where the powerless remain powerless in part because they do not successfully challenge the meaning of terms used to describe their existence, their experiences. These are sites where patriotism and loyalty are attached to "artificial" nations—Yugoslavia, or the Soviet Union.

"Here the words 'I' and 'we' have no certain referent."[14] These are "sites of struggle, where power is conspicuously at work." They "resist knowing in the sense celebrated in modern culture, where to 'know' is to construct a coherent representation that excludes contesting interpretations and controls meaning."[15] The meaning of events occurring in these marginal sites is, accordingly, ambiguous and fluid. When meanings change, revolutions may follow, particularly if institutions created to channel power do not adapt to the pace, depth, and direction of change.

Marginal sites indicate the possibility of fundamental and dramatic changes in the context of world politics. These changes are not necessarily anticipated or taken into account by more conventional theoretical orientations. The existence of marginal sites in social science is akin to Kuhn's notion of anomalous developments in the physical sciences. However, in the case of social scientific studies, it is not only our perception of (social) reality that changes, but also the *reality itself* that changes. Marginal sites, therefore, do not necessarily offer insight into how things are, but *how things are becoming*. They call into question a dominant theoretical interpretation and set us to work modifying and adapting a prevailing theoretical orientation, or lead us toward the development of an entirely new paradigmatic framework for interpreting and studying world politics. The importance of marginal sites has at no time been more apparent than in the continuing political turmoil surrounding events in Europe over the past several years—the disintegration of the Soviet Union, Yugoslavia, and Czechoslovakia, the end of the Cold War and the democratization of Eastern Europe. Ironically, as Eastern Europe moves toward fragmentation, Western Europe is attempting to continue on the path of consolidation and unification. Yet the political outcome in both arenas is likely to take the form of "confederation," or some other relationship involving negotiated cooperation among states enjoying sovereign equality.

The importance of interpretive paradigms to foreign policy analysis is glaringly evident in the case of the breakup of the Soviet Union. The realist paradigm used to interpret U.S.-Soviet relations was formulated in the aftermath of the 1917 Revolution and reinforced during the Cold War era. Coercion is the most salient feature of the state and unrestrained great power competition is mitigated only by the possibility of achieving and maintaining, through preparedness, deterrence and alliances, a power balance among adversaries. Within this interpretive paradigm, the United States intelligence community assigned meaning to information gathered about the Soviet military capability, and made assessments of Soviet political willingness to develop and use increasingly sophisticated nuclear weapons. The dominant paradigm both provided the interpretative context within which "facts" are assigned significance and determined which "facts" are relevant.

According to a realist view, the relevant information for the development of U.S. policy toward the Soviet Union consisted of military budgets, estimates of troop strength, knowledge of troop and weapons locations, weapons capability and numbers, and statements of Soviet military policy. This information was continuously interpreted in light of the assumption that a coercive state will continue to exist as long as its government possesses sufficient coercive capacity to control the population and territory in its jurisdiction.

As early as 1980, however, a "marginal site" of Soviet life came to light that might have foreshadowed the events to come in the Soviet Union. The meaning of loyalty to the Soviet Union, and accordingly, the willingness of Soviet citizens and soldiers to obey the coercive state, was called into question by Soviet soldiers defecting from service in Afghanistan. On this site the meaning of "I" and "we" or "us" and "them"—the language of adversarial relationships—had become ambiguous. On this site of struggle power was conspicuously failing to work. Here the viability of the coercive Soviet state began to show signs of weakness. The morale of Soviet troops was never lower. This is a problem for the effectiveness of any state's foreign policy, as U.S. policy makers learned in Vietnam. The difference in the case of the Soviet Union was that the maintenance of a Soviet regime *within the Soviet Union*, given its heavy reliance on coercion, also depended on retaining the loyalty of Soviet soldiers— on the ability of political elites to maintain effective control over the language of identity internalized by the Soviet soldier. That such control had been lost was evident during the subsequent failed coup in Moscow. While western intelligence analysts focused on the struggle between the western and the Soviet version of reality, the conflict over realities within the Soviet Union—a marginal site to western intelligence operations—became the locus of more significant developments.

INDIGENOUS ACTIVISM AS A MARGINAL SITE

There is now perceptible an agreed upon reality or normative consensus common to global elites that is consistent with European cultural evolution. The establishment of that core has been an enormously violent, coercive, and destructive process from the perspective of non-European peoples who now, through international discourse, seek to influence that core. Although realism may explain why the core is essentially a product of European struggle and influence, it explains neither why the core should exist in the first place, nor how and why non-European peoples might now be effectively influencing it.

Struggles over normative issues often appear as conflicts over language and meaning. Linguistic analysts such as Michel Foucault claim that the allocation of power is embedded within the language we use to talk about power, its nature and residence, its presence in our lives. To attach language to a social event or experience is to interpret its significance, and in that interpretation to crystallize or "institutionalize" a conception of power consistent with the interpretations of a dominant or core group. Thus the use of a term by those who control its meaning is a means of legitimating the normative beliefs of the dominant group. Challenges arise on the margin of power, among those whose normative beliefs are fundamentally at odds with those of the dominant group.

Indigenous activists understand the power of language and have long worked toward the transformation of language within the dominant discourse used to discuss indigenous issues. Of no small importance is the fact that the term "indigenous," as opposed to terms used by their colonizers such as "native," "aboriginal," or "tribal," has been promoted and defined primarily by indigenous peoples themselves. They have, so to speak, grasped the rhetorical high ground and established control over the label and its meaning. By contrast, the terms formerly used interchangeably by colonizers were associated with derogatory meanings including "backward," "primitive," "uncivilized," and "savage."

Indigenous peoples' demand for inclusion in global civic discourse not only challenges status quo meanings, but is also an exercise in the deconstruction of meanings attached to international values such as modernization and development. White policy makers in the United States and Canada no longer aim to "civilize" the indigenous peoples of the Americas, but to "promote their development," "modernize" them, or "bring them into the twentieth century." The term "international development" has become a kind of shorthand among international power elites, where "development" means "the establishment of economic, social, and political institutions to facilitate the development of a capitalist economy which will then interface with the international capitalist economic system." More important are the qualitative assumptions implicit in the meaning of "development." To "become developed" is desirable, even necessary to the survival of those who are not "developed" or are "underdeveloped." To become developed is to end one's savage or uncivilized condition/way of life.

Calling the meaning of "development" and "modernization" into question is central to the movement among indigenous peoples because these concepts rationalize the marginalization and destruction of indigenous values and ways of life. Indigenous peoples' cultural, social, political, economic, and physical integrity has been directly attacked in the name of "development." By challenging the legitimacy of policies which bring forced assimilation, relocation, the introduction of deadly alien epidemics, and the sanctioning of private violence by "settlers," indigenous peoples have targeted the source— the *meaning* of development itself. For instance, representatives of the Yanomamo people in Brazil traveled to the World Bank in the 1980s and argued before Bank officials that "Development can have many meanings. Your interpretation of development is material. Ours is spiritual. Spiritual development is as legitimate as material development."[16]

We can also think of different kinds of development and different kinds of knowledge by considering how knowledge develops in relation to cultural context. European economics, for example, is based on the belief that economic problems are caused by the scarcity of resources relative to human demands. Yet European economics is also based on an uncritical assumption that maximizing surplus value is the primary goal of all economic systems. This thinking emerged during a period of enormous population increases in Europe and following the separation of church and state so that the church no longer exerted a moral restraint on greed and accumulation of wealth. But because the indigenous peoples of the Americas did not, prior to the arrival of Europeans, think of economic problems in such terms does not mean that they were not moving along their own path of cultural evolution, thinking about economic problems in a different context and with different ideas about the management of economic resources. The pre-European indigenous world was perceived to provide resources in abundance relative to human demand, and most indigenous social and religious or spiritual systems contained norms that restrained greediness and fostered generosity (potlatches and giveaways, for instance) as opposed to the accumulation of large material surpluses.

The pan-Amazonian indigenous peoples' alliance known as COICA addressed the issue of different conceptions of development this way in an open letter to the World Bank:

> If you want to know what development means to us, you must be willing to accept that our mode of development is not the same as yours. Many development agents have come into our villages and . . . say to us "Soon you will be able to give up your miserable huts and live in tin-

roofed houses." But we like our houses. . . . For us, tin roofs, while perhaps a symbol of economic wealth and success, turn our houses into
ovens. . . . Our development is not based on the accumulation of material goods, not on the greatest rates of profit obtained at the expense of
our territories. The key to development for us is an extensive, diversi-
fied, integral territory where all its occupants, peoples, animals, trees,
will share the benefits. Our development is our own territory, safe from
invasion and threat, and respect for our right to conduct our activities in
an autonomous way. Our development must emphasize our capacity to
feed ourselves—you call it subsistence farming—and to satisfy the material needs of all our people. When we are able to do this, then we can
begin to look toward the market and learn how to deal with it without
destroying our territories.[17]

It is not "development," "modernity," or "industrialization" that
indigenous leaders rail against, but rather against the excesses, the
lack of restraint, and the uncritical assumption that these ideas are
culturally neutral and inherently good.

Marginal sites not only challenge the dominant narrative that legitimates one version of reality or set of normative beliefs over others, but
also the prevailing interpretations ("facts") of *past* events. The quin-
cententary of Columbus's contact with indigenous peoples of the
Americas has prompted a reinterpretation of events related to the five
centuries of conquest, colonization, and subjugation that followed.
Such reinterpretations of history are not, however, unique to the issue
of Columbus's "discovery." Both the civil rights and women's movements in the United States, and the Bolshevik revolution as well as
the more recent democratic movement in Russia involved important
reinterpretations of historical events or the historical context of
events. Marginal sites are occupied by marginalized and excluded
people whose demands for inclusion alter the content of civic discourse.

The emerging strength of the indigenous voice, evidenced by the
growing acceptance of the validity of indigenous peoples' interpretation of events that for four centuries had been in the exclusive interpretive domain of non-indigenous elites, raises several interesting
questions. First, the marginal site occupied by the experience of
indigenous people is becoming less marginal. Once such a site comes
into focus and receives widespread attention it is no longer, by definition, marginal. Did this occur as a result of indigenous activism or

from some change in the context in which indigenous activism occurs? Or both? And what is the cost to indigenous peoples of "demarginalizing" their concerns? That is, since placing their concerns on the international agenda involves participating in the dominant discourse, how have their own meanings been altered by the process?

Secondly, and of particular interest to political scientists, the emergence of an international indigenous voice (and the responsiveness of power elites to it) indicates a change in the flow and distribution of power and the context in which responsiveness occurs. If indigenous activism is bringing about a transformation of the meaning of something as fundamental to the world social system as "development," then the content of the normative beliefs underlying world order may also be changing. If world order as we know it today is essentially the product of an expanding European influence, then indigenous activism, among other things, suggests that world order must come to terms with the influence of non-European perspectives, norms, beliefs, and values if it is to be an inclusive order. Such things as *excessive* capitalism, the destruction of local cultures and identities, the majoritarian democratic model—which has been replaced by a model of ethnic pluralism in South Africa, for example—are all called into question by the increased participation and influence of non-European peoples. And if indigenous peoples' influence is a consequence of rhetorical practices, rather than the use of force or the control of state institutions, then we must admit that, at least in this case, international politics is beginning to look less like the anarchic environment portrayed by realism and more like a civil society, albeit an imperfect and embryonic one.

THE CHANGING CONTEXT OF WORLD POLITICS IN THE TWENTIETH CENTURY

The study of politics is not only about power, but also about the restraint of power, the use of power to achieve a vision of collective good, struggles over and adaptations of the normative basis of the collective good, and the channeling of power through decision-making institutions where values determine output. Until recently, however, notions of restraint, collective interests, normative struggles, and institutional value allocation were in the main subjects of political inquiry limited to the study of domestic politics. The realist paradigm held that international politics was distinguished from domestic arenas of political activity because in international politics (1) power remains unrestrained, (2) the dominance of self-interest precludes the emergence of collective interests and shared vision, (3) struggles are characterized as contests of power, and (4) the effectiveness of institutional value allocation is severely limited by the absence of mechanisms for enforcing decisions.[18]

The emergence and proliferation of conflicts representing struggles over normative issues suggests that world politics during the twentieth century has undergone a profound transformation—from struggles over power and its tangible manifestations to struggles over normative issues and the values allocated through international institutions, or by collaboration among dominant actors. Interdependence is less a theory or even an "interpretation" of events, than it is an accurate description of the context of world politics impelling conflicts of a political, economic, and ideological nature to rapidly reach global proportions. Terms referring to "world" war, "global" recession, or "intercontinental" ballistic missiles suggest that the problems and conflicts among the most powerful actors possess a global reach making it nearly impossible for any state to remain neutral, isolated, or unaffected by conflicts involving western societies. Through trade and war, conquest and colonization, and the development of technologies that defy national boundaries, the web of interdependence, however unevenly, has been spinning for at least the past century. Violent conflicts arising out of disputes over tangible issues—boundaries determining jurisdiction over people and resources, or contests of power—became the arenas for contests of power among western powers, the outcome of which would determine the future structure of world political leadership.

But during the twentieth century a new dimension was added to these struggles as technological and economic interdependence spread throughout the system. The Napoleonic Wars, First and Second World Wars, and the Gulf War of 1991 were certainly about "who gets control over what." But in each case a new level of discourse was also emerging. Through the dialogue of diplomacy, through war and peace, and through the creation of international institutions of universal membership, power elites—western Europe and wealthy, industrialized former European colonies or "settler states"—began to articulate a set of normative assertions about legitimate and illegitimate uses of power. These normative assertions are directed at both external uses of coercive power by the state—collective and individual self-defense (legitimate) versus (illegitimate) "aggression"—and internal uses of coercive power embodied in the concept of human rights.

Although contemporary conflicts occur primarily in connection with tangible issues, they *also* involve the values and intangible but "socially significant" attributes—such as "status"—represented by them. For instance, it is not only "territory as resources" that is important, but territory as a resource *base* used to support a particular *way of life*, or to enable the survival of a particular version of reality. Or, territorial claims might be sought in connection with aspirations to political status, as in the case of Palestine. The articulation of a shared set of norms regulating the use of force in international relations points to an even more profound development in the evolution of global discourse. Attaining a common understanding regarding the meaning of "security" suggests agreement among elites regarding the values to be secured, thereby giving rise to collective interests grounded in shared normative beliefs. What kind of shared normative beliefs underlie the emergence of the present world order?

MODERNIZATION AS A WORLD VIEW

In attempting to understand the grievances brought by indigenous peoples before the world community today, we must look to the broader socio-historical context of global social mobilization over the past five centuries. The social transformations accompanying this experience have been characterized politically by the rise of the secular nation-state, and economically by the incorporation of non-European societies into an expanding industrial world society, and by the subsequent weaving together of the many nation-states into a world political system.

Modernization is the ideology, or normative basis, of world community-building. Modernization is actually a program or composite of policy behaviors developed to carry out a particular value agenda. This agenda, aggregated in the concept of "development," underlies the social transformations that produce industrial economies and public as well as private bureaucratic systems instrumental to the maintenance of these economies. The presumed superiority of industrial economies and the bureaucratic systems necessary to manage them is frequently cast in moral terms that denigrate and undermine the cultural integrity and viability of indigenous peoples.

The dominant image of the state, consistent with the necessities of hierarchical organization, has been coercive. The concept of consent-based legitimacy, at least among members of the controlling moral community within the state, has modified this image over the past two centuries.[19] Some have even argued that the existence of a political system depends on the existence of coercive capacity. The dominant image of the individual is self-gratifying, ". . . concerned with glory and fame, with self-realization and joy."[20] Political man was a Machiavellian realist, economic man a rational actor, social man restrained only by his own self-interest, and psychological man obsessed with gratification and consumption. Both the individual and the state were freed from the repressive influences of religious doctrines and institutions that had previously demanded self-denial and restraint. These freedoms, in turn, were combined in the concept—or myth—of "progress."[21] And progress made modernization possible.

The liberation of individual and collective creativity unleashed by "progress" produced the modern, bureaucratic state to manage complex industrial economies. The separation of church and state, however, left a vacuum of public or collective morality. The absence of an official, external moral authority makes room for individuals to progress toward moral independence—the capacity to make moral judgments through reason of conscience rather than fear of public retaliation or in response to other mechanisms of social control. On the other hand, it leaves the political community without a clearly defined normative basis.

This "liberal state" in which all conceptions of the good life are equal leaves unanswered questions such as: On what is it everyone in the liberal society agrees? Is there a vision of public good that is shared by members of the community? Is there a guide to the restraint of individual behavior in light of public interest? What individual responsibilities are attached to the liberal vision of individual freedom?

In the absence of any clearly articulated, community-wide, non-material conception of public good and social meaning, the idea of "progress" and other materialist ideologies have taken on special importance among political elites in both national and international contexts. "Progress" or "modernization" can therefore be viewed as a kind of global ideology providing the basis for agreement regarding the allocation of global resources. The belief that economic "development" is a universal good serves as common ground among national elites functioning in the context of cultures arising out of otherwise diverse historical experiences.

In the aftermath of European colonialisation, newly "independent" states were controlled by groups of "indigenous" non-western peoples willing to assume political leadership and join in the global process of industrial development. These new "Third World elites" are frequently members of the same ethnic group, but deculturized and reculturized as a consequence of having been coopted by colonial administrators, educated in the colonists' culture, and returned to their country of origin to carry out the work of "civilizing" and "modernizing" their "countrymen." The political boundaries of these multiethnic states were drawn by the colonial powers with little or no regard for the ethnic boundaries of the indigenous peoples. As a consequence, the postcolonial multiethnic pattern found today in Africa, for example, often involves the political dominance of one educated/resocialized ethnic group in which the values supportive of modernizing programs have been internalized over others who are labeled "backward," "primitive," "uncivilized" and so on. The wars of decolonization thus continue long after the Europeans have gone home, as in the case of Kenya and Somalia.

Indigenous Activism Challenges the Ideology of Modernization: The Struggle for Different Meanings

The international distribution of resources and rights has been shaped to a large extent by the idea that the state exists in order to facilitate modernization. This belief is reinforced by the notion implicit in the myth of progress that the state is an adaptive, natural, and inevitable outcome of universalized social evolution. There are disagreements about how to modernize, or the extent to which other values can be accommodated, traded off, displaced, or suppressed in the short run. But among economic and political elites worldwide there is fundamental agreement about the priority of industrialization for improving the quality of life. The process of incorporation into the world system is often viewed by local communities, however, as a threat to their cultural diversity.[22]

Because modernization is believed to be a good end in itself, a kind of moral community has developed in connection with its implementation, thereby rationalizing courses of action that promote modernization, as well as those aimed at "removing obstacles" to modernization. The treatment of indigenous communities frequently falls into the latter category. Modernization represents the sum of attributes perceived by elites as endowing them with moral superiority, and non-modern societies are therefore, by definition, morally inferior.

Marginal peoples have been dislocated, not only normatively, but to geographically marginal sites. Non-industrial societies have, therefore, survived on the periphery of industrial development, in areas difficult to penetrate geographically, such as the hill country in Bangladesh, the rain forest in South America, or in areas believed to be of little economic value, like deserts and swamps. "Progress" has in the course of "modernization" necessitated building a new highway through the territory used for thousands of years to support the Yanomamo way of life, relocating the Cherokee out of the Appalachian mountains where large deposits of gold had been discovered, flooding the traditional homelands of the James Bay area Cree for a hydroelectric power project, flooding the large tracts of land traditionally occupied by the Chittagong Hill peoples in Bangladesh, or clearing Brazilian rainforest in order to expand the cattle ranching that supplies the American fast-food beef and pet food markets.[23]

It would be incorrect to say, however, that indigenous peoples simply oppose "modernization" or "progress." Instead, they insist on the right to define and pursue development in a manner consistent with their own cultural context. They advocate the right to choose the degree and terms of their interaction with other cultures. Indigenous activists in Ecuador, for example, are attempting to negotiate with oil companies, the Ecuadorian government, and various development agencies to halt the process of oil exploration and exploitation for a period of time during which the indigenous peoples can develop mechanisms to adapt to the changes these processes will bring.[24]

The key to indigenous peoples' advocacy, however, is that local control is understood within a context of global continuity. In a statement formulated by the Akwesasne Mohawk community entitled "Our Strategy for Survival," the philosophical basis for indigenous decolonization was outlined in the following terms:

> The roots of a future world which promises misery, poverty, starvation and chaos lie in the processes which control and destroy the locally-specific cultures of the peoples of the world. Colonialism is a process by which indigenous cultures are subverted and ultimately destroyed in the interests of a worldwide market economy. The dialectical opposite of that process would be the rekindling on a planetary basis of locally based culture.

. . . A strategy for survival must include a liberation theology . . . or human kind will simply continue to view the earth as a commodity and will continue to seek more efficient ways to exploit that which they have not come to respect. If these processes remain unabated and unchanged at the foundation of the colonizer's ideology, our species will never be liberated from the undeniable reality that we do live on a planet of limited resources and that sooner or later we must exploit our environment beyond its ability to renew itself.[25]

An indigenous representative speaking to the United Nations in 1982 offered his version of "realism." Here, "natural law" refers to the immutable laws of ecological balance.

Brothers and Sisters the natural law is the final and absolute authority governing Etinohah—the earth we call our mother.

The natural law is that all life is equal in the great creation; and we human beings are charged with the responsibility, each in our generation, to work for the continuation of life. The Elder circle of the indigenous people of the Great Turtle Island, charged with keeping the first law of life . . . are concerned that the validity of this law no longer is recognized in today's life. This could be fatal to life as we know it.[26]

Conclusion

Marginal sites are important to the study of politics whether domestic or international because they are the loci of changing social contexts. Taking the claims of indigenous peoples seriously suggests that a new context for international relations is emerging—indeed, must emerge—in order to accommodate the demand for inclusiveness on the part of non-Western peoples and world views. International responses to indigenous activism also illustrate the importance of rhetorical practices and normative discourses for the conduct of politics in international arenas. If we continue to base the state's legitimacy, even implicitly, on its ability to represent the interests of a collectivity normatively grounded in a shared world view, then states will continue to suffer from ideologically or ethnically-driven, often violent conflict. Either state boundaries will ultimately be adjusted to coincide with the multiplicity of collective identities or the state itself must be defined in different terms. Given the dominant processes of modernization and globalization—which appear irreversible—the inevitable interpenetration of national identities will further exacerbate conflicts arising out of normative struggles within the state as well as across state boundaries.

If, on the other hand, the normative cores at global, national, and local levels are to become inclusive of the indigenous and other versions of reality, they must be adapted to accommodate the necessity of coexistence among multiple versions of local realities. In this case, the ideal of global community increasingly resembles the ideal of domestic political community—unity within diversity, or the harmonizing of diverse cultures. Global civic culture will be grounded in a recognition that the fate of humanity is intimately and inextricably bound to the fate of all life, and will acknowledge the absolute requirement of living within the limits of the natural world. Indigenous world views may offer us a way of conceiving of our intercultural relationships whereby four thousand versions of reality—intersecting in common recognition of our interconnectedness—are also bound together by acknowledging the interdependence of our destiny.

Notes

1. John Mohawk told this story in a recorded lecture, Hunter College, New York City, 1993.
2. See Winona LaDuke, "Indigenous Environmental Perspectives," *Akwe:kon Journal* 9 no. 2 (summer 1992): 52-71.
3. Bernard Nietschmann gives a figure of between 3,000 and 5,000 in "Militarization and Indigenous Peoples," *Cultural Survival Quarterly* 11, no. 3 (1987): 1-16,
4. Ken Taylor interview, November 1987, Washington, D.C.
5. U.N. Document E/CN.4/Sub.2/1991/40. Grand Council of the Crees (Quebec), Indian Council of South America (CISA), Indian Law Resource Center, International Indian Treaty Council, International Organization of Indigenous Resource Development, Inuit-Circumpolar Conference, National Aboriginal and Islander Legal Services Secretariat, National Indian Youth Council, Nordic Saami Council, and the World Council of Indigenous Peoples.
6. This was the name adopted in March 1990 by the First Congress of the indigenous peoples of the arctic "north Soviet" area.
7. Nietschmann, "Militarization and Indigenous Peoples," op. cit.; Brian R. Ferguson and Neil Lancelot Whitehead, eds. *War in the Tribal Zone: Expanding States and Indigenous Warfare* (Sante Fe, N. Mex.: School of American Research Advanced Seminar Series, 1992).

8. U.N. Document E/CN.4/Sub.2/1991/40, 12. See also the International Work Group for Indigenous Affairs (IWGIA) *Newsletter* July/August 1991 on constitutional reform in Argentina; IWGIA Nos. 51 and 52, 1987 on constitutional reform in Brazil; "The Metis Nation of Alberta Constitutional Process: An Alberta-Made Metis-Driven Report on Constitutional Reform and Canadian Unity;" "Canada's Native Peoples and the Constitution," IWGIA *Newsletter* No. 24, 1980; "Designing a Nunavut Constitution," IWGIA *Newsletter* No. 37, 1984; and "Consensus Government," *Edmonton Journal,* 12 October 1991, G-1.

9. *International Workgroup for Indigenous Affairs Yearbook 1990* (Copenhagen: IWGIA, 1991), 89.

10. This was true of a ten-year energy development program in the Philippines, for example, as well as the Koel Karo Dam in India. International pressures also led Brazilian president Collor to engage national security forces against miners illegally encroaching on Yanomamo territory. See Julian Burger, *Report from the Frontier: The State of the World's Indigenous Peoples* (London: Zed Press, 1987).

11. I.L.O. Convention No. 169 Concerning Indigenous and Tribal Peoples in Independent Countries 27 June 1989.

12. Joe Kane, "With Spears from All Sides," *The New Yorker*, 27 September 1993, 54-79, and Joe Kane, "Moi Goes to Washington, *The New Yorker*, 2 May 1993, 75-81.

13. *International Studies Quarterly* 34, no. 3 (1990). The entire issue was devoted to this theme.

14. Richard K. Ashley and R. B. J. Walker, "Speaking the Language of Exile: Dissident Thought in International Relations," *International Studies Quarterly* 34 (1990): 367-416.

15. Ibid., 261.

16. Paraphrased from an interview with Ken Taylor, former executive director of Survival International-U.S.A., who worked with the Yanomamo during the 1970s.

17. COICA, "To the International Community: COICA for the Future of the Amazon," (Lima, Peru, NGO Meeting on the World Bank, 1990).

18. Normative issues have not been entirely overlooked, but this work generally takes place on the periphery of mainstream international relations studies, for example, Richard Falk, *The End of World Order* (London: Holmes and Meier, 1983), the World Order Studies Project, and the work of Kenneth W. Thompson reflect a normative focus.

19. This relationship between law and politics is captured by the Austinian notion of the "command of the sovereign." The legitimacy of state coercion is also reflected in such international principles as domestic jurisdiction and non-intervention.

20. Michael Curtis, *Great Political Theories*, vol. 1 (New York: Avon Press), 1961.

21. See Lucy Kramer Cohen, *The Legal Conscience: Selected Papers of Felix S. Cohen* (New Haven: Yale University Press, 1960).

22. Raimundo Pannikar, "Is the Notion of Human Rights a Western Concept?" *Diogenes* 120 no. 120 (1982): 75-102, and Ali Mazrui, *A World Federation of Cultures: An African Perspective* (New York: Free Press, 1976).

23. Catherine Caulfield, *In the Rainforest* (London: Heinemann, 1985).

24. "CONAIE Calls for a Halt to the Seventh Round of Oil Licensing!" *Rainforest Action Network*, 22 May 1994, received by NATIVE-L Bulletin Board NATIVE-L@tamvm1.tamu.edu.

25. Akwesasne Notes, *Basic Call to Consciousness* (Rooseveltown, N.Y.: Akwesasne Notes, 1986), 76.

26. Oren Lyons, "Traditional Native Philosophies," in *The Quest for Justice: Aboriginal Peoples and Aboriginal Rights*, eds. Menno Boldt and J. Anthony Long (Toronto: University of Toronto Press, 1985).

Francis A. Beer and G. R. Boynton

Realistic Rhetoric but not Realism

A Senatorial Conversation on Cambodia

The speeches of United States senators are important political data. The Senate has major foreign policy responsibilities under the American Constitution. Senators are substantial American political leaders, playing a significant foreign policy role; their speeches are notable verbal political acts. Actions and events, without words to explain them, are mute. When senators talk, they articulate an American vision of the map of the world. They express many of the thoughts and motivations that lie behind American foreign policy. They give foreign policy a meaning that American citizens can understand.

Some of what the senators say may be "just" talk, public posturing for domestic political constituents and the historical record. Yet, in order to be successful, senatorial rhetoric must also have muscle and substance, a core of integrity. Senators, when they speak, construct a foreign policy world that is a plausible, reasonably hard-headed, tough-minded picture of real-world politics and real-world politicians. As realists might expect, some of the senators' foreign policy discourse is compatible with traditional realism.[1] At the same time, senators describe a world more complex than that of realism. They present a much broader, more comprehensive picture of international relations. For the senators, actors in addition to nation-states are important for world politics. These include international organizations such as the United Nations, domestic political factions, public opinion, and individuals. Criteria beyond material capabilities and military force are significant in assigning weight and rank to international actors in specific situations. Power has important local, contextual dimensions. Interactions are complicated. In the senators' conversations, world political actors are more fully formed agents than realist theory suggests. These agents construct foreign policy using criteria in addition to national interest defined in terms of power, benefits and costs, ends and means.

Senators reason in ways that go well beyond the standard realist formula of comparing costs and benefits for future policy options. Foreign policy talk, and the collective cognition it reflects and addresses, are "thick" and "hot." Motivation is "dense."[2] Senators apply their memories of history, and its lessons, to current policy situations. They are concerned with law, ethics, and morality, at least to the extent of policy justification. They are not afraid to express passion and emotion. Senators use policy stories about prior cases. Senators are very critical and always political. Their reasoning in specific situations highlights internal contradictions and practical problems of alternative paths into the future.

The hearing on Cambodia before the Subcommittee on East Asia and Pacific Affairs of the Committee on Foreign Relations of the United States Senate during 1990 provides a sample of senatorial foreign policy discourse for intensive examination. As we look at the way in which senators talk about foreign policy, as we listen to what senators really say, their rhetoric is less abstract, less formal, less stylized than the language of realism would lead us to expect. Their talk is part of the life world that they share, with each other and with us. It is more realistic than realism in the sense that we recognize the characters as more fully drawn, concrete human beings with whom we can identify. We understand the discussants when they talk and reason, and we recognize them in important ways as ourselves.[3]

Actors in World Politics

Realist doctrine emphasizes nation-states as actors in world politics. Yet, when we look inside nation states, up close and personal, we see many other actors. The first set of actors at this lower level of magnification includes subnational actors within the United States. These cluster around the most important subnational entity of the discourse, the Senate itself. Within the Senate, in turn, are committees, individual senators, and witnesses, all of which stand out as important participants in a very intricate political process.

We see a network of domestic political actors, and also a pattern of domestic political action, that combine realist and non-realist themes. Senators are realists enough, in the sphere of domestic politics, to be jealous of their place within the overall Constitutional separation of powers. Senators are at pains to assert themselves against representatives of the other branches of government, particularly the Executive branch. Subnational power is local and contextual, defined by changing relations between individuals, the sets of groups and institutions to which they belong, and the particular issue at hand.

Interwoven with the text of senatorial power are the hypertexts of collegiality and humane concern, mediating the harsh interplay of interest and conflict. As senators affirm their power, they also construct the institutions and the inner world of the Senate through protocol and precedence, courtesy and civility. The manners of the senators and their consideration for each other create the comity that is necessary for continuing interaction. In their talk senators also legitimate themselves as representatives their electorate, showing a concern with both the national power and rank of the United States and the humanitarian dimension of foreign policy.

The Senators construct, through talk, the world of international relations. Their conversation reflects and creates world politics, maintains and refreshes an agreed real world. Yet it is a world that realists would have a hard time recognizing. Senatorial discussion of Cambodian world politics includes the rhetoric of national interest and power, but mixed with other real world dimensions.

The Cambodian hearing offers senators a chance to participate in an important issue of international politics.[4] The senatorial conversation centers on and rhetorically constructs Cambodia in this political context. From the hearing emerges a detailed conversational map of Cambodia, though the conversation has implications well beyond Cambodian geographical boundaries. The map is not the same map that we should find if we consulted an atlas or a realist textbook. Rather it is a rhetorical map created by political discourse.[5]

One way into this discourse is through a simple frequency count centering on major topics of interest. We begin with the references to major national and subnational political actors, excluding the United States and its subordinate groups and individuals. Each explicit reference in the text was counted once for each time that it appeared. While this procedure does not include allusion and implication, it does provide an efficient and effective method of assessing the relative weight of rhetorical attention and emphasis. National actors, in descending order, received the following number of citations in the hearing: Cambodia, 238; Vietnam, 194; China, 169; Thailand, 22; USSR, 18; Australia, 13; France, 5. Subnational/individual actors got references as follows: Khmer Rouge, 251; Hun Sen/PRK, 195; Sihanouk, 68; Pol Pot, 16; Son Sann, 3.

Realism suggests that the major actors in international relations are nation-states ranked by material power. The above reference count partly confirms this political truth. Many of the actor references in the hearing are to nation-states. In the world of the conversation, however, the national actors are not weighted by material resources. Minor powers have major roles, major powers appear as supporting players. The United States is the principal actor by conversational implication. The discussion takes place in the United States Senate and concerns United States policy. Next, Cambodia appropriately receives pride of place. It is, after all, the subject of the conversation. Vietnam also sits above the salt. The former Soviet Union plays a relatively minor part, overshadowed by many others. China, a major power with a special interest, appears down the list of the nation-states. This is surprising because the traditional realist view would rank China above Vietnam and Cambodia. Dr. Helen Chauncey of Georgetown University's Department of Government expresses this view, ranking China at the top, when she says, "China tends to look at Indochina much the way that the Soviet Union until very recently looked at Eastern Europe. It is something of a *sphere of influence.*"[6] The senators and their guests, however, rank China in their conversation lower than some realists might expect. Local relations between neighbors outweigh a vast disparity of size and resources between Vietnam and China. At the same time, as realist rhetoric might suggest, China is ranked above Thailand. Thailand mediates between China and Vietnam. Senator Robert Kerry (D-Neb.) refers to "the relationship of China to Thailand and Cambodia as a *buffer zone*" and the "desire of China to have a buffer between Thailand and Vietnam."[7]

In addition to the national actors, a striking aspect of the conversational map is the importance of sub-national actors, particularly the Khmer Rouge, the Hun Sen government, and Prince Sihanouk. These sub-national actors are allied with national ones. The "genocidal" Khmer Rouge are supported by China. The Hun Sen government was installed by the Vietnamese in 1978. Prince Sihanouk is supported by all sides but gets little respect. The Son Sann faction is sustained by the U.S. Interestingly, the coalition of China and its client the Khmer Rouge weighs slightly more in the rhetorical scales than the opposing alliance between Vietnam and Hun Sen.

From a realist perspective, the conversation is deformed. Nation-states are not given proper weightings, and sub-national actors receive too much attention. A realistic theory of world politics recognizes that the lattice of actor weightings is subject to instantaneous and continual transformation. Discursive power orients itself around the subject of the conversation. Conversational worlds are constructed with various subjects in different conversations. Sophisticated understanding of the rhetoric of world politics decenters and relocates itself according to the subject or issue immediately at hand.

Agents

Realist rhetoric tells us that the actors of world politics are driven by the concern for national interest defined in terms of power. Senatorial rhetoric does not contradict this. Many of the tropes in the senatorial conversation are realist: nation-states, interest, power, spheres of influence, buffer zones. At the same time senatorial rhetoric includes non-realist themes that describe agents with a thicker subjectivity: history and memory, morality and emotion.

The text of the hearing to some extent confirms the realist axiom that actors think of international relations in terms of interest defined as the maximization of power. Interest(s) appears explicitly 16 times, power and its cognates 52 times. Indeed a major concern of senators and witnesses is the United States interest in the distribution of power in Cambodia. Senator Cranston (D-Calif.) refers to the stakes when he says that "nothing would be more disastrous than to have present peace efforts fail only to be replaced by more conflict fueled by outside powers."[8]

The discourse articulates interest and power concerns in finer detail, suggesting how they play out in the Cambodian context.[9] The text grounds these general, abstract concerns in very concrete ways. For example, former Democratic Senator from Maine and Secretary of State Edmund Muskie describes the Vietnamese interest in trade relations with the United States as follows. "They (Vietnam) want to formalize with us . . . They want to move toward economic development and growth. They emphasized that over and over again. There is nothing belligerent in anything that I encountered." He concluded on a very basic, mundane note, " they would like to sell shrimp in the United States."[10]

Interest and power are very much on the minds and lips of the senators and their guests. At the same time the speakers in the hearing describe a world where actors are broader and deeper than *Realpolitik* suggests. The actors are more fully formed agents, with a subjectivity where cognition, thought and feeling wander freely into and out of grottoes that are not included in a standard realist account. In particular, memory and emotion play critical roles. Senators believe that emotions of grievance and hatred, based on collective historical recollections, drive international politics and motivate the actors. Senator Robert Kerry refers to "the historical enmity between Vietnamese and Chinese." Mr. William Colby, former CIA Director, reiterates: "The Chinese hate the Vietnamese. . . . The Chinese just plain hate the Vietnamese."[11]

Not only hatred, but other emotions also play important parts in this political world. To ignore the importance of these emotions is not to heighten reality but to withdraw from it. We see the emotions clearly in discussions of the negative dimensions of Cambodian domestic politics. Senator Kerry refers to "the fear these people have for a return to power of Pol Potism." Mr. Colby suggests that "the Cambodians vote because of appetite, some out of fear, envy. . . . And historical guilt and shame drive positive emotions and moral sentiments as well."[12]

Sometimes the senators remember their own past, and it compels them to face their own moral obligations. Mr. Muskie reveals the heavy weight of historical guilt when he recalls that, "most of my Senate career, twenty-two years, was involved with the Vietnam war and its consequences and its aftermath. We have intervened, we have changed the history and the lives of that area of the world. So, from that point alone we have a responsibility to try to deal with the consequences of the interests of the people who have been impacted by it."[13] Senator Kerry shared his view when he states that, "I cannot think of many issues in foreign affairs today where the moral imperatives for us in this country are quite as clear, as they are with respect to Cambodia. Our policy in Cambodia was a stepchild directly of our involvement in Vietnam."[14]

Sometimes the senators come to moral obligation through international law. Senator Muskie remembers, "how many years this committee struggled with the genocide convention. . . . And yet we are on a side that refuses to recognize what so clearly has taken place in Cambodia, one of the worst genocides in the history of this century."[15] Senator Muskie's personal experience gives his words special meaning.

REASONING

Realist reasoning is front loaded. The realist future is an abstract matrix of potential costs and benefits; realist decision makers choose policies on the basis of estimated future consequences. Yet, it is clear from just the few excerpts above that the senators' rhetorical and mental maps of Cambodia also carry with them the strong weight of the actors' pasts. Memories of their own actions and the actions of others are the sources of present moral obligation and emotion.

Memory also contains concrete models for decision. These concrete models are the basis for a type of reasoning that operates quite differently from the abstract estimation of utilities favored in standard realist decision theory. This alternative form of reasoning, case-based reasoning, is based on precedent.[16] Precedents supply historically based ideal types, patterns that can be matched metaphorically to current situations through systematic comparison. The best fitting historical precedents are chosen as guides to action and the lessons of the past are applied to the present.[17]

Historical case precedents figure importantly in senatorial reasoning. Senator Kerry mentions four major precedents—Nicaragua, Namibia, the Philippines, and Vietnam. The first three concretely demonstrate the promise of free elections in Cambodia. Senator Kerry says, "it seems to me, Mr Chairman, that the lessons of the recent elections in Nicaragua, the recent elections in Namibia . . . , and the elections in the Philippines must have taught us something about the ability of the international community to assist in bringing about the responsible policy that permits people to choose freely their future." A fourth precedent, Vietnam, recalls the negative consequences of replacing ballots by bullets. "I cannot think of a better moment," Senator Kerry said, "for us to deal with the reality that there cannot be a military solution, that there has to be a political negotiated solution, and that we, because of the bizarre role we have played over the years much of which is psychologically entwined with Vietnam, must be central to the process of bringing about that determination."[18]

The rhetoric of the senators and their guests also includes realism's important future component. After all, it is the formation of future policy and potential U.S. action that are at stake. Senatorial reasoning, however, takes a narrative shape which is quite foreign in form and substance to abstract, academic realism. Senators supplement the past extrapolation of historical cases with the future extrapolation of policy stories.[19]

The senators and their guests construct their discussion of the Cambodian future around a central linear plot. Moving from the past, through the present, to the future, the core Cambodian story includes the prospect of free and fair Cambodian elections and a final ending without the Khmer Rouge. The senators embroider variations on this story as a way of trying alternative developments out for consistency, plausibility, and practicality. They are interested in the reactions of the audience. And they want to make sure that the Cambodian story will end correctly.

Practical policy reasoning is defined, not by abstract calculations, but by the characters and the story lines. American hostility to the Khmer Rouge is appropriate because of the triangular struggle for power between the U.S., China, and Russia, each supporting a particular regional and Cambodian client. China, particularly after the Tienanmen Square debacle, and its ally the Khmer Rouge appear as major power rivals to the United States in the area. The Soviet Union has collapsed politically, becoming less of a threat. Its ally Vietnam is trying to recover from the long war for independence and wishes to normalize relations. The Chinese and U.S. governments also wish to normalize relations. At the same time there is great moral repugnance to the Khmer Rouge. The rhetoric is adamant. Senator Kerry reiterates the intention of the Pell Amendment, "passed in the Senate by a vote of 97 to 1," that "most of all was determined" by a desire to "to prevent the return of the Khmer Rouge to power."[20]

The Khmer Rouge is the major problem in the story. It is defined as the primary enemy character. Mr. David Lambertson, Deputy Assistant Secretary of State for East Asian and Pacific Affairs, emphasizes that "any alternative to the Khmer Rouge that one can think of is preferable, and . . . the prime objective of what we are doing and the prime objective of any negotiated settlement must be to ensure . . . that the Khmer Rouge cannot return to power."[21]

Hostility to the Khmer Rouge is justified by the power calculus. Yet it goes deeper than the struggle for power. Again and again the senators and witnesses place the Khmer Rouge in the context of massive human rights violations, referring to the Cambodian "killing fields," the "genocidal Khmer Rouge," Pol Pot's "atrocious massacres."[22] The violation of these human sensibilities justifies the struggle for power. Human concerns strongly supplement and ethically inform the conversation.

Free elections are also a significant objective. Elections are important for instrumental power considerations. A government in Phnom

Penh that results from free and fair elections will be probably be more symmetrical with Washington and not include the Khmer Rouge. Mr. Colby notes that "every recent visitor to Cambodia says that the Khmer Rouge would lose a free election."[23] Yet the senators and witnesses can imagine free elections also leading to a non-democratic hostile government. Mr. Muskie alludes to this possibility when he suggests that "the Khmer Rouge is in the field with a dominant political force and with the ability, of course, to try to influence the people."[24]

Khmer Rouge participation in the elections is a risk that the discussants are willing to take, either because the senators believe they have no other choice, or because they believe that the risk is small. At the same time, free elections are important in their own right as political legitimation. Senators give important, independent weight to political philosophy and ideology. They identify their power and themselves with the democratic electoral process. What is good for the senators, the Senate, and the United States must be good for the world.

Senators and witnesses all agree that the Khmer Rouge is bad, and should go, and that elections are good and must occur. A major problem is how you get from here to there. The conversation visualizes getting from here to there along "roads," "paths," or "tracks" on various "fronts."[25] Different witnesses support different ways. The administration wants a comprehensive settlement under U.N. auspices. The senators and witnesses are very critical of this and search for a more minimalist solution involving independent national observers to supervise the elections. They also construct a branching narrative, using counterfactual conditional reasoning—what if?—to analyze the permutations of possible Cambodian governments.

Policy stories are the form through which senators and witnesses undertake critical analysis of the strengths and weaknesses of different policy options. For example, the discussion of the administration's proposal for U.N. administration of elections comes up against the fundamental problem of the U.N. presence, the fact that the Khmer Rouge have the U.N. seat for Cambodia. Thus the U.N. presence in Cambodia might be staffed by the Khmer Rouge. Dr. Jeremy Stone points out that "the U.N. lawyers cannot figure out how to deal with the problem that the U.N. cannot administer a country over the dead body of the Khmer Rouge because they hold the U.N. credentials for the country. . . . Once you give the credentials to the country, you cannot do something over their dead body."[26]

Senators and witnesses find basic inconsistencies, contradictions, and circularities in various options. One of these centers on verification of Vietnamese withdrawal from Cambodia. Mr. Muskie charges that the administration has opposed verification of the Vietnamese withdrawal in order to ease the way to Vietnamese approval. Yet without such verification, there would be no way to be sure that the withdrawal took place. Senator Kerry notes that "you indeed have a catch-22 situation . . . you are saying the normalization process is tied to the settlement in Cambodia, but the settlement in Cambodia is tied to verification, but we cannot verify until we have a settlement and you keep going around in this circle.[27]

More importantly, Senators Sarbanes (D-Md.) and Kerry believe that inclusion of the Khmer Rouge in a quadripartite provisional government would weaken the government and strengthen the Khmer Rouge, possibly make a mockery of free elections and lead to the ultimate triumph of the Khmer Rouge. Senator Sarbanes says to Mr. Lambertson, "You want them out. You are saying that your objective is to keep them (the Khmer Rouge) out and yet you are bringing them in . . . ." Senator Kerry continues along the same line. "You said in your statement that if we do nothing, then the Khmer Rouge could sweep to power, but I could not agree more with Senator Sarbanes and others that the things we are doing, in effect, may result in their having greater ability to sweep to power than if we were to pursue other alternatives."[28] The senators' rhetoric will have important corroboration as Cambodian policy and politics play themselves in the months that follow.

RESULTS

After the discussion, Senator Cranston closes the hearing with a prepared statement that supports a policy of (a) Khmer Rouge exclusion from the Cambodian government; (b) elections "this year"; (c) United Nations or private citizen center—like the Carter Center—organization and supervision of elections; (d) condemnation, and United States pressure to remove, Chinese support for the Khmer Rouge.

Of course, the end of the hearing was not the end of the affair. The discourse of the Senate committee was only a very small part of the discourse on Cambodia. Outside the committee, relations with the Soviet Union and China were changing. Other international actors, for example, the nations of the European Community and Australia, were active participants. Within the United States, various other governmental and non-governmental actors considered the matter. The Subcommittee on East Asia and Pacific Affairs of the Committee on Foreign Relations of the United States Senate held three later hearings on the subject during 1990. Participants in these hearings continued to speak about Cambodian "reality" in other venues.[29]

On 23 October 1991, the leaders of the Cambodian government and three major dissident factions signed a peace agreement that promised to end the chronic Cambodian civil war. The peace plan was drawn up by representatives of the Five Permanent Members of the U.N. Security Council (U.S., U.K., France, U.S.S.R., China), Cambodian Prime Minister Hun Sen, and leaders of the three rebel factions— Prince Norodom Sihanouk; former Prime Minister Son Sann, head of the right wing Khmer People's National Liberation Front; and Khieu Samphan, leader of the Chinese backed Khmer Rouge movement which ruled Cambodia from 1975 to 1978.[30]

The solution included U.N. administration of Cambodia; a Supreme National Council, made up of all the factions; U.N. disarmament of warring factions; U.N. supervision of elections; proportional representation of each of the four factions in the national assembly according to their share of the popular vote, with seats distributed according to the proportion of vote received on a province by province basis.

This plan was essentially the plan that Mr. Lambertson of the State Department originally offered to the subcommittee. As Senator Cranston suggested, it gave a major role to the U.N. It did not get rid of the Khmer Rouge, though it did promise to disarm them. It gave the Khmer Rouge a role in the transitional Supreme National Council and proportional representation in the government as a result of free elections. At the same time, the administration abandoned its longstanding opposition to dealing with the Vietnamese-backed Hun Sen government. It corrected, just a bit, the "tilt" toward China and its unwillingness to offend the Chinese.[31]

Case based reasoning and policy stories helped structure critical reasoning by senators and witnesses about the workability of various aspects of the peace agreement. Their practical misgivings turned out to be well founded. In particular, their discussion highlighted the complications involved in U.N. administration as well as the inclusion of the Khmer Rouge in a coalition government. These were and are well seeded minefields on the path to a lasting Cambodian peace in the Southeast Asian quagmire. Senatorial reasoning, even though it did not follow a realist model, contributed to rational decision making by providing early warning of problems to come.

MULTIPLE REALISMS

Reality is much more complex than realist rhetoric. Realism's hard-edged, minimalist parsimony offers too thin a model to describe exhaustively and exclusively the dense and complex cognitions and actions of the real world. Senatorial rhetoric opens the window to a more accurate view, a more complex theory. Senatorial rhetoric reveals dimensions of foreign policy reasoning that traditional realism neglects. It is more down to earth, with a better fit to practical politics. It foreshadows a more sophisticated formulation of foreign policy and international relations.

The realist story fits the rhetoric of the Cambodian case only in part. Nation-states are actors. But the power of national actors is locally weighted within the conversation and according to the specific issue. Subnational actors are important. The privileges and folkways of the Senate give a texture to subnational action that is heavily discounted in more traditional international analysis. Here the culture of foreign-policy decision within national institutions comes into sharper focus, more complex and detailed definition. Cambodian sub-national actors, though they have external national patrons, are extremely significant in their own right, and not only because of their power attributes. The ethical, moral identity of a sub-national actor like the Khmer Rouge, derived from the past historical record of behavior, is a substantial independent determinant of the other actors' reactions to it. Interest defined in terms of power is a motivation that drives the national and sub-national actors alike. But other dimensions are important as well: individual and collective historical memories; emotions of hatred, fear, guilt, revulsion; feelings of responsibility, morality.

Policy reasoning is partly based on the abstract, general power calculus. But it is also practical and local. Politics is the art of the possible. Senators and witnesses are concerned with what is likely to work in the specific context, how it is going to work, and what might conceivably go wrong. They describe the actors in multiple dimensions, including but not limited to power, and imagine how they may react. Their counterfactual, "what if" reasoning explores, in thick detail, alternative paths into the future.

The rhetoric of the hearing does not convey the strong realist current of permanent, immutable laws of international politics moving toward deterministic outcomes. Instead, there is an undertow of unpredictability, contingency. Machiavelli's *fortuna* and Simon's bounded rationality are very much in evidence. The hearing massages contingency with a rhetoric of consultation and participation, as well as exhaustive detailed examination. The discussants work to achieve futures management and surprise control, to hedge against unanticipated outcomes, cognitive and political disasters. They are also sensitive to discourse as legitimation for foreign policy. They have strong opinions, but are flexible and open enough to make room for divergent points of view required by both bureaucratic and democratic ethos.[32]

The world of the senators is not persuasive to everyone. Yet the conversation is plausible and realistic to the legislators and to their audience. The emphasis on the internal, domestic politics of countries suggests a legislative sensibility. The senatorial discourse also reflects a wider popular consciousness. Upon the signing of the peace treaty, the *New York Times* published several stories with headlines and a photo. Major nation-states—Vietnam, China, the U.S.S.R., and the U.S.—appeared in the headline of one of the secondary stories on the front page, but they were not the main focus of attention in the central photo or the lead story. The picture instead showed the individuals leaders of the principal Cambodian factions. The distribution of power was certainly an important element of the situation. But other aspects appeared as well in the journalistic use of such words as "frighten" and "nightmare." The themes of justice, history, and emotion evoked in the hearing reappeared in the media, reflecting deep currents in popular consciousness and mythology.

In the early years of the post-Cold War era, and as we approach the international system of the year 2000, the continuing relevance of international realism remains an important and troubling concern. The senators' conversation is a supplement and a possible alternative to realism. It constructs the world in a way that is more complex, more practical, and more authentic. The rhetoric is real, and it is realistic, but it is not realism.

Notes

1. See also Francis A. Beer and Barry J. Balleck, "Realist/Idealist Texts: Psychometry and Semantics" *Peace Psychology Review* 1 (spring 1994): 38-44.

2. See G. Robert Boynton and Milton Lodge, "Voters' Images of Candidates," in *Presidential Campaigning and America's Self-Images*, eds. Bruce Gronbeck and Arthur Miller (Boulder, Colo.: Westview Press, 1993), 176-89.

3. See also G. Robert Boynton, "The Expertise of the Senate Foreign Relations Committee," in *Artificial Intelligence and International Politics*, ed. Valerie Hudson (Boulder, Colo.: Westview Press, 1991), 291-309; Francis A. Beer and Barry J. Balleck, "Body, Mind, and Soul in the Gulf War Debate," *The Theory and Practice of Political Communication Research*, ed. Mary Stuckey (Albany: SUNY Press, 1996).

4. World attention has come to Cambodia in the context of the Vietnam War and its aftermath. Significant books on the contemporary Cambodian experience include William Shawcross, *The Quality of Mercy: Cambodia, Holocaust, and Modern Conscience* (New York: Simon and Schuster, 1984) and *Sideshow: Kissinger, Nixon, and the Destruction of Cambodia* (New York, Simon and Schuster, 1979). A major movie, *The Killing Fields*, has made Americans conscious of the cruel realities of contemporary Cambodian political life. Cambodian emigrés have become a part of some American communities.

5. See John O'Loughlin and Richard Grant, "The Political Geography of Presidential Speeches, 1946-87," *Annals of the Association of American Geographers* 80 (1990): 504-30; V. M. Sergeev, V. P. Akimov, V. B. Lukov, and P. B. Parshin, "Interdependence in a Crisis Situation: a Cognitive Approach to Modeling the Caribbean Crisis," *Journal of Conflict Resolution* 34 (June 1990): 179-207; Michael J. Shapiro, G. Matthew Bonham, and Daniel Heradstveit, "A Discursive Practices Approach to Collective Decision-Making," *International Studies Quarterly* 32 (1988): 397-419.

6. Senate Committee on Foreign Relations, *Hearing Before the Subcommittee on East Asia and Pacific Affairs of the Committee on Foreign Relations: Prospects for Peace in Cambodia*, 101st Cong., 2d sess., 28 February 1990, 100.

7. Ibid., 15.

8. Ibid., 2.

9. cf. Judith Goldstein and Stephanie Ann Lenway, "Interests or Institutions: An Inquiry into Congressional-ITC Relations," *International Studies Quarterly* 33 (September 1989): 303-27.

10. Senate Committee, *Prospects for Peace in Cambodia*, 26.

11. Ibid., 101.

12. Ibid., 116.

13. Ibid., 13.
14. Ibid., 4.
15. Ibid., 9.
16. See Francis A. Beer, "Words of Reason" *Political Communication* 11 (summer 1994): 185-201; G. Robert Boynton, "Practical Reasoning: Politics in Action" (Iowa City: University of Iowa, unpublished Ms.).
17. Richard Neustadt and Ernest May, *Thinking in Time: The Uses of History for Decision-Makers* (New York: Free Press, 1986); Yuen Foong Khong, *Analogies at War: Korea, Munich, Dien Bien Phu and the Vietnam Decisions of 1965* (Princeton: Princeton University Press, 1992).
18. Senate Committee, *Prospects for Peace in Cambodia*, 5.
19. Emery Roe, *Narrative Policy Analysis: Theory and Practice* (Durham: Duke University Press, 1994).
20. Senate Committee, *Prospects for Peace in Cambodia*, 4.
21. Ibid., 39.
22. Ibid., 1, 4.
23. Ibid., 108.
24. Ibid., 17.
25. G. Robert Boynton and Francis A. Beer, "What Would Happen If? Exploring Paths through the Minefields of U.S. Cambodian Policy," in *Taking Political Talk Seriously*, ed. John S. Nelson (forthcoming).
26. Senate Committee, *Prospects for Peace in Cambodia*, 102.
27. Ibid., 47.
28. Ibid., 43.
29. See, for example, Edmund Muskie, *Exploring Cambodia: Issues and Reality in a time of Transition* (Lanham, Md.: University Press of America, 1992).
30. *New York Times International,* 21 September and 24 October 1991.
31. See Sanjoy Banerjee, "Explaining the American 'Tilt' in the 1971 Bangladesh Crisis: A Late Dependency Approach," *International Studies Quarterly* 31 (June, 1987): 201-16.
32. This is consistent with previous foreign-policy decision research. See, for example John P. Burke and Fred I. Greenstein, *How Presidents Test Reality: Decisions on Vietnam, 1954 and 1965* (New York: Russell Sage, 1989); Irving L. Janis and Leon Mann, *Decision Making: A Psychological Analysis of Conflict, Choice, and Commitment* (New York: St. Martin's Press, 1977).

V
POST-REALISM

FRANCIS A. BEER AND ROBERT HARIMAN

STRATEGIC INTELLIGENCE AND DISCURSIVE REALITIES

The realist is right about one thing: Much of the time, international politics boils down to strategy. The calculation of advantage in the game of nations is the first condition, the final necessity, and—not to be underestimated—the continuing attraction for those who presume to be players. Therefore, it is not enough for post-realists to articulate a broader conception of scientific inquiry; if we are to move beyond realism, we shall have to provide decision makers with better instruments for strategic analysis. It may seem that these two objectives are mutually contradictory. For example, the post-realist perspective exemplifies the strong pluralism recently celebrated in "the third debate" about the conduct of inquiry in the discipline.[1] Precisely because "pluralism" sounds to some like an effortless egalitarianism—everyone welcome, have a nice day—it appears unlikely to foster the mental discipline required for calculation under pressure. Stated in terms of a commonplace of realist analysis, the global pluralist appears to make the mistake of promoting political and intellectual practices that might be appropriate only in the domestic sphere of democratic politics. Further, the emphasis in post-realist work on textual practices seems to weaken not only the autonomy of political science but also its most serious application. When speaking of textual strategies, it seems that the stakes are not so high as when one is observing the fate of nations.

Post-realism begins by recognizing that the relationship between language and action is not so simple. The real world is marked by deeds, and words themselves are also important—indeed, they are important means for altering reality, not least by defining what counts as action. Our understanding of events always is determined by our discourse; much of the time, descriptions of events can become the causes of subsequent events; some of the time, discourse is the primary mode of action; at some crucial moments, all hangs on a phrase. Realist discourse contrasts textual values and real world conditions, but this perspective need not be either true or strategic. The fate of nations can turn on words. Such events can be explained by other traditions of strategic analysis, such as the tradition of rhetoric, that do not depend on the realist's definition of reality or presumptions of autonomy.

The significance of these differences can be summarized by the question: what if the realist's conception of strategy is not strategic? If nothing else, this question suggests the value of a more reflexive realism: that is, one that could assess how its own conventions of understanding could become strategic liabilities in particular situations (the emerging scenarios of the twenty-first century not least among them). In addition, the question suggests that one consider how other discourses—including other, more rhetorically sensitive conceptions of the conditions, agents, instruments, actions, and effects of international relations—also might contain currently unacknowledged resources for strategic analysis. This concluding chapter offers a reconsideration of strategic analysis designed to organize both conventional realist and more interpretative post-realist approaches.

STRATEGY, DISCOURSE, AND RHETORIC

The first step in this reconsideration is deconstructive. Michael Walzer has identified an important inconsistency in the realist valorization of strategic thinking over the conventions of moral discourse. Walzer conceded the realist claim that moral reasoning does indeed depend on precepts that are abstract, ambiguous, and unable to direct their own application reliably. But it also is the case that strategic thinking possesses exactly the same faults in the same degree, and necessarily so.[2] Thus, the realist cannot claim validly to be using a cognitive practice that must provide a better purchase upon reality than the one rejected. There is no guarantee in general that the strategic analysis is accurate and no reason that moral and strategic options have to be at odds in every case. The choice between what one ought to do morally and what one ought to do strategically cannot be settled *a priori*.

This criticism of realist abstraction is significant even if one has no commitment to any standard other than strategic success. If strategic thinking is as unreliable in principle as the moralizing it would displace, then the strategist needs to devise a pattern of reflection that could possibly be on the alert for its internal deficiencies. Realists are not disposed to do this, however, because their basic conception of strategic thinking begins by suppressing the interpretative sensibilities—the cognitive practices—that could supply such reflexiveness. This weakness becomes clear by going a bit further down the road that Walzer has taken and considering why the strategist cannot escape the ambiguity endemic to other forms of practical reasoning.

The realist, like the rest of us, faces not one but two forms of constraint: not only the conditions of material necessity but also the constraints inherent in our limited ability to account for the world in which we live according to the terms of a given discourse or calculation. We are constrained not only by reality but also by our definitions of reality. In the words of Kenneth Burke, our definitions of reality serve as "terministic screens."[3] They filter our perceptions, determining what we can see and what we overlook. Moreover, the realist relies on a particular pattern of definition that, while it has great persuasive power, so walls off alternative accounts that it produces a blind spot of considerable magnitude. We can identify this rhetorical maneuver characterizing realism by recalling the foundational text in the standard intellectual history of the discourse, "The Melian Dialogue" in Thucydides' *History of the Peloponnesian War*. When negotiating the ground rules for this debate between Athenian diplomats and the leaders of Melos, the Athenians make the following stipulation:

> We on our side will use no fine phrases saying, for example, that we have a right to our empire because we defeated the Persians, or that we have come against you now because of the injuries you have done us—a great mass of words that nobody would believe. And we ask you on your side not to imagine that you will influence us by saying that you, though a colony of Sparta, have not joined Sparta in the war, or that you have never done us any harm. Instead we recommend that you should try to get what it is possible for you to get, taking into consideration what we both really do think; since you know as well as we do that, when these matters are discussed by practical people, the standard of justice depends on the equality of power to compel and that in fact the strong do what they have the power to do and the weak accept what they have to accept.[4]

As realists read this passage, it identifies the essential, natural condition of international politics. The complexities of political life are reduced to a calculus of power, justice is reduced to self-interest, appearances are reduced to the reality they conceal, and, ultimately, language is reduced to the world it would represent. When thinking rationally, the text becomes transparent and nature is seen clearly. It is difficult to resist the Athenians' conclusion:

> It is a general and necessary law of nature to rule whatever one can. This is not a law that we made ourselves, nor were we the first to act upon it when it was made. We found it already in existence, and we shall leave it to exist for ever among those who come after us, and we are merely acting in accordance with it.[5]

Yet one should be wary of the interpretive assumptions undergirding the realist reading, not least the assumption that the Athenians' rhetoric represents Thucydides' own voice. Without having to deny entirely the truthfulness of Thucydides' account, one can see something else as well which has direct bearing on how we understand and act in accord with the text. Consider how this dialogue also foregrounds the rhetorical design generating the Athenian discourse. The crucial moment occurs when the Athenians define their claim to know the world against the opposing appeals to justice. Note how at that moment they also align justice with the properties of speech itself: such appeals rely on "fine phrases" and "a great mass of words." The implication is that ideas of justice and the like exist only as words. To dress up this claim a bit in contemporary critical terms, realism persuades by marking all other claims with the sign of the text. That is, realism persuades not by pointing to a clearly observable, natural reality, but through dialectical self-assertion against other discourses that points to their condition as discourses. The alternatives are given a variety of labels—they are called utopian, idealistic, moralistic, legalistic, ideological, or rhetorical—but the label always is there and invariably aligned with some of the attributes of a text. Without the denigration of discourse, there is no realism. The immediate implication is that terms such as "justice" are the fodder of human illusion, while self-interest is not constructed rhetorically but rather is a material condition. The full implication is that the essence of power is "something that is correctly communicated only through artlessness"; the realist "abjures explicit textuality because power is not itself textual. As rhetoric is extrinsic to reality, so power becomes objectified, something existing independently of language, texts, and textual authority."[6]

This point is crucial to understanding realism as a discourse: It identifies both the source of its rhetorical power and its deconstructive moment. The discourse of realism appeals to us by defining itself as hierarchically above other discourses. These other perspectives are identified as inferior vehicles for knowing the political world because they are too discursive, too caught up in their textuality to serve rational calculation. This is the master trope of realist discourse, used repeatedly for local effect in particular debates and especially when establishing the legitimacy of the discourse, as when Machiavelli declares, "I have not sought to adorn my work with long phrases or high-sounding words or any of those superficial attractions and ornaments with which many writers seek to embellish their material."[7]

The realist speaker gives us a real world by contrasting it to a textual world and denigrates opposing perspectives by associating them with their means of expression. In short, realism is not nature's own discourse, and it is very much a matter of style. It is an explicit preference for one style of communication that is presumed to be rational because unadorned. It has the parsimony so admired by William of Occam and his followers, the simple focus of Jomini's strategic line of force. (The belief that representations of the world should be simple is a crucial step in constructing a simple world.) Realism's implicit model is the military memorandum, made famous to generations of schoolboys in Caesar's *Gallic Wars* and carried forward in the *militarisme* of writers like Ernest Hemingway. It is a minimalist program for stylizing oneself and one's world, and it is a means for suppressing other styles more complex than its own. Once this stylistic code has been established, the substance of the realist's argument may safely be articulated. Much of the time, the successful performance of this style may displace actual proof of the claim that one does know what really is the case.

The consequence of this rhetorical design for strategic thinking should be obvious. The realist is disposed by his or her own discursive habits to deny the relevance of any linguistic art to strategic analysis. Because realism is created by the textual practice of defining reality against textuality, turning toward a text must be a turn away from what really is the case, and that could hardly be strategic. Realists do not incorporate explicitly interpretive cognitive practices into their analyses, even when it is strategic to do so. Therefore, unless one presumes that unreflective use of this trope will always be the best means of thinking, there arises the suspicion that the realist may be trapped by his or her own rhetoric. The realist's definition of reality may be a strategic blunder.

The tendency toward such a mistake may be corrected by turning to a more linguistically sensitive model of strategic thinking. The tradition of rhetoric provides such an alternative. Strategic thinking is an ever-present and identifiable dimension of speech and it has been a persistent theme of rhetorical studies. Classical rhetoricians had to be strategic (and realistic) as they were developing the art of speaking for advantage in a competitive arena. If you spoke poorly, you lost. If you mastered the pragmatic skills of effective speaking, you could win. Thus, Aristotle begins his *Rhetoric* by observing that all people speak to attack and defend, and Cicero begins *De oratore* by comparing the personae of the orator and the general. The theme also sounds among contemporary theorists, as when Kenneth Burke makes explicit use of the analogy to emphasize how discourses are strategies for encompassing situations.[8] Our own experience is shaped by this theme as well, for the ordinary language of argument is replete with the diction of war: We advance claims to attack positions to defeat arguments to defend theses in verbal combat.[9] Strategic thinking has long been tied to the experience of political debate, just as advantage has been a goal of rhetorical instruction. Our supposition is that this analogy between rhetoric and war has been pervasive in both the experience and the study of rhetoric because it communicates the structure of a cognitive modality common and crucial to both practices.

A THREE-TIERED MODEL OF STRATEGY

We offer the following three-tiered model of strategic analysis. It is one example of a post-realist approach to this unavoidable concern of international studies. The model does not reject the realist's conventional association of strategic thinking with military action, nor does it abandon entirely the realist's conventional separation of strategic and ethical discourses, but it organizes these constructs within a broader historical and interpretive context. For purposes of illustration, we draw on three texts that have been important repositories of strategic intelligence. These are a remark by Gorgias, one of the founders of rhetorical studies; Machiavelli's *The Prince*, the primer of modern strategic thinking; and Clausewitz's *On War*, the text of central importance within late-twentieth century strategic studies.[10]

Our model arranges three patterns of strategic thinking into a hierarchy of analytical perspectives, each of which is outlined by one of our representative texts. Each level of this hierarchy articulates an important perspective on the process of conflict: Each integrates the cognitive, conceptual, and rhetorical elements of strategic thinking in a characteristic manner for defining and acquiring advantage within that process. The first level of our model, which can be imagined as the broad base of a pyramid, sets out the essential elements of the primitive competitive situation. In this abstract space, we find pervasive scarcity, explicit contingencies, a single objective, and a few individuals who are known only as utility maximizers and who are constantly oriented toward *reacting* to other's actions. The second level of analysis, which would correspond to the narrowing mid-section of our pyramid, incorporates a deeper sense of complexity and less predictive capability, as well as competing objectives, and so emphasizes the development of the strategist's character as a key locus of control. Although well aware of the situational constraints and still reacting to others, this analysis focuses on the *self-control* of the decision maker who will then be able to make more rational calculations while manipulating others. The third level of analysis redefines strategic decision making further by identifying how agents are surrounded by a myriad of discourses, technologies, or other media for analysis that can offer additional knowledge and advantageous perspectives. The decision maker still has to respect the logic of reaction and control character, yet also exercise skill in the *interpretation* of perhaps radically divergent definitions of the conflict in order to gain the most advantageous perspective for long-term success. This level of the model should be imagined as the upper section of a pyramid that narrows indefinitely without ever coming to a single point of completion. We hope the following brief elaboration of this model suggests how realist conceptions of strategy can be unduly limited and how post-realist strategies can be intuitively oriented to discursive realities that could be important elements in the international politics of the twenty-first century.

Competition

The first level of our model of strategic analysis consists of the primitive competitive situation: its motives, constraints, conventional maneuvers, and outcomes. This situation is primitive in several senses: It is simple, adhering to a small though powerful array of conditions and calculations; it is universal, an immanent structure potentially available within all human interaction; it is harsh, as different actions produce starkly different outcomes; and it is logically prior to other, more complex though less comprehensive patterns of interaction. Although one could say that the primitive situation contains all the elements of the more complex definitions of strategic interaction, its analytical power comes in part from keeping them hidden. There is an important sense in which strategic intelligence begins here, in the bracketing of all of life's complexity to focus on one's essential interaction with a competitor.

This primitive conception of strategic encounter is neatly summarized in the report of Gorgias' remark "that you should spoil the opponents' seriousness with laughter and their laughter with seriousness."[11] Gorgias' maxim identifies the essential features of its object, which include abstract outlines of the scene, agent, purpose, agency, and act defining strategic thinking.[12] He assumes an environment of capable adversaries struggling over limited resources (in this case, the scarcity comes from their competition for the approval of the audience before whom they are performing—which was no small consideration in the Greek world). Within such a world, the motive to gain advantage is both dominant and rational, and the speaker naturally works toward the goal of victory. Stated otherwise, there is no other standard for assessing one's actions than their utility in securing advantage. The means of victory in this case are vocalizations used to strike an attitude, but it is clear from the radical symmetry of the examples that they stand for any means whatsoever. Finally, one always should act to counter the actions of one's opponent.

This last point is the key to surviving in this primitive situation. In order to secure victory, one has to react to the actual or likely actions of the other. This *reactivity* is the inner logic of competitive success— the most important component of strategic thinking highlighted in Gorgias' remark. Gorgias thinks of what he should do by thinking of what his opponent has done or might do. If an action is an attempt to use one's environment, a reaction is a response to another's attempt at using a common environment—whether to avoid the effects of the other's actions or to modify the action itself. Within the elemental scene of competition, any act is essentially a reaction and the one competitor is always defining (positioning) himself or herself against the other. Conversely, when a game fails to have a reactive structure it also is devoid of strategic analysis. When this reactive structure is in place, it quickly generates other elements of strategic action: e.g., among reactive players, action quickly becomes characterized by indirection.[13] One proceeds indirectly so as to weaken the opponent's ability to react against one's initiative, and reactive actions encourage local paradoxes (laughing at a serious matter) and extended paradoxes (revolutionary rhetoric rationalizing the status quo).[14] Thus, Gorgias's remark also represents a primitive conception of social life: individual survival comes from relentlessly orienting oneself toward others who are either capable of dispensing the desired goods or are competitors for those goods. This simple calculus generates complex social interactions, which in turn can be analyzed through reduction to their fundamental contingencies of individuals reacting to each other's attempts to gain the same objective.

Maneuvering within these simple alternatives can lead both to familiar interactive routines and to unexpected disruptions by rogue players. Thus, even in its simplest form, the strategic situation involves indeterminate patterns of inference. The essential constraints on and opportunities for advantageous action can be identified, and the probabilities of various outcomes can be determined in general, but actual outcomes still depend on combinations of individual skill and competitive interaction likely to elude prediction. The question then is, on what should one focus to manage this complexity? At this level of analysis, the answer lies in the basic contingencies inherent in the structure of the primitive situation. Gorgias needs to know only what his competitor is doing and what reactions have proven effective in countering specific actions in similar situations. If the other does X, you do Y. If he or she is likely to do XX, then do YY. By adhering to these rules, the strategist is aligned with the essential structure of the situation in which the competition is occurring. This is the kind of thinking that operates as the common sense of realism—its vernacular mentality for understanding ordinary political practices. This mentality works well enough either if the opponent is relatively naive or if everyone agrees on the definition of the situation.

Realists are accustomed to such definitions—disposed stylistically to reduce words to actions, they likewise tend to prefer to reduce actors and acts to a basic situation, whether it is known as a two-person game, a condition of anarchy among states, the international arena, or an equilibrial system.[15] To the extent that they are thinking in such terms, realists will see themselves as severely constrained by their environment, rationally obligated to anticipate and neutralize the actions of other competitors to use the environment advantageously, and rightly unconstrained by any countervailing definitions of their actions that emphasize other purposes than victory or intrinsic qualities of the agents or actions in the situation.

Within the contemporary social sciences, the primitive competitive situation has been the subject of game theory, which has developed powerful explanations of the constraints on and means of strategic choice within a wide variety of political, economic, and social practices. This is not the place to review this well known research program. It is enough for our purposes to point out that its strength is its weakness. Its accomplishments are precisely the result of bracketing all phenomena supplementary to the primitive competitive situation. As a result, game theory provides a parsimonious account of calculation options whenever one is striving for advantage—the primitive competitive situation is always the foundation of a strategic encounter. Yet, as our model suggests, this account might be incomplete whenever there is a more complex situation, or more complex actors. Stated otherwise, game theoretical explanation of many real world events requires an explanatory model that reduces all higher-order dynamics to the causal factors at work in the primitive competitive situation. This causal model cannot itself be validated by the application of game theory, however, and in fact it is highly presumptive. The criticisms that fault the theory for ignoring the historical, contextual, interpretive, social, rhetorical, and other dimensions of political experience all converge at this one point: Actual decision making has to handle variables that cannot be reduced to simple action-reaction relationships. At least one additional independent level of strategic analysis, one that provides the means for managing a wider range of contingencies, is required.

Control

The next level in our analytical hierarchy builds on and surpasses in complexity the elemental competitive calculus. In our formulation, this level corresponds to a mature realism, sophisticated and accustomed to authority; it is the sensibility of the classical realist. This sensibility issues from the learning that can occur from the accumulation of experience. Time has proved to be the key, though hidden, variable in the basic competitive situation, and particularly so for those who would hope to escape from wholly competitive relationships.[16] A sense of time—of both the patterns of the past and, most important, the likelihood of future interactions with the same players—changes the nature of strategic thinking. Not only are particular strategies (and perhaps more long-range strategies) more likely to be selected, but the successful strategist also is likely to develop a stronger sense of contingency. Instead of merely being constrained by a situation, the sense of the situation changes to encompass larger processes that in turn heighten one's sense of the likely fallibility of any strategy (over time). Instead of becoming more confident of one's definition of the situation, the mature strategist (whether an individual or an organization) develops a heightened awareness of how much is beyond anyone's control. The constraints of the original competitive situation do not merely multiply so much as they are transformed into an encompassing sense of indeterminateness or irrationality. So we come to speak of *fortuna* or the uncertainties of the historical process. Thus, the distinctive feature of the second level of strategic analysis emerges, which is emphasis on the self-control of the strategic actor. In this context, the strategist realizes that even the most rational strategy by a master strategist can lead to defeat by inferior players, that one can never gain complete control of the competitive situation itself, and that the key to survival is to control what is most immediate to one's actions—that is, one's own character and its presentation to others.

This more sophisticated analysis of the strategic encounter still recognizes the brute necessity of the primitive competitive situation, yet uses it as background for outlining the strategist. This pattern of definition emphasizes the competitive actor—more specifically, the construction of ethos, the strategic control of one's personality. This locus of control is constructed, first, to ensure the inner environment conducive to making rational calculations and, second, to present a carefully adapted image to influence (intimidate) others. Stated otherwise, the strategist strives to devise the personality that is most likely to prevail in a competitive environment sufficiently complex that it can not be mastered solely through the manipulation of a few preformed strategies. While still thoroughly reactive in the particular case, the strategist prepares not just by assessing what others are doing or likely to do, but by taking pains to control his or her own emotions internally and presentation of self externally. Whereas Gorgias seemed to have no central self—to have nothing inside but a central processor

for making action-reaction choices—our second-order strategist is recognized primarily as someone possessing a particular character.

Not surprisingly, when classical realists articulate their understanding of international politics, they often refer to Machiavelli's *The
Prince*, which is the model for this second order of strategic thinking.[17] Although it is no secret that Machiavelli repudiated a conventional equation of ethical virtue and political success, we have
perhaps overlooked his continuity with the genre of the "mirror-to-
the-prince."[18] Like the other writers of this time, Machiavelli was
writing to craft the character suited to ruling others. Despite being
freed from the conventional virtues, the Machiavellian strategist
nonetheless must regulate his or her own behavior to achieve some
point of stability in a constantly changing environment, conduct the
dispassionate calculations of utility required for effective decision
making, and avoid falling into the snares set by others. Thus,
Machiavelli placed self-control at the center of strategic thinking;
indeed, it was the crucial element in defining the leader's *virtú*. In
other words, one reason *The Prince* has been enormously influential
is that it gives us a *persona* for the strategic thinker—a model of personal character that one can trust to provide political security—and
often realists are granted authority to manage political events because
they imitate this stock character.

This ethos of self-control is evident throughout *The Prince*, for it is
a common characteristic of his portraits of successful rulers while
also evident in the author's own performance. For example, even the
stories of murder—as when Borgia kills the assembled Orsini and his
official Remirro de Orco, Agathocles kills the assembled leaders of
Syracuse, or Liverotto kills the assembled leaders of Fermo—emphasize calculation rather than impulse, anger, or bloodlust. In every
case, the strategist subordinates conquest to self-control. In contemporary terms, we are talking about the Godfather, not Rambo. Other portraits, such as of Philopoemen, leader of the Acheans, fill out this
model of strategic character. The successful prince will be one who is
ever alert to threats within and without, constantly training for war,
always assessing the political utility of any customary activity, and
habitually exercising restraint from distractions and impulses alike.

This construction of a single ethos for strategic success is an important feature of modern realism. The realist is schooled not just in the
logic of strategic analysis but as a political character. This character
sees itself, and not without justification, as rationally and ethically

superior both to those who would rush off to war and to those who would never fight. This thinking may seem to require great strength: One has to master the conduct of forces yet look beyond the immediate field of battle while also resolutely avoiding the many distractions that lie beyond. Perhaps this is why realists have relied on and aspired to portraits of great leaders while communicating their theory of strategy: The personalities of Richelieu, Metternich, and Bismarck loom large in realist history.

By styling themselves in this way, realists develop a more comprehensive and complex strategic intelligence than that represented in the calculus of rational choice theory, as well as a means for persuading others to grant them authority. In fact, this sensibility is relentlessly rhetorical: It characteristically sees everything as a means for persuasion. Since one's own self already is something that has been both won (by subduing one's more risky impulses) and formed for the purpose of intimidating others (by acting the part of the character most likely to prevail in a competition), there is little reason to see anything else as inherently exempt from competitive use. Yet this character is capable of only a limited, instrumental sense of rhetoric, one that sees only the objective of winning and the relationship between victory and the available means of persuasion. Value is defined minimally by the constraints of the competitive situation and most immediately by the intentions and capabilities of the strategic actor, with everything else becoming means of manipulating others.

This level of strategic analysis has other limitations as well. For one, a rhetoric devoted to the construction of character can become a self-perpetuating process. Realist discourse may become more devoted to performance of the character of the strategist, paragon of self-control who avoids emotion and ideology, than to the application of that intelligence to problem solving. As the realist actor becomes a figure of reassurance whose pose is reinforced by audience approval, strategic calculation may become secondary to maintaining the status quo in the conduct of decision making. This tendency hardly is diminished when the realist works on behalf of a superpower or receives extensive promotion through the mass media.

This self-fulfilling tendency offers no check on another dynamic of the second level of strategic analysis. Edward Luttwak observes, "because the dynamic logic of strategy has no end, at least for those who survive its workings, all outcomes—even victory and defeat sealed by formal treaty—are only interim results, destined to be changed by the reactions that they themselves immediately begin to induce."[19] For many strategists, this truism becomes an obsession. The combination of the realist's assumptions of contingency, utility, deceit, and vigilance result in a mind that is always whirring, always exercising its calculus in a world itself ever changing. Put simply, the Machiavellian strategist never knows when to quit. Ironically, the strategist often becomes the most abstract of thinkers and susceptible to hermetic or paranoid narratives. As Plato and Marx each suggested, the prince who turns into a tyrant becomes the most captive subject. Although the next level of strategic analysis cannot escape this problem entirely, it provides the means with which to manage it by incorporating a wider range of cultural materials.

Criticism

Just as the analysis of the competitive situation leads to the development of self-control, so does that reflexive process lead to the third level of our analytical model: the practice of critical interpretation of all available means for understanding and action. Again, the movement up the hierarchy is an attempt to compensate for undue simplicity in the prior patterns of definition. Both the competitive situation and the persona of self-control can be strategic liabilities. To overcome these limitations, the third level of analysis emphasizes the process of revising prior definitions of the conflict. This revisionary inquiry can question the basic sense of the scene, agent, agency, purpose, and act defining (and constraining) the decision maker's options. Its signal operation, however, is to look primarily to the means for action and to see them not as neutral instruments but rather as possible bases for redefinition of the any or all other elements of the conflict. Through careful analysis of how alternative means are elements of or contexts for meaning that make any action possible and advisable, the strategist acquires a capacity for broad explanation and decisive innovation.

The third level of analysis is derived from Clausewitz's strategic theory—generally, we are imitating his movement from the tactical level to the operational level to critical analysis (with the latter defined as an "examination of the means" leading into "the realm of theory").[20] Like Gorgias and Machiavelli, Clausewitz emphasizes the provisional character of strategic thinking: "A critic," he says, "should never use the results of theory as laws and standards, but only—as the soldier does—as aids to judgment."[21] Unlike them, however, he peers deep into the nature of battle to develop a more profound understanding of conflict. For the purposes of this essay, we want to highlight his emphasis on *Kritik*, which is the process of enhancing strategic analysis to incorporate ever more diverse criteria and standards for judgment.

As we would adapt them, the additional considerations at this final level include a number of operations implicit in our analytical hierarchy: evaluating decision making strategically through continued movement in a linked network of perspectives; granting equal status in principle to those viewpoints that otherwise would be dismissed as inappropriate because not strictly pertinent to the competitive situation or ideal strategic character; obtaining the most synoptic and coherent plan of action; specifying detailed actions in multiple fields of competition; and validating one's judgment through continuing examination of the full range of circumstances attending both defeat and victory. The key to all this activity, however, lies in the attention to "originally" extraneous criteria for assessment of the outcome. Clausewitz's discussion of this process of critical review not only introduces higher-order perspectives into strategic calculations—although that is no small addition—but also initiates a different type of analysis. *Kritik* is set over both merely descriptive fact-finding and causal analyses. The analysis of immediate causes and effects and of means-end relations, he argues, can lead to disaster when not given an additional evaluation in terms of more comprehensive considerations. A decision that is rational at the tactical level may be counterproductive at the operational level, and a rational decision there may be counterproductive at the political level, and so forth. "Every stage in this progression obviously implies a new basis for judgment. That which seems correct when looked at from one level may, when viewed from a higher one, appear objectionable."[22] In other words, the conventional definitions of the competitive situation and the consummate strategist need to be loosened up, examined for their own liabilities, and perhaps left behind before one adopts the most carefully considered plan of action.

The application of *Kritik* need not deny the validity of lower-level analyses, but it does allow the strategist to re-introduce considerations that had been bracketed. Furthermore, from the perspective of *Kritik*, no account of the action can be ruled irrelevant simply because it is not directly commensurable with a lower level analysis. Thus, this form of critical thinking, which is not necessary for effective action in respect to more simple conceptions of the competitive situation, involves the comparison and translation between different, perhaps incommensurable, accounts of that situation. The full significance of this idea can be developed by restating it in respect to the linguistic turn. *From this point onward, strategic thinking becomes explicitly a form of interpretation.* The strategist has to be able not only to assess the array of forces, and to gauge political objectives and constraints, and to control dangerous impulses, but also to understand different accounts of the situation that are stated in different discourses. Instead of presuming that state outcomes are determined by the logic of a primitive strategic situation and the natural laws of coercion in a political environment, the strategist presumes that strategic conflicts are meaningful and that meaning is not easily predicated from any one set of variables. Instead of an autonomous mode of analysis and a single language and persona of calculation, the strategist recognizes that different languages offer different selections of reality, different programs for attributing meaning, and different means for motivating reactions. Thus, the strategist has to be able to translate, learn from, and perhaps act in accord with discourses that reflect different cultural practices and communal interests than those explicitly represented in the typical formulations of grand strategy.

The movement upward involves taking seriously the discourses of law, ethics, religion, and others as well, if only because they now are understood as accurately coded representations of more complex processes at work in the social totality. Likewise, this expanded context also attends to the discourses of the peoples caught in the field of conflict, whether they are there as enemies, collaborators, or bystanders, and regardless of their level of "civilization." We cannot presume that any perspective is inadequately informed or inconsequential, but have to look to each for knowledge, symbolic resources, and overlooked constraints potentially at work in the situation. We cannot rule that an argument is not sufficiently "military" or "geopolitical," for the strategist has to consider whether success on those terms could be damaging to "domestic" or "institutional" or "ecological" objectives. In short, there are many levels of discourse impinging upon the strategic situation, and the strategist will be more likely to succeed by recognizing how the "horizontal" means-end calculus within any account of the situation also has to be matched by a "vertical" attempt to gain maximum interpretive power. One's thinking will always be bracketed and the calculation of expediency important, but the genius required is to discern which discourses for interpreting the scene ought to be appropriated and which set aside.

Not surprisingly, this perspective also places a premium on the ability to interact with others. Whereas the first level often involves competition between individual actors, and the second command or manipulation, the third is cooperative. The strategist now looks to succeed competitively by understanding discourses that are grounded in long-standing realms of social experience; to do that one often has to engage deliberatively with others of perhaps quite different training and character. The knowledge that is to be gained from interpretation is not given freely but has to be acquired through argument and negotiation. Perhaps this is an implicit lesson in Thucydides' method of recording or recreating the many speeches framing the other events of his *History*. In any case, this shift to a higher order cognitive practice carries with it collaborative obligations.

It may be difficult for a contemporary realist to appreciate our emphasis here, that is, to see anything other than the familiar conception of grand strategy which would seem to incorporate all extra-military considerations. Certainly, many realists would feel comfortable with Luttwak's formulation, which also is based directly on Clausewitz:

> At the level of grand strategy, the interactions of the lower, military levels . . . yield final results within the broad setting of international politics, in further interactions with the nonmilitary actions of states: the formal exchanges of diplomacy, the public communications of propaganda, secret operations, the perceptions of others formed by intelligence official and unofficial, and all economic transactions of more than purely private significance.[23]

As this statement indicates, grand strategy can be, ironically, a quite limited formulation. The very definition of "the political" often is determined not only by the conditions of conflict but also by the language of international studies. Not surprisingly, Luttwak has drawn on the language of realism, so that broadening the basis for strategic judgment does not go much further than highly conventional and strategically limiting conceptions of propaganda, secrecy, and deception, while continuing the implicit reduction of political power into coercive action. This conception of grand strategy does not easily incorporate a wide range of determinants of state action or recognize long-term changes in the basic conditions of understanding and action in international affairs.[24] Therefore, sound, long-term strategic analysis requires a process of critical review through a hierarchy of perspectives, and this hierarchy needs to motivate interpretation of more diverse or synoptic discourses.

The lack of closure in our visual representation of this model of strategic analysis is intended to suggest the importance of not foreclosing any particular perspective while also recognizing that the terms for strategic analysis always can change. Not only is there continuing need for analysis within any strategic arena, but there always is the possibility that lower level judgments may be overturned by reframing them in a higher order perspective previously ignored. Not only are all resolutions of conflicts merely provisional, but any resolution can be revalued. As one moves into other formulations that are not obviously entailed by the terms of the military-political situation, one enters into a process of learning and interpretation that guards against strategic hermeticism. The fully-activated strategic intelligence can guard against its own tendency to self enclosure precisely because it becomes a pluralistic sensibility. The obsession with individual victory becomes mediated by its multiple definitions; the meaning of victory is defined by many voices.

It is precisely as this expansive process of interpretation becomes dominant that a final paradox occurs. Just as the classical realist could become locked into a narrowing circle of constant calculation, so the post-realist can become paralyzed by perspectivism, a Hamlet who sees too well all sides of any issue. If this critical intelligence is to be a form of strategic thinking, however, it must culminate in action. To do that, ultimately it must return to something close to the primitive competitive situation. Clausewitz knew as much, for *Kritik* properly conducted achieves higher perspective while burrowing ever deeper into the specific conflict.[25] Interestingly, this is also the analytical double movement of moral casuistry, which applies a general principle while modifying it to meet the exigencies of the specific situation. The post-realist may have a sophisticated conception of the social fabric of politics, yet the decision will have to be implemented in accord with fundamental constraints if it is to be effective. The marshaling of complex considerations of language and culture will have to result in actions that may be simple or harsh. Post-realism properly conducted will result in an eternal return to conditions that are hostile to its best intentions.

The Context of Application

The three texts featured in our model present a developmental pattern and a history of strategic thought. Gorgias represents a simple version of the strategic situation that includes a primitive but resilient form of competitive calculation. Machiavelli adds to this calculus a political persona featuring the self-control appropriate to survival in a world of radical contingency. Clausewitz articulates the concept of *Kritik* to incorporate still more complex interpretive considerations and so remedies the major theoretical deficiency of the previous approaches. Although the differences between these models are conditioned historically, they are not necessarily progressive. Any option is available at any time, and recourse to a simpler level of strategic analysis might be the most effective way to understand and master a specific conflict. If we are to see them historically, this should entail close consideration of how changes in historical conditions are embedded in the later models of strategy. Machiavelli was reacting against a tradition of political writing that did not reflect adequately either the political difficulties of small state feuding or the ascendancy of the modern nation-state, and Clausewitz was influenced by the development of modern science and modern warfare. Application of their conceptions is likely to work best as one is encountering similar circumstances. Yet even this approach offers little assurance, for historical conditions continue to change. By giving Clausewitz's model a linguistic orientation, we hope to equip strategists for the problems of learning to compete within a world increasingly moving beyond the bounds of modernist modes of production and discourse.

To summarize the model briefly, we might label the three stages of strategic analysis as simple realism, classical realism, and post-realism. Each is a pattern of definition used to make competition intelligible. The simple realist analysis defines competition in terms of the competitive situation. It locates the key to competitive success in *reactivity*; "quick reaction time," "rapid deployment capability," and similar phrases are signs of this mentality for gearing oneself to the competitive environment. The situation and the other actors are assumed to be largely non-negotiable, fixed constraints. Very little structural knowledge can be gained over time; the acquisition of knowledge is presumed to be expensive.

The classical realist analysis defines competition in terms of the situation and especially the agents involved. Competitive success comes from control of self and others: first and foremost in *self-control* which also will sway others to the extent they can be objects of manipulation. The situation is assumed to be unstable, but largely due to large-scale, impersonal processes of change. Other actors are temporarily changeable—so long as they can be kept under coercive or persuasive control. Knowledge of the situation is expandable but also often subject to error, both from miscalculation (often due to a loss of self-control) and from others' (controlled) use of deceit.

The post-realist analysis defines competition in terms of the situation and agents involved, but most of all in terms of the perspectives implicit in the means available for taking action. Success comes from *interpretive flexibility*: from reading the welter of signs available in any complex environment. It is understood that the definitions of the situation are not fixed save by convention and that they always are open to change via rhetorical practice. Likewise, all other actors are potentially capable of great change, but unpredictably so. Alternative definitions each can contain new, perhaps crucial knowledge for competitive success—true accounts of the environment that can be used advantageously—but knowledge alone is not enough for victory and any one perspective will be self-limiting.

It should be clear that the post-realist analysis cannot dismiss the others. Consider how a particular situation—the war in Bosnia, for example—can be described from each of the three perspectives. At the first order of analysis, the conflict is a simple demonstration that those (the Bosnian Muslims) who do not anticipate the aggressive actions of others will lose. From the second perspective, we see a longer-term, more complex situation in which those (the Western leaders) lacking the requisite strategic character to intimidate aggressors will lose. The post-realist perspective grants the validity of these two analyses, in their place, but also defines the problem in terms of a complex set of discourses including several nationalisms, several Christianities, a secularized Islam, liberal institutionalism (primarily involving the UN and the EEC), and several strands of American neo-isolationism, among others. From this perspective, one can consider more broadly how stable success could be achieved through mastery of these means for reaching agreements, building alliances, disrupting the enemy's ability to continue the war, or developing innovative means of resistance.

This post-realist model of strategic thinking integrates key elements of the realist mentality and seemingly contradictory assumptions from perspectives that often have been counterpoised to realism. It allows the strategist to bracket legal, ethical, religious, or any other considerations that are not strictly in accord with an instrumental calculus, yet it also encourages the reintroduction of such discourses as correctives for the inherent limitations of the realist perspective. Post-realism asserts that the many discourses informing foreign policy are not mere epiphenomena but are both sources of complexity and means of accounting for complexity. Instead of defining discourses other than realism as inducements to vulnerability, they are considered as higher order perspectives that might contain important resources for competitive adaptation in a changing environment. The model recognizes the importance of calculation and self-control yet emphasizes interpretative capability as an important key to strategic action. This is particularly so when one recognizes that the use of the different strategic mentalities will often depend on the context or issue at hand. Thus, post-realism defines strategic thinking in the international arena to be more a rhetorical than a military art, for international competition ultimately is a struggle over meaning.

The three-tiered model has its own limitations, of course—particularly from a realist's perspective. It does not maximize speed in calculation, and sometimes speed is the key to victory. (Although, the post-realist replies, speed also is an unexamined assumption, a constraint on both political reform and long-term stability, and a dangerous norm.) It could habitually require short term costs for long term benefits—costs which many participants are not likely to be willing to pay. (Unless the strategist can tie costs to shorter term benefits in other issue areas.) It admits additional actors with other interests into the process of deliberation and it carries obvious opportunities for distraction. (But what has been a bigger distraction of late than realism itself?) As a traditional realist would be quick to remind us, there are no guarantees. (We accept that, and add that this is more true than any of us, including realists, dare admit when trying to speak authoritatively.) In any case, there certainly is room for consideration of other models than the one offered here. Whatever the suggestion, we believe that the need for a post-realist conception of strategic thinking is likely to become more evident in the coming years.

Refiguring International Relations

Realism now represents a traditional approach to foreign policy. This tradition is centered on the first requirement of sovereignty, the

defense of the state. National strategy, in this sense, is typically oriented toward the international struggle for power. This is negative
power, the power to destroy and prevent, motivated by fear. The story
of the fate of nations remains compelling, but we must become increasingly aware of its limitations.[26] Realists themselves occasionally have
come to this realization. This is the import of Morgenthau's conclusive
emphasis on diplomacy, Kennan's renunciation of the excesses of the
policy of containment, Nye's focus on soft power, and Huntington's
attention to the clash of cultures. Such a conception of realism places
greater emphasis on positive power, the power to create politics and to
influence others in a constructive way. Post-realism develops this shift
in focus. Although it includes traditional realism and its concerns with
security and power, post-realism refocuses on the manifestly political
practices of international relations. To this end, it emphasizes diplomacy and discourse, communication and persuasion. Likewise, post-
realism also includes the legitimate concerns of idealism with
superordinate, collective processes and structures, recognizing the role
of organization generally and of institutions in particular for motivating and constraining action. It is not, however, simply idealism or realism writ large, merely concerned with the creation of power or
agreement at the highest level of international politics. It goes well
beyond both traditional realism and idealism as well in its concern
with multiple agencies and multidimensional cooperation.[27]

This shift in perspective provides a means for operationalizing the
relationship between strategy and ethics. Traditional realism constrains ethics by expediency. Political authority is the necessary context, the essential precondition for any ethic; it identifies and
stabilizes the meanings of core values. As Aristotle reminds us, outside the *polis*, the highly structured arena of domestic life, human
beings are not ethical or even fully human. To live in such an environment, one must be "either a beast or a god." This is the world
described in Hobbes' state of nature and Rousseau's stag hunt. In
international politics, since there is no strong central authority with a
monopoly on violence and based in a sense of shared community,
there can be no recourse to ethical judgment. Thus, realism justifies
itself as the external defense of basically domestic ethical values.[28] In
this harsh external world, realists find it difficult to think in terms of
a Kantian scheme of absolutist/deontological ethics. When transferred
into the international environment, they argue, strong ethics lead to a
Crusader mentality, what Morgenthau called the "messianic" ten-

dency. For realists, a broader, shallower international community implies a weaker, relativistic, pragmatic ethics.[29]

Post-realism transforms realism's relativism into a pluralistic world ethics based in the diverse discourses and experiences of local politics. Instead of assuming that there can be no strong international ethic since there is no central authority, post-realism considers how international ethics articulate norms and practices for living together that do not depend on enforcement by a central authority. Good judgment in foreign policy involves listening to multiple points of view, a line of argument that has been well developed in the social psychology of group decision making in foreign policy formulation.[30] Interactions between polities depend on recognition of the identity, selfhood, and dignity of multiple others. For this reason, the ethics of an emerging superordinate polity are complex and richly textured, tolerant and diverse.

In other words, both realism and post-realism have internally consistent concepts of strategy and ethics. Where the realist identifies morality and expediency as different modes of cognition and subordinates the one to the other, the post-realist sees them as different though related means for managing the world that can correct each other. This sense of similarity ultimately leads to the idea of their likely congruence: One unusual implication of the post-realist perspective is that the strategist ought to consider that in many situations ethical action may prove to be more strategic than acting otherwise. Machiavelli came close to this when he stressed that it is important to appear good. Erasmus, following Quintilian and Cicero, argued that being good is the most expedient way to maintain the appearance of good. If considered empirically, these are claims that can be overturned in any given situation. As Machiavelli taught us so well, the strategist has to acknowledge those cases where immoral action is the shortest route to political success. Stated more theoretically, however, the claim is that continuous, albeit flexible adherence to moral norms will result in economies of action in the long term. These will coordinate one's interests with the more stable resources in the political system.

In terms of the three-tiered model outlined above, as strategic thinking becomes fully articulated into a well functioning system of critical judgment, then it increasingly has to master the most comprehensive discourses in a culture, not least among them those discourses articulating good conduct generally, which will contain important indications of the possibilities for effective action within the expanded field of play. As Walzer has argued, moral discourse also is realistic, and as rhetoricians have long known, communal values are essential means for securing agreement and motivating action. So the sophisticated strategist will consider carefully the mores active in the particular locale and strive to coordinate political initiatives with ethical norms. This is why one must guard against an impulsive bracketing of seemingly "idealistic" claims. Ultimately there still is no absolute resolution, but the practical effect will be that, over time in a complex environment, "good" deliberation will look much the same regardless of whether it is being practiced by someone thinking strategically or ethically.

This congruence of ethical and strategic thinking will seem simplistic to many realists, yet we offer it as a better means for managing complexity. Post-realist theory can provide a more accurate, complex, multi-dimensional map for the emerging world of the twenty-first century. As the world moves toward the millennium, international conversation grows richer and more varied. State elites maintain their local monopolies over the means of violence, but modern technology gradually erodes control over other areas of international interaction as contemporary telecommunications open new channels for discourse. Further, the very nature of international power itself is being transformed. The lesson of Desert Storm is that military muscle remains an arbiter of disputes among national elites, at least in the short term. But the lesson of the former Soviet Union, Germany, and Japan is that economic power does not necessarily grow out of the barrel of a gun. Central and Eastern European revolutions teach us that the soft power of Western democratic values is also important in the emerging world of the early twenty-first century. China offers a test case in the relationship between economic transformation and global politics. In every case, power is determined only in part by the means to compel and sometimes in great part by the invention and negotiation of meaning.

A post-realist international relations is gradually taking shape. New configurations do not replace traditional international practices, but co-develop with them, coming to exist side-by-side in the form of alternative possible realities. More and more activities in all realms of life cross over national boundaries. The dissemination of new vocabularies and discursive practices is encouraged by functional cooperation on different tasks in the contexts of different regimes in multiple international sectors. Increasingly, international economic and cultural activities tie together a wide range of communities, each with its own sense of political action, expediency, and value. International rhetorics are becoming more widespread and more persuasive to an ever larger number of participants in the international conversation. Multiple realisms, international realities alternative to realist realities, thus come into being, schemata available for activation by contemporary events and their interpreters. Such alternative realities are lodged in the categories and discursive practices that contemporary international actors and observers actually use to describe and construct international relations.

Realism compels us because it gives a stable identity to international relations and to the nation-states that are its major political components. Yet we have focused too long on one story, the story of realism, as the only possible or plausible representation of reality. Old stories are good stories. They reassure us in the dark night of critical situations. Yet the old stories have dangerous distortions and blind spots, leaving us unprepared for important dimensions of reality. The older the rhetoric, the less we speak it and the more powerfully it speaks through us.

New rhetoric allows room for critical thinking about the old. It also allows space for innovation and openness. World politics is not one simple story told in multiple contexts. Like the 1001 nights of Scheherazade, there are many stories of international relations waiting to be invented, acted, and told. The stories will continue so long as world politics continues. As recent global events dramatically confirm, neither stories nor actual events need be determined or inevitable—pre-plotted by the master realist always to contain the same few characters, ritually performing the same cramped actions, and ultimately arriving at the same tragic denouement.

NOTES

1. Yosef Lapid, "The Third Debate: On the Prospects of International Theory in a Post-Positivist Era," *International Studies Quarterly* 33 (1989): 244.
2. Michael Walzer, *Just and Unjust Wars: A Moral Argument with Historical Illustrations* (New York: Basic Books/Harper Colophon, 1977), 13 ff.
3. Kenneth Burke, *Language as Symbolic Action: Essays on Life, Literature and Method* (Berkeley: University of California Press, 1966), *A Grammar of Motives* (1945; reprint, Berkeley: University of California Press, 1969).

4. Thucydides, *The Peloponnesian War*, trans. Rex Warner (Middlesex: Penguin, 1954): 401-2.

5. Ibid., 404-5.

6. Robert Hariman, *Political Style: The Artistry of Power* (Chicago: University of Chicago Press, 1995), 24.

7. Machiavelli, *The Prince*, trans. Luigi Ricci, from Max Lerner, ed., *The Prince and the Discourses* (New York: Modern Library, 1950), 3-4; for more extended discussion, see Hariman, *Political Style*, chap. 2.

8. Kenneth Burke, "Literature as Equipment for Living," *The Philosophy of Literary Form* (1941; reprint, Berkeley: University of California Press, 1973).

9. George Lakoff and Mark Johnson, *Metaphors We Live By* (Chicago: University of Chicago Press, 1980), 3-6, 77-86. Kathleen Hall Jamieson, *Eloquence in an Electronic Age: The Transformation of Political Speechmaking* (New York: Oxford University Press, 1988), 47-49.

10. We assume that readers in strategic studies will not need to see that literature cited here. For a general introduction to the history and themes of modern strategic analysis, others can look to Peter Paret, ed., *Makers of Modern Strategy: From Machiavelli to the Modern Age* (Princeton: Princeton University Press, 1986), and to the three introductory essays in Carl von Clausewitz, *On War*, eds. and trans. Michael Howard and Peter Paret (Princeton: Princeton University Press, 1984): Paret, "The Genesis of On War"; Howard, "The Influence of Clausewitz"; and Bernard Brodie, "The Continuing Relevance of On War." See also Edward N. Luttwak, *Strategy: The Logic of War and Peace* (Cambridge: Belknap/Harvard, 1987), and Peter Paret, *Clausewitz and the State* (New York: Oxford University Press, 1976).

11. Aristotle, *Rhetoric* 1419b, trans. George A. Kennedy, *Aristotle on Rhetoric: A Theory of Civic Discourse* (New York: Oxford University Press, 1991).

12. These five terms of scene, agent, purpose, agency, and act were developed by Kenneth Burke for the analysis of human motivation: *A Grammar of Motives* (Berkeley: University of California Press, 1969). Burke claims that any complete attribution of motive necessarily must articulate consistent definitions of these terms (and of "ratios" between some of the terms), which together then encompass the motivational structure of an event. For example, a rise in the murder rate can be attributed variously to the heat (scene), availability of guns (agency), loss of moral values (purpose), etc., with each account having to line up the other elements of explanation explicitly or, more often, implicitly.

13. B. H. Liddel-Hart, *Strategy*, 2d rev. ed. (New York: Praeger, 1967); Sun Tzu, *The Art of War*, trans. Samuel B. Griffith (New York: Oxford University Press, 1963).

14. For discussion of the role of paradox in strategic thinking, see Luttwak, *Strategy*, and Zeev Maoz, *Paradoxes of War: On the Art of National Self-Entrapment* (Boston: Urwin Hyman, 1990).

15. These examples also illustrate how other linguistic devices, including easily identifiable metaphors and more implicit narratives, can work in tandem with scenic definitions. See Roger Hurwitz, "Strategic and Social Fictions in the Prisoner's Dilemma," in *International/Intertextual Relations: Postmodern Readings of Modern Politics*, eds. James Der Derian and Michael J. Shapiro (Lexington, Mass.: Lexington Books, 1989).

16. For example, Robert Axlerod emphasizes the importance of "the shadow of the future" for the development of strategies of cooperation; *The Evolution of Cooperation* (New York: Basic Books, 1984), 126 ff. and 176 ff.

17. For discussion of the debate over Machiavelli's strategic sensibility, see John Geerken, "Machiavelli Studies Since 1969," *Journal of the History of Ideas* 37 (1976): 360 ff. See also Neal Wood, "Machiavelli's Humanism of Action," in Anthony Parel, ed., *The Political Calculus: Essays on Machiavelli's Philosophy* (Toronto: University of Toronto Press, 1972), 41; "Introduction," Niccolo Machiavelli, *The Art of War*, trans. Ellis Farneworth, rev. ed. (Indianapolis: Bobbs-Merrill, Library of Liberal Arts, 1965), liii ff. William Wiethoff, "The Martial 'Virtue' of Rhetoric in Machiavelli's *Art of War*," *Quarterly Journal of Speech* 64 (1978): 304-12.

18. For a more extended version of this analysis of the Machiavellian strategist, see Hariman, *Political Style*, chap. 2.

19. Luttwak, *Strategy*, 190.

20. Clausewitz, *On War*, 157. At least two caveats ought to be mentioned here: (1) Obviously, there is some incommensurability between the German and English terms for *Kritik*/criticism and also between the positivistic conception of theory informing Clausewitz's work and our explicitly interpretive conception of the human sciences. Our usage is intended, like post-realism itself, to be inclusive without erasing awareness of such differences in meaning. (2) Our model probably has affinities with other analytical schemes as well, such as Freud's hierarchy of Id, Ego, and Superego. One should not make too much of these parallels, however. Our intention is not to reproduce or interpret another system, but to identify some of the analytical distinctions we believe necessary and useful for strategic thinking that would work with regard to but not within the constraints endemic to realism.

21. Ibid., 158.

22. Ibid.

23. Luttwak, *Strategy*, 179.

24. Such analyses are not impossible, of course, and Luttwak himself has entertained a broader conception of, e.g., the effect of social practices on state action: Edward N. Luttwak, "Where are the Great Powers," *Foreign Affairs* 73, no. 4 (1994): 23-28.

25. As Gary Wills has noted: "*Kritik* moves simultaneously in two directions, down into the actual details of the engagement and up to ever higher levels for judging that single clash" ["Critical Inquiry (*Kritik*) in Clausewitz," in

The Politics of Interpretation, ed. W. J. T. Mitchell, (Chicago: University of Chicago Press, 1983)].

26. John Lukacs, *The End of the Twentieth Century and the End of the Modern Age* (New York: Ticknor and Fields, 1993).

27. See Ronald L. Jepperson, Alexander Wendt, and Peter J. Katzenstein, "Norms, Identity, and Culture in National Security," in *Culture and Security*, ed. Katzenstein (New York: Columbia University Press, forthcoming).

28. Lea Brilmayer, *American Hegemony: Political Hegemony in a One Superpower World* (New Haven: Yale University Press, 1994).

29. See Terry Nardin and David Mapel, *Traditions of International Ethics* (Cambridge: Cambridge University Press, 1992); Joseph S. Nye, *Nuclear Ethics* (New York: Free Press, 1986).

30. See for example John P. Burke and Fred I. Greenstein, *How Presidents Test Reality: Decisions on Vietnam, 1954 and 1965* (New York: Russell Sage, 1989). Irving L. Janis and Leon Mann, *Decision Making: A Psychological Analysis of Conflict, Choice, and Commitment* (New York: Free Press, 1977).

Contributors

James Arnt Aune is an associate professor of speech communication at Texas A&M University. He is the author of several articles on rhetoric and political theory, as well as *Rhetoric and Marxism*, (Westview Press, 1994).

Francis A. Beer is a professor of political science at the University of Colorado, Boulder. His books include *Integration in NATO: Processes of Alliance Cohesion and Prospects for Atlantic Community* and *Peace Against War: The Ecology of International Violence*, as well as related monographs and an edited volume on *Alliances: Latent War Communities in the Contemporary World*. He has published articles in the *American Political Science Review, Atlantic Quarterly, International Interactions, International Organization, International Studies Quarterly, Journal of Applied Behavioral Science, Journal of Conflict Resolution, Journal of Political and Military Sociology, Peace and Change, Peace Psychology Review, Political Communication, Politics and the Life Sciences, Review of International Studies*, and *Social Epistemology*. He has been President of the International Studies Association/West and co-edited a series of Sage books on "Violence, Conflict, Cooperation."

G. R. Boynton is a professor of political science at the University of Iowa. His current research interest is communication–cognition. The sites of this research are: communication and the formation of public opinion, communication in congressional committees, and communication in international affairs. Much of his current research uses multi-media scholarship.

Paul Chilton is a reader in the department of French studies at the University of Warwick U.K., where he teaches and researches linguistics and political discourse analysis. He was a research fellow at the Center for International Security and Arms Control, Stanford in 1988-90. He is the editor of *Language and the Nuclear Arms Debate* (London: Pinter, 1985), author of *Orwellian Language and the Media* (London: Pluto, 1988), *Security Metaphors: Cold War Discourse from Containment to Common House* (New York: Peter Lang, 1995), and of numerous articles on language, society, and politics.

James Der Derian is a professor of political science at the University of Massachusetts at Amherst. He has taught at Columbia University, the University of Southern California, and Gardner and Lancaster State Prisons. He is the author of *On Diplomacy: A Genealogy of Western Estrangement*, and of *Antidiplomacy: Spies, Terror, Speed and War*, editor of *International Theory: Critical Investigations*, and co-editor with Michael Shapiro of *International/Intertextual Relations: Postmodern Readings of World Politics*. He is currently writing a book on war games, the media, and U.S. foreign policy, called *Virtual Security*.

Roxanne Lynn Doty is an assistant professor in the department of political science at Arizona State University. She is the author of *Imperial Encounters: The Politics of Representation in North-South Relations* (University of Minnesota Press, 1996), and of essays in *International Studies Quarterly* and *Millennium*.

Jean Bethke Elshtain is the Laura Spelman Rockefeller Professor of Social and Political Ethics at The University of Chicago. She is the author of many books including: *Public Man, Private Woman: Women in Social and Political Thought*; *Meditations on Modern Political Thought*; *Power Trips and Other Journeys*; *Women and War*; *Democracy on Trial*; *Augustine and the Limits of Politics*. She is the editor of *The Family in Political Thought*; co-editor of *Women, Militarism, and War*; co-author of *But Was It Just? Reflections on the Morality of the Persian Gulf War*; editor of *Politics and the Human Body*; and editor of *Just War Theory*. She also has written over two hundred articles and essays in scholarly journals and journals of civic opinion.

Roger Epp is an assistant professor of political studies at Augustana University College in Camrose, Alberta, Canada. Much of his research has involved the rereading of various strands of international political thought: Hugo Grotius, Karl Marx, and the Augustinian tradition revived with Martin Wight, Herbert Butterfield, and Reinhold Niebuhr. He has also published work on ethics, international relations as an academic subject, and the prospects for a meaningful democratic politics. From 1992 to 1994 he was co-editor of *Dianoia: A Liberal Arts Interdisciplinary Journal*.

G. Thomas Goodnight is a professor of communication studies at Northwestern University. His major interests are rhetorical theory and criticism with a special focus on the recovery of the public sphere. His publications include several monographs on foreign policy in the nuclear age. Professor Goodnight has been recognized for his scholarship by the American Forensics Association, National Speakers Association, and the Speech Communication Association.

Robert Hariman is a professor of rhetoric and communication studies and Endowment Professor of the Humanities at Drake University. His journal publications include essays in the *Quarterly Journal of Speech, Rhetorica, Journal of the History of Ideas*, and *Journal of Higher Education*. He is the editor of *Popular Trials: Rhetoric, Mass Media, and the Law* (University of Alabama Press, 1990), and the author of *Political Style: The Artistry of Power* (University of Chicago Press, 1995).

Robert L. Ivie is a professor and chair of the department of speech communication and adjunct professor of American studies at Indiana University. His research focuses on the rhetoric of war within the American experience, including most recently the Cold War and its legacy of fear in the post-Cold War rhetorical republic. He is co-author of *Congress Declares War: Rhetoric, Leadership, and Partisanship in the Early Republic* (1994) and *Cold War Rhetoric: Strategy, Metaphor, and Ideology* (1990). He has published widely within communication studies and in interdisciplinary outlets such as *Social Science History* and *American Behavioral Scientist*. He recently was editor of *The Quarterly Journal of Speech*.

Charles Jones spent four years on the research staff of the Institutes of Latin American and Commonwealth Studies in London before taking up his present post in international studies at the University of Warwick in 1977. Earlier publications were mostly in the field of international business history, Latin American studies, and North-South relations. During the past ten years he has devoted more time to international relations theory. He is author, with Barry Buzan and Richard Little, of *The Logic of Anarchy* (Columbia University Press, 1993) and currently is writing a book on E. H. Carr.

Yosef Lapid is an associate professor of government at New Mexico State University. He has published articles and book chapters on international relations theory, nationalism, and border studies, which are his main research interests. He is currently working on a book entitled *Beyond the Third Debate: New Frontiers of International Relations Theory.*

Stephen Majeski is an associate professor of political science at the University of Washington. He is currently working on a manuscript with David Sylvan entitled *Constructing the Inevitable: U.S. Foreign Policy Making and the Vietnam War.* He has published numerous articles on foreign policy making, arms races, and defense budgeting. He is also currently engaged in research on how communication, exit, and payoff structures effect the ability of groups to cooperate in experimental game situations.

Jennifer Milliken is an assistant professor at the department of political science, York University, Toronto, and currently a visiting lecturer at the Graduate Institute of International Studies, Geneva. Her research interests include international relations theory, American foreign policy, comparative foreign policy, and qualitative methods.

V. Spike Peterson is an associate professor in the department of political science, University of Arizona. She edited and contributed to the volume, *Gendered States: Feminist (Re)Visions of International Relations Theory* (Lynne Rienner Press, 1992) and co-authored, with Anne Sisson Runyan, *Global Gender Issues* (Westview Press, 1993). She is currently at work on a book-length manuscript examining subjectivity, sexuality, and sovereignty in the context of globalization.

David J. Sylvan is a professor of international relations at the Graduate Institute of International Studies, Geneva, Switzerland. He has co-authored *A Rationalist Methodology for the Social Sciences*, co-edited *Knowledges: Historical and Critical Studies in Disciplinarity*, and written numerous articles in journals and edited collections. In addition to his work on U.S. policy making with respect to Vietnam, he has also done extensive research on the genealogy of sovereignty in ancient Greece and Renaissance Italy.

Franke Wilmer is an associate professor of political science at Montana State University. She is the author of *The Indigenous Voice in World Politics* (Sage, 1993) and of journal publications regarding ethnicity and marginalized peoples in world politics.

INDEX

A

Acheson, Dean, 70, 208, 209, 218, 311, 312, 314, 318
Adams, John, 147
Alexander, J.C., 244
Alker, Hayward R., Jr., 292
Angell, Norman, 324
anti-imperialism, 112, 336-37
Arendt, Hannah, 182
Aristotle, 36-37, 146-47, 150, 269, 314, 392, 408
Armstrong, John A., 186
Aron, Raymond, 5, 245
Ashley, Richard K., 122, 146, 160-61, 244, 281
Augustine, Saint, 173-74, 283

B

Bacon, Augustus, 340, 341
Bakunin, Mikhail, 99
balance of power, 40, 124, 159, 211, 223, 230
Ball, George, 219-20, 221, 223, 233, 312
Balzac, Honoré de, 287, 295
Bao Dai, 317-319
Barrett, John, 340
Barrington-Ward, Robert, 99, 108, 112, 114-15

Barth, Karl, 79
Baudrillard, Jean, 292-93
Berki, R.N., 67, 68, 244
Bernstein, Richard J., 295
Berry, C.J., 247
Beveridge, Albert, 336
Bevin, Ernest, 115
Bismarck, Otto von, 37, 45-46, 397
Blumenberg, Hans, 6, 145
Bodin, Jean, 5, 176-78, 181-82
Bolingbroke, Henry St. John, 135
Bosnian War, 173, 211, 406
bounded rationality, 381
Bourdieu, P., 241
Brecht, Arnold, 179
Brecht, Bertolt, 278
Bretton Woods, 111-112
Brezhnev, Leonid, 43
British Committee on the Theory of International Politics, 130
Brown, Wendy, 266
Brundtland report (1989), 211-12
Brzezinski, Zbigniew, 282
Bull, Hedley, 5, 130, 136
Bundy, McGeorge, 222
Bundy, William, 219, 227, 229-30
Burke, Kenneth, 292, 305, 389, 392
Bush, George, 281, 312